LONGMAN LINGUISTICS LIBRARY

PIDGIN AND CREOLE LANGUAGES

LONGMAN LINGUISTICS LIBRARY: SERIES LIST

General editors
R. H. Robins, *University of London,*
Martin Harris, *University of Manchester*
Geoffrey Horrocks, *University of Cambridge*

A Short History of Linguistics
Third Edition
R. H. ROBINS

Text and Context
Explorations in the Semantics and Pragmatics of Discourse
TEUN A. VAN DIJK

Introduction to Text Linguistics
ROBERT DE BEAUGRANDE AND WOLFGANG ULRICH DRESSLER

Psycholinguistics
Language, Mind, and World
DANNY D. STEINBERG

Principles of Pragmatics
GEOFFREY LEECH

Generative Grammar
GEOFFREY HORROCKS

The English Verb
Second Edition
F. R. PALMER

A History of American English
J. L. DILLARD

English Historical Syntax
Verbal Constructions
DAVID DENISON

Pidgin and Creole Languages
SUZANNE ROMAINE

A History of English Phonology
CHARLES JONES

Generative and Non-linear Phonology
JACQUES DURAND

Modality and the English Modals
Second Edition
F. R. PALMER

Semiotics and Linguistics
YISHI TOBIN

Multilingualism in the British Isles I: The Older Mother Tongues and Europe
EDITED BY SAFDER ALLADINA AND VIV EDWARDS

Multilingualism in the British Isles II: Africa, The Middle East and Asia
EDITED BY SAFDER ALLANDINA AND VIV EDWARDS

Dialects of English
Studies in Grammatical Variation
EDITED BY PETER TRUDGILL AND J. K. CHAMBERS

Introduction to Bilingualism
CHARLOTTE HOFFMANN

Verb and Noun Number in English: A Functional Explanation
WALLIS REID

English in Africa
JOSEF SCHMIED

Linguistic Theory
The Discourse of Fundamental Works
ROBERT DE BEAUGRANDE

General Linguistics
An Introductory Survey
Fourth Edition
R. H. ROBINS

Historical Linguistics
Problems and Perspectives
EDITED BY C. JONES

A History of Linguistics Vol. I
The Eastern Traditions of Linguistics
EDITED BY GIULIO LEPSCHY

A History of Linguistics Vol II
Classical and medieval Linguistics
EDITED BY GIULIO LEPSCHY

Aspect in the English Verb
Process and Result in Language
YISHAI TOBIN

The Meaning of Syntax
A Study in the Adjectives of English
CONNOR FERRIS

Latin American Spanish
JOHN M. LIPSKI

A Linguistic History of Italian
MARTIN MAIDEN

Modern Arabic
Structures, Functions and Varieties
CLIVE HOLES

Pidgin and Creole Languages

Suzanne Romaine

LONGMAN
LONDON AND NEW YORK

Longman Group Limited,
Longman House, Burnt Mill, Harlow,
Essex CM20 2JE, England
and Associated Companies throughout the world.

Published in the United States of America
by Longman Inc., New York

First published 1988
Fifth impression 1994

British Library Cataloguing in Publication Data

Romaine, Suzanne
Pidgin and Creole languages. — (Longman linguistics library
1. Creole dialects 2. Pidgin languages.
I. Title
417′.2 PM7802

ISBN 0-582-01474-3 CSD
ISBN 0-582-29647-1 PPR

Library of Congress Cataloging in Publication Data

Romaine, Suzanne, 1951–
Pidgin and Creole languages
(Longman linguistics library)
Bibliography: p.
Includes index.
1. Pidgin languages. 2. Creole dialects.
I. Title. II. Series.
PM7802.R66 1988 417′.2 86-27500
ISBN 0-582-01474-3
ISBN 0-582-296471 (pbk.)

Set in Linotron 202 10/11 pt Times
Produced by Longman Singapore Publishers (Pte) Ltd.
Printed in Singapore

Table of contents

Preface viii

1 Introduction to the study of pidgins and creoles 1
- 1.1 Some introductory issues and problems 2
- 1.2 Early studies in pidgin and creole languages: a brief history of the field 4
- 1.3 Present distribution of pidgin and creole languages 14
- 1.4 The scope and structure of this book 19

2 Definitions and characteristics of pidgins and creoles 23
- 2.1 Some preliminary definitions of pidgins 23
- 2.2 Some linguistic features of pidgins 25
- 2.3 Pidgins as simple or simplified codes 31
- 2.4 The pidgin lexicon 33
- 2.5 Some preliminary definitions of creoles 38
- 2.6 Expansion and elaboration of creoles 41
- 2.7 Towards a typology of pidgin and creole languages 42
- 2.8 The minimal structural requirements for pidgins and creoles 46
- 2.9 Twelve features of creole grammars 47

3 The origin of pidgins 71
- 3.1 Baby talk, foreigner talk, simplification and imitation as the source of pidgins 72
- 3.2 Nautical jargon 84
- 3.3 Monogenesis and relexification 86

3.4 Independent parallel development 92
3.5 Substratum theories 102
3.6 Native speakers' theories of origin 109

4 The life-cycle of pidgins 115
4.1 The notion of life-cycle 115
4.2 Stages in the process of pidgin formation 115
4.3 The jargon phase 117
4.4 Stable pidgin 124
4.5 Expanded pidgin 138

5 The life-cycle of creoles: decreolization and recreolization 154
5.1 Creolization 154
5.2 Decreolization and the notion of post-creole continuum 158
5.3 The structure of the creole continuum 161
5.4 The distribution of the copula in the creole continuum 166
5.5 Tense and aspect across the creole continuum 173
5.6 Some criticisms of the notion of creole continuum 177
5.7 Recreolization 188

6 Language acquisition and the study of pidgins and creoles 204
6.1 Transfer vs. universals 206
6.2 Interlanguage 209
6.3 Foreigner talk and second language acquisition 210
6.4 The pidginization hypothesis and second language acquisition 212
6.5 The critical period hypothesis 215
6.6 Comparison of some linguistic features in second language acquisition and pidginization 220
6.7 Relativization and first language acquisition 229
6.8 Children's acquisition of relative clauses in English 231
6.9 Relative clauses and universal grammar 235
6.10 Relative clauses in pidgins and creoles 241
6.11 Relative clauses in second language acquisition 251
6.12 Chains of grammaticalization 252

7 Language universals and pidgins and creoles 256
7.1 The bioprogram hypothesis 256
7.2 The contents of the bioprogram 259

7.3 Tense, mood and aspect 264
7.4 Some evidence from child language acquisition 275
7.5 Other areas of research relating to bioprogram grammar 296

8 Conclusion 311

Appendix I A survey of the pidgins and creoles of the world 315

References 326
Index 357

Preface

This book is about pidgin and creole languages. In writing it, I had a number of aims and audiences in mind. In Chapter 1 I explain why the study of pidgins and creoles is of major concern to linguists. Chapters 2 to 5 describe the linguistic features of these languages and the dynamic developments that bring them into being and lead to changes in their structure. These chapters can be read by anyone who wants an introduction to the subject and who has an elementary knowledge of linguistics. Chapters 6 and 7 place these languages within the context of current issues of central concern to linguistic theory; namely, language acquisition, universals and change. This reflects my own reasons for being interested in these languages. At the risk of being egocentric, I would argue that linguists who study pidgin and creole languages cannot afford to neglect research on language acquisition (both first and second), and vice versa. Historical linguistics should not dismiss these areas of research either. These two chapters are rather more difficult. I hope they will be of interest to researchers in language acquisition as well as to creolists and historical linguists.

Pidgins and creoles are spoken mainly in Third World countries. Their role and function there is intimately connected with a variety of political questions concerned with national, social and economic development and the problems of transition into a post-colonial society (*cf eg* Hall 1972 and Samarin 1980). My main difficulty in writing this book lay in deciding whether to deal with some of the more social issues at the expense of more theoretical ones. The former merit a book in their own right. Valdman (1978) has managed to treat both theoretical and social issues relating to the French-based creoles, but in a book considerably larger than this one. Due to limitations of space, I have unfortunately had to neglect some of the more sociolinguistic aspects of these languages (*cf* however Ch. 8). Although I have tried to provide samples from a wide range of pidgins and creoles, inevitably I have stuck close to the languages I know best in illustrating basic points.

At the time of writing, the question of how large a role creative innovation, transmission or continuity of pidgin structures, or borrowing plays in creole formation has not been resolved. The bioprogram hypothesis proposed by Bickerton (1981a) has figured prominently in discussions of creole origins. In Chapter 7 I have given a review of the research relating to this issue. However, only time will tell how important the research generated by this question will remain in the history of the field.

There are a number of people who have aided me during the preparation of this book, whose help I would like to acknowledge. I am grateful to the series editors R. H. Robins and Martin Harris for suggesting that I write this book. It has forced me to bring together in a fruitful way some of my various research interests over the past few years. I would also like to acknowledge a number of sources of help and encouragement in connection with my research on Tok Pisin, some of which is discussed in this book. The Max-Planck-Institut für Psycholinguistik in Nijmegen provided the primary financial support for this research project [A sociolinguistic study of creolization, language acquisition and change in Tok Pisin], which is still on-going. The results of the first phase are discussed in Romaine and Wright (1986). I received a lot of encouragement and practical help from the Institute directors, W. J. M. Levelt and Wolfgang Klein. The project was conceived while I was a research scientist at the Institute and was launched in cooperation with the Max-Planck-Institut für Verhaltensphysiologie in Seewiesen. Additional financial support was provided by the English Faculty Board of Oxford University and the Higher Studies Fund of Merton College.

Various people in Papua New Guinea were of assistance. I am very grateful to the Papua New Guinea University of Technology for providing me with a research base, accommodation and transport. I would like to thank in particular Moseley Moramoro, the Vice-Chancellor, for allowing me to be attached to the University as a visiting research fellow, and Stewart Marshall for providing facilities in the Department of Language and Communication Studies. The Department was a congenial atmosphere for my work. I would also like to thank Geoff Smith, John Swan, Geraldine Terry and Robynne Walsh in that department for their help. I am also grateful to Sael Misilagen for providing technical assistance and Jill Bebe for helping out with some difficulties in transcription. There were many others from other departments and branches of the university who aided me, whom I would like to thank: Lorna Moramoro provided an introduction to Taraka School; Bob Johns of the Forestry Department helped with the fieldwork in Bulolo; Doug Mackrell of the Department of Civil Engineering assisted with the fieldwork in Indagen and Sid Patchett, head librarian, allowed me to distribute Asia Foundation materials to schools where I worked. These were much appreciated. I am also very grateful to the headmasters who cooperated so willingly with the research: Mr Kaengeri of Taraka School, Mr Elok of Indagen School and Mr Apo of Hompiri School. I owe thanks too to all the teachers who assisted me, in particular, Mrs Boni Vue of Taraka School. Brian Peters of Talair kindly organized travel within Papua New Guinea. It goes almost without saying that I am indebted to all those speakers of Tok Pisin who took part in the study, but I owe a great debt to Sali Bafinu and his family who acted as guides and hosts in Indagen village. Mi laik tokim tenkyu tumas long en na long ol lain bilong en. I would also like to thank the Provincial Government of Morobe Province for granting me permission to conduct research in the province, and in particular, I am grateful for the help of Benson Nablu.

The final stages of the book were written at the University of Hawaii at Manoa, while I was teaching in the Department of English as a Second Language. Various people there provided both practical assistance and intellectual stimulus. I am particularly grateful to Charlie Sato for my knowledge of various aspects of Hawaii pidgin and creole English, and for access to a number of data sources. Byron Bender of the Linguistics Department allowed me to use computer facilities. Mrs Au of the Pacific Collection at the Sinclair Library of the University of Hawaii made available for consultation John Reinecke's collection of pidgin and creole materials. I would also like to thank Martha Pennington for enlightening discussions on a number of topics related to this book. I am also grateful to Roger Andersen for comments on the issues in Chapter 7. I would like to thank too Joseph P. Balaz for contributing the poem on *Da History of Pigeon* which appears in Chapter 3. I am grateful also to Bob Le Page for comments.

At Oxford I am most indebted to my colleagues Peter

Mühlhäusler and Fiona Wright. To the former I owe my interest in Tok Pisin. I have benefited a great deal from many discussions with him about the language and a variety of related issues in linguistic theory. He also made available a draft of his book on pidgins and creoles (1986). Fiona Wright, who collaborated in the Tok Pisin research, provided personal and intellectual support as well as unlimited good cheer when it was needed under what were at times rather arduous field conditions.

Suzanne Romaine
Oxford, September 1986

For Roger

Chapter 1

Introduction to the study of pidgins and creoles

In his speech to the English-Speaking Union Conference in Ottawa (29 Oct. 1958) the Duke of Edinburgh made reference to Tok Pisin (New Guinea Pidgin English), in observing that 'I am referred to in that splendid language as "Fella bilong Mrs Queen"' (Cohen and Cohen 1971:67). This book will deal with a group of languages which linguists call pidgins and creoles, and some of the issues arising from their study.

It would be logical to begin a book on pidgins and creoles by offering definitions of these languages; however, this is easier said than done. Although all scholars would agree that there is such a group of languages, perhaps one of the biggest disputes at present among those who study them centres on how they are to be defined, how they originated and what their relationship is to one another. It is partly for this reason that research in this area is at the moment one of the most exciting and rapidly growing fields of linguistics. Indeed, some now refer to a field of study called **creolistics** (*cf eg* Mühlhäusler 1985d).[1]

Although pidgins and creoles were long the neglected step-children of linguistics because they were thought to be marginal, and not 'real' full-fledged languages, they have now emerged as the centre of attention for a number of reasons. In fact, one creolist, Bickerton (1981a) believes that creoles hold the key to understanding how human languages originally evolved many centuries ago. But even as early as 1914 Schuchardt (who is regarded as the founder of the field of pidgin and creole studies *cf* 1.2) noted that the significance of creoles for general lingustics was not fully appreciated.

If we pause to think for a moment of the circumstances in which pidgin languages arise, (by comparison with so-called 'natural' languages) very suddenly in contact situations, where they are used by speakers with different language backgrounds to fulfill certain basic communicative functions (*eg* trade), it is not hard to imagine that their rise, spread and development should reveal things of interest for linguists concerned with language acquisition, language change and universal grammar.

Hymes (1971:84), for example, describes pidginization and creolization as complex processes of sociolinguistic change. Pidginization involves reduction of linguistic resources and restriction of use, while creolization involves expansion along both these dimensions. Bickerton (1977a) has more recently characterized both pidginization and creolization as processes of acquisition under restricted conditions. In pidginization the acquisition process involves the learning of a second language by speakers of different language backgrounds who have limited access to the language of the dominant group. In creolization the restricted input occurs as part of the first language acquisition process. Bickerton's (1981a) hypothesis is that under such conditions children have recourse to innate universals which govern the process of expansion of the pidgin into a fully adequate native language. Thus, one can justify treating both pidgins and creoles as related phenomena. Both involve developing systems which arise in different contexts of language acquisition (*cf* Chs 6 and 7)

Another kind of link between these languages is historical. Hall (1966), for instance, includes a pidgin origin as an essential feature of creoles. He elaborated the notion of a linguistic life cycle, discussed in Chapter 4, linking the development of pidgins and creoles. Others such as Bickerton, however, have been concerned to identify creole features which have no origin in a prior pidgin stage (*cf* Ch. 2) My discussion in Chapter 2 of various attempts to define and type pidgin and creole languages in terms of shared features shows that there is a great deal of overlap between the two. Chapter 3 treats theories of origin, while Chapters 4 and 5 illustrate the dynamic nature of developments which characterize the pidgin–creole life cycle.

1.1 Some introductory issues and problems

My introductory anecdote about the Duke of Edinburgh's encounter with Tok Pisin serves as a convenient point of departure for some of the theoretical issues to be dealt with in subsequent chapters. There is some truth and falsehood in his remarks.

Elsewhere in his speech the Duke wrongly includes pidgin as a dialect of English. In doing so, however, he touches on some issues of interest to those who study pidgins and creoles: namely, whether these languages are to be regarded as dialects (*ie* socially and linguistically subordinate varieties) of the language which appears to contribute most of their lexicon (*ie* the superstrate, lexifier language or lexical base). In this case, for instance, the question would be whether Tok Pisin is a dialect of English, on a par with say, Scottish English, or whether it is a language in its own right (*cf eg* Chambers and Trudgill 1980 on the problem of defining the terms **language** and **dialect**). From a linguistic point of view part of the problem in coming to a decision on this matter lies in the fact that the vocabulary of a pidgin is usually drawn primarily from the prestige language of the dominant group in a situation of language contact. Its grammar, however, retains many features of the native languages of the subordinate groups. The prestige language which supplies the bulk of the vocabulary is the one which is usually thought of as being pidginized, hence, the name Pidgin English for Tok Pisin and Chinese Pidgin English etc. (*cf* 1.3).

The process of pidginization, as I will argue, involves some universal principles for putting together linguistic material of different origins by speakers trying to communicate over linguistic barriers. Schuchardt addressed these and other questions fairly early, but concluded that in the case of creoles we are dealing with independent systems. Questions about the relatedness of creoles, in particular, to their superstrate languages are still a concern of the field, *eg* in the debate about Black English in the United States in the 1960s and 1970s (*cf* 5.4). Schuchardt included Black English in the category of creole languages.

Thus, the Duke is right in this quotation to refer to Tok Pisin as a language. He is, interestingly, wrong about his designation; he would be referred to as **man bilong (misis) kwin**.

There is, however, still a bit more I can add to the anecdote at this stage, and that is to note the increasing anglicization of some varieties of Tok Pisin through renewed contact with English. Thus, it is probably more likely that the Duke of Edinburgh would be referred to in this kind of Tok Pisin as the **Duke of Edinburgh** or perhaps the **Duke bilong Edinburgh**. In fact, Hall (1966:45) noted the 'weird mixture' in the following report of the Duke's arrival in Rabaul:

> **Today i bikpela de bilong ol i welcomim Duke of Edinburgh i kamap long aerodrome bilong citi Rabaul.**

He says that in 'normal' Melanesian, this should be:

> **Tude i bikpela de bilong ol i heloim Dyuk bilong Edinboro i kamap long ples balus bilong siti Rabaul.**
> 'Today is the big day for all to welcome the Duke of Edinburgh to Rabaul airport.'

Hall remarks (1966:45–6) that:

> *Dyuk* 'Duke' and *Edinboro* 'Edinburgh' would presumably be inevitable loanwords in any case, but the phrase *Duke of Edinburgh* is a crass Anglicism, as are also *welcomim* for normal *heloim* 'to greet', and *aerodrome* for *ples balus* 'airport'; and *today* and *city* are Anglicised spellings for normal *tude* and *siti*.

These kinds of developments will be discussed in Chapter 4.

1.2 Early studies in pidgin and creole languages: a brief history of the field

The study of pidgin and creole languages goes back more than a century. DeCamp (1971a:31) and others recognize Schuchardt as the greatest of the early scholars and the founding father of the field. Schuchardt (1842–1927) is more generally known for his contributions to Romance philology and Basque studies, but within the field of pidgin and creole studies he is known for a series of papers entitled *Kreolische Studien* published in the 1880s. Significant studies have continued to appear since that time. For example, Hesseling's (1897) controversial study of Afrikaans, which claimed creole ancestry for the language, deals with issues which are still being debated today (*cf eg* Markey 1982, and 2.9). Linguistic descriptions of Capeverdean Crioulo also date from the latter part of the nineteenth century, when Coelho published a series of three articles on what he called the **Romance** or **Neo-Latin** dialects of Africa, Asia and America. This study inspired two further descriptions by native speakers, also published at the end of the century (Costa and Duarte 1886 and Brito 1887). Brito's study is actually written in Capeverdean Crioulo with an accompanying translation into Portuguese. Studies of pidgin and creoles written by native speakers of these languages are rare today (*cf* however, Silva 1985 and Rickford 1979 for two examples). As far as I know, no scholarly treatments have been written by native speakers in their own languages except for Brito (1887) and Veiga (1984) on Capeverdean. One volume which deserves mention, even though it is not written by native speakers, is the special issue of **Kivung**

(McElhanon 1975) devoted to Tok Pisin, in which some of the articles are written in that language.

DeCamp (1971a:14) says that since the Second World War, and especially in the 1960s, the nature of pidgin and creole studies has changed radically in several ways. For one thing, the field has become unified. Before the 1950s few linguists dealt with both pidgins and creoles; and few studied more than one geographical area or more than one language. Each language was treated as a separate sphere of interest. One can compare this state of the field with that of the more general state of enquiry into language before concepts such as the general theory of grammar, universal grammar, the logical problem of language acquisition and so on became central to linguistic theory (*cf eg* Smith and Wilson 1979).

Secondly, DeCamp cites the fact that pidgin–creole studies have now become a respectable academic field. In 1969 the Modern Language's Association annual bibliography groups pidgin–creole studies in a separate section rather than treating them as appendages to other languages such as French etc. DeCamp (1971a:14) dates the true birth of the field to 1959, when the first international conference on creole language studies was held in Jamaica. The proceedings of the conference (Le Page 1961) have formed the basis for much discussion and research since. For example, the Portuguese origin hypothesis had been advanced some 60 years earlier by Hesseling, but not until the 1959 conference were its implications discussed seriously from a general perspective, and the possibility of a monogenetic theory of pidgin–creole origin considered (*cf* Ch. 3). DeCamp singles out as the greatest contribution of this conference the fact that a group of scholars recognized that they were 'creolists'.

The second hallmark in the development of the field was the second international conference held nine years later in Jamaica (*cf* the papers in Hymes 1971). There some of the topics raised at the previous conference were considered again, this time by a wider range and larger number of scholars. Other issues were treated such as the possibility of prior creole origins for Black English in the United States and Marathi. The emergent field of pidgin–creole studies benefited from the growing interest in sociolinguistics, and contributions from other fields such as historical linguistics. In fact, DeCamp (1971a:14) says that 'if a genuine sociolinguistic theory ever does appear, it will certainly be indebted to pidgin–creole studies'. Hymes (1971:5) has remarked that pidginization and creolization represent the extreme to which social factors can go in shaping the transmission and use of language. Due to this and also to the fact that pidgin–creole speaking communities usually display a considerable range of varieties of speech, these languages have occupied an important place in sociolinguistics, particularly within that area often referred to as variation theory (*cf eg* Bailey 1973). A number of important methods of analysis, such as implicational scaling (*cf* 5.3) have been introduced into the study of variation by those working with data from pidgin and creole languages.

Since that time conferences in the field of pidgin–creole studies have become regular events (*cf eg* Day 1980; Valdman and Highfield 1980; *York Papers in Linguistics* 1983); and the number of collections of papers and books on pidgin and creole languages continues to increase. At the beginning of the 1980s the field derived new impetus from Bickerton's bioprogram hypothesis (*cf* Ch. 7), and the study of pidgin and creole languages now attracts an even wider range of scholars from fields such as first and second language acquisition. (*cf eg* the papers in Andersen 1983).

Having given this brief synopsis of the growth of the field (*cf* also Hellinger 1985:1.3–4 and Mühlhäusler 1986:Ch. 2), let us now consider some of the reasons why it took so long to become established as a respectable academic discipline. In order to understand them, we have to consider the historical context in which the field of linguistics became established, and how various ideas about language influenced its development. (Robins 1967 provides a useful historical overview.)

The earliest grammarians regarded the so-called classical languages, such as Latin and Greek, as the only ones deserving study. Languages without highly developed inflectional morphology such as modern English or French, were thought of as 'grammarless'; and therefore by definition they fell outside the scope of the study of grammar as it was conceived in earlier centuries. The notion that there were developed and undeveloped languages gave way largely in the late nineteenth century, partly due to the finding that the languages of so-called 'primitive' people turned out to be very structurally complex. Modern linguistics was founded on the principle of descriptivism, which held that languages should be studied on their own terms without reference to externally defined standards of correctness. Mühlhäusler (1986:24) notes that the status of 'true language' was denied until relatively recently to a number of linguistic phenomena, *eg* child language, pidgins and creoles, and second language learners' systems. The study of language systems undergoing development has generally remained marginal to the concerns of mainstream linguistics. Pidgin languages, for example, were regarded as corrupt, simplified versions of donor languages. Children's language was even recently seen as an imperfectly learned or lesser version of the parent's language. Similarly, until systematic research was undertaken into second language learner systems (*cf eg* Klein and Dittmar 1979), these too were viewed as imperfect versions of the target language.

Despite the progress made in the field of pidgin–creole studies many still believe that pidgins and creoles are parasitic rather than independent linguistic systems, which are the result of random mixing (*cf* the discussion of the notion of system in Labov 1971a). Part of the problem in this attitude has been the lack of descriptive models for dealing with highly variable and rapidly changing systems. The existing categories of linguistic analysis are biased towards the description of autonomous, discrete language systems. Moreover, there is no neutral way of recognizing a linguistic entity as a language or a system in its own right rather than as parasitic on or derivative of another.

The majority of early studies of pidgins and creoles, which go back as far as the early sixteenth century, tend, as Mühlhäusler (1986) notes, to be limited in scope and of little relevance to the aims of theoretical linguistics. Some of the earliest reports, and in some cases the majority or only reports, we have for pidgin and creole languages come from gentlemen travellers, administrators and missionaries. Many of their accounts are written to amuse others of languages which were regarded as bastardized versions of civilized European tongues. In the preface to one of the first accounts of Jamaican Creole (Russell 1868, cited in Mühlhäusler 1986:25), the author writes: 'This little work was never intended originally to meet the eye of the public; the writer merely prepared it as a source of social amusement to such of his friends as are of a literary turn.'

Others however, are written with the explicit aim of teaching Europeans something about the structure of the pidgin or creole because it serves as a useful or sometimes the only means of communication between the indigenous and expatriate population. Lloyd (n.d.) prepared a small grammar and vocabulary of what has been called Kitchen-Kafir, a contact language used by speakers of Bantu languages to communicate with the Dutch, Portuguese and English-speaking Europeans whom they worked for. The aim of the book was to allow the European to 'satisfy his immediate needs' and 'cease to trouble about learning Zulu'. Another example of this kind of description can be found in Berrenger (1811:ii) who writes of the creole Portuguese spoken in Sri Lanka that 'it is the common vehicle of intercourse with the inhabitants'. There is 'no other mode of communicating with natives and conducting political negociations [sic] with the Court of Candy'. It is condescending in tone, as can be seen even from the title, where the Portuguese is referred to as corrupted. Its intended audience is 'the English Gentleman in the Civil and Military Service'. In the preface Berrenger (1811:i) writes that the corrupted Portuguese is:

> no longer that impressive and melodious medium by means of which the genuus [sic] of Camoens has immortalized the enterprizing spirit and intrepid valour of his countrymen. It has sunk into a barborous Jargon, scarce intelligible to a native of Portugal, which hitherto no one has dared, or deigned to reduce to grammatical form.

He adds (1811:11) that 'the facility with which this dialect may be acquired is a most inciting advantage it possesses in a climate so discouraging to mental exertion'.

Often such accounts contain a number of real or concocted fragments of the language, which get handed down from one generation of amateur linguists to the next as part of the folk wisdom concerning the speech in question. For the most part attempts to explain aspects of the structure of Pidgin English are confused by the resemblance between English and pidgin words. Pidgin expressions are seen as clumsy, but often amusing and descriptive. Collinson (1929:21), for instance comments:

> That word 'stop' is rather a puzzler until you get used to it. It means 'is present' and not 'finish'. Here is an illustration. If you lost your pencil you would probably mutter to yourself, 'Now, where's that pencil of mine?', but a Solomon Islander would say, 'My gracious, where pencil belong me he stop?' It sounds rather difficult, but in time this curious phrasing comes naturally.

Another example can be found in Collinson's (1929:22–3) observations on pidgin English **wanem** [<what name], a general interrogative marker meaning 'which' or 'what':

> We use the phrase 'What name?' a great deal. It is a sort of general query meaning 'Well, what is it?' If a native came into my store and wandered vaguely about, staring and goggling, I should rap out sharply, 'What name?' meaning, 'Well, young-feller-me-lad, what do you want?'

The Pacific Islands Monthly carried the following examples supplied by readers (cited in Mühlhäusler 1985b:17):

> A European lady: 'Big fella missus he put water belong stink along him.' In other words, the average white woman is best remembered by the natives owing to her use of perfume. A piano:

'Big fella bokus (box) you fightem he cry.' This is highly ingenious–particularly the description of keyboard action. (*Pacific Islands Monthly* 16 Sept. 1930)

A resident of Townsville sends me more lively examples of 'pidgin'. This is how a New Guinea boy says: 'You're bald!': 'Grass belong coconut he no more stop.' 'Picaninny' is a 'baby'; 'deewhy' is a 'tree'–'piccaninny belong deewhy' is therefore 'fruit'. 'Copper' is a covering, such as a roof; therefore 'copper belong "hand"', for 'fingernail', is quite ingenious. 'Lik lik' is 'small'; 'lik lik too much' is 'smaller';' lik lik plenty too much' is 'very small'. (*Pacific Islands Monthly* 16 Dec. 1930)

The various circumlocutions reported for **piano** are part of the mythology about Pacific Pidgin English. Collinson (1929:21), for example, cites the South Sea Islands version of it as **This fella box you fight 'im he sing-out-out**. Mühlhäusler (1986:26) adds the following form from Baron von Hesse-Wartegg (1902:53):

big fellow box spose whiteman fight him he cry too much.

In the same year Daiber (1902:255) writes:

All in all the black does not lack a certain sense of humour. His description of the first piano brought to the German South Seas is also delightful. It was a Papuan who, horrified, told of **big fellow box, white fellow master fight him plenty too much, he cry** (of the big box which the white man beats so much that it screams). Since that time the piano has been called in Pidgin-English **box belong cry**, that is, 'screaming box' or 'screaming trunk'. (translated by Mühlhäusler 1986)

Hall (1943:82–3) cites a tale which he entitles 'The piano arrives' (as described by a 'boy'), which probably explains how such circumlocutions were invented and then passed on:[2]

Wanfela bigfela bakis i-kam long sip. Nau masta i-tok: 'Hariap yufela kisim i-go antap.' Orait. Mifela pulim i-go antap, nau masta i-tok: 'Kisim tamiak i-kam.' Orait. Mifela kisim tamiak, nau brokim bakis. Godamn noderfela bakis i-stap insaid. Nau mi kisim tamiak, mi laik brokim nambatu bakis. Nau masta i holim fas han bilong mi. Bel bilong em i nogud finis. Em i-tok: 'Yu longlong man yu! Yu laik brokim samting bilong misis, a?' Nau mi lukim bakis. I gat tit. Plentifela tit i-stap. Nau masta i-singautim misis, nau masta i kisim sia. Nau misis i-kisim liklik bakis. Masta i-faitim tit bilong bakis. Godamn! I save kraiaut. Nau misis i faitim liklik bakis long stik-liklik haf stik, i olsem banara. Godamn! Disfela i kraiaut olsem pusi!

[Gloss: A large box arrived on the ship. Then the master said: 'Hurry up, you and bring it up.' Very well. We pulled it up, and then he said: 'Bring me an axe.' Very well. We took an axe and broke the box. By heck! There was another box inside. Then I took the axe and started to break the second box. Then the master held back my hand. He was thoroughly angry. He said, 'You crazy man, you! You want to break something of the mistresses, do you?' The master called to the mistress and the master got a chair. Then the mistress took a little box. The master hit the teeth of the box. By heck, it could cry out. Then the mistress hit the little box with a stick – a little piece of stick, like a bow. By heck! This [box] cried like a cat!]

Mühlhäusler (1986) adds a few more circumlocutions to the list:

big fellow bokkes, suppose missis he fight him, he cry too much (Friederici 1911:100)

big fellow box, stop house, suppose you fight him, him cry (reported for Samoan Plantation Pidgin by Neffgen in the *Samoan Times* 27 March 1915).

fight im bokis moosik – 'to play the piano' (Shelton-Smith 1929).

him big fella box, suppose you fight him, he cry (Mihalic 1969:39)

bikpela bokis bilong krai taim you paitim na kikim em (Bálint 1969).

Mühlhäusler observes that none of these sources has the same 'name' for a piano.

Other accounts of pidgins and creoles are more outspokenly pejorative and negative. Silva (1985:48–50) for example, cites the following collection of reports on Cape Verdean Crioulo:

> A governor arriving there [Cape Verde Islands] in 1801 wrote in dismay of the 'ridiculous language of the natives'. Chelmiki in 1841 found a general preference for Crioulo and disdain for Portuguese; he was shocked to find even continental residents accustoming themselves to Crioulo rather than trying to overturn that 'pernicious practice'. In 1844 Lima described the language as a ridiculous slang, a monstrous composition of Old Portuguese and the languages of Guinea.

In the same vein an editorial in the *Rabaul Times* (16 Oct. 1925) deprecates Tok Pisin (cited in Mühlhäusler 1985b:16):

> The pidgin English as spoken in these days is about the most atrocious form of speech perhaps one could find in any corner of

> the globe. It is neither one thing or the other. Consisting of a mixture of Samoan and Chinese here and there, with an occasional word of Malayan, it is conglomeration truly worthy of the Tower of Babel.

It can be seen that many Europeans commonly make the assumption that pidgins are just a special form of their own language. Most often they regard it as a debased and bastardized one. Serious misunderstandings can arise from the assumption that words which look like English ones have the same meaning. Hall (1955a:18–19) cites the following case:

> I was in a certain New Guinea hotel, and witnessed the following scene between the assistant manageress (recently arrived from Australia) and a Papua house-boy. She had not seen him all afternoon, and thought that he had only just come in, so she began to scold him:
> Manageress: **Why you no come this afternoon?** [One would never say 'why' in Pidgin, but **bilong wonem?** Still, the house-boy got her drift, and answered:]
> House-boy: **No, misis, mi kam long belo kaikai**. (*On the contrary*) *madam, I came at noon*.) [**Belo kaikai** is a phrase meaning the *bell for food*; originally a term used on the labour lines in copra plantations, it has now become the general expression in Pidgin for *noontime*.]
> Manageress: **Belly kaikai! That's all you niggers ever think of, is filling your bellies with kaikai**.
> House-boy: **Tasol misis, mi stap long haus kuk**. (*But madam, I was in the kitchen*.) [**Haus kuk** is a phrase of the same structure as **belo kaikai**, with two nouns, the second telling of some characteristic or purpose of the first; it means *room for cooking*, and therefore, *kitchen*.]
> Manageress: **Nonsense! You're not the cook of this house**.

Mühlhäusler (1985a:246) notes some other lexical items that are reported to have led to some confusion, *eg* **baksait** interpreted as *backside* rather than **back, kilim** interpreted as *to kill* instead of *to hit, strike*, and **pusim** *to push* instead of *to copulate*. Murphy (1966:16–17;43) gives a list of pitfalls or *faux amis* for expatriates, and notes too that it is commonly believed that any English word can be translated into Tok Pisin by adding **-fela** or **-im**. He stresses, however, that 'there are no such words as **Whysat, gotim, wantim, tellim, broke, broke'im, callim** (meaning *to call*), **cryout**'. A misunderstanding arising from the similarity between English and Tok Pisin with more serious consequences is reported in Nelson (1972:170–1), in which a Papua New Guinean stumbled against a white woman coming out of the theatre. When questioned by a man about what had happened, the Papua New Guinean replied: 'Mi putim han long baksait bilong misis.' – 'I touched the woman's back with my hand.' The answer, however, cost him half a tooth, his job and three months in prison, due to the confusion between the meaning of Tok Pisin **baksait** and English **backside**.

Mühlhäusler (1981b) has described in detail the features of the variety of Tok Pisin called **Tok Masta** (*ie* European talk). This variety differs from Tok Pisin in a number of ways. Mühlhäusler (1985a:246) illustrates this with a sentence taken from a radio talk on the BBC (15 May 1970):

> **Im fellow Matthew e got im three fellow egg.**
> 'Matthew has three eggs.'

He points out three typical European misconceptions about the structure of Tok Pisin:

1. It is not the case that each noun is preceded by **fellow**. Contrary to what is claimed by many European writers, **-pela** [<**fellow**] is used as a suffix with monosyllabic adjectives, *eg* **blakpela pik** – 'black pig'.
2. **Em [<him]** serves as a third person singular pronoun and as an emphasizer when preceding nouns. The suffix - **im** [<**him**] marks transitivity and causativity with verbs. It is not sufficient or grammatical to sprinkle a sentence with **-im**. The first **-im** in the text is ungrammatical because it is not followed by a noun; the second is unacceptable because **gat** is one of the verbs which do not take **-im**.
3. Many Tok Pisin words, especially those referring to aspects of flora and fauna, are not of English origin. The word for **egg** is **kiau** [<Tolai].

Thus, in ordinary Rural Pidgin, the correct version of the sentence would be:

> **Matthew i gat tripela kiau.**

Even a consideration of the origin of the label **pidgin** for these kinds of contact languages is revealing of some of the characteristics of these languages, as well as of the prejudices of some Europeans towards them (*cf* Hancock 1979b). Mühlhäusler (1986:1) lists five plausible etymologies for the term **pidgin** and concludes that they are equally likely to be genuine. It is in the nature of a pidgin language that multiple or convergent etymologies can be found for a number of its lexical items (*cf* 3.4). The OED says that pidgin is a 'Chinese corruption of English **busi-**

ness'. According to others it could be a Chinese corruption of Portuguese **occupação** – 'business', or is from Hebrew **pidjom** meaning 'exchange or trade'. Another possible source mentioned is that it is a South Seas pronunciation of English **beach** as **beachee**. And still another is that it comes from Yago, a South American Indian language spoken in an area colonized by Britain, which has a word **pidian** meaning 'people'. In popular accounts some of these (and other sources) are given, as in Collinson's (1929:20) remarks about South Sea Island Pidgin:

> Pidgin English! Now in the first place the word 'pidgin' has nothing whatever to do with pigeons.[3] It comes from China, and represents John Chinaman's best attempt to pronounce our word 'business'. So pidgin-English simply means business-English – the queer sort of language used between white men and natives which enables them to understand each other and do business together.

Still another possibility not mentioned by Mühlhäusler is the one noted in Knowlton (1967:228) attributed to Professor Hsü Ti-san at the University of Hong Kong. Ti-San received a copy of Leland's (1924) book on Chinese Pidgin English and on page 3 he has written in the margin that the term **pidgin** may be derived from two Chinese characters, **pei** and **ts'īn**, which mean 'paying money'. This would be consistent with the function of pidgins as trade languages.

It is as well to dispel at the outset of this book the view that pidgins are simply corrupt versions of the superstrate languages with no grammar. As recently as 1986 the *Times Higher Education Supplement* (17 Jan. 1986) carried a report from a newspaper in Ghana complaining about the use of Pidgin English on Ghanaian campuses and recommending that stern measures be taken against it. The report notes that in no other case do the future leaders of the country talk a 'mixture in which all the tenses are thrown to the wind, and words are picked from far and wide, making no sense to the listener'. It is true that pidgins are 'makeshift' languages in the sense that they make do with a minimum of grammatical apparatus. Wurm (1985) comments that any language which is closely related to another in a portion of its vocabulary or structure could, when looked at from the perspective of the other language, be said to be a debased, corrupt or ridiculous version of the other language. One point of consensus reached by those who study pidgins is that they have a recognizable structure of their own independent of the substrate and superstrate languages involved in the original contact. The degree of stability of this structure varies, depending on the extent of internal development and functional expansion the pidgin has undergone at any particular point in its life cycle (*cf* Ch. 4).

1.3 Present distribution of pidgin and creole languages

It would be impossible in a single volume to do justice to the 100 or so pidgin and creole languages spoken in all parts of the world. Inevitably, our knowledge of some of these languages is better than others. Mühlhäusler (1986:19) has noted that research on creoles in the Pacific region of the world is less advanced than it is in the Atlantic regions. This is true, despite the fact that English-based pidgins and creoles have been used in the South Pacific for nearly 200 years (*cf* Clark 1979:3). The study of at least one of these goes back 100 years (*cf* Schuchardt 1883 and 1889), and two of them, Tok Pisin and Hawaii Pidgin English are among the best known and most studied pidgins in the world. At the other end of the extreme, however, is the case of pidgin and creole languages of Australia, which are the least researched (*cf* however, Harris 1984; Dutton 1983b; Mühlhäusler (forthcoming) for an overview of the state of research in this part of the world). Muysken (1980) observes that although there are numerous references to Spanish-based Amerindian pidgins spoken in the upper Amazon, there have been no detailed studies of them. The bias towards the study of Caribbean pidgins and creoles in the field as a whole and their connection with the slave trade, has resulted in a distortion of the historical perspective on pidgins and creoles in general (*cf* Thomason 1980:168).

One can only hope to sample widely from typologically different and historically distant languages so as to obtain adequate coverage and representation. In doing so, the aim of the typologist is to pinpoint certain similarities and differences. The question which must then concern us is how to account for the similarities. A number of possibilities arise: One is that they are due to:

1. shared historical links
2. simplification of the same source language, *eg* Portuguese or English
3. linguistic universals, syntactic, semantic and pragmatic
4. accidental factors
5. shared function
6. a combination of these factors.

I discuss these and other possibilities in Chapter 3.

In his survey of pidgin and creole languages of the world, Hancock (1971:510–11) provides the map shown in Fig. 1.1, on which he locates 80 pidgin and creole languages. In a later count, he (1977) gives the number as 127. In his preface to a collection of papers published in 1979 Hancock says that Meillet and Cohen's (1978) *Survey of Languages of the World* lists 200 pidgin and creole languages. A list of the languages mentioned by Hancock in 1971 and 1977 is given in Appendix 1 to this book.[4] Another indispensable reference source for the field is Reinecke *et al*'s (1975) bibliography of research on pidgin and creole languages. The exact number of such languages is difficult to establish for a number of reasons. One is simply that the number depends on our definitions of what counts as a pidgin or creole. Hancock (1971:520), for instance, wrongly includes Babu as a rudimentary pidgin employed during the British rule in India. He equates it with Hobson-Jobson and Chee Chee (*cf* however, Schuchardt 1891). As Widdowson (1977) has pointed out, Babu is a variety which shows the reverse development to a pidgin in that it represents an elaboration of the expressive component of language. In Chapter 2 I discuss some of the reasons why these languages are hard to define. Hancock (1977) adds a number of new languages to his original list, such as Gastarbeiter Deutsch, *ie* the varieties of German spoken by migrant workers, and reclassifies and omits others. The addition of Gastarbeiter Deutsch can be justified on the basis of the discovery of a number of pidgin-like features in the language of adult foreign workers. In drawing attention to these in 1968, Clyne referred to this variety as Pidgin German (*cf* also 3.1 and 6.3). This idea and term were subsequently taken up by a research group in Heidelberg (*cf* the study described in Klein and Dittmar 1979). 'New' pidgins and creoles are continually being 'discovered'. Hancock could have added Middle English to his list (*cf eg* Bailey and Maroldt 1977); and even more recently, it has been argued that sign languages are creoles (*cf eg* Fischer 1978; Deuchar (1986; and 7.5). In both these cases it has been argued that there has been a disruption in the transmission of the language sufficient to justify calling them creoles (*cf* Ch. 7).

Other reasons which make counting more difficult are illustrated in Mühlhäusler (1986:15ff). He observes that pidgin and creole speakers are often at the bottom of the social scale, and are frequently pushed aside or ignored. It is commonly believed, even sometimes by the speakers themselves, that they speak the same language as that which is recognized as the standard or official one in a particular country. Thus, often there is no

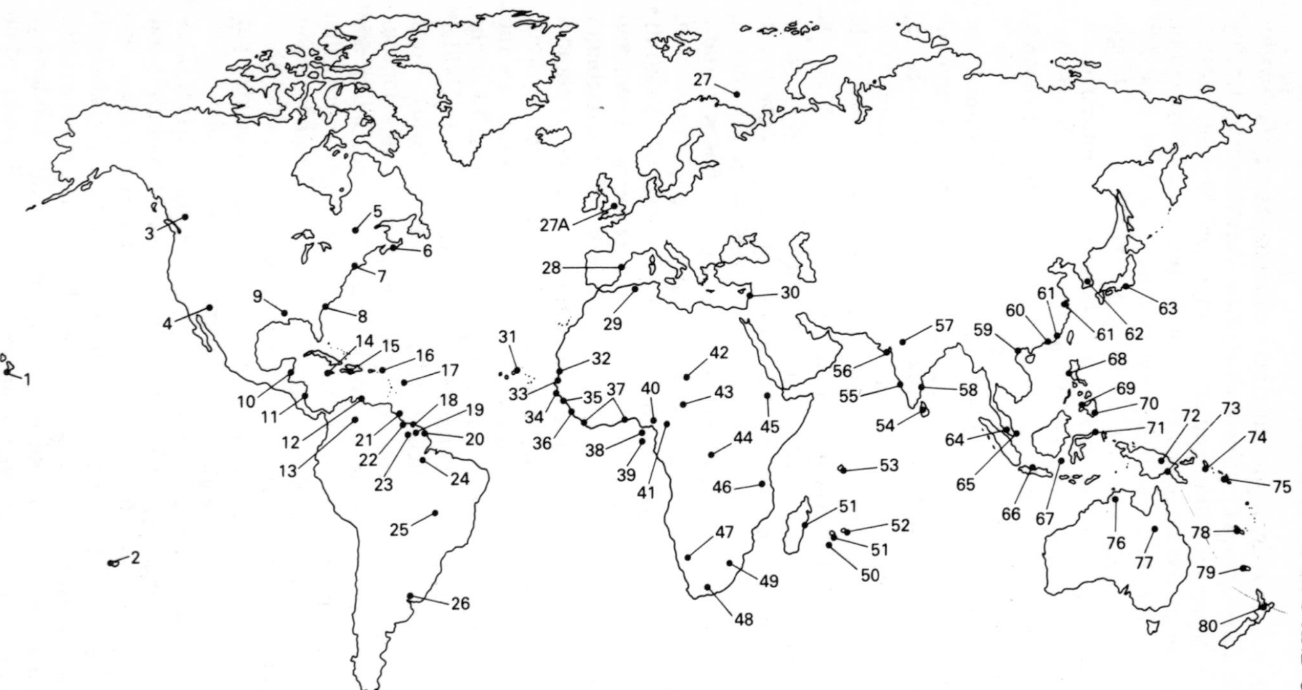

FIGURE 1.1 Map of Pidgin and Creole Languages. Numbers refer to the pidgins and creoles listed in Hancock (1971) and Hancock (1977), given in Appendix 1, pp 315–25.

recognition of a pidgin or creole as a separate language. In the case of Papuan Pidgin English discussed by Mühlhäusler, informants claim to be speaking English not Pidgin. The term 'pidgin' has only recently become known to Pacific Islanders. Mühlhäusler obtained samples of New Guinea Pidgin German by asking his informants to speak German.

Even where a pidgin or creole has a name and is recognized as a separate language or variety, its speakers may be reluctant to admit that they speak it. This reflects the low prestige which these languages very often have.[5]

Mühlhäusler also points out the drawbacks in the customary practice of labelling pidgins with a formula which includes their location and their principal lexifier language, as in the following examples:

(a) Chinese Pidgin English
(b) New Guinea Pidgin English
(c) New Caledonian Pidgin French

This formula is used in textbooks such as Hockett (1958:424). Schuchardt (1891) raises the issue of terminology in connection with his typology of what he called Indo-English, but does not resolve it adequately. These labels are misleading for a number of reasons (*cf eg* the discussion in Walsh 1984). From a linguistic point of view one objection is that such labels imply that the lexicon is separate from the syntax and that the lexicon is more important in deciding relationships among languages. Taylor (1971:293) objects to these labels because they minimize structural similarities between lexically unrelated creoles.

A more sociolinguistic objection is that the first term in such labels can be ambiguous as to whether it specifies a language, a group of speakers or a geographical location. For example, in the case of Chinese Pidgin English the label is now taken to refer to the pidgin spoken by speakers of Chinese origin rather than the kind of pidgin spoken along the China coast. In the case of Hawaiian Pidgin English the adjective Hawaiian is ambiguous because it could refer to the geographical location of Hawaii, to the people of Hawaiian ethnic descent or to the Hawaiian language. I will use the terms Hawaii Pidgin and Creole English here rather than the customary adjectival form Hawaiian in the designation of these varieties following the practice of Sato and others. There is a strong local reaction from people of native Hawaiian background to the traditional labels due to concern in the community that outsiders may think that it refers to a pidginized (and therefore stigmatized) form of the Hawaiian language.

As speakers of these languages are becoming aware of the negative connotations of the term 'pidgin', new names have been introduced for some of them, such as Tok Pisin, officially recognized in 1981 as the name for New Guinea Pidgin English, or Broken for Torres Strait Pidgin English.[6] Other names have often been invented by linguists, such as the use of the term Neomelanesian for Tok Pisin by Hall (1966).

Another problem is the high geographical mobility of the speakers of these languages. For example, Mühlhäusler (1986:14) says that what is called Pidgin Fiji appears to be Kanaka English transported from Queensland. Baker and Corne (1982) show that the label **Indian Ocean Creole French** is a misnomer because the social and linguistic histories of Mauritian and Reunion Creole French are separate. Mühlhäusler concludes that it is inadvisable to associate pidgins and creoles too closely with a single location.

A further complication arises from the fact that a pidgin may change its lexical affiliation at different stages of its development. This is referred to as **relexification** (3.3). Present day Hiri Motu may be partially relexified Papuan Pidgin English (*cf* Dutton and Mühlhäusler 1979). This poses a further question of historical continuity and identity over time, which is discussed in more detail in 3.4.

There are of course no doubt a number of extinct pidgin and creole languages for which we have no evidence. There are also a number of nearly extinct ones which are in great need of research (*cf eg* Urry and Walsh 1981 on the Macassarese language in Northern Australia). For the moment, however, I will note a few things about the present distribution of these languages. They are spoken all over the world, but particularly in tropical and subtropical regions of West Africa, the Caribbean and the South Pacific. Most of these languages are European-based, *ie* have a European language as their main lexifier language. Hancock (1977) lists only 37 non-European based pidgins and creoles.

As far as numbers of speakers are concerned, DeCamp (1971a:17) makes the following estimates. He says that two to three million speakers probably use some form of pidgin daily in at least some situations. Creoles are spoken by more than six million persons. Given all the difficulties mentioned previously, these estimates can only be rough indicators, but world-wide, it is certainly true that there are more speakers of pidgin and creole languages than there are speakers of Swedish.

DeCamp (1971a:17) says that French-based creoles claim the largest number of speakers, probably around 45,000,000. There are four major dialects of French Creole in the Caribbean: Haiti, French Guyana, Louisiana and the Lesser Antilles. It is also spoken on the islands of Reunion and Mauritius in the Indian Ocean. There is some dispute as to whether French-based pidgins exist; much more research needs to be done in the Pacific (*cf eg* the discussion by Reinecke 1971 of Tây Bôi spoken in Vietnam). The status of French-based Bichelamar and its relationship to other pidgins in New Caledonia and the New Hebrides is disputed (*cf eg* Hollyman 1964 and 1976). Valdman (1978) provides a good introduction to the study of French-based creoles (*cf* also Green 1987).

English-based creoles are used in West Africa, the Cameroons and Sierra Leone, and throughout the Caribbean and the Pacific. Spanish- and Portuguese-based creoles are widely used in Asia. Three Portuguese creoles are in use on islands off the West African coast, *ie* Cape Verde, Annobon and Saõ Tome. Papiamentu is the only such creole in the Caribbean spoken by the inhabitants of the Southern Caribbean Dutch-owned islands of Aruba, Bonaire and Curaçao. A Dutch-based creole is spoken by a few speakers in the Virgin Islands; and if one includes Afrikaans as a Dutch-based creole (*cf eg* Markey 1982, and 2.9), then another three million or so speakers can be included for Dutch-based creoles. Non-European based creoles can be found in Africa and the South Pacific, *eg* Swahili in parts of Africa, and Hiri Motu in Papua New Guinea.

1.4 The scope and structure of this book

It is perhaps easiest to explain the scope and structure of this book by comparing it with the other available introductions to the field. Hall's (1966) work constitutes what would probably be called the first major attempt to treat pidgin and creole languages from the perspective of modern descriptive linguistics. His book did much to put the field on the map, and also to define the kinds of languages which were taken to be within its scope. The three sections of Hall's book give us an overall view of the main areas he was interested in: (i) nature and history; (ii) structure and relationships; and (iii) significance. Hall (1966:xi) argued in his introduction that pidgins and creoles were of major importance. He writes (1966:xv) that from a scientific point of view one can learn a great deal about language history from the origins of pidgins and creoles; the study of their structure is of great value for the general theory of language. Hall, however, treated pidgins and creoles as self-contained wholes, and adhered strongly to the genetic model of historical relationship in accounting for the origins of pidgins (*cf* 3.3). By using the family tree model Hall was able to establish the fundamental structural similarity of pidgins and creoles to their related European lexifier languages.

The next major book in the field is Todd's (1974), an extremely useful introduction, which treats issues such as the origin of pidgins and the process of development from pidgin to creole (*cf* Rickford's 1977 review). Todd's (1984) more recent work is restricted to English-based pidgins and creoles (as is Hellinger 1985). It contains detailed descriptions of the lexicon and grammar of two pidgins, Cameroon Pidgin English and Tok Pisin and allows us to make some comparisons between the two.

One respect in which the treatment of pidgin and creole languages I will offer here is distinctive lies in the attention I will give to language acquisition, language change and universals (*cf* Chs. 6 and 7). Jespersen noted some time ago the similarities between language learning and pidginization. His book on language was noteworthy for its inclusion of a chapter entitled *Pidgins and Congeners*. In commenting on the status of Beach-la-Mar (now Bislama, a variety of Pidgin English spoken in Vanuatu), Jespersen (1922:225) says that it is 'English learnt imperfectly, in consequence partly of the difficulties always inherent in learning a totally different language, partly of the obstacles put in the way of learning by the linguistic behavior of the English-speaking people themselves'. Jespersen (1922:233) saw parallels across acquisition, loss of language and pidginization in attributing the results to the 'same mental factor . . ., imperfect mastery of a language'. A more recent statement is made by Samarin (1971:126) to the effect that 'there is something in pidgin languages, imperfect learning of a second language, loss of one's own language and restricted codes that is common to them all'. Given the rapid growth of the field of pidgin and creole studies and second language acquisition there is now a sufficient number of studies, emergent theoretical consensus and models to allow us to make comparisons between the two (*cf* especially the papers in Andersen 1983).

The most recent book on pidgins and creoles is Mühlhäusler's (1986) *Pidgin and Creole Linguistics*. Its aim is (1986:xi) to clarify what constitutes the dynamic character of pidgins and creoles and to isolate the most important forces underlying it. He pays attention to the social forces which are constitutive of pidginization and creolization. He argues, for example, that the structural viability of a creole is dependent on its social viability (*cf* Ch. 3). He stresses (1986:94) that pidgins and creoles can be understood only if they are seen as social solutions to discontinuities in social and linguistic traditions. Since the social pressures to develop cross-linguistic communication differ from case to case, this makes it very difficult to establish a coherent definition of these languages.

Mühlhäusler also attaches a great deal of importance to the role of universals rather than influence from substratum and superstratum languages in pidgin development. Despite the renewed interest in creoles raised by Bickerton's bioprogram hypothesis, Mühlhäusler chooses to mention it only in passing and does not discuss it in detail. In this book I have devoted a chapter to this topic and related issues.

Another difference in emphasis between this book and Mühlhäusler's is my concern to relate the study of pidgins and creoles to the more general study of acquisitional processes, and to a lesser extent (due to limitations of space), historical change. Mühlhäusler (1986:261–5) devotes only one section of his Chapter 6 on the relevance of pidgins and creole studies to linguistic theory to a discussion of some of the implications for language learning. He comments (1986:261) that 'pidginization and creolization can be regarded as the unmarked case of language acquisition and should therefore be studied before acquisition in contextually more complex situations'. Wode (1980:21–2), however, says that man's capacity for language acquisition can only be characterized if the various types of language acquisition are brought within the scope of one integrated theory that describes both the similarities and differences between various acquisitional types, *ie* first and second language acquisition and pidgins and creoles. He argues that the commonalities which recur across all these types are due to non-age specific, non-language specific, and hence universal strategies of language acquisition. Because there are such regularities which apply to all acquisitional types, pidgins necessarily have specific properties which they share with all developing systems.

Notes

1. It is interesting that this term subsumes the study of pidgins, creoles and much more. Markey (1981) recognizes three basic processes: (i) diffusion; (ii) fusion (between two languages); and (iii) pidginization and creolization.

2. I have transliterated this text into normal orthography from Hall's phonemic transcription.
3. The similarity between the two words **pidgin** and **pigeon** does, however, have some interesting consequences, as shown in 3.6.
4. I am grateful to Fiona Wright for making this comparison.
5. A similar situation is true of many minority languages which are not pidgins or creoles.
6. The name Tok Pisin is not universally used by its speakers. Children whom I interviewed in Lae did not use this term, but referred instead to the language simply as pidgin.

Chapter 2

Definitions and characteristics of pidgins and creoles

2.1 Some preliminary definitions of pidgins

DeCamp's (1977:3) comment on the lack of agreement over definitions of pidgins and creoles is a useful starting point for my discussion:

> There is no . . . agreement on the definition of the group of languages called pidgins and creoles. Linguists all agree that there is such a group, that it includes many languages and large numbers of speakers, and that pidgin–creole studies have now become an important field within linguistics. Yet even the authors of this book [in Valdman 1977b SR] would not agree among themselves on a definition of these languages. Some definitions are based on function, the role these languages play in the community: *eg* a pidgin is an auxiliary trade language. Some are based on historical origins and development: *eg* a pidgin may be spontaneously generated; a creole is a language that has evolved from a pidgin. Some definitions include formal characteristics: restricted vocabulary, absence of gender, true tenses, inflectional morphology, or relative clauses, etc. Some linguists combine these different kinds of criteria and include additional restrictions in their definitions.

Let us take a look at some problems in attempts to define the terms 'pidgin' and 'creole'. It will soon become apparent, as Traugott (1981:1) points out, that 'despite attempts to define the terms "pidgin" and "creole" in homogeneous ways, they have proved to defy such definitions'. DeCamp (1971a:15) defines a pidgin as a:

> contact vernacular, normally not the native language of any of its speakers . . . it is characterized by a limited vocabulary, an

elimination of many grammatical devices such as number and gender, and a drastic reduction of redundant features.

A pidgin represents a language which has been stripped of everything but the bare essentials necessary for communication. There are few, if any, stylistic options. The emphasis is on the referential or communicative rather than the expressive function of language. As Hymes (1971:84) puts it: 'Pidginization is that complex process of sociolinguistic change comprising reduction in inner form, with convergence, in the context of restriction in use . . . Pidginization is usually associated with simplification in outer form.' It appears that pidgins should be recognized as a special or limiting case of reduction in form resulting from restriction in use, since other varieties of language display similar properties, *eg* dying languages, second languages, koinés, etc. (*cf* Chs. 6 and 7).

If we use Todd's (1974) definition of a pidgin as a marginal language which arises to fulfil certain restricted communicative needs among people who have no common language, then pidgins are probably more generally the outcome of any situation of language contact. Indeed, one could extend this idea, as Le Page (1977:222–3) has done, to refer to the communicative act of a speaker on a given occasion as an 'instant pidgin'. In other words, Le Page is pointing to the on-going need in all human communicative settings for speakers to negotiate a common set of meanings through the linguistic means available to them. Speakers in any situation will need to accommodate to one another even if they speak the 'same' language (*cf* Giles *et al.* 1973 on the notion of accommodation theory).

There has been some dispute in the literature over the number of languages which are necessary input to produce a true pidgin. DeCamp (1971a:22) says that any two languages in contact can result in an 'interlingual improvization' but more than two languages in contact are required for the development of a true pidgin. Whinnom (1971) too stresses that a pidgin always arises from a situation involving a target language and two or more substrate languages, where the socially superior target language is sufficiently inaccessible to the substrate speakers that there is little motivation to improve performance and where a defective version of language can be functionally adequate. Others, such as Schumann (1978), would say that similar conditions can occur when any individual foreign learner of a language has only limited exposure to its speakers and limited motivation to acquire it. In such cases even though there is only one 'substrate' language involved, he would speak of a process of pidginization at work in the acquisition process (*cf* 6.4). If we accept Whinnom's criterion, then it would not be appropriate to extend the term pidginization to refer to all situations which involve contact between only two languages. This would rule out situations of 'foreigner talk' (*cf* 3.1), or immigrant languages or the type of makeshift communication between tourists and guides described by Hall (1966) as a pidgin. In cases where speakers of more than two different languages must converse through a medium which is native to none of them, the kinds of restructurings are more radical than in these other cases.

2.2 Some linguistic features of pidgins

Among those who stress social explanations for the reduced and simplified nature of pidgins is Hudson (1980:63), who comments in particular on their characteristic lack of inflectional morphology. He suggests that inflectional morphology may in some sense be an unnatural mechanism for expressing semantic and syntactic distinctions. He notes too that it is strange that inflectional morphology is so widespread among natural languages, given that it benefits nobody, and makes a language more difficult to learn. It is often the finer details of language such as variable pronunciations of inflectional suffixes (*eg* the plural marker, as in **house/houses** and the past tense, as in **pack/packed**) which are socially diagnostic of the speaker's social class, sex, style etc. Hudson speculates that if a language variety is a pidgin, which no one uses as a means of group identification, there is no pressure to maintain inefficient aspects of pronunciation and grammar. Presumably there are also difficulties in borrowing and integrating inflectional morphology in the early stages of a pidgin's development.

A number of linguists have tried to explain the similarities which pidginized speech varieties show in the expression of grammatical categories and syntactic relationships by appealing to more general principles of linguistic organization motivated by specialization to the referential function. One such principle is that of paradigmatic univocity, as defined, for example, by Hjelmslev (1938:285), which refers to cases in which a stable relationship exists between form and meaning. For example, in standard Swahili, prefixes and infixes are used to express the subject and object of the verb, *eg* **ni-ta-m-piga** [I future him hit] – 'I will hit him'. The language gets significantly reduced in form and function the further away one travels from the East African coast since it is used by many second language speakers as a trade language. Some have referred to these varieties as pidgins (*cf* however, Scotton 1979:111), while others such as Nida and Fehderau (1970) speak of koiné varieties of African vernacular languages (*cf* also Siegel 1985 on koineization). A koiné is a less drastically reduced variety than a pidgin. It shares mutual intelligibility with the superordinate language. At any rate, in these vehicular varieties of Swahili affixes are replaced by full and invariant pronominal forms, *eg* **yeye alipiga mimi** – 'he hit me' [*cf* full Swahili **alimpiga**]; **mimi tapiga yeye** – 'I will hit him' (*cf* Manessy 1977:137 and also Heine 1979:94–5). In most Bantu languages the object precedes the verb, but in the pidginized varieties, the object follows the verb so that word order becomes SVO. The grammatical category of tense tends to get lost. Embedding tends to be replaced by conjoining as a means of linking sentences; the listener is left to make the connections.

Mühlhäusler (1986:158–9) identifies a number of features of pronominal systems which characterize pidgins. He notes that the pronominal systems of stabilized pidgins illustrate the minimal requirements of pronoun systems in human languages. The most minimal system is evidenced by Chinese Pidgin English where there are three pronouns, first, second and third person, but no number distinctions. In Pacific Jargon English many utterances appear without an overt pronoun, where we would expect one in Standard English. Mühlhäusler (1986:158) cites the following from 1840 as an example:

> **Now got plenty money; no good work**. – 'Now I have lots of money so I do not need to work.'

This feature also emerged in Schumann's (1986) attempts to create pidgins artificially in an experimental setting. He gave learners a lexicon of 220 words (based on Bickerton and Givón 1978) and got them to communicate in specific tasks such as giving locations or directions on a map. Sokolik (1986) reports examples such as the following in Farsi pidgin, which show that there is a tendency to omit subject pronouns:

> **naxeir fahmidan**. [no understand] – 'I don't understand.'
> **naxier xastan mundan inja**. [no want stay here] – 'I don't want to stay here.'

There is a major typological difference between languages which allow sentences without subject pronouns and those which don't. Chomsky (1982) refers to this distinction as the pro-drop parameter. Languages like English which require subjects to be realized lexically are considered non-pro-drop languages. We would predict that if speakers were applying the rules of their native language in inventing a pidgin that they would follow the parameter settings in that language. Thus, in the case of speakers of pro-drop languages, we would expect that parameter to remain in force. Then the absence of pronouns in the resulting pidgin could be said to be due to substratum influence. In the case of Farsi pidgin, however, the speakers' native language was English, so this explanation does not hold. Much the same argument applies to other cases of second language acquisition. White (1985), for example, has claimed that native speakers of Spanish (a pro-drop language) learning English transfer this parameter. It is interesting that in other instances of second language acquisition Meisel (1983b:202) claims that deletion of pronouns can be found irrespective of the first language backgrounds of the speakers. This suggests that pro-drop constitutes the unmarked case. Hyams (1983) has argued this for first language acquisition.

The pronominal systems of pidgin languages generally do not encode distinctions of gender or case. Thus, in Tok Pisin, the third person singular pronoun **em** can be used to refer to masculine, feminine and neuter subjects and objects, *eg* **em i go long maket** – 'he, she, it is going to market'; **mama bilong mi i lukim em** – 'My mother sees him/her/it'. This is a consequence of the fact that full lexemes are usually preferred at the expense of inflectional morphology to mark grammatical categories. This can be seen in the case of plural marking, where it occurs in pidgins. Mühlhäusler (1986:157–8) cites the widespread absence of number distinctions in nouns as typical of pidgins. In vernacular forms of Hausa, the formation of noun plurals involves a dozen suffixes and various modifications of the noun stem, *eg* partial or total reduplication and vowel alternations. In the vehicular variety of Hausa, the plural is formed by the addition of the full lexeme **deyawa** – 'much' to the singular form (*cf* Manessy 1977:140). Thus, there is a drastic reduction of allomorphy (*cf* also Heine 1979).

Another aspect of the principle of paradigmatic univocity is that it eliminates agreement markers which require the redundant expression of the same unit of meaning in several places in an utterance. For example, in the following English sentence, plurality is indicated in the noun and its modifier, as well as in verb agreement in the third person singular present tense: **Six men come** (*cf* **One man comes**). The equivalent utterances in Tok Pisin show no variation in the verb form or the noun: **Sikspela**

man i kam/Wanpela man i kam. Thus, there is a tendency for each grammatical morpheme to be expressed only once in an utterance, and for that morpheme to be expressed by a single form. Heine (1979:97) contrasts this Standard Swahili sentence with its equivalent in Kenya Pidgin Swahili to illustrate the elimination of redundant expressions of number, tense and agreement:

Standard Swahili: **Juma alileta vikombe viwili jana**
[Juma he past bring plural cup plural two yesterday]
Kenya Pidgin: **Juma naleta kikombe mbili jana**
[Juma aorist bring cup two yesterday]
'Juma brought two cups yesterday'

In Fanagalo (Pidgin Zulu), for example, the complex system of positive and negative conjugations of the verb forms, which are found in Southern Bantu languages, are replaced by a single negative element, **aikhona**, which appears in preverbal position (*cf* Heine 1973:133). Similarly, the allomorphy of the negative morpheme in standard Swahili is considerable. However, in the pidgin Swahili of West-Central Kenya negation is expressed by means of the invariable preverbal word **hapana**, as in the examples cited by Haiman (1985:164): standard Swahili: **simuoni** – [I not see him not] – 'I don't see him' [**mu** is the third person pronoun **him** + negator]; pidgin Swahili: **mimi hapana one yeye** – [I not see him] – 'I don't see him'. This means that analytic constructions as opposed to synthetic ones prevail in pidgins and pidginized varieties so that complex forms are decomposed into their component morphemes. A language which is analytic in structure indicates syntactic relations by means of function words and word order as opposed to synthetic languages, where such formal relationships are expressed by the combination of elements (*eg* prefixes, suffixes and infixes) with the base or stem word. The structure of words in an analytical language is morphologically simple, but complex in a synthetic language. In vehicular Swahili, for example, the locative suffix has been replaced by a preposition, *ie* a function word. This means that in standard Swahili a single word, albeit a morphologically complex one, encodes the meaning of constructions indicating location, *eg* **dukani** – 'in the shop', where **-ni** is the locative suffix. In vehicular Swahili, however, two words are required to express the equivalent meaning, *eg* **kwa dukani**, where **kwa** is a preposition meaning 'in/at' (*cf* Duran 1979). In one of the previous examples from Tok Pisin, I showed how possession is marked by a prepositional phrase headed by **bilong**, *ie* **mama bilong mi**.

Thus, where English can have possessive constructions such as **John's house**, where the inflectional suffix **-s** marks the possessive, Tok Pisin has the analytical construction **haus bilong John**.

Mühlhäusler (1986:160) cites as a characteristic feature of pidgins the fact that they make use of a few prepositions to indicate grammatical relations. For example, in the principal stable pidgins of the Pacific there is a one or two preposition system of indicating grammatical relations. **Long** [<'along'] is the most common form. Some also have the form **belong** [<'belong'], which shows a shift of function from verb to preposition. Chinook Jargon has only one preposition, **kopa**.

Haiman (1985:162) says that the phenomenon of grammatical agreement seems a clear case of the victory of the indexical aspect of language over its iconic aspect since categories such as number and case, properly associated with nouns, are copied onto verbs and adjectives. He adds that conjugation categories, noun class systems and the verbal concord systems to which they give rise, are notoriously dysfunctional. Generally there is little semantic homogeneity to the members of a noun class system and none at all to a verb conjugation. Similarly, pidgins often lack the copula, whose function is basically to mark tense and to distinguish between stative and non-stative predicates (*cf eg* the discussion in Ferguson 1971). Not surprisingly, there is a sharp reduction or disappearance of all these features in pidgins. Haiman concludes (1985:165) that pidgins seem 'to strip themselves spontaneously of this kind of luxury. Pidgins offer only one means of packaging redundancy: massive and wholesale repetition of the entire message. Repetition is stylistic rather than obligatory and (grammatical).'

Concomitant with the tendency to eliminate allomorphy pidgins usually display a fixed and invariable word order. In Haiman's (1985:162) terms, they avoid allotaxy, *ie* the use of different word orders for the expression of the same grammatical relationships. For example, in standard German different word orders are required in main and subordinate clauses. In main declarative clauses the finite verb must appear in second position, while in subordinate clauses it must be in final position. Thus, we can contrast:

> **Morgen kommt Frau Weber/Frau Weber kommt morgen** – 'Mrs Weber is coming tomorrow'
> **Morgen kommt Frau Weber nicht, weil sie krank ist/Frau Weber kommt morgen nicht, weil sie krank ist** – 'Mrs Weber isn't coming tomorrow because she is ill'

Or one could also have the subordinate clause preceding the main clause, in which case the verb of the subordinate clause is in final position. However, since the clause counts as one element in the larger sentence, the verb of the main clause occurs immediately after the verb of the subordinate clause. Thus:

Seitdem sie krank ist, kommt Frau Weber morgen nicht – 'Because she's ill, Mrs Weber isn't coming tomorrow'

Rabaul Creole German, however, has SVO word order (*cf* also Stammler 1922–3 on the German spoken in Estonia). It arose at the turn of the century as a lingua franca of the Catholic mixed race community in Vunapope near Rabaul. It became creolized in one generation. In the following sentence (cited by Volker 1982:49), we can see that the verb **muss** follows the subject instead of precedes it: **Wenn der Baby weinen, der Mama muss aufpicken** – 'When/if the baby cries, the mother must pick it up'. The verb form **weinen** is the infinitive form of the verb. Standard German would have the inflected third person singular form **weint**. We can see also the lexical influence of English in the words **aufpicken** – 'to pick up' and **baby** – 'baby'. Another characteristic feature is the lack of a gender system. Where standard German has a three gender system, Rabaul Creole German has only an invariant definite article **de** (pronounced **der** by some speakers). Standard German has **der**, **die**, **das**, variable forms which indicate gender, number and case distinctions. Rabaul Creole German shows deviation from standard German in certain declarative clauses which involve the use of complex verb forms. In Standard German when a verb form is made up of a finite (*ie* a form of the verb inflected for person, tense etc.) and a non-finite form, such as: **Ich habe das Buch gelesen** – 'I have read the book', the finite form (in this case, the inflected form of the auxiliary verb **haben**) must occupy second position, and the non-finite form (in this case the past participle) must go to the end. In Rabaul Creole German, either the auxiliary is omitted or the two verb forms appear in second position. Thus **I hat gelesen Buch** or **I gelesen Buch**.

Other pidgins show a tendency toward SVO order. For example, Pidgin Fijian and Chinook Jargon. With regard to the former Siegel (1983:11) says that Standard Fijian has a preference for VSO. Similarly, Thomason (1983:844) says that SVO is not a statistically dominant word order pattern in any of the Indian languages spoken in the Northwest. The basic word order is VSO. There are, however, pidgins which do not show a tendency towards SVO order. Hiri Motu seems to be OSV. Trader

Navajo, like Navajo, is verb initial or VSO (*cf* Silverstein 1972b) and Eskimo Trade Jargon is SOV (*cf* Stefánsson 1909). Another aspect of word order that has been noted in connection with pidgins is the lack of variant word orders for interrogatives and declaratives.

Givón (1979b) has claimed that SVO order is most common in pidgins because it is the easiest to process. That is to say that, in languages in which subjects precede objects, and the subject is separated from its object, the possibility of confusion between the two is reduced. Just as the tendency towards analytical structure makes the morphology of pronominal systems invariable, the invariable nature of pidgin word order leads to a greater isomorphism between form and meaning. Because pidgins are weakly grammaticalized, they depend heavily on context for their interpretation.

2.3 Pidgins as simple or simplified codes

These kinds of changes can be thought of as reductions in complexity. Southworth (1971:260), for example, notes that the most obvious characteristic of pidgins is their lack of complexity. The notion of simplicity is often invoked in the discussion of pidgins. In many popular accounts of pidgins simplicity is attributed to an alleged lack of grammar. For example, French (1953:58) says about Pidgin English in New Guinea:

> If the attempt to simplify vocabulary is fraught with difficulties, the attempt to simplify grammar is simply disastrous. The standard grammar has been jettisoned, and a new crude, and incredibly tortuous form of grammar has been built up in its place . . . So, far from being an independent language, pidgin takes over a whole ready-made phonetic and morphological system, crudely distorted by false ideas of simplification.

A number of linguists however have pointed to the lack of agreement in defining simplification and specifying the role it plays in pidginization. Hymes (1971:72) makes an important distinction between what is simple for the speaker in terms of production and what is simple for the hearer in terms of perception. The linguistic economies which result from the process of pidginization are of aid primarily to the speaker. Hymes (1971:73) observes that:

> . . . invariance in form, rather than allomorphic variation; invariant relation between form and grammatical function, rather than derivational and inflectional declensional and conjugational

variation; largely monomorphemic words, rather than inflected and derived words; reliance on overt word order; all have in common that they minimize the knowledge a speaker must have, and the speed with which he must decode, to know what in fact has grammatically happened.

Corder (1975) argues that simplification does not correspond to any psychological process of the learner because learners cannot simplify a system which they have not internalized (*cf* however, Meisel 1983a). He proposes instead that second language learners have recourse not to strategies of simplification but to a universal linguistic base reflected in less elaborated varieties of a language, *eg* pidgins, children's speech, and second language learner varieties. Fully formed adult speech represents a complexification of this universal base to which language learners approximate by means of a process of elaboration. Linguistic elaboration is determined by the communicative demands and function of the discourse. Thus, Corder distinguishes between structurally simple codes, *eg* foreigner talk, and the simplified use of a complex code, *eg* mothers' speech to babies (*cf* 3.1).

I will use the term **simplification** here in the sense in which Mühlhäusler (1974:5.4) defines it as an increase in regularity. Similarly, Traugott (1973:315) points out that simplification is a 'descriptive term accounting for relationships within particular grammars, not an explanatory one accounting for what goes on in language'. I will look further at the notion of simplification as a psycholinguistic strategy applied to a target language in 3.1. Nevertheless, even as Mühlhäusler defines it, simplification will have psycholinguistic consequences, since one can expect that greater generality of rules and fewer exceptions in grammar make a language easier to learn.

Simplification of form does not necessarily entail impoverishment of meaning, *ie* loss or lack of certain means of expression (*cf eg* Mühlhäusler 1974:5.4 and also Samarin 1971:125). For example, in Tok Pisin there is a regular principle by means of which causative verb forms can be derived from adjectives by adding the suffix **-im**, thus: **bik** – 'large': **bikim** – 'to make large/enlarge'; **brait** – 'wide': **braitim** – to widen/to make wide'; **doti** – 'dirty': **dotiim** – 'to make dirty'. We can see that English expresses the Tok Pisin equivalents of these causative verbs with a variety of means, *eg* with a verb plus prefix or suffix, and by a periphrastic construction involving the verb **to make**. In the case of the causative equivalent for **dirty**, the only option available to English is to encode the meaning analytically. Thus, to the extent that there is no single lexeme to encode the meaning 'to make something dirty', English can be thought of as more impoverished than Tok Pisin with respect to this feature of its lexicon. All languages differ of course in terms of codability, *ie* categories which have single word names are more codable (*cf eg* Brown 1958:235–41). English is also less simple or regular in that it has several forms to express the same meaning (*cf* also 7.2).

It is widely believed in popular accounts that pidgins are inadequate for the expression of certain ideas and concepts. Chatterton, for example, commented in a news bulletin (NBC 23 June 1976):

> My eight years in the House of Assembly [in Papua New Guinea SR] convinced me that Pidgin [Tok Pisin SR] as it is now is an inadequate medium for conducting the business of a modern nation. It could only be made so by a massive infusion of concise neologisms to express the often sophisticated and difficult concepts involved. I offer no opinion as to the possibility of this happening. I can only say that in the twelve years since the establishment of the House of Assembly in 1964, it has not happened, either in Pidgin or Hiri Motu. The tendency has been just to stick to an English word, and in the case of Pidgin prefaced by the disarming phrase 'ol i kolim'.

A look at some statistics on the use of Tok Pisin in transactions in the House of Assembly shows a dramatic increase from 40 per cent in 1964 to 95 per cent in 1973 (*cf* Noel 1975:78). In the first four-year period of its use it was restricted to certain topics or specific purposes. Now any business arising in the House of Assembly can be discussed in pidgin. In a survey of self-estimates of use of Tok Pisin on the part of students at the Papua New Guinea University of Technology in Lae, Swan and Lewis (1986) found that there was no evidence of any significant decline over the four years and no indication of a move towards the use of English. Some of the younger students appear to be using more Tok Pisin at university than at any previous time in their educational career since Community School. Swan and Lewis interpret the data as an indication of a very positive attitude towards the language even in an environment which strongly favours the use of English.

2.4 The pidgin lexicon

The most obvious place for impoverishment to take place is in the lexicon. Hall (1953:23), for example, compares the number of lexical items which a speaker of an ordinary language has, *ie* 25–30,000, by comparison with the number of lexical items in Neomelanesian, *ie* 1,500.[1] He adds however that these 1,500 words can be combined into phrases so as to say anything that can be said in English. The implication is that there is no reduction in the overall semantic domains covered by a pidgin, but merely in the number of items used to map them. There have been few attempts to demonstrate systematically the nature of lexical reduction. Samarin (1971:119) counted the number of basic morphemes in Sango and found there were 700–1,000. This is nearly the same number which Swadesh (1971) found for natural languages.

Moag (1978:80) suggests that we need studies which compare the lexical inventories of a pidgin versus the first language of the same speakers. Another possibility would be to obtain identical texts in the pidgin and first language (*cf* also Samarin 1979). Moag (1978:80) has compared a selected lexical sample for Standard Fijian and Pidgin Fijian to illustrate that items in the pidgin cover a wider semantic domain, As an example, we can look at the words for different kinds of containers or baskets:

Meaning	*Standard Fijian*	*Pidgin Fijian*
case, box, basket	**kato**	**kato**
fishing basket	**noke**	
coconut leaf basket	**sū**	
woven leaf tray	**i lalakai**	

The general pidgin term **kato** covers a domain which is lexicalized by four different items in standard Fijian.[2] The small lexical inventory of pidgins is a consequence of their context-dependence. Generally, only a very small part of the vocabulary of the lexifier language is taken into the core of the pidgin lexicon. Pidginized African languages, for instance, show a drastically reduced ideophone inventory. Ideophones are words that alter in some way the meaning of another. The closest analog to their function in English would be semi-reduplicative forms found in expressions such as **hurly-burly**, or **teeny-tiny**. Some 8–9,000 ideophones are reported in Gbeya. However, pidgin Sango has only some three dozen. Samarin (1979) suggests that pidginization of function is responsible for pidginization of form leading to the loss of ideophones. Since pidgins communicate only a referential minimum, it is to be expected that items which further specify others would fall out.

Mühlhäusler (1986:165) observes that not only is the number of actual pidgin lexical items highly restricted, but also the conventions as to the lexical information found within each item. I gave examples in 1.2 of words in Tok Pisin which had an English derivation but differed in meaning.

Haiman (1985:166) says that there is an inverse correlation between the lexical expansion of a language and the iconicity of its grammar (*cf* Saussure 1969:183). Haiman makes a distinction between 'lexical' and 'grammatical' languages. A lexical language has a large stock of primary roots, while a grammatical one has a small stock and makes up the deficit in periphrastic constructions. For example, in Tok Pisin, circumlocutions like **singsing long taim maus i pas** [to sing when the mouth is closed] – 'hum' are well known. Long-established languages are relatively more lexical, while pidgins, trade languages, second language learner varieties and child language are more grammatical. Pidgins have the properties of both lexical impoverishment and analytic structure. Established analytical languages like Chinese, however have only the characteristic of greater isomorphism. To the extent that analytical languages exhibit greater isomorphism, they are more iconic, less arbitrary and presumably more grammatical than synthetic languages like Sanskrit.

Let us compare some examples of the lexical structure of Tok Pisin and English:

Tok Pisin	*English*
gras	**grass**
mausgras	**moustache**
gras bilong fes	**beard**
gras bilong hed	**hair**
gras bilong pisin	**feather**
gras antap long ai	**eyebrow**
gras nogut	**weed**
han	**hand/arm**
han bilong diwai	**branch of a tree**
han bilong pisin	**wing of a bird**

The fact that meanings such as **grass**, **beard**, **feather** and **weed** are all expressed by means of separate, unrelated lexemes in English is an indication of its greater degree of lexicalization. In Tok Pisin, however there is a kind of diagrammatic iconic relation between these items, which is expressed by the fact that they are all encoded by means of constructions incorporating the word **gras**. That is to say that the words are motivated. I am using the term **diagrammatic iconic relation** in the sense used by Haiman (1980:515) to refer to a systematic arrangement of signs, none of which necessarily resembles its referent, but whose relationships to each other mirror the relationships to their referents. Thus, one could say that **grass** has the same relationship to the ground or earth that feathers have to a bird, a beard to a face, etc. They are all coverings on different surfaces. Similarly, a hand is an appendage to a tree or bird just as a hand or an arm is an appendage of a person. The English words **arm** and **branch** are by comparison unmotivated and lexically arbitrary.

It is a direct consequence of their impoverished vocabulary that pidgins exhibit a high degree of motivation and transparency in compounding. As Haiman (1985:158) puts it, 'the greater the lexicon, the greater the opacity; the smaller the lexicon, the greater the transparency and iconicity of the linguistic (sub)system.' Voorhoeve (1962) claims that the relationship between size of vocabulary and number of grammatical rules is optimal in pidgins and creoles.

It is obvious that there will be gaps in the pidgin lexicon, particularly in the early stages of its development. These may be filled by borrowing or circumlocution, as seen in 1.2. Only at a later stage does the pidgin develop productive internal resources for expanding its lexicon (*cf* Mühlhäusler 1979; Jones 1983). Circumlocution is a strategy which involves letting the syntax make up for the lack of productive morphological processes which would be used to form words in the lexifier language. A stereotypical view of this process is given in Helton (1943:5):

> When you are stuck for a pidgin word to describe anything, think of what it is used for and use the word **something** for its name and state its use. For instance, a stud is used to fasten your collar, therefore a request to a native to **bring im something belong pass im neck** (collar) would have the effect of a native producing a stud.

Although this characterization of the improvisation process has some truth in it, once an innovation has caught on and used, it will become conventionalized in shortened form. Some evidence in support of this comes from Master's (1986) study of noun compounding in experimental Farsi pidgin. He found that learners often used the words **place** or **thing** as lexical anchor points in coining new words. These were then modified by other words. Thus, in Farsi pidgin terms such as **neveshtan chiz mahal** [write thing place] and **xandan chiz mahal** [read thing place] were introduced for 'bookstore'; **kone chiz mahal** [old thing place] or **mundan kone chiz borzorg mahal** [stay old thing big place] for 'museum'; and **felez mahal** [metal place] or **mundan felez mahal** [stay metal place] for 'bank'.

Initially these expressions served as descriptions. At this stage there was a preference for high analytical coding at the expense of economy. Later, however in response to the demands of efficient communication speakers economized. Once these forms had been used several times they were reduced and stabilized compounds developed. For example, in pidgin German an expression denoting 'restaurant' – **platz wo kaufen diese dinge fur essen** [place where buy these things for eat], became shortened and stabilized as **essen kaufen platz** [eat buy place]. Here we see what was originally a description becoming a name or referring expression once the post-nominal modifiers become prenominal.

Stable pidgins often develop phrase-like formulas for the description of new concepts. Mühlhäusler (1986:171) gives the Hiri Motu formula O-V-**gauna** – 'thing for doing something to an object' as an example. It parallels the word formation process in experimental Farsi pidgin. Thus:

kuku ania gauna	[smoke eat thing]	'pipe'
lahi gabua gauna	[fire burn thing]	'match'
traka abiaisi gauna	[truck raise thing]	'jack'
godo abia gauna	[voice take thing]	'tape recorder'

Out of the raw material of a lexicon speakers create morphology and syntax. A similar process of conventionalization can lead to the introduction of inflectional morphology in the later stages of a pidgin's development. For example, many pidgins have affix-like classifiers which are attached to various elements, *eg* **-pela/fela** [<**fellow**] in Pacific Englishes. Mühlhäusler (1986:153) says that in Pacific Jargon English this element was found variably in a number of positions following and preceding nouns and following adjectives. It was also used as a kind of lexical anchor in the sense noted above in circumlocutions such as **fellow belong open bottle** – 'corkscrew'. Here **fellow** seems to mean 'thing'. For indigenous speakers, however, a gradual reinterpretation took place which served to grammaticalize **fellow** as a affix marking the word class of attributive adjectives.

There is also a correlation between brevity and opacity. As the lexicon of a pidgin expands the clumsy, but motivated compounds and periphrastic constructions disappear, *eg* Tok Pisin **kot bilong ren** is now **kotren** or **renkot**, and **waia i go antap** [wire it goes on top] is now **aerial**. Lexical expansion is motivated by a desire to give common concepts a reduced expression. As Zipf (1935:29) puts it: 'High frequency is the cause of small magnitude.'

Another property of the pidgin lexicon is multifunctionality. Wurm (1971:8), for example, says that 'a characteristic feature of Pidgin is the presence of many universal bases, *ie* words which can function as nouns, noun and verb adjuncts, intransitive verbs and transitive verbs. The functional possibilities of pidgin bases are fundamental to the grammar of pidgin.' For example, in English the lexeme **ill** functions as an adjective, as in **he is ill**, or **an ill woman**. However, the corresponding noun is **illness**, derived by addition of the nominalizing suffix **-ness**. In Tok Pisin, however, the lexeme **sik** can function as both noun and adjective, *eg* **mi sik** – 'I am sick'; **sik malaria** – 'malaria'; **em i gat bikpela sik** – 'he has got a terrible disease'. Similarly, the lexeme **askim** can function as both verb and noun, *eg* **Mi laik askim em** – 'I want to ask him/her/it'; **Sapos you gat askim em i orait** – 'If you have any questions, it's alright (to ask)'. Silverstein (1972a:381) observes that the freedom from lexical specification increases the information content of each unit in the lexicon. The great majority of the lexicon of Chinook jargon (and probably most jargons *cf* 4.3) is made up of words which are grammatically and semantically ambiguous. Pidgins lack word formation rules with which to expand their lexicons. Although the use of the same lexical item in a number of grammatical functions constitutes a gain in simplicity, it also has the consequence that it violates the principle of one form equals one meaning (*cf* also Voorhoeve 1981 for a discussion of the theoretical consequences of multifunctionality).

2.5 Some preliminary definitions of creoles

The term **creole** [<Portuguese **crioulu** via English and French] originally meant a white man of European descent born and raised in a tropical or semitropical colony. The meaning was later extended to include indigenous natives and others of non-European origin. The term was then subsequently applied to certain languages spoken by creoles in and around the Caribbean and in West Africa, and then more generally to other languages of similar types which had arisen in similar circumstances.

The development from pidgin into creole involves an expansion of expressive forces in response to communicative needs. In Hymes's terms, the process of creolization involves an expansion of inner form and complexification of outer form. Valdman (1977a:158–9) refers to both these aspects as elaboration. Thus, a creole language is defined as (DeCamp 1971a:16):

> the native language of most of its speakers. Therefore its vocabulary and syntactic devices are, like those of any native language, large enough to meet all the communicative needs of its speakers.

As part of the process of creolization a great many iconic features are lost. Independent words become grammaticalized and begin to exhibit allomorphy (*cf eg* Sankoff and Laberge 1973). Reduced forms become crystallized and obligatory; reduced forms are reinforced by independent words, giving rise to agreement systems. For example in Tok Pisin, Sankoff (1977) discusses the process whereby the subject pronoun **he** has become generalized and cliticized as a preverbal predicative marker **i**, *eg* **yupela i kam** – 'You (pl) come'. Once the pronoun has undergone a process of phonological reduction from its full form, it is bound to the verb, and loses its force as a full pronoun and marks a purely grammatical function. Earlier in its history there is textual evidence of the full form **she**. Schuchardt (1889) has examples such as: **Woman she finish thing me speak him** (*cf* Mühlhäusler 1986:164). Churchill (1911) cites four cases. However, even at the time Churchill was writing **he** was the predominant form, *eg* **Queen Victoria he look out** (Churchill 1911:49).

The development of predicate markers can take place in the stabilization phase of a pidgin rather than as part of creolization. Mühlhäusler (1986:163–4) mentions the use of anaphoric pronouns as generalized predicate markers as a feature which is widespread across pidgins. It is found, for example, in some of the Indian Ocean Creoles, as in the example from Corne (1974–5:69) in Seychelles Creole:

ban zanimo i tan sa – 'The animals hear that'

Thomason (1983:847) reports its use in the speech of some speakers of Chinook Jargon (*cf* also 4.3) as in:

t'alap'as' pi lilu laska məlayt ixt-ixt laska haws
[coyote and wolf they live one-one they house]
'A coyote and a wolf lived with their houses side by side'

It is not always possible to tell, in cases where pidgins have developed predicate markers, whether equivalent constructions in the lexifier and or substratum languages provided the input. In the case of Chinook Jargon Thomason (1983:851) says that almost all the Indian languages whose speakers use Chinook Jargon have pleonastic subject pronominals, at least to a limited extent. However, the positioning of these markers does not always agree with their consistent preverbal position in the jargon. She says that it is not possible to conclude on the basis of present evidence whether the appearance of the subject markers should be expected as the outcome of native speaker simplification. Tolai, which provided input to Tok Pisin, had a similar construction. However, Mühlhäusler claims that the use of **i** in Tok Pisin appears to be reinforced by it and not derived from it since Tolai uses different forms of the pronoun for different subjects. With third person singular subjects **i** is used. Mühlhäusler (1986:164) says that it is this coincidence with English **he** that probably promoted the rapid stabilization of **i** as a predicate marker in Tok Pisin (*cf* however, Keesing (forthcoming) for a substratum explanation).

Creoles can even develop case suffixes. This has happened in Sri Lanka Portuguese Creole with the result that the language is now typologically very like the Indo-European and Dravidian languages Sinhala and Tamil, rather than Portuguese. Portuguese influence was removed in 1658, rather early in the development of the creole. This meant that the substratum languages provided input during the creolization phase. Case suffixes have developed from postpositions, which were unstressed and gradually reduced. For example, the case marker **-ntu** is derived from the full form **junto** – 'joined'. The dative **-pə** is derived from a reduced from of the preposition **para**. The genitive comes from a reduced form of **sua**, the third person possessive pronoun. In some varieties the postposed genitive co-exists with the postposed case-marked construction. Compare these examples from Smith (1977:366–8): **pa:nu de mæ:zə** – 'cloth of table'/**mæzə-su pa:nu** – 'table's cloth'. In these next examples from Smith (1978:73) it can be seen that the creole is more similar in structure to Tamil than to Portuguese:

Portuguese: **Eu tinha dado o dinheiro a/para João**
[I aux have give past participle article money to/for John]
Tamil: **nān calli-yay jon-ukku kuṭu-tt iru-nt-an**
[I money-accusative John- dative past give past Aux was 1st singular]
Sri Lankan Portuguese: **ẽw diñeru jon-pə jā-dā tiña**
[I money John-dative already give past]
'I had given the money to John'

This typological shift has involved a movement away from the Portuguese type which is SVO and prepositional to a Dravidian type which is SOV and postpositional with case marking.

It was apparently Bloomfield (1933:474) who first suggested a historical relationship between pidgin and creole. Hall (1953) carries this idea much further when he makes a pidgin origin an essential feature of his definition of a creole and postulates a linguistic life-cycle beginning with the spontaneous generation of a pidgin followed by its evolution to a creole. Hall's notion of life-cycle will be examined in greater detail in Chapter 4. Others, such as Bickerton (1981a), emphasize the discontinuity between a newly emergent creole and the antecedent pidgin based largely on the fact that creoles share a great many semantactic similarities which cannot be traced to their respective pidgin ancestors. These newly created features must in his view be the result of innate language universals, These will be looked at in 2.9 and Ch. 7.

2.6 Expansion and elaboration of creoles

Valdman (1977a:175) has observed that an important question in pidgin and creole linguistics is the degree of elaboration undergone by the terminus a quo of existing creoles. The standard view voiced by Hall and others is that pidginization and creolization are mirror image processes. This implies two stages in the development of creoles. The first involves rapid and drastic restructuring which produces a language variety which is reduced and simplified with respect to the base language. The second step consists of the elaboration of this variety as its functions expand and it becomes nativized.

It is by no means clear that all of the kinds of changes which typically go on in the expansion of a pidgin and under creolization involve an increase in complexity. For example, one characteristic of creoles is that they tend to have particles to express tense and aspect distinctions. Pidgins normally use adverbial expressions. Valdman (1977a:157) notes that it is not readily apparent how the signalling of tenses by means of particles instead of adverbs introduces greater complexity. Bickerton (1975a) traces the development of the verbal system of Guyanese Creole from a basically aspect-oriented system to a tense-oriented system via successive restructuring rather than the addition of new categories and more elaborated means of expressing them (*cf* 5.5). Labov (1970/1977) comments that although a language which relies on adverbs to express temporal distinctions may be rudimentary, it is hard to show that it is inadequate. It is not easy to understand why creoles develop obligatory tense markers, when there is no conceptual advantage in doing so, *ie* such a change does not increase the referential power of the language or add a new category. He concludes (1970/1977:36) that the main advantage which tense markers possess is their stylistic flexibility. They can be contracted or expanded to fit in with the requirements of different speech tempos. Thus, this seems to be a case of simplification, but not impoverishment. Sturtevant (1917:166,175) points out a related aspect of simplicity. He notes that analytical languages are more economical in terms of the number of syllables required to communicate a given message because they avoid redundant repetition. Haiman (1985:165), however, says that this kind of economy is possible only if each morpheme is heard with total clarity. Frequent repetition results – by economy – in the diminution and decay of each morpheme. This, in turn, results in a demand for redundancy.

2.7 Towards a typology of pidgin and creole languages

In attempts by Stewart, Hymes, Fishman and others (*cf* especially Stewart 1962) to develop a typology to categorize kinds of languages/varieties according to their sociolinguistic characteristics, the main difference between a pidgin and creole lies in terms of the feature referred to as vitality. This means whether the language has a viable community of native speakers. Otherwise, pidgins and creoles share six features. That is, they lack standardization, historicity, and autonomy, but are reduced, mixed languages with de facto norms.

The feature **standardization** has to do with whether a language possesses an agreed set of codified norms which are accepted by the speech community and form the basis for teaching of it either as a first or second language. Codification has to have taken place and be accepted before a language can be said to be standardized. It isn't sufficient for a language to have grammars and dictionaries. Jamaican Creole, for example, has both (*cf eg* Bailey 1966; Cassidy and Le Page 1967), but it is not a standard language. Although its speakers have norms for use of the language, as is probably the case in all speech communities, these are not sanctioned by any externally recognized authorities of language or appealed to as arbiters in normative teaching. Standardization is a feature which is imposed on a language and not inherent in it, and may take place at any time. Some present-day standard languages have pidgin origins, such as Bahasa Indonesia, which is a standardized variety of pidgin Malay (*cf* Hall 1972 and Samarin 1980).

The feature **historicity** refers to whether the language has grown up through use by some ethnic or social group. This attribute is intended to divide first from second languages, on the assumption that the latter tend not to be used as markers of social identity or in an affective function. **Autonomy** has to do with whether the language is accepted by its users as distinct from other languages or varieties. Speakers do not usually claim autonomy for non-standard varieties of a language, or for a pidgin or creole. This too is a difficult criterion to apply to a language as a whole since speakers may have differing attitudes towards its status. Sandefur (1984), for example, says that Kriol is regarded as a European language by second language and first generation creole speakers. Second generation creole speakers however regard it as an Aboriginal language and do not use it in the presence of whites. In the case of Tok Pisin many speakers regard it as an indigenous language, while others regard it as a language of colonialism (*cf* 4.3).

Tok Pisin is spreading as a general language of solidarity among Papua New Guineans of diverse ethnic origins. As indicated in 2.3 it is widely used and preferred in the House of Assembly. The former Prime Minister, Michael Somare, has on occasion chosen to speak abroad in Tok Pisin rather than English, even though he publicly endorses the use of English as the language of international relations. The *Post Courier* (14 Dec. 1977) carried the following report:

> Shortly before he met the Japanese Prime Minister, Mr Fukuda, a few days ago, Mr Somare surprised Japanese officials by requesting a three-way interpretation. When the talks got underway, Mr Somare, whose English is excellent, spoke in pidgin. The secretary for Foreign Relations, Mr Tony Siagura, translated the pidgin into English, and this in turn was translated for Mr Fukuda by the Japanese interpreter. A Papua New Guinea Official said later Mr Somare believed he should use pidgin because he could express his thoughts better.

Somare's attitude towards the role of the two languages can be seen in the following report from *Wantok* (10 July 1976):

> Na praim minista i bin tok olsem: 'Miting yumi mas yusim Tok Inglis long skul na long bisnis na long toktok wantaim arapela kantri. Na mi no laikim Tok Pisin long wanem em i gat planti Tok Inglis insait long en. Miting planti yumi long olgeta hap i yusim Tok Inglis pinis, olsem mi laikim em i kamap na nasenel tok ples bilong PNG.' Na taim em i mekim dispela tok, em i yusim Tok Pisin.
>
> [The Prime Minister spoke thus: 'I think we must use English in our schools and for business and discussions with other countries. I don't like Tok Pisin which is mixed with a lot of English. I feel very strongly that we've used English for all sorts of purposes, and I want it to become the national language of Papua New Guinea.' At the time he made this speech, he was using Tok Pisin.

Here we see a desire expressed for the two languages to remain separate and to be used in different domains. English is viewed as the language to be used in an international context. It is interesting, however, that Somare takes a decidedly negative attitude towards the adoption of English words into Tok Pisin. Although he favours English as the best choice for a national language, it is clear that Tok Pisin has positive affective value for Papua New Guineans (*cf* also 4.3 and Romaine 1986).

The remaining two distinguishing features of pidgins and creoles are formal. **Reduction** means that the language makes use of a smaller set of structural relations and items in the syntax, phonology and lexicon than some related variety of the same language. **Mixture** has to do with whether the language consists essentially of items and structures derived from no source outside itself.

There are problems with virtually all these features when applied to either pidgins and/or creoles. With regard to the criterion of mixture, for example, it can be said that no language develops in isolation. There are hardly any 'pure' languages, though as Hall (1966:117) noted, some are purer than others (*cf* 3.4). There do not seem to be any clear criteria for determining how much mixture there must be in any given case of language contact before deciding that we are dealing with a case of pidginization or creolization as distinct from the effects of borrowing and interference. It is also not clear how much weight should be attached to mixture at the phonological as opposed to syntactic and lexical level. Some have defined a pidgin as a mixed language, which has the grammar of one language (the substrate) and the lexicon of another (the superstrate, *cf eg* Adler 1977:12). As Hoenigswald (1971:478) puts it 'The historian's problem is whether the outcome of nearly total lexical borrowing from one language (B) into another (A) can be distinguished from the outcome of the acquisition of B by speakers of A with substratum effects from B. In one case the outcome could be said to be a continuation of A, despite the B vocabulary, while in the other, the outcome could be said to be a continuation of B despite the A grammar.' A pidgin cannot be defined as simply the result of heavy borrowing from one variety into another since there is no pre-existing structure into which items may be borrowed. Thus, a so-called English-based pidgin is not a variety of English which has borrowed a substantial amount of its syntax from other languages. In fact, it seems that mixing at the syntactic and morphological level is virtually impossible in the formative stage of pidgin development. It becomes more important once stabilization and expansion have taken place (*cf* Mühlhäusler 1981b). As I have already shown in the case of Tok Pisin, it becomes more prominent when a pidgin comes into renewed contact with its original lexifier language. In Chapter 4 I will look further into this issue.

With regard to reduction, we can say, following Gilbert (1981:209), that there has been a tendency to define pidgins in terms of what they lack, *eg* copula, articles, inflectional morphology, etc. Moreover, this comparison tends to be carried out between present-day standard varieties of the lexifier languages and the pidgin without regard for the fact that both would have changed considerably. Moreover, the pidgin was more likely to have had more input from regional or non-standard varieties of the lexifier language. Posner comments (1983:195) that some of the developments which have been attributed to substratum influence in Haitian Creole may simply be ordinary internal developments which are not too far removed from what is going on in Canadian French today (*cf* also 3.5).

As far as the sociolinguistic features of standardization, autonomy, and historicity are concerned, Tok Pisin is a difficult case to assess. Firstly, it has undergone considerable standardization through its use by missionaries in publications, and the issue of standardization has been debated extensively by linguists (*cf* especially the papers in McElhanon 1975). Wurm (1985) discusses various attempts to develop standardized orthographies for the language. A proposal by Hall (1955b) was approved by the Director of Education and the Administrator of the Territory of Papua and New Guinea and by the Minister for the Territories in Canberra. In an official publication issued by the Department of Education in 1956 it was recognized officially and was used with a few minor changes in Mihalic's grammar and dictionary (1957). A modified orthography was used in the translation of the New Testament (*Nupela Testamen* 1966). In 1969 an Orthography Committee was set up, and it recommended that the spelling system employed in *Nupela Testamen* be recognized as the official orthography, and that the variety of Tok Pisin spoken along the north coast of mainland New Guinea should be the standard. However, in the absence of official endorsement, the proposals were largely ignored by government departments and agencies. Even after independence in 1975 recognition is lacking. In 1981 the name Tok Pisin was accepted as the official designation of the language, and it now has official status along with English and Hiri Motu. This orthography is however accepted widely, as it appears in a more recent edition of Mihalic's (1971) grammar and dictionary, in a course for foreign learners (Dutton 1973) and in *Wantok*, the weekly newspaper which has a circulation of over 10,000. There is considerable linguistic documentation of the grammar of Tok Pisin in the recent *Handbook of Tok Pisin* (Wurm and Mühlhäusler 1985) which could serve as the source of an official standard, and the basis for language planning and development. So far, however, there is no recognition of an official grammar.

Moag (1978:85) says that Pidgin Fijian meets the criterion of standard language if we take the main characteristic of such a language to be minimal variation in form. Siegel (1975) however has claimed that there are several kinds of Pidgin Fijian based on different regional dialects. Moag, however, ignores the aspect of codification, which does not exist for the language.

Another aspect of standardization which pidgin languages generally fail to meet is that although there is minimal variation in form in a standard language, there is maximal elaboration of function. Pidgins by definition are generally used for restricted communicative purposes. Expanded pidgins, such as Tok Pisin and West African English, however, may show a wider range of uses, and in some cases these may be equivalent to those which a native speaker of a non-pidgin language might command. Both Nigerian Pidgin English and Tok Pisin, however, have viable creole communities while continuing to serve as second languages for most of their speakers. In such a situation a speaker's dominant language may not be the language first acquired. This suggests a revision in our terminology, along the lines suggested by Mafeni (1971:112), who writes of his own language skills:

> I have the feeling I speak Pidgin more fluently than any other Nigerian language which I know and use. Although my mother tongue is Isako, Yoruba seems to be the dominant substrate in my variety of Pidgin.

We can use the term **primary language** to refer to the language which is best mastered by a speaker. This is not necessarily the first acquired language (or mother-tongue). All other languages of a bilingual person are secondary languages.

2.8 The minimal structural requirements of pidgins and creoles

If we start from a linguistic point of view in defining the characteristics of pidgins and creoles, we could ask what the minimal structural requirements for such languages are. Koopman and

Lefebvre (1981:216), for example, suggest that young pidgins are characterized by two features: (i) a vocabulary defined in terms of major features, nouns and verbs (*ie* [+N,−V] and [−N,+V]. Except for a few quantifiers, they show no class of words defined in terms of minor features; (ii) minimal sentence structure. That is to say, that there are no morphosyntactic categories, *eg* auxiliary. The impossibility of clefting, embedding and topicalization are accounted for by the fact that S is the highest node. They propose a simple phrase structure rule, S → (adverb) NP VP (adverb). Adverb positions are filled by adverbs which encode tense, mood and aspect and also negative markers.

As far as the minimal structural requirements for a creole are concerned, Koopman and Lefebvre (1981:216) propose the following: (i) vocabulary defined in terms of major syntactic categories, *ie* noun, verb, preposition, adjective, and in terms of morphosyntactic features, *eg* tense; (ii) the structure of the lexicon is reflected in base rules containing positions defined in terms of major and minor features. For example, there may be a provision for auxiliaries and determiners. Assuming SVO word order, the minimal sentence structure for creoles is: S → NP (Negative) AUX VP (adverb), with further scope for embedding, topicalization and clefting provided by rules such as $\bar{S}$ → [±TOP] S.

The problem with such characterizations is that they are static and purely formal. They ignore the fact that pidgins and creoles are developing systems which may overlap in terms of the structural complexity reached at any point in their life-cycle depending on their functions. A more recent attempt to pinpoint specific features as typological traits of creoles can be found in Bickerton (1981a), which I will look at next.

2.9 Twelve features of creole grammars

Bickerton (1981a:Ch. 2) identifies twelve features which he believes to characterize creole grammars (*cf* also Taylor 1971:294 for twelve features, some of which are different):

(i) movement rules
(ii) articles
(iii) tense – modality – aspect systems
(iv) realized and unrealized complements
(v) relativization and subject-copying
(vi) negation
(vii) existential and possessive
(vii) copula

(ix) adjectives as verbs
(x) questions
(xi) question words
(xii) passive equivalents

Some of these features have already been mentioned in connection with my discussion of the features of pidgins and some will be looked at in more detail in subsequent chapters (*cf* especially 7). For now, it will suffice to define and exemplify them briefly. First, however, it should be pointed out that Mühlhäusler (1986) cites (x) and (xi) as characteristic features of pidgins which apparently had no input model. In other words much the same solutions tend to recur wherever pidginization occurs regardless of the lexifier and substratum languages involved. Their presence in creoles illustrates the problem in drawing a sharp boundary between the two and also indicates that there can be some continuity in development from pidgin to creole. That is, creoles may have inherited these features from a prior pidgin stage, rather than re-invented them independently. Mühlhäusler (1986:155–65) lists nine syntactic features which are salient for stable pidgins: SVO word order; invariant word order for questions and statements; sentence-external qualifiers; lack of number in the noun; pronoun systems; prepositions; lack of derivational depth; bimorphemic wh-questions words; and anaphoric pronouns. Of these six are considered to be criterial features of creoles by either Bickerton, Markey or others.

By movement rule Bickerton means the placement of focused constituents at the front of the sentence. He notes that many languages mark focus by means of movement rules, focusing particles, stress or tone patterns. Creoles, however, have not adopted these alternative strategies. As an example, Bickerton cites the fronting of subjects and the adjoining of the copula **a** in Guyanese Creole. A sentence like **Jan bin sii wan uman** – 'John had seen a woman' can be converted into a sentence in which the subject NP is focused: **a Jan bin sii wan uman** – 'It was John who had seen a woman'. The object can also be focused on, as in **a uman Jan bin sii** – 'It was a woman that John had seen'. Other constituents such as the verb or adverbs can also be focused on in a similar manner. As we will see in 3.5, this feature is one of those which many creolists believe to be a feature incorporated into various creoles from African substratum languages such as Yoruba.

Bickerton (1981a:56) observes that there seems to be hardly any variation at all in the way that creoles handle articles. He claims that virtually all creoles have a system identical to Hawaii Creole English. A definite article is used for presupposed-specific NPs, an indefinite article for asserted-specific NPs, and zero for non-specific NPs. He gives the following examples from Seychelles Creole (1981a:57):

mô pe aste sa banan – 'I am buying the banana' (presupposed-specific NP)
mô pe aste ban banan – 'I am buying the bananas' (presupposed-specific plural NP)
mô pe aste ê banan – 'I am buying a banana' (asserted-specific NP)
fakter i n amen let is? – 'Did the postman bring a letter here?' (non-specific NP)

I will look at this feature in more detail in 7.2.

It is with regard to the nature of creole tense-modality and aspect systems that Bickerton has based some of his more far-reaching claims. He states that the majority of creoles express these grammatical categories by means of three preverbal free morphemes, which occur in the order (if they co-occur): tense, mood and aspect. Bickerton also claims that the range of meaning of the particles is the same across unrelated creoles. The tense particle expresses the meaning [+anterior], *ie* past before the past, for action verbs such as **run**, and past, for stative verbs such as **think**. The modality particle expresses [+irrealis] as in conditionals and hypothetical and unrealized events. The aspect particle expresses [+non-punctual]. The stem form in isolation expresses the unmarked term in these three oppositions, *ie* present statives and past non-statives. More will be said about the creole TMA system in 7.3 (*cf* also Table 3.1 and 5.5).

In his discussion of realized and unrealized complements Bickerton says (1981a:59) that complementizers are selected according to the semantics of the verb. That is to say that all realized complements are either unmarked or marked with a different complementizer from the one(s) used with unrealized complements. For example, in Baker's (1972) Mauritian Creole texts all the realized complements are marked with **al** or zero, and all unrealized complements are marked with **pu** or **pu al**. Thus:

li desid al met posoh ladah – [she decide go put fish in it]
'She decided to put a fish in it' (cited in Bickerton 1981a:60)

The complementizer **al** is chosen here since the action is realized, *ie* she did what she decided to do. In the next sentence the complementizer **pu al** is chosen since the subject of the action was prevented from carrying it out:

> **li ti pe ale aswar pu al bril lakaz sa garsoh-la me lor sime ban dayin fin atake li** [He tense-mood-go one evening for go burn house that boy the but on path plural witch completive attack him] – 'He would have gone that evening to burn the boy's house, but on the way he was attacked by witches' (cited in Bickerton 1981a:61)

Jansen, Koopman and Muysken (1978:153) note a similar contrast in Sranan:

> **a teki a nefi foe koti a brede, ma no koti en** – 'He took the knife to cut the bread, but did not cut it'

The complementizer **foe** marks unrealized complements and zero is used with realized complements. Bickerton (1981a:61) comments that the distinction between realized and unrealized complements is not attested in any non-creole language. The identity of the construction across creoles is striking in that it applies to both syntax and semantics. It extends even to the source of the lexical items chosen as complementizers. For example, French **pour** – 'for' is the source of **pu** in Mauritian and other French-based creoles; English **for** is the source of Hawaiian Creole English **fo**, Jamaican Creole **fi**, Sranan **foe**; French **aller** – 'to go' is the source of Mauritian Creole **al**, and English **go** is the source of Hawaii English Creole **go** and Jamaican Creole **go**.

I will discuss relativization in considerable detail in Chapter 6. However, for the moment I can note Bickerton's claim that most creoles, unlike pidgins, have relative pronouns, at least when the head noun is also subject of the relative clause, as in a sentence like **The man who lives next door is John's brother**. Later I will show that there are many similarities between unrelated creoles with regard to the source of the lexical items chosen as relativizers.

With regard to negation, Bickerton (1981a:66) observes that non-definite subjects and VP constituents must be negated in addition to the verb (*cf* also Labov 1969 for discussion of negative concord in Black English). Thus, in Guyanese Creole, the negative marker **non** is attracted to the NPs **dog** and **cat** and the verb is also preceded by the negative **na**:

> **Non dag na bait non kyat** – 'No dog bit any cat'

The feature existential and possessive refers to the fact that in many creoles the same lexical item is used to express existentials (*ie* 'there is') and possessive (*ie* 'have'). This is not true of any of the superstrate languages. Bickerton (1981a:66–7) cites the following examples:

Guyanese Creole: **dem get wan uman we get gyal pikni** – 'There is a woman who has a daughter'
Haitian Creole: **gê you fâm ki gế you petit-fi**' – 'There is a woman who has a daughter'
Hawaii English Creole: **Get wan wahini shi get wan data** – 'There is a woman who has a daughter'

In Portuguese-based creoles, but not in Portuguese, possession and existence are marked by derivations of **tem** – 'to have', as in Malaccan Creole Portuguese (*cf* Markey 1982:193):

irmang-machu teng na rua [brother have in street]
'My brother is in the street' (existence)
yo teng irmang-machu [I have brother]
'I have a brother' (possession)

I have already noted the fact that creoles characteristically lack the copula. Since adjectives function as verbs, they require no surface copula. Thus, in Jamaican Creole, we can have sentences like **di pikni sik** – 'the child is sick'. Bickerton (1981a:68) notes a general tendency towards semantic transparency. That is, there are separate forms for each of the semantically distinct functions fulfilled by the copula, *eg* attribution (*cf* **John is a good man**), with adjectives (*cf* **The child is sick**), locatives (*cf* **John is in the garden**), etc. The lack of the copula and the functioning of adjectives as verbs in various creoles will be discussed in more detail in 5.4.

With regard to questions, Bickerton states (1981a:70) that no creole shows any difference in syntactic structure between questions and statements. If a creole has special question particles, they are sentence-final and optional. In Guyanese Creole the following sentence is not formally distinguishable as an interrogative or a declarative. The difference between the two sentence types is marked by intonation:

i bai di eg dem – 'He bought the eggs/Did he buy the eggs?'

This is an interesting and salient typological feature of creoles when taken in conjunction with the fact that most creoles tend to have SVO word order. Greenberg (1963:81) proposes an implicational universal to the effect that if a language has sentence-external question particles, these tend to occur initially in prepositional languages (*eg* SVO), but sentence-finally in postpositional (*eg* SOV) languages. The creole protoype violates this expectation.

In many creoles question words are bimorphemic. The first morpheme is generally derived from a superstrate word, *eg* Guyanese Creole **wisaid** – 'which side' = 'where', and similarly Haitian Creole **ki koté** – 'which side = where'. Other forms include Cameroons Creole **wetin** – 'what thing' = 'what', Guyanese Creole **wa mek** – 'what makes = 'why', and Haitian Creole **lakoz ki** [<**la cause que**] – 'the reason that = 'why'' **ki fer** [<**qui faire**] – 'what makes' = 'why'. The same is also true of many pidgins. Tok Pisin, for example, has **wanem** [what name] = 'what/which' and **husat** [who's that] = 'who'. Pidgins based on African languages also have similar forms, *eg* Kenya Pidgin **saa gani** [hour which] = 'when'; Swahili **sababu gani** [reason which] = 'why'; Fanagalo **ipi skati** [where time] = 'when' (*cf* Heine 1973). Taylor (1977:171) notes that these bimorphemic constructions are found in many African languages. However, in the experimentally created pidgins mentioned in 2.4, bimorphemic expressions emerged for question words too, *eg* in Farsi pidgin **che so'al** – [what ask] = 'why' and **che vaqt** – [what time] = 'when'. A number of these bimorphemic constructions may have been taken over from the related superstrate languages. English, for example, has 'what time' = 'when', 'which way' = 'where', etc.

Finally, Bickerton (1981a:71) says that passive constructions are rare in creoles. In the relatively few creoles where such constructions do exist, they are either marginal to the language or relatively recent superstrate borrowings (for further discussion *cf* Markey and Fodale 1983; Corne 1977a; and Wright 1984). For example, in Jamaican Creole, we can find the following pairs, where no formal distinction between active and passive is marked on the verb:

dem plaan di tree – 'They planted the tree'
di tri plaan – 'The tree was planted'

Some creolists like Ferraz (1976), however, have attributed the absence of passives to African substratum. In this particular case, he argues that four Portuguese-based creoles of the Gulf of Guinea (São Tomense, Angolor, Annobonese and Principense) have been influenced by Kwa.

Markey (1982) considers some of the same features and some additional ones in evaluating the question of whether Afrikaans is a true creole. Earlier, Hesseling (1897) had argued that Afrikaans was on its way to becoming a creole, but the process was stopped short of completion. He described it as a semi-creole patois. In his discussion Markey rightly observes (1982:170) that to label creoles simply as contact languages is vacuous because all languages are in some sense the product of contact. Likewise, to call all languages creoles is equally fatuous. There are marked genetic and typological differences between Haitian Creole French and post-Norman Conquest English.

Markey considers the syntactic innovations of creoles to be paramount in their typological definition. Creoles are uniquely distinguished by the disruption of grammatical input patterns on every linguistic level. Creoles are characterized by discontinuity and form their own new creations, but they also show phenomena inherited from source languages. Markey notes that all languages borrow, dissolve and create grammar, but that the generation of new grammatical, particularly syntactic innovations, is typical of creoles. Above all, creolization is characterized by catastrophic, non-uniformitarian change.

The distinction between catastrophic and uniformitarian change played an important role in theories of geological change in the 19th century. The so-called uniformitarians followed Lyell's view that change was slow and gradual. Others, however, believed that change was catastrophic or abrupt. More recently, Thom (1975) has elaborated a catastrophe theory to deal with any discontinuous transition that occurs when a system can have more than one stable state or can follow more than one stable pathway of change. The catastrophe is the jump from one state or pathway to another. Scientists who subscribe to this theory argue that on the smallest scale change is sudden and discontinuous. For example, electrons jump from one energy level to another without passing through states in between. The notion behind catastrophe theory is however controversial to biologists and geologists (and even linguists), because it proposes a new view of change which is contrary to mathematical principles which were ideally designed to analyse smooth, continuous change (*cf* also 5.6).

We can take as a linguistic example the case of **wen** and **bin** in Hawaii English Creole. Bickerton (1977b) argues that **bin** is the original basilectal creole marker of [+anterior], *ie* past before past. The zero or unmarked form of the verb marks the present tense. However, some speakers also use **wen** for the simple past, *eg* **wi wen mek fren** – 'We made friends'. Bickerton hypothesizes that **bin** 'developed into' **wen** via a series of regular and gradual phonological processes or rules. In other words there is a series of uniformitarian changes connecting the progression from **bin** to

wen. Presumably an intermediate stage would be one in which the initial labial approximant /w/ becomes a stop, or conversely one in which the stop becomes weakened to an approximant /w/. Thus, /bin/ → /wɪn/ → /wɛn/. Sato, however, disagrees with this analysis for several reasons. One is that **bin** and **wen** users seem to be mutually exclusive, which suggests that the forms are in free variation. Another is that **bin** seems to be used to mark the simple past, just as **wen** is. She therefore believes that the two markers emerged independently. This would be an example of a catastrophic development because there would be no series of gradual stages in the emergence of this item (other than of course the original English **been** and **went** from which these markers derived).

Others, such as Bailey and Maroldt (1977), consider the issue of continuity and degree of disruption of transmission to be more criterial for creolization. In considering whether Middle English is a creole they say (1977:21) 'by creolization the authors wish to indicate gradient mixture of two or more languages; in a narrow sense, a creole is the result of mixing which is substantial enough to result in a new system that is separate from its antecedent parent system'. They conclude that in this case there was sufficient mixing in the process of transmission from Anglo-Saxon to Middle English to warrant calling the resultant language a creole. However, Bailey and Maroldt do not argue that Middle English developed out of a prior pidgin (*cf eg* Gumperz and Wilson 1971 and the discussion in 3.1). Therefore, unlike Hall and others (*cf* Chapter 4), they do not consider the emergence of a creole to be dependent on a pre-existent pidgin. The question of the status of Middle English is far from resolved. Albert (1922) for example, has considered another aspect of the question, namely, what was the French spoken in England during this time like? He has argued that there was a kind of English-French jargon among the lower classes. Among its characteristics, which Albert identified in thirteenth-century texts, are a reduction in allomorphy and the tense paradigm, and peculiarities of pronunciation.

Markey assesses the case of Afrikaans by comparing it primarily to Negerhollands, a Dutch-based creole spoken in the Virgin Islands until the 1940s. It is the only form of creole Dutch that is well recorded; it also has the longest tradition of documentation of any creole. Magens (1770) is one the first grammars of a creole. Markey's (1982:200) checklist of features in relation to Afrikaans and Negerhollands is as follows [where + means creole-like; – means non-creole-like, and *a* means more or less]:

	Features	*Afrikaans*	*Negerhollands*
(i)	gender	+	+
(ii)	number by anaphora	–	+
(iii)	SVO order	–	+
(iv)	anaphoric unity	–	+
(v)	nominal case	+	+
(vi)	comparatives	*a*	+
(vii)	tense-aspect markers	*a*	+
(viii)	non-finite verb forms	–	+
(ix)	passives	–	+
(x)	semantic repartitions	–	+
(xi)	negation	–	+

Negerhollands has all of the features cited by Markey as typical of a true creole, whereas Afrikaans has only two, and is creole-like in two additional areas. I will look firstly at the features shared by both languages. We have already seen that grammatical gender is a feature which is generally lacking in pidgins and creoles. By grammatical gender Markey (1982:177) means the lack of inflectional gender marking or classifiers such as is found, for example, in German, where all nouns fall into one of three gender classes: masculine, feminine or neuter. One area of the grammar in which gender marking has consequences is in the noun phrase, where modifiers of the noun agree with it in gender. Thus, in German, the definite article for masculine nouns is **der**, **die** for feminine nouns and **das** for neuter nouns (in the nominative singular). Modern Dutch has a bipartite gender classification, masculine and neuter *eg* **het huis** – 'the house', a neuter noun preceded by the definite article; **de brief** – 'the letter', a masculine noun preceded by the definite article. Both Afrikaans and Negerhollands lack grammatical gender.

The feature nominal case refers to the general lack of nominal case inflection in creoles. We have already seen that this is a feature common to pidgins and creoles. There are no bound, but segmentable affixes used to indicate various case relations such as direction, possession, instrumentality, etc. Both Afrikaans and Negerhollands lack case inflection. However, the same is true of Dutch (and other primary European superstrate languages at the time of creole formation) as well as many substrate languages such as Yoruba, etc. Absence of nominal case marking is however a non-distinctive feature for creoles, since some creoles have created a system of prepositional case marking via cliticization of what were formerly serial verbs, *eg* **go**, **gi**, etc.. This has happened in some of the Atlantic creoles as well as in other languages which have no creole origin, *eg* Kwa (*cf* Lord 1976). In the following examples, the serial verb constructions are used for marking functions such as direction, benefaction, dative and instrumental. These grammatical relations would in other languages be marked either by inflectional case or prepositions (Bickerton 1981a:118–9):

Sranan: **a waka go a wosu** – [he walk go to house] directionality
'He walked home'
Guyanese: **li pote sa bay mo** – [he bring that give me] benefactive
'He brought that for me'
São Tomense: **e fa da ine** – [he talk give them] dative
'He talked to them'
Djuka: **a teke nefi koti a meti** – [he take knife cut the meat] instrumental
'He cut the meat with a knife'

This is not the only way in which creoles can express case relations. For example, Djuka also has the preposition **anga**, and thus an equivalent sentence to the one above would be **a koti a meti anga nefi** – 'He cut the meat with a knife' (*cf* Huttar 1975). Bickerton (1981a:119) says that serial verbs represent a more marked means of expressing case relations than do prepositions. Therefore, it is unlikely that a language which already had prepositions to mark case would develop serial verbs. It is also unlikely that a language which originally had only serial verbs as a case-marking device would later develop prepositions (*cf* also 3.5 for further discussion of serial verbs).

The feature comparative in Markey's typology refers to the use of non-indigenous comparatives in creoles. Generally speaking, creole comparatives are readily identifiable as input specific. For example, both Negerhollands and Afrikaans form the comparative either by the addition of **-er** to the positive or by introducing Afrikaans **meer** – 'more' or Negerhollands **me**. Both of these constructions are transparently Dutch in origin, *eg* **lang/langer** – 'tall/taller'; **Jan is meer lang dan Kees** – 'Jan is taller than Kees'. Where Dutch has **dan**, Afrikaans has **as wat** or **as waar** + preposition (*cf* Markey 1982:183).

Markey does not however mention the important fact that a number of creoles have a primary or secondary option of forming a comparative construction, whose main characteristic is that the noun which serves as the standard of comparison is the direct object of a transitive verb whose meaning is 'surpass or exceed'.

For example, in Cameroon Pidgin English, the following comparative constructions are found: **pas mi fo big** – 'he is bigger than I'; **i big pas Bill** – 'He is bigger than Bill'. Reflexes of English **pass** are used in Jamaican Creole, Krio, Gullah and Sranan. Some French and Portuguese-based creoles have a similar construction based on the lexeme meaning 'pass' (*cf* Valkoff (1966:101 – 2) on the **pasa** comparative construction in the Portuguese-based creole Principe). For example, Haitian Creole has **bel/pi bel/pi bel pase tout** – 'beautiful/more beautiful/more beautiful passed all' (*cf* standard French **bel/plus bel/ le plus bel**). In Sranan the following two types of comparative construction are found (*cf* Voorhoeve 1962):

> **Hugo can lon moro betre leki Rudi** [Hugo can run more better like Rudi]
> 'Hugo can run better than Rudi'
> **A koni pasa mi** [he smart surpass me]
> 'He is smarter than me'

The so-called exceed comparative (*cf* Stassen 1985 for this term and discussion of the type) has been clearly modelled on the serial verb construction. Thus it has been argued that the exceed comparative is a West African substratum feature (*cf eg* Hall 1966:82; Gilman 1972).[3] It can be found in the West African languages Ewe, Yoruba, Twi and Igbo (*cf* Twi: **ketwa sene me** – [small surpass me] – 'smaller than I'. Modern Sranan has largely discarded this construction in favour of the **leki-** comparative, a borrowing from the **like-** construction in English. Whatever the source of the construction, it would not be surprising to find it occurring independently in pidgins or creoles because it represents a weakly grammaticalized and transparent means of expressing the notion of comparison. Seuren and Wekker (1986) suggest that creole languages in general will tend to have a smaller set of secondary grammatical constructions.

Markey argues that Afrikaans is creole-like with regard to its use of three tense–aspect markers, a creole feature to which Bickerton attaches a great deal of weight. Markey too draws attention to the fact that despite formal differences in these markers between and among creoles, they always cover roughly the same semantic space and are concatenated in the same order. There is a major typological difference between pidgins and creoles with regard to this feature. Propositional qualifiers in pidgins, which are functionally equivalent to creole markers of tense–mood–aspect, are sentence external (*cf* also Kay and Sankoff 1974:64). In creoles the markers are sentence internal and always preposed to the verb. Markey (1982:185*n*) cites Portuguese Pidgin use of sentence initial and final **ja** [<Portuguese 'already, now, at present'] as an example: **Já mim disse isso já** – [already me say this now] – 'I have said this'. Mühlhäusler too (1986:156–7) cites the use of propositional qualifiers as a major typological characteristic of pidgins. As part of the process of creolization sentence-external modifiers become integrated into the sentence as part of the verb phrase. For example, in Tok Pisin, Sankoff discusses how the sentential modifier **baimbai** became phonologically reduced to **bəmbai** > **bai** > **bə** and prefixed to the verb.[4] Thus, in creolized Tok Pisin one can find a sentence like **mi bai go** [*cf* **baimbai/bai mi go**] – 'I will go'. A counterexample to this is found in Sango. Despite the fact that there is now a second generation of creole speakers, the future marker **fade** [identical to the adverb **fade** – 'right now'] always occurs first or early in the sentence and is never phonologically reduced (*cf* Samarin 1975). Nor has its use become obligatory, *eg* **fae tongana kété nginza ti mo ake, mo goe mo vo á-Nivaquine quoi** [if small money of you is, you go buy Nivaquine] – 'If you should have a little money, you ought to buy some Nivaquine (anti-malarial medicine)' (*cf* also 7.3).

There are cases where negation is sentence initial, *eg* as in Chinook Jargon discussed in 4.3, or sentence final, as in Principense, where the negative morpheme **fa** is placed at the end of the sentence as in **podi nda fa** [can walk negative] – 'He cannot walk'. Ferraz (1976) attributes this to substratum influence from African languages. On the whole, however negation is a general exception to the tendency to place propositional qualifiers in sentence external position. Negation is usually preverbal in pidgins rather than sentence external (*cf* also Chapter 6). This tendency emerged too in the study of experimentally created pidgins. Sokolik (1986) reports that 97 per cent of negation in Farsi pidgin is preverbal.

Markey (1982:188) points out that the Afrikaans verbal system is radically different from that of other Germanic languages in that it has largely lost vowel gradation as a means of distinguishing tenses.[5] It has also lost the so-called dental preterite as well as the distinction between strong and weak preterites. For example, in English and other Germanic languages, there are classes of verbs which show vowel gradations such as the following: **sing**, **sang**, **sung** (*cf* German **sing**, **sang**, **gesungen**). The marking of preterites with a dental suffix is also a Germanic typological trait. Compare, for example, English **jump/jumped** and **grab/grabbed**, where the past tense is formed by the addition of either /t/ or /d/, depending on whether the previous consonant is voiced or voiceless. The verbal system of the Germanic languages is also organized into classes of strong and weak verbs. Strong verbs are irregular with regard to the formation of their past tense, *eg* **write**, **wrote**, **written**, while regular verbs mark the past tense with a dental suffix. By comparison with the other Germanic languages Afrikaans has become more analytical.

With respect to all the other features in Markey's typology, Afrikaans does not fit into the class of true creoles. Three of these features are equivalent to Bickerton's, namely negation, the lack of passives, and semantic repartitions. Markey (1982:197) observes that creoles generally display an expanded scope and range of negation that is lacking in the main European lexifier languages. Preverbal negation appears to be the prototypical pattern for creoles. I have noted that this is true in pidgins too. The negator is also invariant in form. There are also differences in the scope of the negative in true creoles. The feature which Markey calls negative spread is equivalent to negative attraction or negative concord, as discussed above (*cf* Ch. 5), *ie* the spread or attraction of the negative to all the NPs in a sentence, as in Black English: **I ain't got no money nohow**. Negation is also cumulative, *eg* Afrikaans **Ek kom nie na jou to nie** [I come not to (see) you not] – 'I'm not coming to see you'. Afrikaans does not, however, have negative spread. In addition, negation is preverbal only in subordinate clauses. Compare **Hy kom nie** [he comes not] – 'He is not coming', and **Hy se dat hy nie sal kom** [He says that he not will come] – 'He says that he will not be coming'. Thus Markey (1982:199) concludes that Afrikaans is not a creole in terms of its properties of negation.

Markey, like Bickerton, claims that all true creoles lack morpho-syntactically full passives in which a semantic agent is expressed. The kinds of passives typically found in the European superstrate languages in which the passive is indicated by, amongst other things, a change in verb morphology, do not appear in true creoles although they do emerge in decreolization. In English, for example, the morphosyntactic hallmarks of the passive are: a form of the copula plus past participle, *eg* **was found**; and a promotion of the patient, or direct object to subject role and position via a movement transformation, and corresponding demotion of the agent to a prepositional phrase usually headed with **by**, *eg* **John was hit by a car/A car hit John**, or deletion, *eg* **John was hit**. Markey says that the only Atlantic creole with a full passive is Papiamentu as spoken in Aruba (*cf* also

Corne 1977a on the passive in Indian Ocean creoles). Both the verb form and agentive marker are borrowed from the superstrate (Dutch and Spanish/Portuguese). Thus, **mi a wórde imbitá dor su ruman** [I anterior passive invited by his/her brother/sister] – 'I was invited by his/her brother/sister'. The auxiliary **worde** and the preposition **dor** are Dutch. The Hispanic **sér** and **di** can also be used as auxiliary and agentive marker respectively. Afrikaans has a morpho-syntactically marked full passive, as does Dutch, as in:

Piet skryf die brief – 'Peter is writing the letter'
Die brief word deur Piet geskryf – 'The letter was written by Peter'

By semantic repartitions Markey means the creole feature whereby possession and existence are expressed by the same form. I have already given some examples of this. Markey (1982:193) adds too the fact that the copula tends to be absent in equative constructions, and the locative copula is used to mark the progressive. In other words both location and progression have the same marker. Compare the use of Papiamentu **ta** [<Spanish/Portuguese **estar**] in these examples:

E buki ta riba mesa [the book is on table]
'The book is on the table'
E ta come pan [he/she/it eat bread]
'He/she/it is eating bread'

Afrikaans does not share any of these features with true creoles.

There are still four features in Markey's typology which are not found in Bickerton's, namely, anaphora, SVO order, anaphoric unity and non-finite verb forms. Afrikaans shares none of these with true creoles. The first of these characteristics refers to the fact that in creoles nouns are generally pluralized by the addition of the third-person plural pronoun, *eg* Papiamentu **buki-nan** – 'the books' and French Guyanese creole **fam-ya** – 'the women'. Negerhollands postposes anaphoric **they** to pluralize nouns, *eg* **di kine sine** – 'the children', but Afrikaans plurals are formed as in Dutch primarily by suffixation, *eg* **broer/broers** – 'brother/brothers'. Many words such as **broer** that have **-s** plurals in Afrikaans have **-en** plurals in Dutch. Hesseling (1897) observed some time ago that French was not a probable source for the introduction and expansion of **-s** pluralization in Afrikaans since this was no longer a productive pluralizer in seventeenth-century French. Neither does the spread of **-s** seem to be due to English influence. It seems instead to be an independently motivated development in

Afrikaans (*cf* Markey 1982:179). There are, however, differences between creoles with regard to the position of the pluralizer (*cf* for example, the discussion on French creoles in Valdman 1977a). The pluralizer operates on definite, but usually not on indefinite nouns (*cf* Markey 1982:178). This strategy of pluralization is not unique to creoles. It is found in a wide variety of West African and Oceanic languages (*cf* also 4.4), some of which provided input for some creoles. Some have therefore argued for a substratum explanation for this property in creoles (*cf* 3.5). For example, Valdman (1977a) believes that the use of the third-person plural pronoun as a plural marker in French-based creoles such as Haitian Creole (*eg* **liv-jo** – 'the books', where **yo** is from French **eux** – 'them') is an early innovation. This feature is absent from the Indian Ocean Creoles which were little influenced by African substratum.

The fact that creoles tend to have SVO word order has already been noted. Markey (1982:179) says that this is the typical order for analytical languages, and that contact situations appear to precipitate a change towards this ordering pattern. As an example he cites a split in the word order of the native languages of New Caledonia. In the more isolated languages spoken in the northern part of the island the dominant word order is VOS, while in the southern portion of the island around Nouméa as a contact centre, the dominant word order is SVO. There is a broad transitional zone in between in the southern mid-section of the island with alternative VOS/SVO ordering. The shift to SVO in the indigenous languages of the island is presumably due to contact within the last century. Afrikaans, like German, Dutch and indeed all the Germanic languages except English, is a verb-second language. After certain subordinating conjunctions such as **nogtans** – 'nevertheless', SOV order is used (*cf* the German and Rabaul Creole German examples in 2.2). Thus, Afrikaans does not conform to the true creole word order pattern. Markey notes however, that Afrikaans may be moving towards SVO order.

By anaphoric unity Markey (1982:185–6) means certain properties of the pronominal system of creoles, some of which have already been noted in 2.3. All creoles make a distinction between singular and plural anaphoric pronouns, and all creoles have just three persons and two numbers. They universally fail to distinguish gender in the singular, *eg* Haitian **i** – 'he/she/it', and only infrequently make a subject–object distinction. Loss of gender is correlated with the general lack of nominal gender (*cf* 2.2), and the loss of anaphoric case is tied to the general loss of case marking. Afrikaans makes no subject–object distinction in the plural forms of the personal pronouns, *eg* **ons** – 'we/us' (*cf* Dutch **wij/ons**). However, throughout the singular it distinguishes between subject and object *eg* **ek/my** – 'I/me', and distinguishes gender in the third person, *eg* **hy/hom**, **sy/haar**, **dit** – 'he/him', 'she/her', 'it'.

The last of Markey's features refers to the fact that creoles lack non-finite verb forms, whether inflected or not. Non-finite verb forms are those forms of the verb which are not limited by person, number or tense, *ie* the participle, the gerund and the infinitive. Afrikaans, however, like the other Germanic languages has non-finite verb forms.

More work needs to be done on this feature to determine how characteristic it is of creoles. Koopman (1986), for example, claims that Haitian Creole has infinitival forms. Although Mufwene and Dijkoff (1986) dispute this, they note that some Bantu-based pidgins and creoles, *eg* Lingala and Kituba, have infinitives which are morphologically different from other inflections and derivations. However, in a language which is largely isolational or analytical in its morphology, it is not clear that purely syntactic features will suffice to distinguish the infinitive from non-infinitive forms of the verb. Mufwene and Dijkoff explore the connection between serialization, which is a correlate to isolating morpho-syntax, and the absence of infinitival forms. In Kituba when the infinitival prefix **ku-** is omitted, a serial-like construction results, as in the example:

Pe'telo kwisáa o-súsa kisálu.
'Peter came (to) look for a job'

Markey's conclusion (1982:201–2) is that Afrikaans is clearly neither a true creole or non-creole. It is a transitional language located on a continuum between creole and non-creole. He adds that English would pattern very similarly to Afrikaans since both languages are the result of fusion.

Gilbert and Makhudu (1984), however, have shown that Markey's conclusion reflects the fact that his analysis was based on a normative grammar of Standard European Afrikaans. If the Afrikaans of whites, coloureds and blacks is distinguished, it can be seen that the latter two are more creole-like (*cf* also Janson 1983). The Afrikaans spoken by blacks shows 9 out of 13 features.[6] Afrikaans is then a loose label for a set of varieties ranging along a scale from highly European-like (*ie* similar to Dutch) to moderately creole-like (*ie* similar to Negerhollands).

Mühlhäusler (1986:222–5) has compared Tok Pisin, Unserdeutsch, English and German to Bickerton's twelve features of creole grammar. He concludes that Unserdeutsch differs drastically from Bickerton's true creoles. It shares with them only movement rules, questions and question words. Two of these features, namely movement rules and question words, are also shared by English and German. Tok Pisin, however, shows considerable overlap with true creoles. It shares eight out of the twelve characteristics. The only true creole features it lacks are definite article, TMA system (*cf* Chapter 7), complements and negation.

As indicated above, Bickerton and Markey ignore phonological features in their typologies. Others such as Bender (1987) have argued that phonological properties may be part of a set of pan-creole features. He proposes that there are some constraints on phonological inventories and on phonotactics, *ie* the permissible combinations of items. Some have proposed similar constraints on pidgin phonology. For example, Hall (1966) and others have commented on the small size or reduction of pidgin phonological inventories when compared to their lexifier or substratum languages. The same has been noted in connection with the number of phonological contrasts. A number of marked sounds in the lexifier language tend to be represented by a single phoneme in the pidgin. Thus, in Fanagalo as used by speakers of non-Bantu languages the clicks are replaced by /k/. In English-based pidgins the interdental fricatives are typically replaced by the corresponding stops /t/ and /d/. Heine (1979) cites similar features as characteristic of African-based pidgins. He notes in particular the difference in syllable structure between, for example, Fanagalo where words tend to be bisyllabic and Zulu where they tend to be tri-syllabic.

Bender (forthcoming) gives the following inventories for consonants and vowels in creoles:

consonants: /p, t, k, b, d, g, f, s, m, n, l- r, w, y/
vowels: /i, u, e, o, a/

Creoles also have no initial or final consonant clusters. They have a simple syllable structure which consists of alternating consonants and vowels, *eg* CVCV. Johnson (1974:119) proposes the latter two as universal morpheme structure rules in English-based creoles, but believes that they may turn out to be universals of pidginization.

The effect of these constraints on word structure results in a simplification by dint of the insertion of epenthetic vowel, or by deletion of particular consonants when they occur in clusters.

For example, Johnson (1974:121) cites the following word list for **worm** in a number of English-based creoles to illustrate the application of vowel epenthesis in breaking up an impermissible cluster sequence of /r + m/:

Krio	**worom**
Sranan	**woron**
Saramaccan	**wanu**
Cameroons	**wom**
Guyana	**worm**
Jamaican	**worom**
Gullah	**βurum**

Mühlhäusler (1986:149) however cautions against the simplistic view that the phonologies of stabilized pidgins represent the lowest common denominator of the languages involved. Pronunciation has often been singled out as the area where substratum influence can be felt most strongly. However, whether or not one believes that these generalities in surface phonological structure are due to substratum influence or universal natural phonological processes, there are some exceptions which are difficult to explain (*cf eg* the case of Chinook Jargon in 4.3). Mühlhäusler (1986:141) for example cites Ross and Moverley's (1964:143) finding that although consonant clusters did not occur in Tahitian, they do in Pitcairnese, which stabilized from the contact between Tahitians and the mutineers from the *Bounty* on Pitcairn and Norfolk Islands.

The case of Pitcairn-Norfolk deserves more careful attention for other reasons. One is that the conditions under which Pitcairnese developed were exceptional. Until 1790 Pitcairn Island was uninhabited. More is known about the details of the linguistic input than in most other cases. We know, for example, that there were 28 original inhabitants of the island, which included nine mutineers from *HMS Bounty*, six Polynesian men, twelve Polynesian women and one small child. The birthplaces of most of the settlers and details of the education and background of some of the Englishmen are known. For the first 33 years the settlers lived in almost complete isolation. Thus, during the formative period of the language there was little outside influence. It is known too that half of the Englishmen died within four years and all but one of them within ten years, so it is possible to make some intelligent guesses about the relative influence of various individuals on the language of this small community.

The only systematic treatment of the language is found in Ross and Moverley (1964) and Harrison (1972), and these are by no means complete. The latter is a study of the speech of Norfolk island, where most Pitcairners were moved permanently in 1856. From Harrison's description it would appear that Norfolk Island speech displays at least nine of the characteristics mentioned by Bickerton or Markey as features of true creoles. For example, it uses adjectives as verbs, preverbal negation (though no negative spread), bimorphemic question words (*eg* **whatawe** [what way] = 'how'), lack of inversion in questions, and existential/possessive **get**. The base form of the verb is the same as the infinitive and is used to express the simple present, past and future. The plural marker, where it occurs, is derived from the plural pronoun **them**, *eg* **em gel** – 'the girls'. It also lacks the copula and passive construction; relatives are not overtly marked. Not enough information is given about the article or TMA systems to assess their status.

Harrison, however, who is not a creolist, rejects the idea that pidginization played a major role in the formation of Norfolk speech. She says (1972:223) that the features of Norfolk do not appear to conform to the creole type (1972:223). It is not entirely clear why she says this since she then goes on (1972:272–3) to compare Norfolk speech to Jamaican Creole and Hawaii Creole English and finds considerable overlap in 14 areas.

Another reason why comparisons of this type have been made is to look at so-called natural languages in terms of their distance from creoles (*cf* 3.4) in order to be able to find evidence of prior creole origins. Aikiba-Reynolds (1983:23) claims that the old Japanese system of TMA marking strikingly resembles Bickerton's creole prototype and takes that as an important piece of evidence for the pidgin–creole origin of Japanese. Doi (1984:49) however, points out that there are a number of problems in interpreting this claim because the basic word order of Japanese is SOV. In an SOV language we would expect that the TMA markers would appear after the verb in the order AMT.

After examining a total of 31 creole features noted by Bickerton and others, Doi (1984) concludes that both Modern and Old Japanese agree in approximately one third of these. He notes (1984:80) that these figures are not as high as those of creoles but are much higher than those of Indo-European languages. They yield about the same degree of 'creoleness' as some of the vernacular languages of Africa such as Swahili. This can be seen in Fig. 2.1 (from Doi 1984:133):

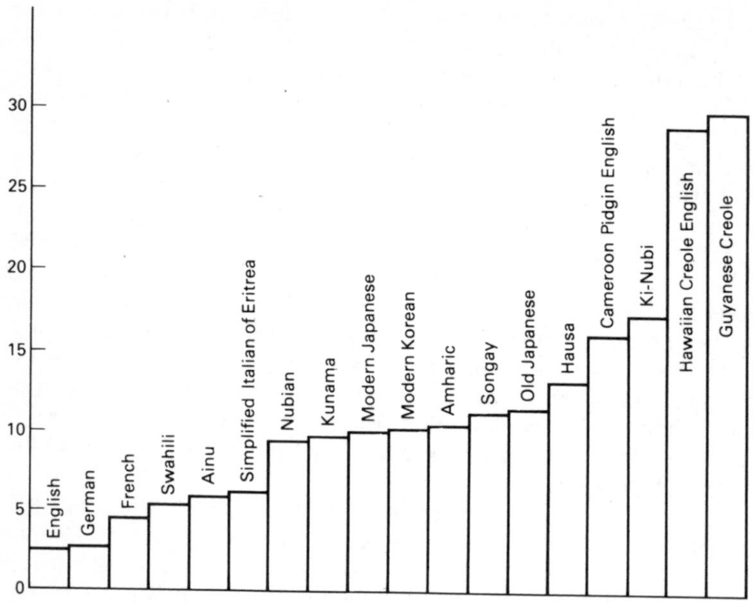

FIGURE 2.1 Summary of occurrence of Bickerton's pan-creole features in selected languages.

Can we conclude that some of the languages which are close to creoles are in fact post-creoles? The case of Japanese is particularly interesting since Old Japanese is closer to true creoles than is modern Japanese, thus suggesting evolution away from the creole prototype. Doi (1984:101–2) says that the results might support the interpretation that Japanese was partially creolized at an earlier stage in its history. The position of English too in this rank ordering is interesting given the claim that Middle English is a creole. Or does this simply reflect the fact that modern English has developed in a direction away from its prior creole-like stage?

Part of the problem in such typological exercises lies in the choice of features taken to characterize the prototype, and another part lies in certain assumptions behind linguistic typology. It is important to bear in mind with regard to the latter that there are no absolutes in typology. Kihm (1983b) goes so far as to say that the term 'creole' has no meaning in linguistic typology since linguists have failed to demonstrate that creoles develop differently from other languages. None of the properties discussed here are unique to creoles. Creoles change like other languages subsequent to creolization and the direction of change is often away from these characteristic features (*cf* also Givón 1979d:19–22 on the feasibility of defining creoles typologically).

Questions of prior creolization and pidginization in the history of a language cannot be decided by appealing solely to typological similarities with present-day creoles. In comparing the present-day form of creoles with present-day languages we are assuming that no major changes have taken place in the relevant features. Additional information is needed. Rickford (1977) suggests four identification procedures: information from external history; simplification of grammar; admixture from substratum languages; and divergence from the dialects of a lexically related language. The question which needs further investigation is which of these features constitute sufficient grounds for prior creolization. Mühlhäusler (1986:270) feels that mixture *per se* cannot be a reliable index of creolization. It can be the result of long and continuous or brief and sudden encounters. Mixture over a long period of time involving two or more fully developed languages has results that are different from mixture involving systems which are changing from less complex to more complex. In addition, mixing is not characteristic of certain stages in the development of pidgins and creoles. Moreover, natural internal developments and the results of mixing are often indistinguishable.

The relationship between these sets of distinctions and the process of nativization has been debated. I noted earlier that in the sociolinguistic typologies proposed by Stewart and others the main distinguishing social feature between pidgins and creoles is vitality. As Todd (1974) says, a pidgin is nobody's first language; and Bloomfield (1933:474) notes that a pidgin is a reduced variety of language which must be native to no one. This raises the question of whether there are changes which have to take place before a pidgin acquires native speakers. Or do the changes take place because the language acquires native speakers? In other words, do languages need native speakers in order to change, in particular to undergo syntactic expansion? Or put in another way, how significant a process is creolization in the evolution of human language?.

Views on this question differ widely. Labov (1971), for example says:

> Full competence in a pidgin grammar is still less than competence in one's native grammar . . . we have objective evidence that pidgins do not provide all of the features which native speakers seem to demand in a language. When pidgins acquire native speakers they change.

The objective evidence which Labov refers to however shows mainly that the kinds of changes which typically accompany creolization increase the stylistic rather than referential power of the language. Thus, in discussions of notions like adequacy these two dimensions must be distinguished. More importantly, however, Labov does not recognize that there are qualitative differences in the languages which have been given the general label of pidgin depending on the stage they have reached in their life cycle (*cf* Ch. 4). For some, like Mafeni (1970:2.7), a pidgin functions as a primary language.

Hudson (1980:67–8), on the other hand, says that creoles are ordinary languages apart from their origins and the special circumstances which give rise to a chain of varieties linking them with their superstrate languages, *ie* a post-creole continuum (*cf* Ch. 5.3). The differences between varieties which co-exist in such a situation are greater than one might expect in an ordinary community fragmented by the normal processes of dialect formation, particularly in terms of the amount and degree of syntactic variation. Otherwise, Hudson believes that creoles do not add anything to our understanding of language in general, or at any rate those which are well established. In the early stages of creole development however, when it is acquiring native speakers, one might expect to see two kinds of changes which may be of more interest for linguistic theory. Firstly, there are those which are due to the variety being learned as a first rather than second language. If it is true that children are innately endowed with the ability to acquire only 'natural' languages (*cf eg* Chomsky 1981), then to the extent that a pidgin does not possess the properties of such languages, we can expect to see changes which are the result of children's adaptations. Secondly, since the emergent creole will be used in an increasing set of social functions, including affective ones, we can expect certain changes to take place in line with changing communicative needs.

Sankoff has expressed the view that creolization is a crucial process from the perspective of linguistic universals defined in terms of the features which are basic to natural language. However, of seven major developments occurring in Tok Pisin, which she studied, only two (having to do with sentence embedding) show a time frame that is possibly coincident with creolization. Each of the other changes seems to have been complete before a community of native speakers existed. She also was not able to find any evidence that native speakers had been the innovators in developing new strategies for sentence embedding. Adult pidgin speakers seem to be responsible for the structural changes, which are introducing, among other things, strategies for relative clause formation (*cf* Chapter 6). If this is true, then stabilization seems to be the key factor in expansion, not nativization. Thus, we can conclude that the dichotomy between pidgin and creole stated in terms of the feature of vitality places undue emphasis on the criterion of native speakerhood, and that the extent to which there are structural differences between pidgins and creoles depends very much on the stage reached in their respective development (*cf* Ch. 4).

Notes

1. Murphy (1966) estimates that it has about 1,400. Bálint's dictionary (1969) lists 2,000 entries for various sporting terms, but these are largely neologisms. Hall's and Murphy's estimates are in line with my own findings for Tok Pisin speaking children between the ages of 7 and 15. They have an active vocabulary of about 1,000 words. In urban areas it is as high as 1,500, but this is largely due to the incorporation of English words. As yet, the longitudinal aspect of children's vocabulary development in a pidgin language has been uninvestigated.
2. A similar process has been observed in cases where convergence between a number of unrelated languages in contact has given rise to restructurings in the lexicon, but the resultant language is not a pidgin. The Scollons (1978:138–45) discuss such a case in Fort Chipewyan in Alberta where Cree, Chipeywan (Athabaskan languages), English and French have been in contact. Although some of the forms are still quite separate the meanings have converged. English **today** and **now** have been collapsed into one meaning, which is translated into Chipewyan by the word **dúhú**. Some speakers say **today** meaning both 'today' and 'now' and others say **now** for both meanings (*cf* also 3.1).
3. Gilman (1972:178–9) points out that in seventeenth-eighteenth century French and English the verbs **passer/pass** were occasionally found to express comparative notions. For example, in Samuel Johnson's dictionary (1775) we find an example from Ben Jonson quoted: 'But in my royal subject, I pass thee.' From the *Dictionnaire de l'Academie Française* (8th ed. 1932–5), we find: 'Le Prince Jesus . . . qui passait en beauté les vierges et les anges' – 'The prince Jesus who surpasses in beauty the virgins and angels'.
4. The phonological reduction involved here is attested in some dialects of English. For example, the *English Dialect Dictionary* (Wright 1893–1905) cites **bimeby(e)**, and the *Linguistic Atlas of New England* (*cf* Kurath *et al* 1939–43 vol. 3:71) reports **bambai** in New England.
5. Yiddish too has lost vowel gradation.
6. Gilbert and Makhudu (1984) have 13 features because they split Markey's feature (ii) into the associative plural, *cf* Jamaican **Jan dem**,

formed by the third-person plural pronoun, and the non-associative plural formed by the third-person plural pronoun. Feature (iv) is also split into lack of case distinctions on the one hand and lack of gender distinctions on the other.

Chapter 3

The origin of pidgins

We must be careful to distinguish between the origin of pidgins and creoles on the one hand and their development on the other. Similarly, we must be careful to distinguish between these processes in relation to pidgins as opposed to creoles. In the past the same explanations of origin have been applied to both; an exception is Bickerton, who has proposed the only theory which deals specifically with the origins of creoles. The question of pidgin origins and development is one of the oldest issues in the field, and continues to be debated today. The discussion of the competing theories is not always very clear, and it is often difficult to tell how many different theories have been proposed and who adheres to any particular one.

In assessing the state of the field in the early 1970s, DeCamp (1971a) says that opinion was divided between two theories, monogenetic and polygenetic. Todd (1974), however, classifies the theories into four groups:

(i) the baby talk theory
(ii) independent parallel development
(iii) nautical jargon
(iv) monogenetic/relexification

She then proposes her own fifth theory which synthesizes these four. Mühlhäusler (1986:Ch. 4) lists six theories grouped under two broader headings:

(i) language-specific theories
  (a) nautical language theory
  (b) foreigner talk/baby talk theory

(ii) general theories
  (c) relexification theory
  (d) universalist theories
  (e) common core theories
  (f) substratum theories

I will now examine some of these in more detail.

3.1 Baby talk, foreigner talk, simplification and imitation as the source of pidgins

Hesseling (1897 and 1933) put forward the view that pidgins arose out of the imperfect learning of the model language on the part of the slaves. This argued against the ideas of Schuchardt (particularly 1909 and 1914) that the reduced structure of pidgins came about as the result of a conscious effort at simplification by whites in a master/slave relationship typical of colonial situations. Schuchardt (1914) described this process as follows:

> To the master as well as the slave it was solely a matter of the one making himself understood to the other; the former stripped himself of everything specific to European languages, while the later restrained everything specific to his language . . . The white was teacher to the black; the latter repeated the former. And the white always used the most emphatic expressions, exaggerations as they occasionally occurred to him too, in communication with his compatriots. He did not say: 'you are very dirty', but 'you are too dirty,' and thus it may be explained that 'very' in Pacific Beach-la-mar is *too much* and *tumussi* in Sranan Black English. (Citation from English translation 1979:74)

We can see again some of the ethnocentric ideas and racist notions at work here in the suggestion that the white master acted as the teacher and simplified his language for the blacks, who were unable to acquire it.

In 1924 Father Jaffré, a missionary, explained the formation of Kitubu (a vehicular form of Kikongo, a Bantu language, one of those with official status in Zaire) by means of a reciprocal process of simplification. He comments (cited in Manessy 1977:149):

> By means of an inexorable correlation, as we deliver to our wards a disfigured language, these giving us back our formulas, present theirs to us in a deformed form. Thus, to give an example, instead of 'il est allé le chercher', one utters 'lui y en a aller le chercher ça', and blacks to conform themselves to the mold of our thought, calque their translation: yande kele konenda mon bonga iaou. [The

> Kituba should be: **yandi kéle kẃenda mu bonga yawu**, and the Kikongo: **welé ya bonga** SR]. They ignore the real form which exists, as adequate as the French form, short, clear and as easy as **ouele (il ėst allé ia (le) bonga (prendre)**.

Manessy comments that this hypothesis of a translation from Kitubu to Petit Negre or vice versa is hardly likely. The latter existed long before French and Belgian colonization, and Petit Negre is employed far beyond the Kongo-speaking area. Petit Negre is a pidginized form of French, formerly employed in French-influenced West Africa. It is highly unlikely that it ever constituted a stable pidgin.

Bloomfield (1933:472–3) was one of the more influential figures who elaborated this view and used the term 'baby-talk', which has since become a label for another theory concerning pidgin origins. The general idea however, is present in Leland's (1876) comment to the effect that Chinese Pidgin English presents no difficulty to 'anyone who can understand Negro minstrelsy or baby talk'. In sketching out the scenario, Bloomfield introduces the idea that a conventionalized jargon emerged as the result of a process of mutual imitation, or of the slave's imitation of the master's imitation. He writes:

> Speakers of a lower language may make so little progress in learning the dominant speech, that the masters, in communicating with them, resort to 'baby-talk' . . . This 'baby-talk' is the masters' imitation of the subjects' incorrect speech. The subjects, in turn, deprived of the correct model, can do no better now than to acquire the simplified 'baby-talk' version of the upper language. The result may be a conventionalized jargon. During the colonialization of the last few centuries, Europeans have repeatedly given jargonized versions of their language to slaves and tributary peoples. Portuguese jargons are found at various places in Africa, India and the Far East; French jargons exist in Mauritius and in Annam; a Spanish jargon was formerly spoken in the Phillippines; English jargons are spoken in the western islands of the South Seas (here known as Beach-la-Mar), in Chinese ports (Pidgin English), and in Sierra Leone and Liberia . . . In spite of the poor recording, we may perhaps reconstruct the creation of speech forms like these. The basis is the foreigner's attempt at English. Then comes the English-speaker's contemptuous imitation of this, which he tries in the hope of making himself understood. This stage is represented, for instance, by the lingo which the American, in slumming or when travelling abroad, substitutes for English, to make the foreigner understand . . . The English speaker introduces such foreign words as he has managed to learn (**kai-kai** 'eat' from some Polynesian language) . . . he does not discriminate between

> foreign languages (**savey** 'know', from Spanish, figures in all English jargons). The third layer of alteration is due to the foreigner's imperfect reproduction of the English speaker's simplified talk, and will differ according to the phonetic and grammatical habit of the foreigner's language.

We can see that the theory which goes by the name of baby talk conflates two processes, one which is initiated primarily by the upper or dominant group of speakers, who simplify their language, and another which is initiated by the lower or subordinate group who simplify the language they hear while trying to acquire it. In the first case the lower group merely imitate what they hear from the upper group. In the second case the active role is played by the lower group, and the upper group simply reinforce their errors.

In his review of Todd's book, Rickford (1977:489) refers to these as Baby Talk I and Baby Talk II; the former referring to the case in which the lower group are the active agents, and the latter referring to the case in which the upper group are the active ones. He notes that the arguments cited by Todd against the baby-talk theory are all directed against Baby Talk II. In order to evaluate the evidence we need to consider whether imitation and simplification play a significant role in the context of certain types of language acquisition, to the extent that they could give rise to a language variety which has the characteristics of a pidgin.

Since the 1960s researchers in the field of child language acquisition have played down the emphasis on the role of imitation. Ervin (1964:172), for example, notes that imitation is not 'grammatically progressive . . . There is not a shred of evidence that progress towards adult norms of grammar arises merely from practice in overt imitation of adult sentences.' Many researchers were eager at this stage in the development of the field to avoid the behaviourist views of Skinner (1957), which suggested that acquisition of language amounted to storing up rehearsed utterances. Both Ervin and Berko (1961) emphasize the creative nature of language competence. Berko, for example, showed that children were able to extend the inflectional morphology of plural and progressive formation to new items of vocabulary. That is, given a nonsense word like **wug**, they were able to form the correct plural **wugs**. Ervin also pointed to the fact that when children first learn the plural forms, they go through a stage in which they overextend the **-s** form, giving such forms as **foots**, which are then later replaced by the correct irregular form **feet**. The overextension of the plural is taken to be a reflection of the rule's productivity. There is evidence to indicate that even at a stage where children's productions do not match those of adults, they can discriminate between 'correct' adult productions and adult imitations of their own incorrect productions (*cf eg* Smith 1973).

In more recent research on children's acquisition more attention has been paid to 'baby talk' or 'motherese', partly in reaction to prevailing views on the innateness of language and the idea that language skills unfolded in a predictable way without regard to input or social context (*cf* in particular, the papers in Snow and Ferguson 1977). There is now a great deal of evidence to support the view that mothers introduce forms and meanings to their children in a principled way, and thus organize the child's input. Within the context of research on children's acquisition of conversational competence in interaction with caretakers and others, imitation has been seen to play a more positive role (*cf* in particular, Peters 1984). Studies have identified a number of characteristics of motherese. It tends to be highly fluent, redundant and simple, and produced with a higher pitch. Snow (1977:47) says that the semantic content of mothers' speech is largely limited to constructions the child has already learned. The MLU (*ie* mean length of utterance) of mothers' utterances is closely associated with the child's rate of psycholinguistic development (*cf* Cross 1977:166).

It is difficult to argue, however, as some have done, that the mother's input is syntactically simple, at least when measured by the usual yardstick of derivational complexity or history. Mothers also use a wide range of sentence types in talking to their children. The only sense in which baby talk is simpler is that utterances are shorter. Each sentence tends to encode one proposition at a time. It is this semantic limitation which produces the ostensible grammatical simplicity. Mothers tend to use coordinate or subordinate clauses in addressing children. This means that MLU is measuring something quite different from syntactic complexity, and that syntactic complexity is not isomorphic with propositional complexity. MLU reflects semantic more than syntactic complexity. Virtually the same amount of semantic information can be conveyed in one proposition as opposed to two. How semantic information is conveyed in surface structure syntax largely depends on the options available at a particular stage within a linguistic system and to a learner for encoding it.

Communication between mother and child is of course not directly comparable as a context of language learning to the asymmetrical situation of master–slave communication in a context of pidginogenesis for many reasons. For one thing, the child is not a cognitively mature language learner, unlike the adult, who already knows his first language. However, the general issues of whether simplification aids language acquisition and of whether acquisition proceeds largely by means of imitation are relevant to both cases. Just by demonstrating the special characteristics of mothers' speech to children, one does not prove that it is better for the language learner. But more importantly, there are no universal design features which delimit this type of speech from all others and make it unique.

I have already noted in Bloomfield's discussion the idea that there is some similarity between the speech of the master imitating the slave and that of the foreign tourist attempting to make himself understood. The comparison is drawn in more detail by Ferguson (1971), who compares baby talk, in the sense of motherese, foreigner talk, *ie* the speech addressed to foreigners, and pidgins. He identifies a number of characteristics shared across these modes of communication, *eg* repetition, absence of copula, short MLU. Ferguson (1971:143) suggests that:

> . . . many, perhaps all speech communities have registers of a special kind for use with people who are regarded for one reason or another as unable to readily understand the normal speech of the community (*eg* babies, foreigners, deaf people). These forms of speech are generally felt by their users to be simplified versions of the language, hence easier to understand and they are often regarded as an imitation of the way the person addressed uses the language himself. Thus, the baby talk which is used by adults in talking to young children is felt to be easier for the child to understand and is often asserted to be an imitation of the way children speak. Such registers are, of course, culturally transmitted like any other part of the language and may be quite systematic and resistant to change.

Ferguson goes on to say that many languages have foreigner talk registers which need systematic investigation. In his view (1971:147–8) the foreigner talk of a speech community may serve as an incipient pidgin. He concludes that the grammatical structure of a pidgin is based on the systematic simplification of lexical source language found in the foreigner talk register of its speakers, rather than in the grammatical structure of the language(s) of the other users of the pidgin.

Similarly, Corder (1975) suggests that there are 'simple codes', among them baby talk, foreigner talk, pidgins and interlanguage. All of these are characterized by a simple or virtually non-existent morphological system, a more or less fixed word order, a simple personal pronoun system, a small number of grammatical function words and grammatical categories, little or no use of the copula and absence of an article system. Corder argues that language learning begins with the acquisition of a simple code, which is nearer to the universal or underlying structure of all languages. The process of language acquisition is thus one of progressive complication. The initially acquired simple code becomes more complicated in ways specific to the actual language being learned. As I will show in Chapter 7, this view bears some similarity to Bickerton's views on the relation between bioprogram grammar and cultural grammar.

Later Ferguson (1975) conducted experiments to elicit foreigner talk, and similar experiments have been carried out for other languages. Ferguson gave sets of sentences such as **I haven't seen the man you're talking about**, and asked informants to transform them into a version suitable for a group of non-English speakers who are illiterate and non-European. In a repetition of this experiment at Oxford, Mühlhäusler elicited the following responses for this sentence:

I haven't seen man you talk.
I no see man you say.
I no see that man.
I no see man you speak.
That man you talk. I not see.
I no see man you talk about.
The man you talk of, I not see him.

I obtained very similar results from a group of native and non-native speakers of English at the University of Hawaii. In just one example we can see some consensus about the kinds of alterations speakers of English would make, *eg* preverbal negation **no/not**, invariant verb form, omission of article, etc.

Further evidence to support the pervasiveness of simplification in foreigner talk has emerged from a study done by Henzell-Thomas (1982). He elicited English foreigner talk from 22 non-native speakers of English, who came from ten different first language backgrounds. Statistical tests indicated that these non-native speaker simplifications were not specific to their first languages. The fact that both native and non-native speaker English foreigner talk had very similar characteristics strongly supports Corder's (1977) view that learners have internalized universal rules for simplifying grammars, which are not learned, but remembered.

There is now a sizeable body of data on foreigner talk (*cf* especially Clyne 1981). Hinnenkamp's research (1982 and 1983) is particularly valuable because it deals with German and Turkish foreigner talk. Examples of German foreigner talk were collected by Turks who recorded everyday encounters between themselves and native-speakers of German. Turkish foreigner talk was recorded in interactions in a Turkish village involving native speakers of Turkish and German tourists. Hinnenkamp (1983:4) lists ten typical instances of simplification:

(i) loss of pre- and postpositions
(ii) loss of nominal inflection and agreement
(iii) deletion of the copula
(iv) generalization of the infinitive
(v) change in word order
(vi) loss of overt question mark
(vii) external placement of propositional qualifiers
(viii) juxtaposition of subordinating clauses
(ix) lexical and grammatical multifunctionality
(x) periphrasis

As an example of loss of the copula (iii), we can take the following German sentence:

Turkisch Mann, Du?
[Turkish man, you?]

The full form in German should be:

Sind Sie ein Türke/Sind Sie ein türkischer Mann? (or in the familiar form **Bist Du**) 'Are you Turkish?'

The following Turkish sentence illustrates the deletion of the third-person singular copula in the past tense:

Vakit yok dün
[time there (isn't) yesterday]

The full form should be:

Dün zaman-im yok-tu
[yesterday time-my there isn't -it was]

The next example illustrates four of the features: (i) the loss of preposition plus contracted article **zum** – 'to the'; (iv) the use of the infinitive rather than the inflected finite forms of the verb. In this case it appears in the sentence finally (v) rather than in second position (though compare the full German sentence with the modal which occupies second position). Finally, there is the use of reduplicated **immer** which combines modality plus aspect.

Immer immer immer Betriebsrat gehen
[always always shop committee go]
full form:
Sie sollten immer zum Betriebsrat gehen 'You should always go to the shop committee'

Hinnenkamp (1983:7) emphasizes as the most important finding the fact that:

> two structurally so widely differing languages like Turkish and German approximate each other in simplification, yielding nearly an identical surface structure. A hitherto agglutinating morphology in Turkish is transformed into analyticity by way of *de-agglutinization* and likewise a hitherto inflectional morphology in German by way of *de-inflectionalization*.

This sort of mutual restructuring is attested by Gumperz and Wilson (1971) in Kupwar, where Kannada, Marathi, Urdu and Telegu are spoken. Almost all local men are bilingual or multilingual. The language of local intergroup communication is Marathi. The land-owning group in the village is Kannada-speaking, and Urdu is spoken by Muslims. Despite the fact that each language functions as a marker of ethnic and/or religious identity for those who use it, the constant code-switching required by daily interaction has had some far-reaching effects on the grammars of Kannada, Marathi and Urdu. Historically, Marathi and Urdu are related (*ie* Indo-European), but Kannada (a Dravidian language) is not related to either. Nevertheless, in this village the similarity among the three is now so great that Gumperz and Wilson report that they could analyse all three local varieties of the language without having to postulate syntactic categories or rules for one language which were not present in the others. Thus all three now seem to have a single syntactic surface structure. The three local varieties are also identical at the phonetic level, although they have different morphophonemic rules. A process which Gumperz and Wilson describe as convergence and creolization has brought about the gradual adaptation of grammatical differences to the point where only differences of lexical shape remain. Urdu has adapted its gender system and radically restructured its system of agreement markers in the direction of Kannada. Kannada has adapted to Marathi in that it has restructured copula constructions, interrogative suffixes and subordinate clauses. Marathi has changed least. Change has been in the direction of Urdu in five cases, in the direction of Kannada in ten and Marathi in ten. However they found no changes which involved just two languages to the exclusion of the third. Thus, we can summarize the changes as follows:

Urdu + Marathi > Kannada (vi)
Kannada > Urdu + Marathi (v)
Urdu > Kannada + Marathi (iv)
Urdu + Kannada > Marathi (i)

Note that Kannada and Marathi do not change towards Urdu, either singly or jointly. All changes are convergences involving the three languages as a set; changes are of the type: one towards the other two (*ie* L1 > L2 + L3), or two towards the other one (*ie* L1 + L2 > L3). The Indian case is interesting from the general perspective of borrowing since it has generally been believed that grammar and syntax are most persistent in language contact, and that lexis is the most easily borrowed (*cf eg* Haugen 1950). In Kupwar, however, it is grammar which has been most adaptable and lexical shape most persistent. This case is also interesting in the light of Hinnenkamp's remark about convergence between German and Turkish foreigner talk at the level of surface structure, since some of the changes involved in the convergence of Kannada, Marathi and Urdu could also be described as simplification. Gumperz and Wilson (1971:164) state that almost all the changes can be interpreted as reductions or generalizations that simplify surface structure in relation to underlying categories and relationships. The changes in gender categories, for instance, make gender form predictable semantically. The other changes show either a reduction in the number of environments in which a category is marked or reduction of the number of categories marked. The result is a more 'natural' surface structure. In referring to this case as an example of creolization, Gumperz and Wilson (1971:151,165) observe that:

> language contact can result in such far reaching changes that the affected language assumes a different structural type. There seems to be no reason therefore to draw an *a priori* distinction among pidginization, creolization and other diffusion processes; the difference may be merely one of degree.
>
> The Kupwar varieties have processes of reduction and convergence suggestive of pidginization and creolization. To say that the varieties have in fact undergone these processes would of course be misleading, if creolization is defined as requiring a pidgin as its starting point. We have no evidence of a pidgin-stage in the history of the village, or reason to suspect one.

They conclude that the present state of the languages in Kupwar is creole-like, in that one finds grammatical structure and lexical shape pointing to different sources. However, they are unlike pidgins in that the varieties in Kupwar seem to have undergone **re-syntactification** rather than relexification. The latter is thought to be a major process in pidginization.

We can note in parallel to the Kupwar case, that the outcome of the simplifications involved in German foreigner talk to Gastarbeiter has not resulted in a pidgin, even though the variety has some of the characteristics of such a language, and the processes involved are similar. Ferguson (1977:39) for instance, maintains that:

> The varieties of German used by and to immigrant workers are examples of foreigner talk and broken language phenomena, and the verbal interaction between native speakers and foreign workers are examples of the pidginization process at work.

Hinnenkamp (1982:10), however, concludes that the typical western European city in which foreign workers and the dominant society interact is not conducive to the rise of a pidgin. Moreover, with regard to the potential role of foreigner talk in pidginization he says that the inconsistency and high variability of foreigner talk does not allow us to attribute to it a decisive role as an input source for the target language learner. In the German data, for example, Hinnenkamp reports that only a quarter of the Germans simplified their speech at all, and among those who did, its use was inconsistent and variable. In their attempt to elicit Polish foreigner talk Krakowian and Corder (1978) also noted variability, but were able to establish a continuum of simplicity–complexity, with identifiable patterns ordered in an implicational hierarchy. Their data suggests that simplification begins with the verb, extends to the noun, then the copula, and then finally the pronoun system.

There is some disagreement over the role played by learned cultural conventions vs. innate principles in the transmission of foreigner talk. Mühlhäusler (1986:106) notes that foreigner talk tends to be a mixture of cultural conventions and genuine natural intuitions about language simplification. Because of its inconsistent nature it is not the ideal simple model some have claimed it to be. Therefore, he concludes that the importance of foreigner talk in pidgin formation is probably confined to the relatively early stages of development. The latter conclusion is supported by research Mühlhäusler conducted on Tok Masta in Papua New Guinea (*cf* 1.2). He found that it continued to be used in spite of the fact that it was badly understood and indigenous Tok Pisin had developed along totally different lines.

There are other cases of deliberate simplification reported in the literature. For example, Taylor (1977:885) says that the early European and Polynesian missionaries around Port Moresby were taught a pidgin form of Motu by its speakers. Early Bible translations are marked by many features of pidgin Motu. Later, when the difference between Motu and pidgin Motu was recognized, the missionaries opposed its use because they considered it inadequate for teaching and religious purposes. This Motu pidgin was not however the same as Hiri Motu (formerly called Police Motu), a pidgin form of Motu used on trading expeditions called hiri along the Gulf of Papua. It later became more widely spread as a lingua franca and is now one of the three official languages of Papua New Guinea along with English and Tok Pisin. There are similar cases from North America, where the Delaware Indians used pidgin to keep outsiders at a distance (*cf* Thomason 1980). Europeans apparently mistook Delaware-based Trader's Jargon for Delaware. Indian communities in Louisiana used Mobilian Trade Jargon for similar purposes (*cf* Silverstein 1975).

Mühlhäusler (1984) has discussed two deliberate attempts to create a pidgin German. Both of these (Weltdeutsch and Kolonialdeutsch) were written during the First World War in expectation of Germany's victory. They were seen as a means of social control within the context of German plans for colonial expansion. A principal motivation was to counteract the spread of English, especially pidgin English, as a lingua franca in the Pacific and Africa. The Germans arrived early in the Pacific; the first trading depot to be established by a German firm was in 1856 in Samoa. Although their influence as colonizers dates from 1884, all their possessions were lost as a result of the First World War after less than 30 years of administration.

A somewhat more controversial case to evaluate however is that of Portuguese pidgin. In arguing against the baby talk theory Todd (1974) says that no evidence has been found of deliberate simplifications in seventeenth-century texts. Naro (1978), however has uncovered earlier textual sources and concludes that the Portuguese did deliberately simplify their language for use in trading along the West African coast. He also argues that they did not imitate the errors of West Africans in learning Portuguese. Moreover, he claims that pidginization took place in Portugal rather than along the West African coast. Naro shows that captured Africans were taught simplified Portuguese in Portugal by order of Prince Henry in 1435 so that they could act as interpreters on ships sailing to Africa. Naro's evidence is strong support for Goodman's (1964) claim that European languages had been deliberately and systematically simplified. It constitutes evidence against the claims of others such as Whinnom (1971) and Taylor (1963) to the effect that the upper language speakers played a minimal or no role at all in the pidginization process. Whinnom (1971) says that pidgins do not develop in order to facilitate communication between master and servant, but rather in order to serve the needs of subordinate groups with mutually unintelligible dialects or languages. Taylor (1963:810) in particular says that it is impossible to account for the predicative systems of Martinician, Haitian and Sranan Creole as reduced versions of those found in any variety of the respective superstrate languages at any time. Whinnom (1971) attributes a major role to what he calls 'tertiary hybridization' among substrate speakers in pidginization. In view of Naro's evidence Koefoed (1979:37) said that the baby talk theory was not as easily refutable as DeCamp (1971a:19) had believed.

Moag (1978:88) maintains that Pidgin Fijian has resulted from deliberate attempts by Fijians to simplify their language. Moreover, its formation clearly antedated the plantations, where labourers were mostly Indians and overseers were Australians who often spoke Hindi. The Fijians did not have a master–slave relationship with outgroup members with whom the pidgin was used. They rarely worked on the plantations; the pidgin was formed in trading relations with Tongans, European traders and missionaries. All of these situations were, however, bilingual ones, involving only two groups in contact at any one time.

Another source of data for foreigner talk is found in literary representations and a variety of second-hand reports. or what Ferguson (1975:2) calls secondary foreigner talk. Corder (1977), for example, examined the speech created by Richard Adams in *Watership Down* for Kehaar, a black-headed gull. The story is about a group of rabbits who abandon their warren to find another one. They are helped by Kehaar, whom they befriended, fed and nursed back to health when they found him hurt and unable to fly. The rabbits in the story are said to speak Lapine, which is a language not known to the other animals. They communicate with other animals in what the author calls a 'limited lingua franca' or 'hedgerow patois'. Kehaar is said to have a 'strange and gutteral accent' and his speech is described as distorted. In his initial conversations with Kehaar the Chief Rabbit, Hazel, also uses this lingua franca, but soon resorts to Lapine, which is realized by the author as Standard English of a conversational informal style with the addition of a small number of Lapine lexical items. It is worth looking at the following extract to see to what extent it conforms to any of the principles mentioned above in cases of primary foreigner talk, and to see what support it lends to the idea that there are intuitive strategies of simplification (Adams 1974:265):

> 'You're a good friend to us, Kehaar.' 'Ya, ya, 'elp you for get mudders. But now ees dis, Mister 'Azel. Alvays I vant Peeg Vater now-alvays, alvays. Ees hearing Peeg Vater, vant to fly to Peeg Vater. Now soon you go for get mudders. I 'elp you, 'ow you like. Den, ven you getting mudders, I leave you dere, fly away, no come back. But I come back anudder time, ya? Come in autumn, in vinter I come live 'ere vid you, ya?' 'We shall miss you, Kehaar. But when you come back we'll have a fine warren here, with lots of mothers. You'll be able to feel proud of all you did to help us.' 'Ya, vil be so. But Meester 'Azel, ven you go? I vant 'elp you but I no vant vait for go Peeg Vater. Ees hard now for stay, you know? Dis vat you do, do heem queek, ya?'

Apart from the phonological peculiarities of this variety, we can note a number of features we have seen before, *eg* the lack of inversion in questions, or unmarked interrogative forms. Presumably, intonation marks utterances such as **ven you go?** as questions. Unmarked forms of the verb are used for present and future time, *eg* **I** (will) **leave you dere**, (I will) **fly away**, **and** (I won't) **no come back**. We can also see the use of reduplication, *eg* **alvays alvays**, and preverbal negation. More work needs to be done on literary representations of foreigner talk (*cf* Mühlhäusler 1984 for a discussion of German literary foreigner talk).

3.2 Nautical jargon

Not much support can be found for the nautical jargon theory as the main source of pidginogenesis. This theory takes the view that a nautical jargon used on ships for communication among sailors of different nationalities was passed on to Africans, Asians and others. It then formed the basis of a pidgin which these groups developed. There are a number of textual references to the unusual nature of sailors' speech from about the seventeenth century onwards. It is noted, for example, that they had a 'dialect and manner peculiar to themselves' (*cf* Matthews 1935:193). Unfortunately, there is little direct evidence of what this kind of speech was like. There is also a nautical element in the lexicon of all European-based pidgins and creoles, although this shouldn't be surprising given the fact that pidgins tend to be located near a marine expanse (*cf eg* Samarin 1962).

Both Reinecke (1937) and Hall (1966) mention the role of nautical jargon in pidgin formation. Reinecke (1937:434) says that merchant vessels are a favourable site and the 'seaman is a figure of the greatest importance in the creation of the more permanent makeshift tongues'. He observed further that the multilingual crew of one ship had developed a common vocabulary of about 300 words within a few months. Hall (1966:120) says that Pidgin English is an approximation to features of lower-class seventeenth-century English speech used in the 'lower reaches of the Thames, on either bank of the river, in the docks and settlements in such parts of London as Bermondsey, Rotherhithe, Wapping, Shadwell and Limehouse, and in other English seaports such as Plymouth'. These features were spread through trading, black-birding and colonizing activities. Attempts have also been made to trace French creoles to a French nautical jargon (*cf eg* Faine 1936). Baker and Corne (1982) tried to assess the influence of this kind of French. They (1982:243) say that there is no evidence to indicate that just one nautical patois existed (*cf* also Hancock 1976 on the nautical element in the Atlantic creoles).

Nevertheless, the role of sailors in spreading linguistic features across vast areas accounts for some lexical sharing between such distant pidgins as Hawaii Pidgin English, Chinook Jargon and Eskimo Jargon. Thus, the term **kanaka** for 'man' [<Hawaiian – 'person/human being/man'] occurs in both English- and French-based pidgins throughout the Pacific. It is also found in Chinook Jargon, where it and other items spread after the development of the fur trade along the northwest coast of North America in the late eighteenth century. Similarly, Eskimo Jargon has **kaukau** – 'food', itself a loanword in Hawaiian, introduced from Chinese Pidgin English **chowchow**. At this time contacts across the north Pacific became routine. The Hawaiian Islands became frequent ports of call and wintering places for ships. Keesing (forthcoming) places a great emphasis on sailors in the spread of Pidgin English throughout the South Pacific. After 1859 about 50 per cent of American seamen on whaling ships in the Pacific were black. As yet, no attempts have been made to assess the significance of this fact for the development and spread of pidgins.

As is typical of pidgins (*cf* 3.4) it is often not possible to trace lexical items to a unique source. Chinook Jargon, for example, has the word **lima** – 'hand/arm/finger/sleeve, thumb/handle'. Hawaiian also has an identical form **lima** which means 'arm/hand/sleeve/finger'. However, the most likely source for the Chinook item is French **le main** – 'the hand' (*cf* Drechsel and

Makuakane 1982). Another etymology for **kanaka** frequently given by Europeans, which is almost certainly erroneous, is that it derives from English **cane hacker**.

3.3 Monogenesis and relexification

As indicated in 1.2, it was Hesseling (1933), who first drew attention to the question of creole origins in his study of the role of Malayo-Polynesian in the formation of Afrikaans. Indeed, some have regarded him as the father of the theory which has been given the name **monogenesis** (*cf eg* DeCamp 1971a). This explanation is based on the view that European-based pidgins and creoles are relexified versions of a fifteenth-century Portuguese pidgin first used along the African coast and later carried to India and the Far East. This pidgin is itself related to Sabir, the Mediterranean lingua franca.

Despite the emphasis which Hesseling placed on the spread of Portuguese, to the point where he suggested that one could expect in every creole dialect 'some Portuguese words from the nautical and slave language that was widely distributed along the Gold and Slave coasts' (1905:68), it would be incorrect to say he was a proponent of the theory of monogenesis. Muysken and Meijer (1979:xvii) maintain that the idea is 'nowhere present in Hesseling's work. What is present is the idea of relexification'. We can see perhaps how this misinterpretation of Hesseling's work arose if we consider the relationship between monogenesis and relexification. I will show that monogenesis assumes relexification, although the reverse is not true: relexification does not imply monogenesis.

The essence of the monogenetic theory of pidgin origin is that all pidgins are genetically related to one proto-pidgin. Thus, one accounts for their similarities by virtue of the fact that at some distant point in time they had a common ancestor from which they are descended. The differences are accounted for by appealing to the process of relexification, which as Hall (1966:183) puts it, consists of the 'substitution of vocabulary items for others with the maintenance of a stable syntactic base'. Because relexification can create similarities between apparently unrelated languages, we cannot conclude anything about genetic relationships without more evidence about the process of historical transmission and relexification. Another problem is that we should expect to find lexical affinities between English-based pidgins and creoles, or between Spanish and Portuguese creoles anyway because they are related to the same respective base language. Similarly groups of pidgins or creoles could share similarities which are due to a shared substratum language.

The proto-Pidgin language of the monogenesis theory is hypothesized to be a fifteenth-century Portuguese pidgin, which may have been a relic of Sabir, the medieval Lingua Franca believed to be the language of the Crusaders and a common Mediterranean trading language. It is claimed that this language was relexified as it came into contact with various other European languages such as English and Dutch. Naro (1978) has suggested that the role of Sabir may have been overestimated. He notes that the Sabir of which we have evidence in fifteenth- and sixteenth-century Portugal is not destructured enough to provide a direct source of what he calls the reconnaissance language, *ie* the Portuguese contact pidgin used along the African coast. The fact that Sabir had few features in common with the reconnaissance language does not necessarily disprove the theory. As noted above, it was Hesseling who first detected the Portuguese origin of creoles which were ostensibly based on other languages. In 1909 Schuchardt noted that in Guiana a Portuguese creole had opaquely developed into an English creole. More evidence accumulated in subsequent years. Navarro Tomas (1951) demonstrated the relationship between Papiamento, a Caribbean creole and the Portuguese West African slavers' pidgin. Whinnom (1956) traced several Philippine Spanish creoles to a common Portuguese origin. And Taylor (1957) drew a number of parallels between these and Caribbean creoles. Subsequently Voorhoeve (1973) demonstrated a Portuguese base for Sranan and Saramaccan, but not Ndjuka, a third creole language spoken in Surinam (*cf* also Hancock 1987) for further evidence of relexification of Sranan and Saramaccan).

Thompson (1961) promoted the theory in an article, where he linked New World and Old World creoles to a common pidgin Portuguese. He says (1961:113) that it may have been the model for 'all the West Indian creoles, just as in the Eastern and Pacific worlds Portuguese creole dialects, well known to Europeans of many nationalities may have provided the model for the two great branches of Pidgin English, China Coast Pidgin and Neo-Melanesian'. One of Thompson's main pieces of evidence was the similarity in function and encoding of the categories of tense, mood and aspect in the Surinam and other creoles despite the considerable difference in their lexical composition. He compiled (1961:110) the list shown in Table 3.1:

TABLE 3.1 Markers of tense, mood and aspect in Surinam and other creoles

Markers	Durative	Perfective	Contingent or Future
Cape Verde	**ta**	**ja**	**lo**
Indo-Portuguese	**ta/te**	**ja**	**lo/di/had** (neg. **nad**)
Macao/Malacca/Java	**ta**	**ja**	**logo** (neg. **nadi**)
Philippine Spanish	**ta**	**ya**	**de/ay**
Papiamentu	**ta**	**taba**	**lo**
Saramaccan	**ta**	**bi**	**sa**
Sranan/Tongo	**de**	**ben**	**sa**
Jamaican	**a/da**	**ben/min/mi**	
Haitian	**ap**	**te**	**a**
Dominican	**ka**	**te**	**ke**

Huttar (1972) did a lexicostatistical comparison of the Surinam creoles, which shows that Saramaccan retains the highest degree of the original Portuguese lexical element, and less English influence.

Todd (1974) draws the hypothetical family tree in Figure 3.1 showing the derivation of all European-based pidgins and creoles.

Let us now look specifically at evidence for relexification of pidgins. In his discussion of this Mühlhäusler (1986:108) says that relexification is not a plausible solution for pidgins in the early stages where they have no stable grammar. However, stable pidgins may undergo relexification either abruptly or gradually. He illustrates the difference between the two from Tok Pisin. In case (a) the change is gradual. Continuity is maintained by the joint use of both lexical items in a synonym pair (*cf* a similar process in the history of English where French and English pairs occur, Jespersen 1968). In the second case, (b), the word for **bi** was introduced twice at different stages in the development of the language by different speakers.

	(a) gradual change	(b) abrupt change
Stage 1	**beten** – 'to pray'	**binen** – 'bee'
Stage 2	**beten o prea** – 'to pray'	
Stage 3	**prea** – 'to pray'	**bi** – 'bee'

Gradual relexification is found in the context of a prolonged period of bilingualism and the simultaneous presence of more than one prestige lexifier language. In the case of German New Guinea, both German and English were available for lexical borrowing for a considerable part of the history of Tok Pisin. The

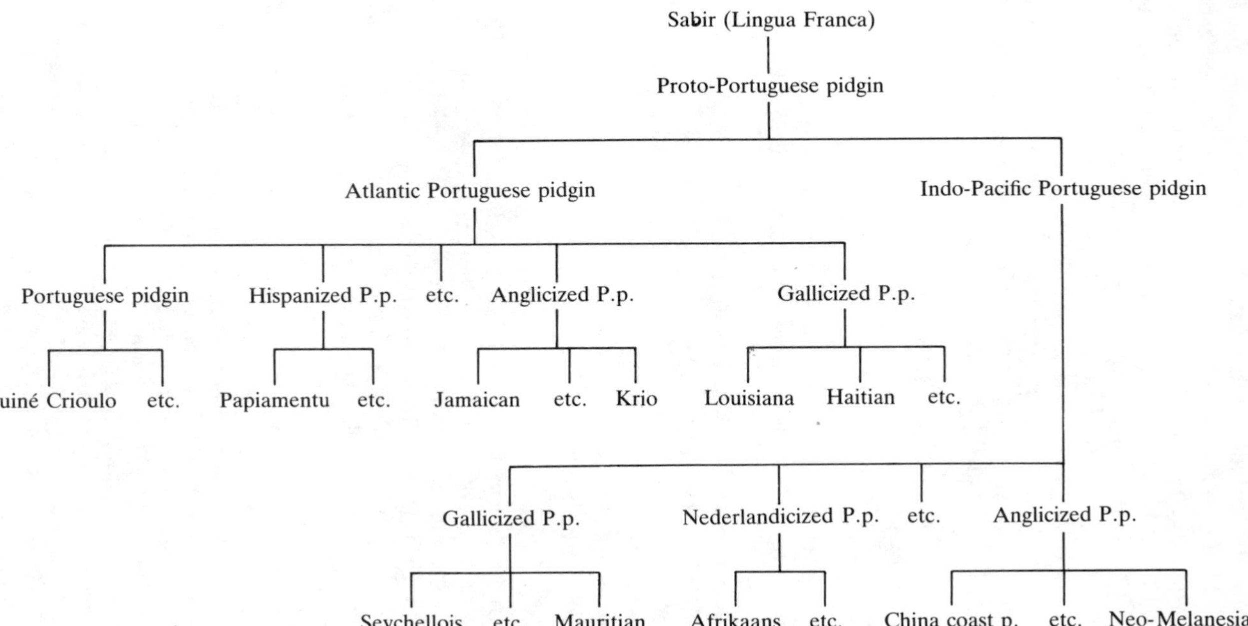

FIGURE 3.1 Family tree for all European-based pidgins and creoles

relative status of German and English changed over time, but at the height of German colonial control a number of New Guineans who already spoke English-based Tok Pisin began to introduce more and more items of German origin. This gave rise to mixed German/English forms of pidgin and predominantly German forms of pidgin. Mühlhäusler (1986:108–9) cites the following text from a speaker of Ali Island, who is a fluent speaker of Tok Pisin. The text is very close to Tok Pisin and probably the result of relexification [PG = Pidgin German; TP = Tok Pisin; E = English]:

> PG: **Ja fruher wir bleiben, Und dann Siapan kommen.**
> TP: **Yes, bipo mipela stap. Na bihain Siapan kam.**
> E: Yes, at first we remained. Then the Japanese came.
> PG: **Wir muss gehen unsere Boot. Wir bleiben und bikples, a Festland gehen.**
> TP: **Mipela mas go bot bilong mipela. Mipela stap na go bikples.**
> E: We must go to our boat. We stayed for a while and then
> PG: **Festland gehen**.
> TP: **Mipela stap na go bikples.**
> E: We went to the mainland.

Mühlhäusler says that a similar process of relexification occurred in the German colony of Kiautschou in North East China, where English and German were prestige languages. Pidgin English was a common trade language used by the Chinese with Europeans. The increasing importance of German led to a changeover to Pidgin German via intermediate mixed varieties. Mühlhäusler (1986:109) cites an example of this from Hesse-Wartegg (1898:10):

> The proprietor with his friendly smile had already learned German. '**Ik sabe Deutch**', he addressed me while making deep bows. '**Gobenol at gebene pamischu open Otel, Kommen Sie, luksi, no hebe pisi man, no habe dima, bei an bei**.' Since this Spanish-English-German-Chinese dialect differs from native to native, I want to add the German translation: 'Ich kann Deutsch, der Governeur hat mir Erlaubnis gegeben, ein Hotel zu eröffnen, kommen Sie, besehen Sie es; ich habe noch keinen Gast, weil ich keine Zimmer habe, aber nach und nach.' The words **pamischu**, **luksi**, **pisi**, and **bei an bei** are not German, but belong to the lingua franca used between the Chinese and Europeans, the so-called

Pidgin English. **Pamischu** is 'permission', **luksi** means 'look see', **pisi** stands for 'piece', for the Chinese do not say 'one man, two men', but **one piece man**, **two piece man**; **bei an bei** is English 'by and by'.

There are a number of examples of relexification of creoles, and the initial evidence supporting the monogenesis theory was drawn from a variety of creoles, as we have already seen. Although relexification appears to be of minimal relevance to the formative stages of a creole, it often occurs in the later stages of development, *eg* decreolization and recreolization (*cf* 5.7). Creolization of a partially or totally relexified pidgin may then take place, or relexification may occur after creolization. It is possible, for example, that Hawaii Pidgin English was a relexified pidgin Hawaiian (*cf* also 5.2). This pidgin, **olelo pa'i'ai** – '(pounded but undiluted) taro language', was allegedly originated by the Chinese who took over the cultivation of taro from native Hawaiians (*cf* Bickerton 1981a:7).

It is clear that relexification is a powerful individual force in pidginization and in the creation of new languages (*cf eg* the case of Media Lengua discussed by Muysken 1981c, where the grammar is Quechua, but the lexicon Spanish). However, it is not clear to what extent it played a role in the history of European-based pidgins to the degree necessary to support the monogenesis theory. One would have to provide detailed evidence for relexification in all of these cases. In addition, one would need to have more information about the original process of relexification of Portuguese pidgin. The most likely site for this is Ouidah (Juda or Ajuda) in Benin, where for several centuries an English, Portuguese and French fortress and slave depot co-existed. Some slaves were kept for a long time in these depots and then sent to other parts of the world.

Koefoed (1979:52) provides a good assessment of the status of the monogenesis/relexification theory when he says that it is essentially correct to assume that a language can change its lexical affiliation almost completely. Thus the absence of a reasonable number of lexical correspondences does not disprove a common origin for pidgins and creoles. However, most of the common features (Koefoed lists ten) shared by pidgins and creoles seem to be 'universals of pidginized speech rather than the result of a unique historical event'. Furthermore, as Todd (1974) notes, the theory does not account for the origin of non-European based pidgins and creoles.

3.4 Independent parallel development

The name of Hall is associated with the theory of independent parallel development of pidgins and creoles (*cf eg* Todd 1974:31). The essence of this theory is that pidgins and creoles arose independently (*ie* by polygenesis), but developed in parallel ways because they used common linguistic material (*eg* from Indo-European and West African languages in particular) and were formed in similar physical and social conditions. Stated in these terms there is a universalist element to this theory, just as there is to the baby talk/foreigner talk view; namely that certain types of codes emerge in response to particular communicative circumstances. However, it is not so easy to give one label to Hall's various formulations of his views on the origins of pidgins and creoles. Mühlhäusler (1986:118–9), discusses Hall's contribution to what he calls a common core theory; namely, the idea that pidgin grammar is a common core between the grammars of the languages in contact. Hall (1961) depicted this as shown in the diagram in Figure 3.2, where the structural resources of the pidgin grammar are built from the area of overlap of the parent languages.

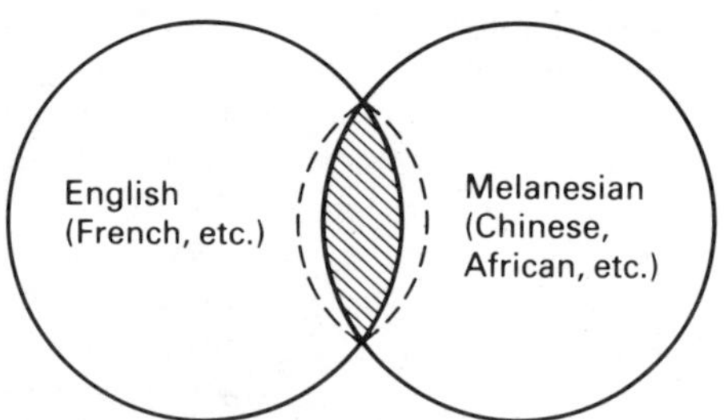

The structural resources of a pidgin language. Hatched area represents the overlapping of the 'parent' languages.

FIGURE 3.2 The common core of pidgin grammar

At the same time, however, Hall was one of the strongest proponents of the family tree model in accounting for the historical relationships among various pidgins and creoles, even though he recognized that many of the doubts various scholars had expressed about the comparative historical method of reconstruction were justified by the evidence from pidgins and creoles. As

Hall (1966:116) saw it, the central questions posed by the existence of pidgins and creoles were:

> How far can structural borrowings go before they affect our classification of a language? Can structural borrowings submerge the inherited system so thoroughly that later inspection cannot discover the actual 'genetic' affiliation of the language? Is it possible for such borrowings to result in a language that actually has many 'ancestors' rather than one?

Hall says that such questions did not arise previously because it was assumed that genetic relationships were 'pure', and that a given language could be related to one and only one language family. Schuchardt, however, was one scholar who disputed this assumption, and undertook pidgin and creole studies to undermine this and other prevailing Neogrammarian ideas about the nature of language change. Hall then goes on to remark that notions of purity have now been rejected in favour of the view that all languages are mixed. Some, however, 'are more mixed than others' (1966:117). In principle, he acknowledges the possibility that we might one day uncover a language where a perfect balance of mixture made classification impossible, but notes that in practice this has never happened. In the existing creoles and pidgins the contribution of the superstrate is always greater than that of the various substrata. Thus, he concludes (1966:118) that the 'ancestral form of any given group of related pidgins and creoles can be reconstructed, using the accepted techniques of comparative linguistics'. Furthermore, the 'proto-pidgin' which is reconstructed in this way will show a reasonable correspondence to certain features of the 'source' language.

Elsewhere Hall (1961:414) draws a family tree illustrating the Proto-Pidgin-English ancestor of modern-day Pidgin Englishes. As can be seen in the diagram in Figure 3.3, he traces its origins to lower-class seventeenth-century English (*cf* also 3.2).

At the same time as Hall defends the family tree model and the procedures for identifying the correspondences which underlie it (*cf eg* his list of Proto-Pidgin-English correspondences in Table 8 1966:119), he is critical of those who propose the monogenetic/relexification theory of pidgin origin. The latter assumes that lexical change can take place on such a scale so as to obscure historical origins, and radically shift genetic affiliations. In criticizing this view, he says (1966:122) that it is just a more sophisticated version of the old idea that a pidgin or creole is simply a 'native language spoken with a European vocabulary'. Hall specifically queries the argument of relexification theory which

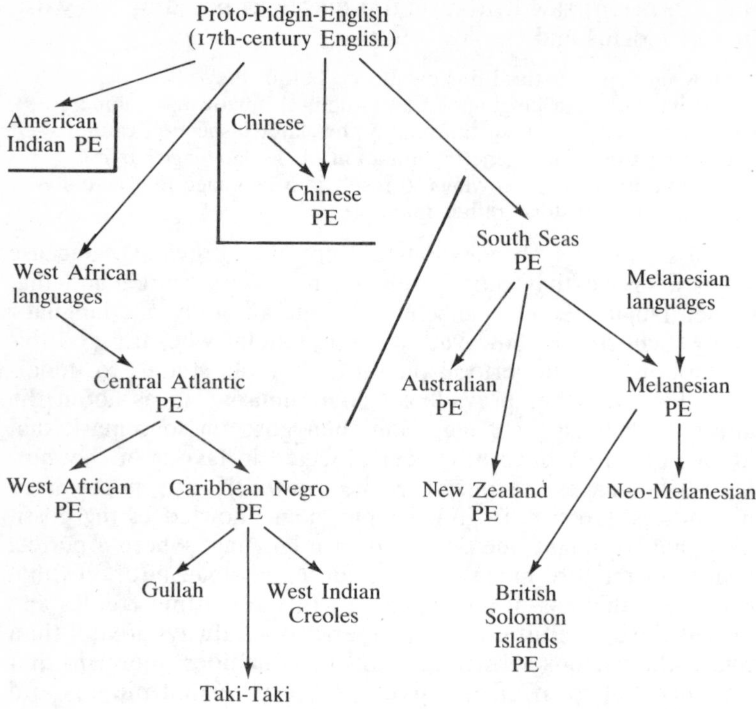

FIGURE 3.3 Family tree for Proto-Pidgin-English

is based on the assumption that only abstract syntactic (and not phonological and morphological) patterns are valid criteria for determining linguistic relationships. (Note, however, that if we applied this criterion to the case of Kupwar, we would be led to the erroneous conclusion that there was a genetic relationship between Kannada and Urdu and Marathi. Other problematic cases are discussed by Heath 1978 and Scollon and Scollon 1978.) Hall compares the history of Sranan and English, and observes that English has been extensively relexified with French and Latin material, but yet can still be classified as a Germanic language on the basis of its phonological and syntactic correspondences with other Germanic languages. Similarly, in the case of Sranan, the fact that its lexicon has taken in a great deal of Dutch vocabulary does not affect its basically English affiliation.

There are special problems, however, in applying the usual kinds of measures to pidgins and creoles to determine the degree of lexical affiliation. I showed above, for example, that in the case of the Surinam creoles significance was attached to the fact that Saramaccan had a greater number of words from Portuguese origin than either Sranan or Djuka (*cf eg* Voorhoeve 1973:138*ff*). In and of itself this tells us nothing about historical relationships, especially if these can be obscured by relexification. One method which has been widely used is glottochronology (*cf eg* Swadesh 1971 and Dyen 1975), although it has a number of drawbacks, some of which are noted by Hall (1966:123–4). The method relies on the assumption that linguistic change takes place at a steady and predictable rate, which can be quantified and compared with a list of core vocabulary. The core vocabulary consists of between 60 and 200 basic items that are alleged to be free of cultural influence, and it is believed that replacement of the words for these meanings proceeds in all languages at approximately the same rate.

Using this method one can compare the vocabularies of any two or more related languages and calculate the approximate time at which they diverged from their common ancestor. Hall (1966:124) describes the absurd result one would obtain if this method were applied to Neo-Melanesian (*cf* Hall 1959 for further discussion of pidgin languages and glottochronology, and Hall 1958 on creoles and genetic relationships):

> If we calculate the presumed relationship between Neo-Melanesian and Modern English, using Swadesh's revised basic list of one hundred words, we obtain a figure of two to three millennia of separation between the two languages if we assume that Neo-Melanesian is directly descended from English, or between one and two millennia if we assume that the two are cognates, descended from the same proto-language. Either of these figures is, of course, wildly divergent from what we know to be the actual length of time involved in the formation of Neo-Melanesian – not over a century and a half since its earlier possible beginnings in the eighteen twenties or thirties.

Hall uses this example to make the point that the main difference between pidgins and creoles and other 'normal' languages lies in the faster rate of change found among the former (*cf* also Woolford 1979:108 for a more recent statement of this idea and also 5.2). DeCamp (1971a:25) points out that this is the major reason why glottochronology should not be relied on unless we know that a language has not passed through the pidgin–creole cycle. This is however only one of the reasons why glottostatistics do not work well for pidgins and creoles. The assumption of a culturally unbiased core basic vocabulary, which can be used as a yardstick of comparison is a questionable one. It is often difficult to decide the origin of any particular vocabulary item, as was demonstrated in 3.3.

Mühlhäusler (1982) has discussed some of the problems in assigning etymologies to words in Tok Pisin. According to some estimates Tok Pisin contains about 79 per cent of English items. If we look however at some of the words which have been classified as being of English origin, it can be shown that other etymologies are equally plausible. For example, take the case of Tok Pisin **bel** – 'belly, stomach, seat of emotions' discussed by Mühlhäusler (1982:101–2). Mihalic (1971) attributes an English origin to it (<'belly'). However in Tolai, the most important substratum language involved in Tok Pisin's development, there is a word **bala** meaning 'stomach, seat of emotions'.[1] Mühlhäusler says that it was probably due to the similarity between both English and Tolai which led to the selection of **bel**. This is not an isolated instance. It was apparently Nevermann (1929:253–4), who first pointed out a number of Tok Pisin items which could be related to English in addition to a local language. He writes:

> Some Pidgin words which at first glance appear to be English have, however, only a chance similarity to it. Thus, the Tolai word **kiap** 'chief' has nothing to do with 'captain' but is native. **Pusi** 'cat' also seems not to be connected with English 'pussy' but is probably Samoan. The word for 'women' **mari** or **meri**, which is usually derived from the name 'Mary', popular among sailors, seems to me to be connected rather with the Tolai word **mari** 'to love' or **mari** 'pretty, beautiful', if it is not to be derived from **married**.

The number of Tok Pisin words which can be assigned plausible German or English origins is also considerable, not surprisingly, given the historical relationship between English and German (*cf eg* Tok Pisin **gaden**, German **Garten**, English **garden**). In other cases the origin of an item may be obscured by the application of natural rules of phonolgical reduction (*cf eg* Tok Pisin **abus** – 'animal' < English 'animal' via /l/ vocalization, loss of unstressed syllable and replacement of /n/ with homorganic nasal. *Cf* Mühlhäusler 1982:115).

A more recent investigation into the comparative and historical relationships between Pidgin Englishes in the South Pacific (Clark 1979) takes a somewhat different point of departure in selecting the basic items to be compared across the languages. Clark takes 30 features of vocabulary and grammar, which are all innovations with respect to standard English. In other word, he avoids precisely the features in these languages which are essentially the same as English. He also attempts (1979:9) to rule out 'those innovations likely to occur more than once independently as a result of universal processes of simplification, *eg* such as the elimination of inflections and most grammatical morphemes, the use of preverbal **no** as negator, etc.'

On the basis of his comparison Clark (1979:19) recognizes the following four classes of features according to their distribution:

(i) **World**: features shared by Pacific pidgins with English-based pidgins and creoles elsewhere in the world. These are **along** (with), **been** (past or anterior preverbal tense maker), **by and by** (future tense marker), **got** (have), **him** (transitive verb suffix), **piccaninny** (child), **plenty** (quantifier 'much, many'), **savvy** (know, understand), **something** (thing), **suppose** (if), **too much** (very very much), and **where** (relative clause marker).
(ii) **Sino-Pacific**: features found in China Coast pidgin and most of the South Pacific languages, but not elsewhere. These are **all same** (like, the same as), **catch** (get, obtain, receive), **got** (existential), and **stop** ('be in a place').
(iii) **Southwestern**: features shared by the Melanesian pidgins and Australian creoles, but not found elsewhere. These are **all** (third person plural pronoun), **all together** (quantifier 'all'), **along** ('to, at, from'), **belong** ('of'), **bullamacow** ('bull, cow, ox'), **fellow** (suffix to various pre-nominal modifiers), **fellow** (plural suffix in personal pronouns), **he** (preverbal predicative marker), **kaikai** ('eat/food'), **kill** ('strike, beat'), **pigeon** ('bird'), **what name** ('what, which'), **you me** (first person inclusive pronoun).
(iv) **Melanesian**: features not found outside the Melanesian group. These are **all** (plural marker) and **man bush** (noun compound where modifier follows head).

Clark (1979:22) draws the diagram of the relationships established on the basis of this comparative evidence shown in Figure 3.4.

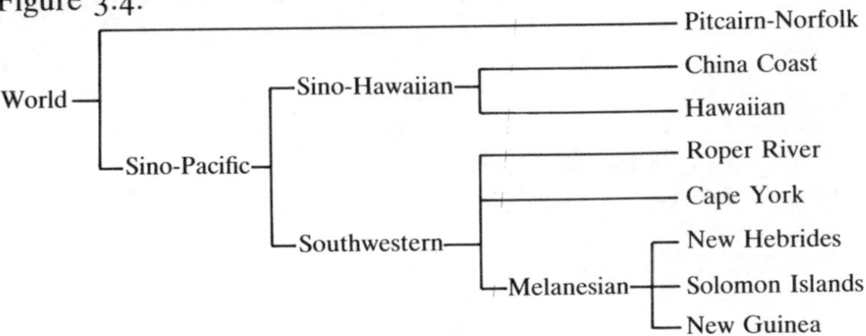

FIGURE 3.4 Relationships among Pacific Pidgin Englishes

On the basis of this comparative evidence Clark says that the features common to all of the languages indicate that the Pacific pidgins and creoles were not independent local developments, but had some links with pidgin and creole languages elsewhere. He suggests an eighteenth-century worldwide nautical English jargon as a possible ancestor. A few features have a defective distribution, *ie* are not found in all the Pacific pidgins and creoles; one such case is **where**, the relativizer, and another is **piccaninny**. This could be explained by loss or independent innovation in some of the languages. Only a few features exist to support the hypothesis that a China Coast pidgin was the ancestor for the South Pacific pidgins. The fact that there are a number of features shared uniquely by the Australian creoles and the Melanesian pidgins supports a close historical link (*cf eg* Crowley and Rigsby 1979, who trace Cape York Creole to Melanesia). A possible explanation for the existence of uniquely Melanesian features is the separate development of creoles in Australia, under the influence of heavy anglicizing pressure (*cf eg* the discussion in Harris, J. W. 1984).

Clark then compares this evidence with documentary data from various sources on the language situation in the Pacific before 1880. He presents (1979:48) the diagram shown in Figure 3.5 to show the revisions necessitated to Figure 3.4 by the documentary evidence.

The documents establish a South Seas Jargon (a foreigner talk/broken language variety) in use in various parts of the Pacific from the 1830s onwards. It was used primarily between European seamen and islanders who sailed with them. The great majority of the World and Sino-Pacific features are attested for this stage. The World features which appear later are probably innovations. Pitcairn-Norfolk creole, which shares only seven New World features of the 30 comparative ones with the other language does not show any distinctly Pacific characteristics. Thus it was probably formed independently of South Seas Jargon (*cf* also 2.9). The linguistic evidence is consistent with the fact that Norfolk people did not have contact with the pidgin English spoken by Solomon Islanders and New Hebrideans until the late nineteenth and early twentieth centuries.

The next stage in the development of this South Seas Jargon probably occurred in the 1840s when a form of it was introduced into southern Melanesia under the quasi-plantation conditions of the sandalwood and beche-de-mer industries. This jargon was locally known as Beche de Mer or Sandalwood English and was used widely between European and Melanesians in New Cale-

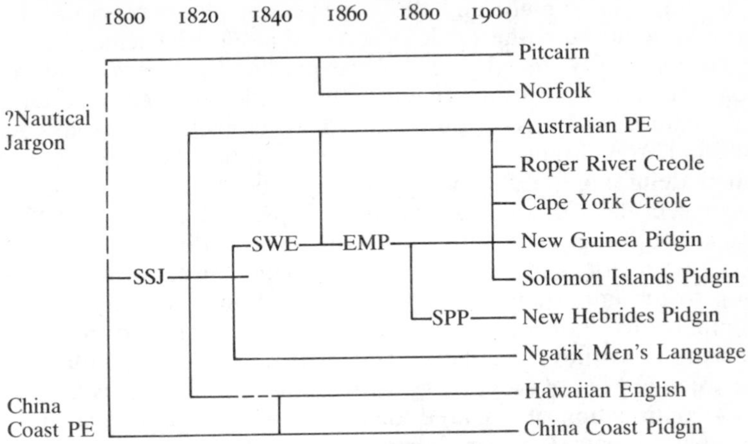

SSJ = South Seas Jargon (Polynesia and Micronesia)
SWE = Sandalwood English (New Caledonia, Loyalty Islands, New Hebrides)
EMP = Early Melanesian Pidgin (New Hebrides, Solomon Islands, Queensland, Fiji)
SPP = Samoan Plantation Pidgin
(For the sake of simplicity, the positions of vernacular languages have not been shown.)

FIGURE 3.5 Historical relations among Pacific pidgins and creoles established by comparative and documentary evidence

donia, the Loyalty Islands and the New Hebrides. In the 1860s it was taken to the plantations of Queensland and Fiji by Melanesian indentured laborers. There it developed rapidly and by the 1870s can be recognized as an early form of Melanesian pidgin. Labourers from the Solomons and New Hebrides took this pidgin to Samoa in the late 1870s, where it was learned by others. Present day Tok Pisin is a result of distinctive developments in New Guinea. However, the documentary evidence does not support this hypothesis that there was a separate period of Melanesian development established on the basis of the comparative evidence cited above. That is, the two features, **all** and **manbush**, which do not appear in Australia are not later developments, but are attested in documents at the same time as **kaikai, belong** and **he**.

Mühlhäusler (1986:16–19) notes a number of difficulties with Clark's analysis, particularly with regard to his interpretation of the plural marker **all**, and the third-person plural pronoun **all**, and the relativizer **where**. He observes that all the Pacific pidgins have apparently encoded the plural marker by means of **all** at some stage in their development. Papuan Pidgin English exhibits this feature before 1890, but in later texts **oltugeta** is used instead of **all**. Torres Straits Pidgin used **oltugeta** in the 1890s and developed a plural marked by **ol** only in the 1970s. Thus, a comparison of present-day Torres Strait Pidgin or Cape York Pidgin with Tok Pisin would suggest a false shared linguistic tradition (*cf* also 4.4 for further discussion of pluralization). Mühlhäusler draws attention to the importance of taking variability into account in such comparisons, not only between languages, but also regional variations within one language. Where we find similarities between any set of pidgins at any point in time, these may be due to a continuation of a shared linguistic tradition, as well as independent innovation, or borrowing. Mühlhäusler suggests a different procedure in comparing pidgins, namely to look at the sequence in which grammaticalization occurs, since pidgins may develop according to a universal program of grammatical expansion governed by linguistic and external factors. Mühlhäusler (1981a) has done this in the case of the plural marker and finds there are a limited number of sources for pluralizers which are in agreement with universal expansion patterns for pidgins.

Mühlhäusler (1986:16–19) concludes that the comparative method will give very misleading results. It is likely to be particularly unreliable at the level of morpho-syntax. He says that even the more restricted goal of constructing family trees on the basis of lexical evidence cannot be achieved unless the nature of the resulting trees is changed drastically. Firstly, we would have to acknowledge that there is only partial continuity in the development of pidgins. Therefore, a different family tree would be required at each different point in time. Secondly, we should abandon any attempt to trace pidgins back to a single ancestor. Mühlhäusler provides (1985d:477) a sketch of what this kind of 'family tree' would look like for Tok Pisin around 1880 and 1975 (*cf* Figures 3.6 and 3.7). We can then compare this with the 'tree' he constructs for Pidgin English in the South Pacific around 1880 in Figure 3.8 and compare it with Clark's reconstruction in Figure 3.5. We can see that Mühlhäusler's 'trees' are much less orderly. With regard to the place of Tok Pisin, it can be noted that the links between Tok Pisin and other Pacific varieties of Pidgin English are entirely replaced or restructured at a later stage (*cf* however, Keesing, forthcoming).

Another line of approach to the problem of establishing relationships between pidgins and creoles has tried to look for typological traits believed to be characteristic of them in other so-called natural languages, like English and Japanese (*cf eg* Doi 1984 for a review of the pidgin–creole origin hypothesis for

——→ direct linguistic influence
- - - - → indirect or weak linguistic influence
←——→ mutual influence between varieties
TP = Tok Pisin (New Guinea Pidgin English)
SPP = Samoan Plantation Pidgin English

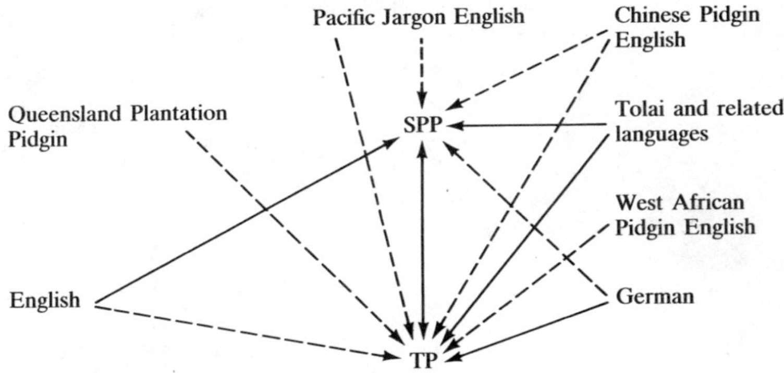

FIGURE 3.6 Linguistic influences on Tok Pisin around 1900

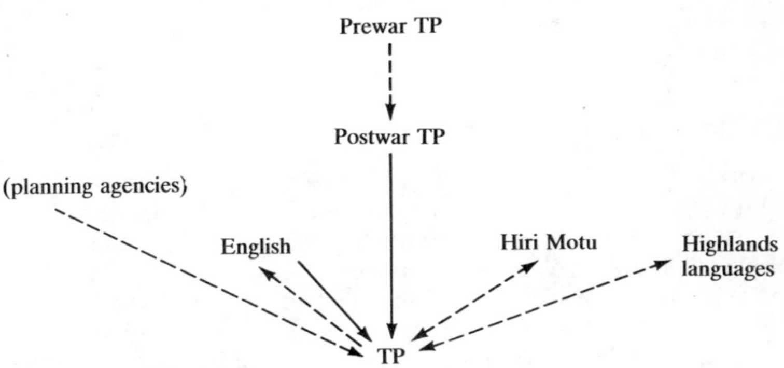

FIGURE 3.7 Influences on Tok Pisin around 1975

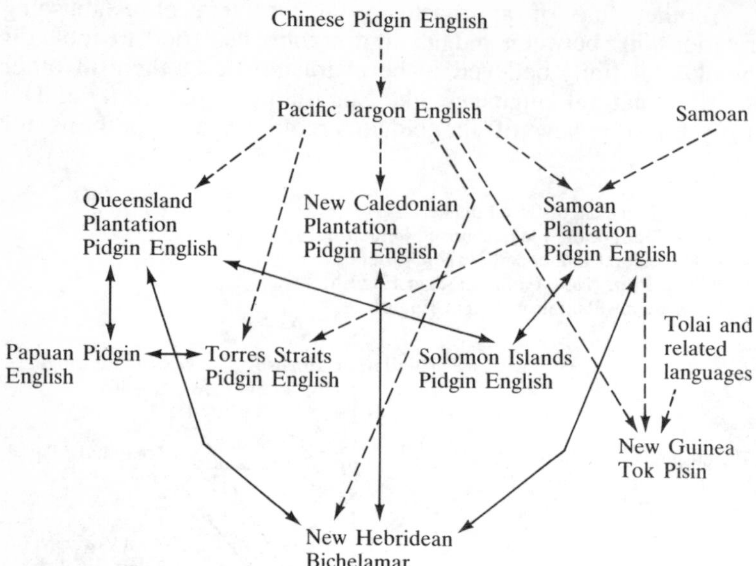

FIGURE 3.8 Pidgin English in the Pacific around 1880

Japanese). This has come in response to a recognition that pidginization and creolization may have been important stages in the life cycles of many 'natural' languages (*cf eg* Southworth 1971 on Marathi). More recently, others such as Bender (1987) have applied Bickerton's (1981a) features of true creoles (*cf* 2.9 and Ch. 7) to other languages to see to what extent there is an overlap.

3.5 Substratum theories

Various features, phonological, syntactic and lexical, widely found in pidgins and creoles have been attributed to the influence of African substratum. Goodman (1964), for example, has argued that only a West African origin for all French creoles can explain the extensive similarities. Hall (1966:109), who is, as I have said (*cf* 3.4), generally reluctant to attribute too great a role to substratum influence in the development of pidgins, nevertheless, comments that 'the entire inflectional system of the Haitian Creole verb with its loss of tense and person – and number – endings and its use of aspectual prefixes, is straight African'.

Bentolila (1971) argues more specifically that the verbal system of Haitian Creole originates in Fon. His conclusion is based on the fact that each has three tense–aspect markers with comparable semantic range and (with the exception of the anterior and irrealis) the markers occur in the same position relative to one another.

While there is no doubt that the verbal systems of many French-based creoles are strikingly different when compared to that of modern standard French, the latter should not be used as a yardstick of comparison. Comhaire-Sylvain (1936:106) argues that it is impossible to account for the verbal system of Haitian Creole in terms of normal evolutive change from French; however, she then mentions a large number of periphrastic constructions with aspectual meaning found in vernacular varieties of French. Valdman (1977a:181) notes that analyticity in the expression of verbal categories and the absence of person–number inflection are not alien to certain types of overseas French. Therefore, appeal need not be made to any special process of decreolization to account for the presence of these features in creoles.

In his analysis of the Reunion verbal system, Corne (in Baker and Corne 1982) claims that the morpho-syntax and semantics derive mainly from seventeenth-century varieties of French, and that the primary semantic distinctions are temporal, with aspect and modality functioning in a secondary role. Reunion has a relatively complex verbal morphology in which the copula carries markers of tense and aspect, as in French. Unlike French, however, **êt(re)**, the copula, does not function as an auxiliary. There are nevertheless some important creole features which distinguish it from French, such as the use of **fin(i)** plus past participle/adjective to mark the completive in stative predicates, *eg* **li fini fatigé** – 'he has become tired' (Baker and Corne 1982:17). Corne (Baker and Corne 1982:101*n*3), however, raises the possibility of Bantu substratum in connection with the equivalent marker **fin/in/n** in Isle de France Creole since it does not seem in any sense other than an etymological one to be a natural development of any variety of French.[2] This marker and its semantic function are shared by other Indian Ocean creoles. We can note here too a similarity of structural origin and function in the completive marker, **pinis**, found for example in Tok Pisin (*eg* **mi painim pinis** – 'I found it'), and other English-based pidgins and creoles. Otherwise, in Isle de France Creole, by contrast with Reunion Creole, the predicate system is mainly aspectually oriented with tense playing a secondary role. All distinctions of tense and aspect are marked by preposed particles, which, as I will show in more detail in 5.5 and Chapter 7, is a characteristically creole way of organizing the verbal system.

Among some of the other features attributed by creolists to African origins are: the copula construction (*cf* 5.4 for more detailed discussion), serial verbs, pronominal systems, and verb topicalization. Koefoed (1979:39) proposes an African source for the affixation of the third-person plural pronoun to form the plural of a noun in French, Spanish and English-based creoles in the Caribbean area, *eg* Jamaican Creole **de pikni dem** – 'the children'. Let us look in more detail at verb topicalization and serialization.

In many creoles it is possible to topicalize verbs. Alleyne (1980:103), for example, cites the following examples from Sranan and Krio:

Sranan: **a pley mi ben pley nang a wroko**
[It is play I played with the work]
'I merely played with the work'
Krio: **Na waka a bin a waka**
[It is walk I was walking]
'I was walking'

Corne discusses a similar double predicate focusing construction in Isle de France Creole, where a predicate head is copied into sentence initial position. An example is given from Corne (Baker and Corne 1982:85):

Mauritius Creole: **batté li capavé batté**
[Beat he can beat her]
'He can beat her as much as he likes, it will be in vain'

Although there are no formal parallels to this construction in either English or French, we can compare the following examples of verb topicalization or fronting from two Kwa languages (*cf* Alleyne 1980:171–2 and also Holm 1980 and Huttar 1975):

Yoruba: **Mi mu ni won mu mi**
[me take is they took me]
'They actually arrested me'
Twi: **hwe na kwasi hwe ase**
[fall is Kwasi fell down]
'Kwasi actually fell'

Corne (Baker and Corne 1982:89) however rejects the possibility of Kwa etymology in the development of the Isle de France construction for two reasons. The first is the alleged implausibility of borrowing a highly marked syntactic structure in the absence of evidence for other borrowings. The second is that none of the items in the lexicon of Isle de France Creole of Kwa etymology belong to the core vocabulary. Corne asks how it could be possible that Kwa contributed such a marked syntactic construction while having so little lexical influence.

Corne may be right to reject a substratum explanation, but his arguments for doing so are not well founded in light of what we know about the kinds of borrowing which can take place in contact situations. While many agree that topicalized and focused constructions are generally stylistically as well as syntactically marked in that they involve movement rules (and these, as seen in 2.9, tend to be lacking in pidgin syntax), Corne is obviously evaluating the notion of markedness on the basis of a frequency metric, *ie* what is less frequently attested in languages of the world is more marked. However, that is only one consideration. One needs to look also at how the semantic category is encoded by the syntactic construction (or other device) which realizes it (*cf eg* Mayerthaler 1981). It may be that both the semantic category and the construction, *ie* a movement rule, are more marked than other categories and their exponents, but the relationship between form and meaning may still be partially iconic. In other words, it is not unnatural for focused constituents to be fronted by movement rules, although it is possibly more natural for them to be highlighted by prosody. Compare, for example, the marking of WH-questions by intonation as opposed to subject–auxiliary inversion. Given the perceptual salience of focused constituents a movement rule is no less likely a candidate for borrowing than anything else, provided it can be integrated into the syntactic base. It may be, as Givón (1979d) has suggested, that only those substratum features which are compatible with universal grammar can be preserved.

As far as Corne's second argument is concerned, there are precedents for large-scale syntactic convergence and borrowing with minimal effects on the lexicon, as I have shown in the Kupwar example (*cf* 3.3). There is also evidence that syntactic constructions are widely diffusable as patterns divorced from their lexical content (*cf* Nadkarni 1975).

Bickerton (1981a:Ch. 2) outlines another route of development in which fronting rules emerge in creole independently of substratum influence because languages invent rules when they are 'demanded by the structure of the language plus functional requirements'. Bickerton argues that most creoles do not have VP as a major category, only V. Thus, if they were to have a fronting rule which moved only the verb to the front, preposed particles would remain stranded, unless there was also provision for copying the fronted verb at the extraction site. That is, the movement rule must be one which copies without deletion.

I will look at one more structure which has been attributed to substratum influence, the serial verbs. These are chains of two or more verbs which have the same subject. They can be transitive or intransitive. If the first verb is transitive, an object appears after it. The following examples are from Bailey (1966:41,134):

im swim we gaan
'He has swum away' V1 and V2 are intransitive.
di bwai faaldong brok im fut
'The boy fell down and broke his leg' V1 is intransitive and V2 is transitive
im tek im fut kik me
'He kicked me with his foot' V1 and V2 are transitive.

In these examples it can be seen that in some cases the two verbs make up a complex semantic unit, which can be translated into English with a single verb. The first verb is often **go**, **come**, **take**, etc. From the perspective of English these constructions parallel coordinate constructions which would have to be derived by a rule of Equi-NP deletion,[3] which deletes the subject of the second clause, as in:

The boy fell down and [the boy] broke his leg.

Another example of this type can be found in Tok Pisin. The following was recorded in a rural village from a twelve-year-old girl who was talking about hunting animals in the bush:

Mipela save kisim kukim kaikai
'We usually catch [and] cook food'

Only the last of the Jamaican Creole examples is a case of what Woolford (1977:176) refers to as strictly defined serial verbs, *ie* a string of two verbs with an intermediate noun such that the noun is the object of the first verbs and the subject of the second. In Tok Pisin there are examples such as this one from an eleven-year-old girl I recorded in Lae:

em wetim olgeta go autsait
'He waited for all of them to go outside'

In this sentence **olgeta** is the object of the verb **wetim** and the subject of the verb **go**.

Eze (1980) describes what he calls superserialization in Nigerian Pidgin English. He (1980:77–81) gives examples of three or more verbs which are concatenated together across a multiple clause structure:

> **Dem come take night carry di wife, go give di man**
> 'They came in the night and carried the woman to her husband'
> **A come enter train, come find one place, sidon, come dey happy**
> 'I entered the train and was lucky to find a seat'

Eze says that the length of such multiple clause sequences is in principle unlimited. The rationale behind the ordering of verbs in superserialization is iconic. The main verbs appear in the order of the actions they are intended to represent. However, the main verb is the initial lexical verb in the sequence and the others are secondary verbs, which complement its action.

Those who attribute serial verb constructions to African substratum have cited parallel examples from the Kwa languages (*eg* Alleyne 1980:167ff):

> Twi: **akoroma no kyeree akoko no wee**
> [the hawk caught the chicken ate]
> Jamaican Creole: **di haak kets di tsikin iit it**
> 'The hawk caught the chicken and ate it'

In the case of the serial verb constructions in Tok Pisin Bradshaw (1979:32*n*) has suggested substratum influence from Austronesian languages. For example, he compares a construction with verbs like **kilim** in Tok Pisin with an equivalent causative serial construction in which the grammatical object of the preceding verb acts as the subject of the following verb. The first verb indicates the cause and the second the result. The Austronesian examples are from Manam, a language of western Madang Province, and from Iwal and Numbani, languages of Morobe Province.

> Tok Pisin: **Ol i kilim indai pik** [they hit die pig]
> Manam: **boro di-rau-mate-i** [pig they-hit-die-it]
> Iwal: **e-s bwelk vunu** [they-hit pig dead]
> Numbani: **ti-lapa bola uni** [they-hit pig dead]
> 'They killed the pig'

In Tok Pisin we can see that the serial construction **kilim indai** is equivalent to the causative constructions in the other languages. On its own **kilim** means simply 'to hit/strike'.

In summary of the role played by substratum in the formation of pidgins we can say that similarities involving isolated subsystems (even if complete) between two languages are not sufficient to involve a link. They could just as well be explained by appeal to linguistic universals. A possible alternative origin for some of the constructions I have examined here would be to attribute them to general principles of simplification which operate in the process of acquisition. That is, the tendency for learners to substitute periphrastic expressions for complex lexemes which they do not know. Another tendency is for semantic processing strategies to converge on SVO (subject–verb–object, where subject is the agent) as the canonical word order (*cf* also Romaine 1984a:Ch. 3 for a discussion of word ordering strategies in children's language acquisition). In his study of English foreigner talk of speakers with different first language backgrounds Henzell-Thomas (1982) found that paratactic syntax and chronological ordering replaced hypotactic syntax and logical organization. He suggests that the former features, which are developmentally earlier, are inherently easier to process.

I will examine some of the principles which operate in second language acquisition in Chapter 6, in particular the theory which predicts that the transfer of native language structure plays a critical role in learning another language.

A number of more general lessons can be learned from this examination of theories of origin. Surface similarity of form is no guarantee for a common genetic origin, or for the semantic equivalence of systems. Neither can commonality of structure be equated with sameness of function. Even Hall (1966:58) was misled into thinking that 'all varieties of Pidgin English and creoles that have grown out of them have an underlying identity of structure with English, and similarly for the French-based, Spanish-based and Portuguese-based pidgins and creoles . . . they still maintain a basically Indo-European pattern'. Baker and Corne (1982:5) say that the view that 'all Indian Ocean Creole French languages belong to the same semantactic tradition results on the one hand from a Eurocentric analysis of the facts and on the other from a concept of language which appears to confuse etymology with function'.

Sankoff (1984:104) has observed that recourse to either substrate or universals has generally been little more than an exercise in pattern matching. Some claims for substratum influence have been motivated by what Dillard (1970) and others have referred to as 'the cafeteria principle' (*cf* also 5.4) *ie* the idea that creoles were mixtures of various rules from different regional varieties of British English. In other words, features were randomly picked out and attributed to substratum influence without regard for how they might have been borrowed or incorporated into the pidgin or creole in question. Welmers (1973), Manessy (1977) and others have emphasized the fact that the so-called 'African substratum' is typologically diverse, and that combinations of substratum languages varied from place to place. If substratum influence was at all significant in creolization, how could such diversity of origin lead to uniformity in structure?

More specifically, Sankoff argues that neither can explain the dynamics of the development of the verb phrase in Tok Pisin. In order for any particular syntactic structure to surface and be sustained, it must prove to function as a viable discourse strategy. Sankoff points to the vast number and diversity of first languages used by speakers of Tok Pisin as a further problem in appealing to substratum. One can always find at least two or three potential sources for anything. She says that discursive practices are better candidates for areal features than specific features of morphology and syntax. Tok Pisin grammar has been reinvented, not copied, from the specifics of various substratum languages. Some of the common discursive practices found in the languages of Papua New Guinea include clause chaining patterns (*cf* also Bradshaw 1979). One could even invoke universals at a more general level and say that narrative schemata are universal and subject only to minimal cross-cultural variation (*cf* the discussion in Romaine 1984d).

3.6 Native speakers' theories of origins

By way of contrast to the various theories proposed by linguists to account for the origin of pidgins I would like now to make a few observations about some of the explanations given by native speakers. The first of these comes from Papua New Guinea and is about the origin of Tok Pisin.

One speaker of Tok Pisin explained the origin of the language by describing it as the result of Papua New Guineans imitating the whiteman's English. This popular account matches in some respects some of the various ideas I have examined in connection with the foreigner talk, baby talk and simplification theory in 3.1. He says:

> Bifo ol i kolim Tok Pisin, tok bilong pisin. Ol i makim nating. I no olsem. Ol waitman i kam. Ol i no save long harim tok bilong ol Niu Guini. Ol Inglis tok, Ol Inglis tok olsem: '/yu kam/'. Ol tok Inglis tasol long yu kam. Na ol Niu Guini ol hat tru ol ting em

> wanem tok ol inglis tok yu kam. Ol tok: '/hu xam/' i go i go kain olsem i go i go i go na ol i kisim tok pisin. I narapela tok ples bilong ol Niu Guini. I go i kam olgeta ol tok tok long inglis tasol. Nau Niu Guini man i tok i go i kam em narapela inglis, wantok bilong narapela. Na ol bihainim disfela. Em tok, 'Yu kam', I go i kam i go i go. Ol i kisim. Em i narapela tok olsem. Ol i kolim tok pisin. I no pisin ol i toktok nogut. Ol i makim nating.
>
> [Before, they called it tok pisin, the speech of birds. They didn't mean anything by it. It wasn't that way at all. When the whiteman came they didn't know the languages of New Guinea. The English people spoke like this: '/yu kam/'. They just said it like this: '/yu kam/'. And the New Guineans were puzzled. They thought, what kind of language is this that the English people speak. The English people said: '/yu kam/', and they said, '/hu xam/', and it went on like this, and that's how they got tok pisin. It's another of the local languages of the people of New Guinea. They just kept on like this. They themselves spoke only in English, English only, and New Guineans kept speaking another kind of English, a related variety of it, and now they all speak this variety. They kept on saying: '/yu kam/'. They acquired it. It's another language. This is how they got tok pisin. It's not bird language. That doesn't mean anything.]

In order to understand the full significance of this explanation, it is important to know that in many parts of Papua New Guinea, birds play a large role in the culture. For example, among the Kaluli studied by Schieffelin (1979), birds are believed to be spirits of the dead. People hope that when they die, they can become birds. However, they try to prevent the association of young children with birds, and they avoid eating pigeons which make sounds like birds. In the early stages of language development children have not learned the phonology specific to their native language, and they typically babble. Schieffelin found that when children made cooing noises and sounded like birds, the mothers corrected them and told them not to talk like birds. The Kaluli fear that children might become like birds and die. Therefore they must protect the children's language development at a stage when the children's language is not 'hard', *ie* fully formed.

Here the speaker seems to be concerned that people may be misled by the name of the language, Tok Pisin, due to the fact that **pisin** is the pidgin word for 'bird'. This has occurred via natural phonological reduction of the affricate /dʒ/ to /s/. Therefore, he is careful to explain that 'pidgin talk' is not the same as 'bird talk'.

My next example of a native speaker's theory of origin is of a different kind. It comes from Hawaii and was composed by

Joseph P. Balaz, who is a local writer who sometimes uses the medium of Hawaii Creole English, or 'pidgin' as it is called locally. He is of Czechoslovakian, Irish and Hawaiian ancestry and lives in Punalu'u on the island of O'ahu. He is the author of *After the Drought*, a book of poetry, and the editor of *Ramrod*, a literary and art publication of Hawaii.

Balaz's account takes its motivation from what he refers to as the 'phonic association' between the linguistic term 'pidgin' and the bird 'pigeon'. His version was written for an oral presentation which he made at a Colloquium on Pidgin and Creole Languages at the University of Hawaii at Manoa in Honolulu on 1st August 1986, where Balaz was reading some of his poetry. He explained that when he had been invited to the university to read some of his work in pidgin, he decided to preface his presentation with this account of the origin of pidgin. Two days before the Colloquium reading he visited a public library to research written material on pigeons with the intent of weaving this information into a humorous parallel. In his investigation he came upon the origin of the word **pigeon** in English, which fit his idea for the poetic parallel. The result is a very creative and skilful combination of some of the ideas mentioned in this chapter in connection with various linguistic theories of pidgin origin expressed through the medium of Hawaii English Creole. There is no standardized orthography for Hawaii Creole English which is accepted in the community, so I have reproduced this story as Balaz wrote it.[4]

Da History of Pigeon

(*in phonic association to pidgin*)

Like different kind words, da world was full of different kind birds: yellow birds, blue birds, red birds, love birds – and den came da pigeon.

Da history of da word pigeon is li'dis – Wen da French-speaking Normans wen conquer England in da year ten-six-six, dey wen bring along wit dem da word pigeon, for da type of bird it was. Da resident Anglo-Saxons used da word dove, or D-U-F-E, as dey used to spell 'um, to mean da same bird. It just so happened dat terms in Norman-French wen blend wit Old English sentence structure, to form what we know as Middle English. In da process, da French word became da one dat referred to da pigeon as food. Today in England, if you look for dem, you can find recipes for pigeon pie.

Food for taught, eh – Even back den, da word pigeon wen blend with pigeon for get some moa pigeon.

> So now days get pigeon by da zoo – get pigeon on da beach – get pigeon in town – get pigeon in coups – and no madda wat anybody try do, dey cannot get rid of pigeon – I guess wit such a wide blue sky, everyting deserves to fly.

A number of the phonological features which are specific to Hawaii Creole English have been represented in the orthography. For example, the use of spellings like **da (the)**, **dis (this)**, **den (then)**, **dey (they)**, **dem (them)**, **dat (that)**, **wit (with)**, **taught (thought)**, **everyting (everything)** illustrates the tendency for the English interdental fricatives /θ/ and /ð/ to become /t/ and /d/ in creole. Spellings like **moa (more)** and **madda (matter)** indicate the absence of postvocalic /r/ in certain environments where it would be present in standard English (*cf* Odo 1975). In two cases Balaz uses apostrophes to indicate that there is a difference between the creole pronunciation and English. For example, **li'dis (like this)** indicates that in Hawaii Creole English the full form **like** /laik/ is reduced when it is followed by **this** or **that**. In the other case he uses an apostrophe to indicate that the creole word is altogether different from English, *ie* **'um** instead of **it**. Hawaii Creole English does not mark gender, number or case distinctions in its pronoun system. Thus, **'um** can refer to **him**, **her**, **it** or **them**, *eg* **I see 'um** – 'I see him/her/it/them'. Historically it may be derived from a phonetically reduced form of **them** (or **him**), and hence the apostrophe is used to indicate that something is missing. Elsewhere, however, Balaz uses **dem**, *eg* **if you look for dem, you can find recipes for pigeon pie**. Perhaps this full form is used here because the reference is cataphoric rather than anaphoric. Another feature is the use of the particle **eh**, or /æ/ as it is pronounced, to seek the understanding or affirmation of the listener (*cf* Perlman 1975).

It is of course impossible to convey in ordinary standard English orthography the full extent of the differences between the creole and English pronunciation and prosody (*cf eg* Bickerton and Odo 1976). The problem of representation of the pronunciation features is particularly difficult for the creative writer who wises to use Hawaii Creole English as a medium. That is, since the creole does not have its own orthography, the writer is faced with the dilemma of how to make the creole look different from standard English. This issue is more easily dealt with at the level of syntax.

There are also some syntactic features specific to Hawaii English Creole, such as the use of **wen** as the marker of the simple past, *eg* **wen conquer** – 'conquered'.[5] Other past tense forms occur with English past tense marking such as **referred**. The construction **for get some moa pigeon** is also characteristic of the creole, which uses **for get** as a complementizer where English would just use **to** or **in order to**. Another feature is the use of **get** in existential/locative constructions (*cf* also 2.9), *eg* **get pigeon by da zoo** – 'there are pigeons by the zoo'. This phrase also illustrates the lack of plural marking, although elsewhere the English plural forms are used, *eg* **birds**. In this case, however, the fact that Hawaii Creole English allows for zero plural marking means that the plural form of **pigeons** and the term for the language **pidgin**, are homophonous. Thus, Balaz is drawing on the phonic association between pidgin and pigeon to make a pun. The fact that both the birds and the language are ubiquitous makes them hard to get rid of. Other features of grammar are more clearly mesolectal or acrolectal (*cf* 5.3), such as the use of **cannot** rather than **no can**, *eg* **dey cannot get rid of pigeon**.

As far as content is concerned, *Da History of Pigeon* draws on the mixing of languages, borrowing and relexification as important factors in the creation of a pidgin. It draws too on the fact that English has a number of semantically equivalent terms for animals 'on the hoof' as opposed to meat on the table, *eg* **cow/beef**, **pig/pork**, etc. This reflects the fact that the Anglo-Saxon word was confined to the barnyard and domestic contexts while the newer Norman-French borrowing was used in more refined contexts. The creative account evokes too the controversy which has emerged over the status of English after the Norman conquest. Balaz wisely leaves this question unresolved.

Notes

1. It is estimated that 11 per cent of Tok Pisin's vocabulary is of Tolai origin.
2. Isle de France Creole is a term used to refer to the Creole French languages of Mauritius, Seychelles and Rodrigues. Isle de France is the name given to Mauritius under French rule.
3. Equi-NP deletion is a rule which obligatorily deletes the subject of a **for-to** or **poss-ing** complementizer clause just in case it is coreferential with the subject of the matrix clause. Thus, in a sentence like **Sam wants very much to go to college**, it is assumed that the underlying structure is: **Sam wants very much for Sam to go to college**, and that a rule of Equi-NP deletion applies to remove the subject of the complement sentence, which is coreferential with the subject of the matrix sentence (*cf* also 6.10).

4. I am very grateful to Joseph P. Balaz for allowing me to include his work in this book.
5. The use of **wen** as a past marker also occurs in Jamaican Creole, where it is a variant of **en**, **min**, and **ben** (*cf* Cassidy and Le Page 1967).

Chapter 4

The life-cycle of pidgins

4.1 The notion of life-cycle

Hall (1962) is generally credited with the notion that pidgins have life-cycles, although the idea is present in the work of Schuchardt.[1] He uses the term to contrast the different histories and social functions of pidgins by way of comparison with 'natural languages'. He observes (1966:126) that:

> 'normal' languages do not have life cycles; a language is not an organism, but a set of habits handed down from one generation of speakers to the next, so that the customary expressions 'mother language', and 'daughter language' are, at best nothing but metaphors. A normal language is one handed down from generation to generation through transference to children who learn it as their first language, and its life is conditioned only by the length of time its speech community lasts . . . From the point of view of social function, the chief difference between pidgins and creoles is in the type of speech community whose needs they meet. Unlike 'normal languages' a pidgin language usually comes into existence for a specific reason, lasts just as long as the situation that called it into being, and then goes quickly out of use . . . A pidgin acquires a longer lease on life only by becoming the native language of a group of speakers (becoming creolized), and thereby passes over to the status of a 'normal' language. From this point of view, we can speak of pidgins as having 'life-cycles', and of their being 'inherently weak' in that, not their linguistic structure, but their social standing is normally not hardy enough to enable them to be used outside of their original context.

4.2 Stages in the process of pidgin formation

Todd (1974:53–69) distinguishes four phases in what she calls the creolization process:

(i) marginal contact
(ii) period of nativization
(iii) influence from the dominant language
(iv) the post-creole continuum

Mühlhäusler (1974; 1986) has refined this idea considerably in drawing attention to the qualitative differences in the stages of development of a pidgin and creole. For example, he lists the following stages together with examples (1974:15):

Stage	Example
Pre-pidgin continuum	Varieties of Bush pidgin in New Guinea in areas that have only been recently opened
Minimal pidgin	Butler English of Madras
Pidgin	Chinese Pidgin English, Chinook, Police Motu
Highly sophisticated pidgin	New Guinea Pidgin
Initial creole	New Guinea Pidgin, Hawaiian Creole
Extended creole	Sranan, Papiamentu
Post-creole continuum	English creoles in the Caribbean

Mühlhäusler's scale and the examples show the relativitity of the terms **pidgin** and **creole**. Mafeni (1971:95) comments that although the distinction between a pidgin and creole is a useful one, it is not always possible to make such a neat separation. There are languages like West African Pidgin, which 'run the gamut all the way from true creole – as a mother-tongue and home language – to what one might call "minimal pidgin", the exiguous jargon often used between the Europeans and their domestic servants' (Mafeni 1971:96). The same is true of Tok Pisin; there is a continuum of varieties which correlates with the age at which the language is learnt.

Mühlhäusler (1979) has refined this model considerably in order to draw attention to three major types of creole which can be distinguished on the basis of their developmental history. He (1979:43) depicts the pidgin–creole life-cycle as in Figure 4.1, where the expansion of pidgins in a post-pidgin continuum, and the expansion of creoles in a post-creole continuum are dimensions of the some process. Sankoff and Laberge (1973; reprinted in Sankoff 1980:198*n*) use the terms **creolization** and **depidginization** synonymously. This serves to emphasize the point that it

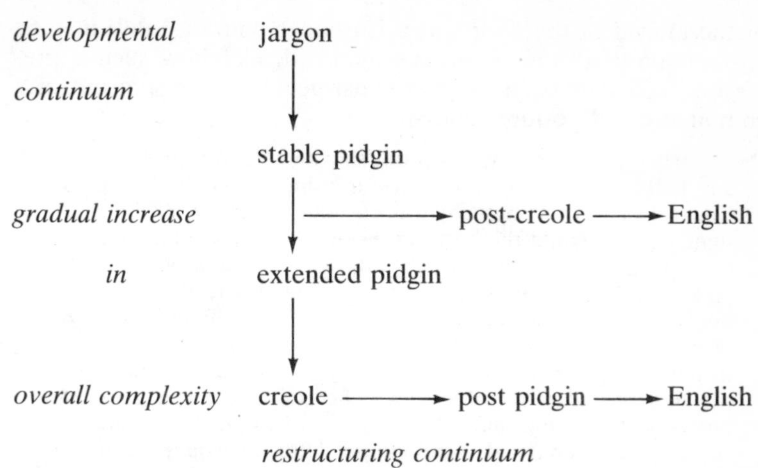

FIGURE 4.1 Pidgin–creole developmental continuum

is difficult to study pidgins and creoles as two separate phenomena rather than as two aspects of the same linguistic process. Expansion may occur without a language acquiring a community of native speakers, in which case we might technically speak of depidginization rather than creolization in characterizing the changes. Charpentier (1983), for example, says that in Bislama in Vanuatu there is depidginization without creolization because the language is used only as a second language. Among the developments involved in depidginization is increasing anglicization leading to fragmentation of the language into two varieties. This is parallel to what is happening in Tok Pisin (*cf* 4.4), except there the process is occurring within the context of creolization.

Of particular insight is Mühlhäusler's distinction between a **restructuring** and **developmental continuum**.

Let us look first at the main stages in the pidgin continuum, *ie* jargon, stable pidgin and expanded pidgin. Mühlhäusler characterizes each in terms of structural properties and functional characteristics.

4.3 The jargon phase

In the jargon phase, we find great individual variation, a simple sound system, one or two word sentences and a very small lexicon. Jargons are used for communication in limited referential domains, *eg* trade, labour recruiting. The following account of the arrival of the Dolphin, a European ship in Tahiti in 1767 (Robertson 1948:136–7) gives a good idea of how such a pre-jargon makeshift language was constructed on the spot out of a combination of gestures and speech:

> . . . when they came within pistol shot they lay by for some time – and lookt at our ship with great astonishment, holding a sort of Counsel of war amongst them mean time we made all the friendly signs that we could think of, and showed them several trinkets in order to get some of them onb[d] after their Counsel was over they paddled all round the ship and made signs of friendship to us, by holding up Branches of Plantain trees, and making a long speech of near fifteen minutes, when the speech was over he that made it throwd the plantain branch in to the sea, then they came nearer the ship and all of them appeared cheerful and talkt a great dale but non of us could understand them, but to pleas them we all seemed merry and said something to them, their language is not Gutteral but they talked so very fast that we could not distinguish one word from another . . . we made signs to them, to bring of Hogs, Fowls and fruit and showed them coarse cloth, Knives sheers Beeds Ribons etc., and made them understand that we was willing to barter with them, the method we took to make them understand what we wanted was this, some of the men Grunted and Cryd lyke a Hogg then pointed to the shore – others crowd Lyke cocks to make them understand that we wanted fowls, this the natives of the country understood and Grunted and Crowd the same as our people, and pointed to the shore and made signs that they would bring us off some . . .

Schuchardt (1883:113) uses the term **jargon** in referring to the Malayo–Spanish of the Philippines. He draws a distinction between it and the Portuguese Creole of Macao or Malacca. The former is in Schuchardt's terms 'kein fertiges patois' ('not a ready language'). By that he meant that it existed in many varieties which showed varying degrees of influence from Spanish and greater or lesser use of Malay words. Portuguese Creole on the other hand was for Schuchardt a 'fertiges patois'.

Without using the term jargon, it is this phase of the development of a pidgin which Labov (1970/1977) captured in his examination of the speech of Obasan, a Japanese woman in her 70s, who came to Hawaii when she was eighteen. She spent most of her life working on a small plantation and never was part of a plantation system. Like other isolated individuals, she did not acquire Hawaii pidgin English, but worked out her own form of linguistic expression which she uses in communication with non-Japanese speakers. Labov says (1970:8) that under these circumstances an ingenious and original mode of expression arises, which combines knowledge of the native vernacular with an imperfect grasp of the other languages in the new environment. The resulting language variety is far less regular than the pidgin and much harder to understand. In fact, he notes that Obasan appears to be understood only by one close friend, an English speaker. The language which she uses in these situations seems to have a predominantly Japanese syntax with lexical items supplied from Japanese, English and Pidgin. For example, Labov reports (1970/1977:8–9) that she conveys the meaning of 'Soon it ended' by the utterance:

Baimbai pau ni natteta

Baimbai is the standard Hawaii Pidgin English adverbial marker of the future. **Pau** also comes from Hawaii Pidgin [<Hawaiian] and means 'finish'. The particle **ni** comes from Japanese and is normally attached to adjectives. The verb is the past tense form of the Japanese verb **naru** – 'become'. The word order of Obasan's utterances normally follows that of Japanese, *ie* SOV or verb final, while Hawaii Pidgin English is SVO. The negative marker **ni** however is a particle preceding the verb, as in HPE rather than a final verb itself, **-nai** as in Japanese. Where a HPE speaker would say **I no like meat** – 'I don't like meat', Obasan would say:

Me wa niku ga no riku

In this sentence the English subject **me** is followed by the Japanese topicalizing particle **wa**, and the Japanese word for 'meat', **riku**. The Japanese verb would have been **sukinai**, with the negative particle **-nai** at the end. Instead, however, the pidgin construction **no like** has been altered by phonological restructuring. That is, l > r, and a vowel /u/ has been inserted after the final /k/ of **like** to bring the utterance more into line with the preferred Japanese CV, *ie* consonant–vowel syllable structure.

Labov remarks that Obasan appears to be relexifying a basically Japanese grammar with words from another source. She is also capable of utterances which approximate more to Pidgin grammar, *eg*:

I think water ga no more – 'I don't think there is any water'

Here the English subject and verb appear at the beginning, followed by **water** with the topicalizing **ga** and the pidgin predicator **no more**. The use of the English tag **I think** commits her to a basically English word order, but she ends up with the pidgin equivalent of the Japanese verb.

Labov contrasts Obasan's jargon with the speech of O-san, a Japanese man of about the same age, who uses Hawaii Pidgin English, a language which has socially sanctioned norms. He quotes (1970/1977:9) the following extract from a narrative about wild pig hunting:

> **Go bark bark bark. All right. He go . . . He stop see. Go for the dog. Go for the dog. He no go for you, the man. He no care for man. He go for the dog.**
>
> The dog starts barking. Alright. He's looking. (The pig) goes after the dog. He goes for the dog. He doesn't go after the man. He's not interested in the man. He goes for the dog.

Further discussion of the features of the Hawaii Pidgin English of Japanese speakers can be found in Nagara (1972).

In the jargon stage there is what Silverstein (1972b) calls a double illusion which makes communication possible. That is, the contact jargon is systematically relatable to both parties' native languages, and is perceived as a kind of lexical extension of some variant of the native grammatical system. As an example, Silverstein (1972b:14) cites a report (1633) from Father Paul de Jeune, a French Jesuit, who resided among the Montagnais at Quebec in which de Jeune tells of his progress in learning Montagnais, a Central Algonquian language:

> I have noticed in the study of their language that there is a particular jargon between the French and Indians, which is neither French nor Indian, and nevertheless when the French use it, they think they are speaking Indian, and the Indians in taking it up think they are speaking good French.

I will illustrate how this works in practice by taking some examples from Chinook Jargon, a trade language spoken along the Northwest coast of North America from the eighteenth-twentieth centuries. Some of the evidence indicates that it was not spoken before white contact, but was initiated by eighteenth-century European traders who purchased furs in the area; however, this is not agreed by all scholars. Some, like Thomason (1983), say that it was an important trade language before the Europeans arrived. In support of this she cites the markedly Indian rather than European structure of the language. Thus, she disagrees with Silverstein (1972a), who stresses the unsystematic nature of the jargon and the lack of independent grammatical norms.

Johnson (1975) describes the phonology of Chinook Jargon as a reduction or generalization of the phonological distinctions which occur in the speakers' native languages. Speakers generally used only those sounds which were present in their native languages. When the phonological systems of their native languages permitted, they maintained the phonological distinctions of the native American Indian languages in words derived from those lexical sources. The distinctions made by English in the labial series /b, p, v, f/ were not matched by distinctions in the native Indian languages such as Kwakiutl, which has /p, p^h, p'/ and Quileute, /p, p'/. Depending on the language origin of the speaker, different allophones may be used, *eg* [p] or [b], [f], [v]. All these distinctions were reduced to /p/ in the jargon used by most Indian speakers. English and French speakers sometimes maintained these distinctions. Thus, for the word 'fish' an English speaker might say /fis/, while a Kwakiutl might say /pis/. This means that lexical items exist in competing forms, *eg* 'fire' may be /paya/, /faya/ and /baya/. Most English speakers reduced /x, ẋ, n/ to a single phoneme in Chinook jargon, namely /h/. Thus, English speakers pronounced the word 'outside' as /klahani/, while Indian speakers pronounced it as /ʔaxni/. The English speaker's substitution of /h/ for /x/ can be accounted for by the fact that the series of back stops found in the Indian languages was much larger than in English. Thus, while English has only /k, g/ as stops, and only /h/ as a back fricative, the Indian languages had /k, q, k', k^w, q^w/ and /x, ẋ, x^w, $ẋ^w$, h/. The English speaker also replaces the initial segment, a voiceless lateral fricative, by /kl/ or /tl/.

Much the same happens at the level of grammar, where there is no inflection *per se*. However, speakers may introduce rules from their own language to create idiosyncratic forms, which may then be picked up by others. Johnson mentions the use of English plural forms ending in **-s** by English speakers, *eg* /ikta/ becomes /iktas/ – 'things'. Salish speakers may add the nominalizing prefix to words, *eg* /lahal/ – 'bone game' becomes /slahal/. This means that a number of competing forms exist at this level too. In some cases there is no semantic distinction between the competing variants, while in other cases, semantic specialization has affected one of the items. For example, in some areas (*eg* Bella Coula and Vancouver) /iktas/ took on the specialized meaning of 'clothing', while /ikta/ has a wider meaning of 'thing', 'clothing', 'what', 'something'.

There was also variation in word order. In the case of negation, in nearly all varieties of Chinook Jargon, the negative marker is placed at the beginning of the sentence. Thus:

helo naika tiki okok kamoks – [no I like that dog] –
'I don't like that dog'

Sentence initial negation is a regular feature of the Indian languages of the Pacific Northwest. In some varieties, however, it is possible to put the negative marker before the verb, as in:

naika helo tiki okok kamoks [I no like that dog]

As indicated in 2.9 this preverbal ordering is a salient characteristic of stable pidgins. The fact that Chinook Jargon has SVO as its basic word order pattern is also taken by Thomason (1983:844) as an indication of the existence of independent grammatical norms. The dominant order in the Indian languages is VSO.

The illusion of double communication is likely to persist for some time, at least on the part of the subordinate population. For example, in the case of Tok Pisin, it is probably not until around 1940 that there are indications that Tok Pisin is perceived as a separate language from English (*cf* 2.7). Speakers of Tok Pisin assumed that the white men were speaking their own language. One village elder in Indagen (a village in the Kabwum District of Morobe Province) related to me his impressions of first hearing Tok Pisin while working as an indentured labourer outside the district. He and many others thought it was the white man's language, *ie* English. The conversation went as follows:

SR: Long taim yupela harim tok pisin pastaim, yupela ting em tok bilong waitman o nogat?
Mipela ting em tok bilong waitman ia. Mipela ting tok bilong waitpela. Bihain ol i tok em i tok insait long namel i tasol. I no bilong waitman. Mipela askim kiap ol kiap mipela askim kiap. Mi tok, 'Em tok ples bilong yu?' Em tok, 'Nogat'. Disfela tok pisin em i bilong yupela bilong Niu Guini. Mipela longlong. Mipela ting em bilong kiap ia bilong gavman, tok ples bilong en, nau. Nogat.

SR: When you first heard Tok Pisin did you think it was the white man's language?
We thought it was the white man's language. We thought it was the language of white people. Then they said that there's only a little bit [of English SR] inside of it [*ie* Tok Pisin]. It's not the white man's. We asked the kiaps [Australian administrative officials]. We asked the kiap. We said, 'Is this your native language?' He said, 'No. This pidgin language is your language, a New Guinean language.' We were wrong. We thought it was the kiap's language, the government's language, their native language, but it wasn't.

Tok Pisin was introduced into this part of Morobe Province after the arrival of the first white men, German missionaries, in 1919. Many village men learned it outside the Kabwum District in another part of the province while working as contract labourers in the gold fields of Bulolo. Thus, it was introduced by New Guineans in many areas rather than by whites themselves. The shift from vertical to horizontal communication, *ie* between superordinate and subordinate to equals, is a main force in the stabilization of a pidgin.

On the previous day one of the village elders had said that he still remembered some German and counted in German. The German missionaries followed the practice of selecting an indigenous language (*ie* tok ples) for religious purposes. In this case it was Kâte. These mission languages were, however, in competition with varieties of pidgin English. In German New Guinea pidgin English was firmly established as a territory-wide lingua franca by 1914. This was the result of early European visits, as well as trade and labour contacts with Samoa. By the time German missionaries established themselves in Indagen, New Guinea had already been taken over by Britain and Australia in 1914. The position of German as a lingua franca outside the mission stations was very weak. One of the linguistic effects of renewed contact between English and Tok Pisin as a result of this change in administration was the replacement of German lexical items by corresponding English ones in the domestic context and in the police force. Because religious instruction remained very much in the hands of German-speaking missionaries, many German words used in this domain were preserved. For example, the village elders used the word **beten** [German – 'to pray'].[2] This term is still preserved in the church variety of Tok Pisin, as standardized, for example, in *Nupela Testamen*.

It is interesting that the elders also commented that they were aware that German and English were related, but different languages. One man noted the following:

> **ol bilong Germany ia tok strong liklik. Nau long England tru astokples bilong ol em England. Ol i go long asples bilong toktok na Germany em narafela. Toktok** [bilong en SR] **mipela sigarapim em narapela kain toktok, tok bilong strong.**

> The Germans speak harshly. But in England itself, this is the mother country for them [those who speak English SR]. They go back to the place of origin of this language. But Germany, that's different. We compared the language [of Germany with that of England] and it is different. It's a forceful language.

The following letter written by a reader of *Wantok* (3 May 1972) is interesting because it expresses on the one hand puristic sentiments, and on the other indicates an awareness of English and Tok Pisin as separate languages. It also affirms the symbolic status of Tok Pisin as a language which belongs to the people:

> **Sapos yumi mekim dispela pasin nogut, bai bihain tok pisin bilong bus na tok pisin bilong taun tupela i kamap narakain tru. Long bus bai ol toktok long tok pisin stret na long taun bai ol toktok long narapela tok pisin i pulap tru long ol wot bilong tok inglis. Olsem bai tok pisin i bruk nabaut nogut. Nogut yumi hambak nabaut na bagarapim tok ples bilong yumi olsem.**
>
> If we follow this bad habit, then bush pidgin and town pidgin will become quite different from one another. In the bush they will all talk genuine pidgin and in the town they will all talk another pidgin full of English words. Thus pidgin will be broken up into a number of varieties. We must not mess around and ruin the language of our country in this way.

Mühlhäusler (1979:141) cites the ability to distinguish between varieties of Tok Pisin as a direct reflection of the increased awareness of norms for the language among its speakers. The ability to make and label such distinctions as **tok pisin bilong bus** – 'rural or bush pidgin' and **tok pisin bilong taun** – 'urban or town pidgin' is a fairly recent phenomenon. It is significant too that it is the bush variety of the language which has acquired the status of the 'real' or 'pure' language. This dimension of the development of pidgin will be discussed in more detail in 4.4 and 4.5.

4.4 Stable pidgin

A stable pidgin has both simple and complex sentences; but more importantly, there are social norms and a consensus concerning linguistic correctness. It is used for communication in a fixed number of domains, for social control and to a small extent, self expression. A good example of a pidgin which probably belongs in this category is Russenorsk (Russo–Norwegian) a trade pidgin which was used in northern Norway (Finnmark and Troms) by Russian merchants and Norwegian fishermen during the Pomor trade. Although there is some dispute in the literature about the status of Russenorsk as a jargon or stable pidgin, I think it is clear from the linguistic and social characteristics which will be considered here, that it fits the description of a stable pidgin, albeit in some senses, a short-lived one. It is possible too that it was to a certain extent repidginized from year to year in accordance with the seasonal fluctuations in trade.

The descriptions of the language from the nineteenth century do not agree on the extent to which the language was considered to be solid and permanent. However, we must bear in mind in our assessment of these reports that Russenorsk was often compared to full languages such as Russian and Norwegian, and by comparison it was often stereotyped as broken and grammarless. For example, Lund (1842:62) calls it 'the most constructionless mode of communication imaginable'. Others call it a 'crow language', in which there are ridiculous misunderstandings (*cf eg* Daa 1870:162). Helland (1899:781) refers to it as an idiotic mixture of certain Norwegian, Russian and English words. Others such as Reusch (1895:47) compare it with other established pidgins such as China coast pidgin English. He claims that Russenorsk is 'not a simple mixture of the two languages [Russian and Norwegian] which each individual makes up as best he can when he needs it, but it is really a fixed idiom [en fæstnet taleform]' (compare Schuchardt's distinction between 'kein fertiges patois' and 'ein fertiges patois'). The first modern scholar to compare Russenorsk with other pidgins in detail was Neumann in 1965.

Broch and Jahr (1984:51), however, argue that Russenorsk was already a fully developed contact vernacular early in the nineteenth century. By that time its use had spread to the most important trading centers in Finnmark and Troms. They (1984:50) believe that in order for the language to have been this widespread, it must have achieved a certain degree of stability. They characterize it as a restricted pidgin. By comparison with many other pidgins the language was exceptional because it existed for quite a long time without expanding or creolizing. The time between the first attested occurrence of the language (in a lawsuit of 1785) until its extinction at the time of the First World War and the Russian Revolution, which put an end to trade relations between the two countries, is 141 years. The main reason why Russenorsk apparently existed for such a long time without expanding was that it was used for seasonal trade in the summer months. The texts examined by Broch and Jahr however suggest that Russenorsk was also used between trade seasons, and could have developed functionally and grammatically if trade between the Russians and Norwegians had intensified.

The precise origins of the language are disputed. Fox (1973), for example, claims that Russenorsk was developed by the grammaticalization of an international Northern European base vocabulary. He suggests that this vocabulary was brought northwards by soldiers, among others, and that there was a soldier's slang. However there is no evidence of this vocabulary. Broch and Jahr, however have found evidence of a pidgin language in the northern area which pre-dates Russenorsk. Högström (1747:76–7) reports a Swedish–Lappish auxiliary language which the Lapps call Borgarmålet [merchant language]. He writes:

> . . . while there are different peoples in Lappland who trade with each other, Swedes, Lapps, Finlanders, Danes [= Norwegians], and Russians, all of whom have their own languages, they still have a common language, *lingua communi*, which they use regularly and all understand. In Lule–Lappland Lappish is used, which Finlanders and Swedes can somehow manage to understand. In Tornedalen and Kemi-Lappland, Finnish is the generally accepted language, which everyone (Swedes, Lapps, Russians and others) understands so well that they can manage to communicate.
> In the Southern parts of Lappland a large proportion of the Lapps understand Swedish, and a large proportion of Swedes understand Lappish. But in some places nearly everyone can express themselves in a language they call Borgarmålet. I do not know why some members of the Borgerskap [merchants] in the market towns who trade with the Lapps and have dealings with them annually at their usual places of business, have started to use a language which is distinct from both Swedish and Lappish.

From the few examples given by Högström, it seems that the vocabulary is predominantly Swedish and the syntax Lappish. It remains to be seen how much influence this pidgin had on the development of Russenorsk. It may be that Russenorsk is a relexified version of this pidgin. Lunden (1973) suggests a connection between Russenorsk and a Sino–Russian pidgin of Kjachta, on the Sino–Soviet border due to the fact that the pronouns **moja** and **tvoja** [me/you] are found in the same form in both pidgins (*cf eg* Neumann 1966). It may be that Russian merchants who had links with China and Norway introduced the pronouns from Kjachta into Russenorsk.

Let us look now at some of the characteristics of Russenorsk in relation to the features of stable pidgins. The data for the language comprise isolated words and sentences, conversations in the form of dialogues, and word lists. Most of the texts were collected from the Norwegian side. Other users include Finns and Lapps, but there is only one Finnish text.

As far as the lexicon is connected, there are approximately 390 words, half of which are *hapax legomena*, *ie* only single occurrences. This means that there was a core vocabulary of about 150–200 words. Russian and Norwegian provide the bulk of the lexical material. Fox (1973:62), for example, estimates that approximately 47 per cent of the vocabulary is of Norwegian and 39 per cent of Russian origin. Other words come from Dutch and

Low German, French, Swedish and Lappish. Broch and Jahr (1984:47) note the existence of many doublets as a characteristic of the Russenorsk lexicon. Verbs, nouns and in particular, adjectives tend to have parallel forms, *eg* **bra-good-dobra-dobro-korosjo** – 'good, well' [<Swedish, English/(German?), Russian, Russian, Russian]. This may be evidence for different varieties which arose at various stages through relexification. Those semantic domains of the lexicon which deal with bartering do not however exhibit doublets. Grammatical words tend to have only one source language.

The texts provide evidence of a number of productive rules of word formation by suffixation, compounding and reduplication.The suffix **-a** is used to form nouns, *eg* **klokka** – 'time, clock'. The origin of the suffix may reflect the convergence of a number of possible sources. It could have come via Swedish, or Norwegian (*ie* the **a-** ending in the singular definite form of all feminine nouns), as well as from Russian (*ie* the feminine nominative or masculine/neuter genitive). It might also come from Lappish. There is also a suffix **-mann**, *eg* **Russman** 'Russian'. An example of compounding is **morradag** – 'tommorrow day' for 'tomorrow' [<Norwegian **imorra** – 'tomorrow' + **dag** – 'day']. There is one example of reduplication, **morra-morradag** – 'day after tomorrow'. There are some circumlocutions too, *eg* **stova på Kristus spræk** [house on Christ speak] for 'church'; however, the Norwegian word for **church** appears in another circumlocution for **baptize**, *ie* **lille junka pa kjerka vaskom** [little boy on church wash].

In general, the morphology of the language is simple. In fact, Weinreich (1953:43) uses Russenorsk to illustrate the abandonment of most 'obligatory categories expressed by bound morphemes'. There are no inflections, and categories such as gender, number, tense, case, aspect, etc., which are present in Norwegian and Russian and marked morphologically, are almost non-existent in Russenorsk. There is no copula and no verb 'to have', although the lack of these verbs is also a feature of Russian. Verbs are uninflected and are generally marked with the suffix **-om**, *eg* **betalom** – 'to pay' [<Norwegian], and **robotom** – 'to work' [<Russian]. Most of the verbs with this suffix are of non-Russian origin. Broch (1927:249) suggests the Swedish hortative form as its origin, *eg* **sjungom** – 'let's sing!'. Compare Russenorsk: **Værsogo pa skib kastom!** – 'please on ship throw!' Both the **-a** and the **-om** suffix could be indications of a historical link between Russenorsk and Borgermalet.

The preposition **på** is used as an all-purpose preposition (*cf*

Russian **po** and Norwegian **på**). The selection of this preposition was probably motivated by its presence in both languages. It indicates various case and other relationships. Broch and Jahr (1984:45) cite the following examples:

possessive: **klokka på ju** [watch on/at you] – 'your watch'
locative: **principal på sjib?** [captain on ship] – 'Is the captain on board the ship?'
temporal: **på morradag** [on tomorrow] – 'tomorrow'
directional: **moja tvoja på vater kastom** [me you in water throw] – 'I will throw you in the water'

As for word order in Russenorsk, Broch and Jahr (1984:41) say that sentences which consist of a subject and verb or subject verb object normally have the word order SVO. Normal Norwegian word order in main clauses is also SVO, but Norwegian, like other Germanic languages except English, has a verb-second rule which requires the verb to be the second element. If some sentence element other than the subject appears in first position, this means that the subject will then follow the verb. Word order in Russian is less constrained, but normal word order is also SVO. An example of SVO word order in Russenorsk can be seen in the following: **moja kopom fiska** [me buy fish] – 'I will buy some fish'. In sentences containing an adverbial, the verb usually occurs in final position, *eg* **Moja tri vekkel stannom** [me three weeks stay] – 'I stayed three weeks'. This order is impossible in Norwegian, but possible in Russian if the sentence contains no object. The negator (either **ikke** < Norwegian, or **njet** < Russian) is restricted to second position, *eg* **moja njet vros** [me not lie] – 'I'm not lying'. In questions there is no inversion of subject–verb, *eg* **kor ju stannom pa gammel ras?** [where you stay on old time] – 'Where did you stay last year?' The Norwegian equivalents of these sentences would have subject–verb inversion, although Russian has SV order in questions beginning with a WH-word when the subject is a pronoun. Often interrogatives are signalled by rising intonation, *eg* **tvoja fisk kopom?** [you fish buy] – 'Will you buy fish?'

The syntactic possibilities of Russenorsk are quite limited. Sentences are generally paratactic without embedding or subordination. Coordination is achieved by juxtaposition or the use of **så** – 'so', *eg* **mojå pa anner skip nakka vin drikkom, så moja nakka lite pjan** [me on other ship some wine drink, so me some little drunk] – 'I drank some wine on another ship, then I got a little drunk'. Some cases are ambiguous between subordination and coordination, *eg* **moja smotom ju kralom** [me see you steal]

– 'I saw you steal'; **moja ska si:ju grot lygom** [me shall say: you much lie] – 'I must say that you lie a lot'; **kak ju vina trinke, Kristus grot vre** [if you wine drink, Christ much angry] – 'If you drink wine, Christ will be very angry'. The word **kak** (<Russian 'how') appears to be used as a subordinating conjunction here. (*cf* however, Slobin 1977:201 who says that Russenorsk has no conjunctions and there is no evidence for subordination.) We can see that there is a considerable overlap between the features of Russenorsk and those described in 2.9. and 2.3. Slobin (1977) cites Russenorsk as an example of a language which is extremely close to universal grammar.

It is difficult to conclude much about phonology on the basis of the written texts, but Broch and Jahr (1984:31) say that the pronunciation varied depending on the language and dialect background of individual speakers. Phonemes which occur in only one of the base languages tend to disappear.

With regard to the social characteristics and functions of Russenorsk, there is some evidence to indicate that the language was more than a trade jargon. Broch and Jahr (1984:37) say that many Russians stayed on in Norway during the winter after the trading season. This makes it likely that the language was used for communication about topics other than trade, even though the majority of the transactions recorded in texts deal with trade. Children also apparently played an important role in the transmission of Russenorsk from one generation to the next. Interviews conducted with people who had participated in the Russian trade establish the fact that children had contact with the Russians. In these contacts it is mentioned that the children knew Russian and were therefore able to speak to the Russians in Russian. It is difficult to know what is meant by the label **Russian** here. There were no doubt fishermen and children who did know Russian.

In many cases though it is likely that the term Russian refers to a knowledge of Russenorsk. The children would have no way of knowing whether the Russians were communicating with them in Russian or Russenorsk in their initial contacts. In practically all the reports about the language the double illusion of communication is referred to. Adler (1977:40) gives a detailed and somewhat patronizing version of this story, without realizing however, that this is a much more general phenomenon:

> What is especially interesting about Russenorsk is the fact that both parties concerned were firmly convinced that they were speaking the other language. The reason for this may be that the Norwegians had never visited Russia and the Russians never

> entered Norway proper but stayed for short periods only in the borderland of that country. It may also be assumed that a certain prestige was attached to thinking that one could speak the other language properly, and this the more so because the two languages have very little in common although they are both of Indo-European origin. It is a kind of auto-suggestion which is pleasing to those who are subject to it, and it did not matter that the grammar of Russenorsk was very simplified because the ordinary people who spoke it were not interested in the peculiarities of each language and had not the mental apparatus to become aware of them.

Fox (1973) disputes this view because of the existence of separate labels for Russenorsk. Apart from Russenorsk there was 'moja på tvoja' and 'kakspreck'. This indicates that Russenorsk represented a variety distinct from Russian and Norwegian. It is possible however that a label like 'moja på tvoja' was simply interpreted as 'Russian as we speak it'. Furthermore, there was a turning point in the language around 1850. Before that time Russenorsk was used by both fishermen and merchants in their dealings with the Russians. Thereafter most of the merchants began learning Russian. The use of Russenorsk was devalued as a result of its social marginalization.

Mühlhäusler (1981a:46) believes that the stabilization stage is the most central one in the life-cycle of a pidgin or creole because it is during this phase that the direction for the future development of the language is determined. A pidgin becomes a linguistic system with a well-defined set of potentialities for further expansion. He illustrates this in detail by describing the development of the category of number in Tok Pisin. He finds that the order in which plural marking appears is governed by universal principles of language development. I will now take a look at some of the stages in this process.

In the earliest stages of its development there is a great deal of inconsistency with regard to plural marking. In jargon texts examined by Mühlhäusler there were lexical items with plural markers, *eg* **binen** – 'bees' [<German **Bienen** – 'bees'], **bis** – 'bead' [<English **beads**], which became fossilized in this form. Other lexical items are unmarked, and some variably marked, *eg* **fellow/fellows**. Mühlhäusler accounts (1981a:40) for the general absence of plural marking in the early stages of pidgin development by virtue of the fact that the plural is a marked semantactic category, and thus 'late' in any developmental hierarchy. In other words, it is a category acquired late by children learning their first language as well as by learners of a second language (*cf*

Chapter 6 for further discussion). Another factor is simply that inflectional morphology gets reduced or lost in language contact or early acquisition. This means that irrespective of whether speakers of various substratum languages have a morphologically marked category of plural in their vernacular, they will not carry over any conventions for plural marking into the pidgin during its formative period.

The development of conventions for plural marking appears first in the pronoun system. In Samoan Plantation Pidgin, for example, Tok Pisin's predecessor, there are no plural pronouns in early texts such as those collected by Schuchardt (1889). The singular **he** is also used as the third-person plural pronoun. There were two formatives which competed as markers of plurality, **-pela** and **ol**, *eg* **mipela/mi ol** – 'we'. The plural is expressed in an analytic manner by means of quantifiers such as **plenti** – 'plenty/many', **olgeta** – 'all together'.

According to Mühlhäusler, stabilization of Tok Pisin occurred first in the area around Duke of York, New Britain and New Ireland, and later on other islands and the New Guinea mainland. During this time (around 1880), Tolai was the most important indigenous language which was a potential source of structural and lexical innovation. The Samoan Plantation Pidgin pluralizer **ol** in the pronoun system, *eg* **mi ol/yu ol/em ol** – 'we/you (pl.)/they' gave way to **pela**, resulting in the plural pronouns **mipela/yupela/hipela** – 'we/you (pl.)/they'.[3] **Hipela** later disappeared, but the others became standard usage. **Mipela** is an exclusive first-person plural pronoun, *ie* refers to the speaker and others, but not the addressee. **Yumi** was introduced as an inclusive first-person plural pronoun, *ie* referring to the speaker and addressee. This distinction between inclusive and exclusive pronouns is found in Tolai and a number of Oceanic languages.

In the noun system, **ol**, **olgeta** and **-pela** competed as plural markers. Mühlhäusler (1981a:42–3) says that this may explain why these markers cannot be combined in present-day Tok Pisin, *eg* ***olfela man/*olgeta ol man**. Throughout the stabilization phase pluralization is variably marked. In a corpus of texts from speakers in the 50–70 year-old group Mühlhäusler (1981a:43–4) found that the appearance of the plural marker **ol** was governed by two factors: (i) the semantics of the noun involved. Plural marking is favoured in nouns denoting humans > animates > count nouns > mass nouns, in that order; and (ii) the syntactic environment in which they appear, *ie* the case or grammatical relation in which the noun appears. Thus, plural marking is favoured in subject > direct object > after preposition **long** (indirect object or locative) > after preposition **bilong** (possessive), in that order. Thus, the appearance of the plural marker is conditioned by a semantic and grammatical hierarchy of environments which are implicationally ordered. (The notion of implicational hierarchy is discussed in more detail in 5.3.) This finding is significant in the light of work on universals and typology (*cf eg* Comrie 1981), in which it appears that a number of grammatical processes are hierarchically controlled, *eg* relativization. Comrie (1981: Ch.9), for example, discusses a number of grammatical phenomena, such as case marking and verb agreement, which are controlled by an animacy hierarchy, which is ordered as follows: human > animal > inanimate. The accessibility or case hierarchy of grammatical relations predicts that grammatical relations are ordered as follows in terms of their accessibility to certain grammatical rules and processes:

> subject > direct object > indirect object > oblique (object of preposition) > genitive.

I will discuss it in relation to the expansion of relative clauses in 6.9. In commenting on Mühlhäusler's finding Comrie (1981:223) says that it is not surprising to learn that number marking is first made obligatory with human nouns, given the universal that the plural distinction is more likely higher up the animacy hierarchy.

Mühlhäusler (1981a:44) cites the following text to illustrate that nouns referring to humans always take **ol** if they are semantically plural, but all other nouns are variably marked [semantically plural nouns are underlined]:

> **I-tokem mi wanfela stori olosem: I-gat wanfela ples bilong ol. I-gat planti kakaruk i-stap. Kakaruk men na meli i-stap long disfela ples, orait, wanfela man em i laikim kisim mani na em i-go singaut long em. Orait i-go was long em na i-stap nau, olo disfela kakaruk i-kamap, singaut na i-laik holim pas i-nogat. Mekim mekim i-nogat.**
>
> He told me the following story: There was this place of theirs. There were many chickens. There were roosters and hens in this place. Well, one man wanted to make money and he called them. He watched them for a long time. These chickens came, they were cackling, he wanted to grab them, but he was unsuccessful. He tried again and again without success.

Mühlhäusler characterizes the development of **ol** in the function of a plural marker as an example of expansion in which the language acquires a new category which makes it referentially or otherwise more powerful.

Other changes such as the development of complementizers

out of previously existing verbs, prepositions and adverbs also increase the power of the language. Expansion can be found in late stages of a pidgin life cycle and in newly developing creoles. The mechanism of the change illustrates a process referred to as **grammaticalization**. Meillet (1912) identifies this as one major source of grammatical change in language (the other is analogy), in which autonomous words become grammatical markers. A case in point is that of **baimbai** mentioned earlier (2.9 and 4.5) in which **baimbai** loses its autonomy, becomes phonologically reduced to **bai**, and then is used as a pre-verbal marker of tense. Another such case is discussed by Kihm (1983a:9) in Guinea Bissau Creole Portuguese (Kriol), where a fully grammaticalized tense/aspect marker, **nin**, has emerged as the result of phonological condensation of **na** (a punctual marker) + **bin** (a marker of punctual future).

Mühlhäusler's findings appear to weaken considerably claims of substratum influence in the development of the category of number in Tok Pisin, and more generally, claims to the effect that substratum influence is the major determinant of developments in the stabilization phase of pidgin development. Developments during the expansion stage are largely a continuation of those found at the previous stage. He notes (1981a:48) that while Tok Pisin is developed enough to borrow grammatical categories from other linguistic systems, the large number of languages which it is in contact with, makes borrowing a less likely option. Mühlhäusler attributes developments which occur at this stage to natural internal growth, and concludes that developing systems of restricted complexity are incapable of integrating complex structures from the languages with which they are in contact. Thus, it is not likely that Tolai or other Melanesian languages provided the source for Tok Pisin plural marking. In fact, Mühlhäusler (1981a:71) says that very little structural borrowing occurred at the stage in Tok Pisin's development when it was in closest contact with Tolai and other substratum languages, *ie* between 1880–1910, when speakers of Tok Pisin were mainly speakers of Tolai and related languages.

Plurality in Tolai and the related languages of the Duke of York Islands and New Ireland is indicated by reduplication or pre-nominal markers which are either numerals or indefinite quantifiers. The plural markers are not identical with the third-person plural pronoun, as in Tok Pisin. A particularly strong argument in favour of the view that borrowing does not take place at this stage, can be found in the fact that Tok Pisin did not use reduplication. One would expect reduplication to be a favoured strategy of indicating plurality since it is a case of iconic encoding, and is found in other pidgins, as well as in the principal substratum language. Hall, however, (1943:194) says that 'reduplication is not of grammatical significance in Pidgin [Tok Pisin SR]'. Reduplication entered the structure of Tok Pisin at a very late stage (*cf* Mühlhäusler 1979:347ff, 515–33). Samarin (1971) regards reduplication as a salient but not a substantive characteristic of pidgins.

Although Mühlhäusler attributes this development to universal principles governing expansion, Keesing (forthcoming) argues that in most of the Oceanic languages of Melanesia there is a human plural marker which is the same morpheme as the third person plural pronoun. Thus, substratum influence could have provided the pattern for the use of **ol** as a plural marker. Keesing, however, believes that Mühlhäusler has overestimated the extent of independent development in the history of the Pacific pidgins (*cf* 3.4). He argues that a Pacific pidgin was nativized early in the 1850s and was then repidginized in various places throughout the Pacific. He claims that by 1880 most of the features which subsequently stabilized are already represented in texts. According to Keesing Tok Pisin split off from this Pacific pidgin only after 1887, which is later than Mühlhäusler's estimated (*cf* 3.4). If Keesing is right, then Mühlhäusler's claims about the role of universals at this stage of pidgin development need to be reassessed.

Mühlhäusler (1981a:73–5) similarly discounts the role of superstratum influence at this stage of development. There are few shared features between Tok Pisin and English with regard to the marking of plurality. Systematic pluralization by affixation is not found at any stage in the development of the language. We have already seen plural forms such as **anis**, which appear to have been isolated borrowings which were unanalyzed. Hall (1956:99–100) documents the use of **-s** plurals for twelve items in Tok Pisin. In recent years the use of **-s** plurals has become a feature of urban Tok Pisin. It can be found, for example, in articles in *Wantok*, and in letters written by readers, *eg* **ol gels** – 'the girls'. One of Mühlhäusler's informants (1981a:58) described this process by saying that 'I gat singular na plural i kam insait long namba tri Tok Pisin'. – 'Singular and plural are now entering the third [*ie* urban] variety of Tok Pisin'. Mühlhäusler (1981a:60), however, says that the emergence of this **-s** in the more anglicized urban varieties of Tok Pisin does not follow the grammatical and animacy hierarchy governing the introduction of pluralization in rural Tok Pisin. The introduction of **-s** appears to be unsystematic by contrast appearing in recent loans, *eg* **bisnisgrups** – 'business groups', as well as with established items, *eg* **yias** – 'years', and also occurring in conjunction with the plural marker **ol**. In spite of the fact that Tok Pisin and German were in contact at a time when Tok Pisin had reached a considerable degree of stability it did not borrow the German plural suffix **-en** as a productive marker. Mühlhäusler cites the introduction of the English suffix **-s** into Tok Pisin as a case of mixing between two systems which have roughly the same degree of complexity. Borrowing which occurs at this stage between such languages results in unnatural developments, *ie* changes which upset the regularity of the language. When borrowing occurs between a developing system and another of greater complexity and stability, it is highly selective and restricted by universal principles of language development.

Some examples of the disruption caused by the borrowing of English plural forms can be illustrated with some examples from young children's creolized Tok Pisin (*cf* Romaine and Wright 1986). One of the tasks we asked the children to perform was to name toy animals. It emerged that the lexical field of animal terms was becoming increasingly anglicized. For example, we found the English terms **duck** competing with Tok Pisin **pato**; **chicken** vs. **kakaruk**; **cow/bull** vs. **bulmakau**; **sheep** vs. **sipsip**; **animal** vs. **abus**. (The latter is particularly interesting since **abus** is indeed English **animal** borrowed in the early stages of development and subjected to various natural phonological changes as indicated in 3.4).

All languages borrow. What is interesting is the extent to which any language can integrate what it borrows without undermining its grammatical and semantic integrity. It is not always the case that a language borrows from another because it lacks vocabulary. Tok Pisin has **kakaruk** so has no need to borrow **chicken** from English. It also has the equivalent for the semantic distinction of gender encoded in English pairs such as **rooster/hen** (Tok Pisin **kakaruk man/kakaruk meri**). The significant difference of course lies in the way the two languages encode this grammatical distinction. In Tok Pisin there is a regular and iconic relation between form and meaning. Thus, the meaning of 'chicken + male/female' is derivable from the component parts of the expression **kakaruk man/meri** in a way that it isn't in English **rooster** and **hen**. The English terms are arbitrary (compare English **boar/sow** and Tok Pisin **pig man/pig meri**). The more regular a language is, the easier it is to learn. The more exceptions it has, the harder it is to learn. In some cases borrowing from English is making the structure of Tok Pisin more irregular.

In other cases borrowing is not disruptive. Some of the children use English plural forms in alternation with Tok Pisin ones, *eg* **ol animal** vs. **animals**. One of the girls, however called one animal **fɔk** [< **fox**] erroneously analysing the final **-s** as a plural, *ie* /fɔks/. She segmented it and arrived at **fɔk** as the singular. But she didn't then use **fɔks** as the plural; instead she said **tupela fɔk**. She has borrowed the word and incorporated it. It has been integrated it into the structure of Tok Pisin without having any disruptive effects on the grammar. This shows that there are qualitative differences in borrowing.

There is also another aspect of borrowing in evidence in the children's naming of the animals, *ie* semantic specialization. When a language has a word to cover a certain meaning and it borrows another one, one of the terms tends to be restricted in meaning. Some of the children sometimes use the English terms for animals to refer to the babies, *eg* **pato wantaim duck or ducklings** – 'adult duck with its ducklings'; **kakaruk wantaim chickens, chicklets** – 'adult chicken with its chicks or chicklets'.

These processes of borrowing and semantic specialization are operative in the history of languages and child acquisition more generally, not just in pidgins (*cf eg* Kuryłowicz 1949). In creating the new form **fɔk**, the child has resorted to a process called **back formation**. There are many examples of this in the history of languages. For example, in English the **-s** plural was not as widely used as it is now. There was once a larger class of nouns like **ox** which formed plurals like **oxen** by adding **-en**. The word **chicken** was once a member of this class. However, the **-s** ending was becoming so pervasively the sign of the plural in English by analogical extension from other plural forms that anything that didn't end in **-s** was taken to be the singular.[4] Thus, **chicken** was thought of as singular and a new plural, in effect, a redundant one, **chickens** was created. What was historically the true singular form **chick** became semantically specialized so that now it refers only to the baby animal.

Another piece of evidence in support of the view that universal principles govern development at earlier stages comes from Mühlhäusler's examination of comparative evidence on plural marking in other Pacific varieties of Pidgin English. He found that all of the languages investigated proceeded from a numberless jargon stage to number marking in certain semantactic contexts. In no case can the origin of pluralization be traced back to a proto-pidgin, unless stabilization occurred much earlier (*cf eg* Keesing, forthcoming). Plural marking is also optional in all the African pidgins studied by Heine (1973:181–4). In the pidgins based on Bantu languages the plural marker is a prefix (or prefixes) taken over from the source language. In Hausa pidgin a word denoting 'multitude' is used (*cf* Gunther 1973:56–7 on the use of **ban** in Seychelles Creole French and **mõci** in Principle Creole). In the Ful pidgin of Adamawa, pronominal elements are used as suffixes (Lacroix 1959).

The case of **nan** as a pluralizer in Papiamentu (*eg* **buki/bukinan** – 'book/books') illustrates again the more general problem of assigning etymologies to items of lexis or grammar in pidgins and creoles (*cf* 3.4). In outer form Papiamento **nan** has no resemblance to the third-person plural pronoun or nominal pluralizers of Spanish or Portuguese. A number of sources of origin are possible, *eg* African substratum (*cf* Van Wijk 1958:173), universal grammar (or independent development) and internal evolution. DeBose (1974) argues that the Spanish or Portuguese plural verb form **estan/estam** – 'they are' could have provided the input to the historical process of phonological reduction and assimilation resulting in **nan**. In certain contexts **estan** could have been interpreted as a third-person plural pronoun or as a nominal pluralizer.[5] In discussing the origin of the Gullah plural marker **dem** Mufwene (1986:56–7*n*18) suggests that an anaphoric interpretation is plausible, since this would be one possibility available to an isolating language (*cf* also Markey 1982 and 2.9). Thus, the full form **dem** when used as a subject following a topic could have been reanalysed as a plural marker, *eg* **The boy(s), they (dem) went to school** → **boy-dem went to school** (*cf* the origin of the predicative marker **i** in anaphoric pronouns in Tok Pisin in 2.5).

Janson (1984:318) points out that there seem to be three options for selecting the morpheme used as plurality markers in pidgins and creoles: a pronoun, a noun denoting multitude, or a suffix/prefix inherited or reintroduced from the source language. A variety of these may be used in any given case, as is illustrated by the system of plural marking in Naga Pidgin (Sreedhar 1977:158–60). The Sema variety marks human plurals with the item **log** – 'people', *eg* **suali** – 'girl'/**suali log** – 'girls' (*cf* also Chinese). Other Southern varieties of Naga Pidgin mark humans and animates with the suffix **-k^{h}an**, *eg* **sualik^{h}an** – 'girls'; **kurkurk^{h}an** – 'dogs'. It is interesting that the varieties follow the animacy hierarchy to different degrees depending on their stage of development. Janson concludes (1984:319) that since the same tendencies are found in such a large number of languages which have nothing in common except the fact that they have gone through a period of disruptive change, the similarities cannot be due to substratum influence, borrowing or common origin. They must therefore be explained by reference to universal properties of language users, and constraints on the shape of grammars.

4.5 Expanded pidgin

An expanded pidgin has a complex grammar, a developing word formation component, and an increase in speech tempo. It is used in almost all domains of everyday life, for self-expression, word play, literature and is instrumental in providing cohesion in heterogeneous groups. Since the process of expansion takes place only in special social circumstances, the number of expanded pidgins is fairly small. The best known expanded pidgins are West African Pidgin English and Tok Pisin. I will now take a look at some of these developments which increase the referential and expressive potential of the language.

Labov (1970/1977a:24ff) established that there was a significant difference in the rate of articulation of fluent Tok Pisin and Buang speakers on the basis of some data collected by Sankoff. Although there have not been any systematic experimental comparisons of the speech tempo of 'natural' languages and pidgins, it seems to be the case that pidgins are articulated at a slower rate of delivery. This is true for several reasons. One is simply that a pidgin is a second language for its speakers. The more basic the pidgin is, the more likely it is that speakers will rely on strategies which maximize naturalness of encoding and decoding. It is only in a community of fluent second and first language speakers that rules which greatly enhance rate of production will have a chance of acceptance.

One effect of the introduction of allegro, *ie* fast, speech styles is an increase in the depth of the phonological component. That is to say that the surface forms are derivable by rule from underlying forms. Sankoff and Laberge (1973), for example, discuss the phonological reduction of the earlier future marker **baimbai** in Tok Pisin to **bəbai**, **bai** or **bə** in the process of its transition from a sentence adverbial to verbal prefix. Similarly, the aspect markers **save** and **laik** may be reduced to **sa**, and **la**.

The amount of phonological reduction in the speech of young children acquiring creolized varieties of Tok Pisin can be quite considerable, as illustrated by narratives collected by Smith (1986) from 6–7-year-old children in the urban areas of Lae and Goroka. Among the forms he cites as typical are the following:

wanem ia > **nem ia** and **husat ia** > **sæt ia**. (These are forms which are used as fillers when thinking of a word for a person or thing). There is also considerable reduction in the markers or quotation frames used to introduce reported speech, *eg* **tok** > **to**, **olsem** > **sem/em**, **kirap na tok olsem** > **kra to sem**. The prepositional phrase **bilong em** and **long em** become **blem** and **lem**; similarly, the preposition **bilong** becomes **blõ**. **Bihainim** is pronounced **byeinim/beinim**. The demonstrative and article **wanpela**, **dispela** become **nla**, **disla/disa/disia**; and the pronouns **yutupela** and **mitupela** becomes **yutra/yuta** and **mitla**. Verb forms like **givim** are reduced to **gim**. Some of these features can be seen in the following text which I recorded from an eleven-year-old boy in Lae (*cf* also Romaine and Wright 1987). He is looking at a sequence of pictures which depict a sick child being taken to the doctor by his parents. The full forms are given in brackets:

> **Fes tru, disla** [< dispela] **man na meri blem** [< bilong en], **ol sa** [< save] **lukautim pikinini blol** [< bilong ol] **gutpla** [< gutpela]. **Pikinini blem** [< bilong en] **sik nau. Ol kisim go lo** [< long] **dokta nau. Dokta lukim em nau, em sik nogut tru nau. Ol karim em long disla** [< dispela] **rum nau. Na dokta givim shoot finish nau. Em kambek laus** [< long haus] **nau. Orait nau holim bal na em plei stap na ol lain blem;** [< bilong en] **wok lo** [< long] **wok**.
>
> In the first one this man and his wife, they are taking good care of their child. Their child is sick now. They take him to the doctor. The doctor looks at him. He's very sick. They carry him to this room. The doctor gave him an injection. He comes back home now. He's alright now. He holds a ball and is playing and all his family are working.

Sankoff (1977:71) believes that it is in the area of phonology in general that children appear to differ most significantly from adult Tok Pisin speakers at present. As one feature which distinguishes children's from adults' speech Sankoff cites a decrease in the use of the **i**-predicative marker. The use of **i** was once more widespread. It apparently reached a peak around the 1930s and has since declined. However, children show even less use of the feature than adults now (*cf* also Smith 1986). She suggests that once the **i** marker lost its semantic and syntactic weight, it could be subject to morphophonological condensation and subsequently deleted. Sankoff describes its present decline as a reversal of the earlier trend to cliticize **i**, and sees it as part of what Givón (1979b) has called the cycle of change. As Givón puts it, pragmatics gives rise to syntax, and syntax in turn gives rise to grammatical morphology which then decays via phonological attrition. Human languages keep renovating their syntax via syntacticizing discourse.

Sankoff and Laberge (1973) also note an alteration in stress patterns as the result of morphophonemic reductions. For example, in adult Tok Pisin one would find full forms such as **Mi go long haus**. A child by comparison is more likely to say **Mi go l:aus**. The child's version has three syllables rather than four and one primary stress falling on **l:aus**. Sankoff and Laberge observe that the presence of native speakers of a language does not necessarily create sudden and dramatic changes in a language, but their presence may be one factor in influencing the direction of change.

During the expansion phase there are also a number of developments which increase derivational depth in the syntactic component. There have now been several detailed studies of the process whereby embedding is introduced in pidgin grammars (*cf* in particular, Woolford 1979; Sankoff and Brown 1976). Woolford (1979), for example, discusses the development of complementizers in Tok Pisin. Three different complementizers have been created through the re-analysis of the following items:

(i) preposition **long** – 'to/of/for'
(ii) adverb **olsem** – 'thus'
(iii) conjunction **na** – 'and'

The examples given by Woolford illustrate identifiable stages in the reanalysis of **long**. In each case a phrase marker is given to indicate the syntactic relations between **long** and other sentence elements:

(i) **long** used as preposition

Yupela i go antap long ples.

$_{PP}$[P NP]

'You (pl.) go up to the village'

(ii) **long** used in a purpose clause

No gat stori long tokim yu.

$_{PP}$[P S. . .]

'I don't have stories (for) to tell you'

The second use of **long** in purpose clauses provides the transition stage for a reanalysis of $_{PP}$[P S. . .] structures to

$_{\bar{S}}$[COMP S] ones. The next example illustrates the completed reanalysis.

(iii) **Ol i no save long ol i mekim singsing.**
$_{\bar{S}}$[COMP S]

'They did not know that they had performed a festival'

According to Woolford, the reanalsyis of **long** has proceeded in implicationally related steps so that a verb is first subcategorized to take a $_{PP}$[P S] complement before it is then subcategorized to take an $_{\bar{S}}$[COMP S] one. Thus, the phrase structure rule $\bar{S} \rightarrow$ COMP S is being gradually added to the base component of Tok Pisin grammar through the syntactic reanalysis of the $_{PP}$[P S] complement. Interestingly, however, there is a group of speakers who still have a set of verbs subcategorized to take $_{PP}$[P S] complements, while all speakers have a set of verbs subcategorized to take $_{\bar{S}}$[COMP S] complements. In between these two poles there exists a group of verbs subcategorized to take different complements by different speakers. Thus, two grammars exist at one time in the speech community. Transition between one grammar and the next is marked linguistically on the one hand, by a group of verbs which display 'squishy', *ie* variable category membership or subcategorization with respect to complement type, and socially on the other hand, by the variable usage of speakers. The micro-dimension of syntactic change can be characterized as lexical diffusion, since the change is diffusing through the lexicon affecting different items at different times. This is a term which is used by historical linguists to describe a change (usually phonological) which spreads differentially through the lexicon (*cf eg* the papers in Wang 1977). More specifically, in this case, what is happening is that a change in the choice of complement type specified in the lexical entries of individual verbs is diffusing through the lexicon at different rates for different speakers. From the more general perspective of historical linguistics Woolford's analysis is interesting because it illustrates how a syntactic change may take place by variable and gradual diffusion in the lexicon. Thus, a language can get from one analysis of a construction to a different one by means of a stage in which the language alternates between two analyses/constructions at the same time.

We can now look at the process by which **olsem** becomes grammaticalized as a complementizer. It can be seen from the first of Woolford's examples that **olsem** in its use as an adverb preceeding a direct quote is in a likely position to be reanalysed as a complementizer.

(i) **Olsem** used as an adverb

Elizabeth i tok olsem, 'Yumi mas kisim ol samting pastaim.'
Adv. [S. . .]
'Elizabeth spoke thus, "We must get things first".'

In the next sentence we can see the reanalysed **olsem** functioning as a complementizer.

(ii) **olsem** used as complemetizer

Na yupela i no save olsem em i matmat?
$_{\bar{S}}$[COMP S]
'And you (pl.) did not know that it was a cemetery?'

The tree diagrams in Fig 4.2 (from Woolford 1979:117–8) show how the change from the phrase markers in (i) to those in (ii) gives rise to the possibility of embedding sentences.

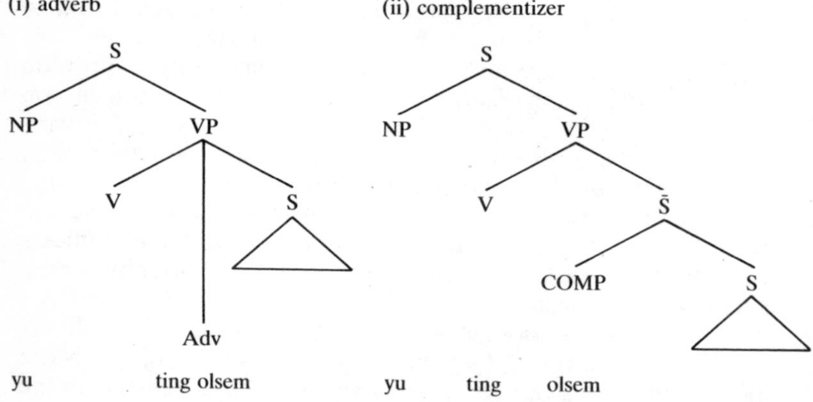

FIGURE 4.2 Reanalysis of **olsem** as a complementizer

Since the conjunction **na** can be used to conjoin words, phrases and sentences (just like its English counterpart **and**), and since it can also appear in a position immediately preceding clauses, it is also in a likely position to undergo reanalysis as a complementizer. An example of the reanalyzed **na** is given below:

Gutpela na yu kam
$_{\bar{S}}$[COMP S]
'It is good that you come'

A parallel process of grammaticalization has resulted in the use of **pu** as a complementizer in Haitian Creole. Koopman and Lefebvre (1981:203–4) give the following examples, which illustrate the use of **pu** as a preposition and complementizer:

pote sa pu mwê [preposition]
'Bring this for me'
li difisil pu m fe sa [complementizer]
[it difficult for me make that]
'It is difficult for me to do that'
m vle pu l vini [complementizer]
[I want for he come]
'I want him to come'

Pu is also used as a modal particle with the meaning of both obligation and futurity. Koopman and Lefebvre argue that the modal use of **pu** provides the source for the complementizer. Washabaugh (1980) has discussed a similar development from a locative or directional preposition to complementizer in Providence Island Creole.

There is more that can be added about the grammaticalization of complementizers from a more general perspective. In Tok Pisin there is now a 'new' marker available to introduce speech, as in the following example from a young boy in Lae:

Em i tok se: 'plis no go rausim mi.'
'He said: "Don't chase me away".'

Here **se** is being used to introduce quoted speech. It can be translated as equivalent to the English complementizer **that**. Mihalic (1971:43) mentions this use of **say**, but doesn't comment on it. Similar examples involving **spik** are reported by Hall, as in:

Nau mi tokim masta, mi spik: "O mi no laik go wantaim yu.'
'And I spoke to the master saying, "Oh, I don't want to go with you."' (Hall 1966; Mühlhäusler 1986:150)[6]
Em i tok i spik: 'yu no ken grisim mi.'
'He spoke, saying, "You can't get around me by flattery."' (Hall 1943:85)

Mühlhäusler (1985c:188–9) postulates the following steps in the grammaticalization of **se**. First, **se** becomes collocationally restricted so that it is used together only with other verbs of similar semantic content, as in:

em i tok i se – 'he said, he was saying'

In the next stage the predicative marker **-i** preceding the second verb **se** is dropped, as in:

Em i tok se: 'Mi laik kam.'
'He said: "I want to come."'

Then, sentences in which the speaker is non-coreferential with the agent of the reported event neutralize the distinction between direct and indirect speech, as in:

em i tok se: 'papa i gat sik.'
'He said: "the father is ill." /He said that the father was ill.'

Finally, **se** is reinterpreted as a complementizer following certain verbs, rather than as an independent verb concatenation. Conventions are then introduced for the treatment of pronouns in the indirect quotation, as in:

em i tok se em i laik kam
'He said that he'd like to come.'

In Tok Pisin **se** occurs with only a small number of verbs, but in other pidgins and creoles this solution has been adopted and is more widespread. For example, in Cameroonian pidgin English **se** can introduce practically any verb. It occurs too in many of the Atlantic English-based creoles such as Jamaican Creole (*cf eg* Bailey 1966:111, and also 5.7), Sierra Leone Creole (Hancock 1964) and Gullah (Turner 1969:210). Hancock (1964:127) gives the following example from Sierra Leone Creole:

A do tel am sê i nô fo ka nayá
'I told him that he shouldn't come here'

Both Mühlhäusler and Mohan (1978) believe that the use of **se** in this new function represents an independent innovation. Sranan, for example, has a corresponding form **taki** [< English **talk**], which bears only a semantic resemblance to **say**, but has a similar function. I have already pointed out the example of English **spik** used in the same function in Hall's Tok Pisin texts. Guy (1974:41) also gives examples of grammaticalized **se** in Bichelamar, a variety closely related to Tok Pisin.

em i talem se: 'yes'
'He said, "yes"'
Mi harem se papa plong yu i sik
'I heard that your father was sick'

Herskovitz and Herskovitz (1936:286) give the following example from Sranan:

a go taig konu taki en sa kiri na foru
'He went to tell the king that he would kill the bird'

Others such as Hancock (1964:27) and Cassidy and Le Page (1967:396) believe that the form **se** is a borrowing from African substrate. The coincidence between **se** in creoles and English **say** is thus accidental. In Akan the form **sé** has a similar distribution to **se** in English-based creoles. Berry and Aidoo (1975:225) give the following example:

Okráá no sé ommra
'He sent word that he should come'

In Akan the form **sé** does not occur in sequence with the verb **say** (Berry and Aidoo 1975:330).

My own view of the Tok Pisin examples is that for some speakers, particularly children, it is equally likely that **se** is derived from a phonologically reduced form of **olsem**, when it occurs in the quotative frame **em i tok olsem**. I indicated earlier that **olsem** may be reduced in the speech of children to **sem** or **se** thus giving **tok se** as a sequence. Children also are more likely to dispense with the predicative marker **i**. The route of grammaticalization is presumably the same as the one traced by Mühlhäusler. Namely, that from the use of **se** preceding reported speech, it has become generalized to other environments. The difference is that the origin is different. In one case **se** has a verbal origin, and in another it comes from an adverbial. If I am right, then children are regrammaticalizing this distinction from another source. There is a parallel for this kind of development in Sri Lanka Portuguese Creole, where Smith (1977) says that the reportative marker **-ski** is a phonologically reduced form of Portuguese **diz que** – 'says that'.

Mohan (1978) analyses these sequences of **tell . . . say** as a serial verb configuration (*cf* 3.5), in which the second verb has become grammaticalized or lexically empty. It then undergoes a category shift to become a non-verbal marker. This lexical emptying frees **say** from an exclusively quotative function introducing reported speech and allows it a broader scope with a function more nearly that of a complementizer. In some cases however, it still retains its verbal behavior. For example, in Jamaican Creole Bailey (1966:133) says that **se** cannot occur in sequence with the verb **say**, as in the examples:

Ruoz-dem se a Klaris mash di pat
***Ruoz-dem se se a Klaris mash di pat**
'Rose and the others said that it was Klaris who broke the pot'

Mohan says that **say** is redundant in this context because the pure verb **say** incorporates the same quotative function with reported speech.

Mohan (1978) cites a case from Trinidad Bhojpuri where the

grammaticalization of **bole** as a marker of reported speech appears to be on-going, but is not complete. Bhojpuri is a transplanted variety of Hindi, which shows some characteristics similar to a creole. The form **bōlē** derives from a habitual/narrative present tense form. In the following example, the verbal and non-verbal uses of **bōlē** are contrasted:

buṛhiyā ōkē bolāwal bōlē āō
'The old woman called out to him, saying, "Come"'
ta pūchēlā bōlē kāhē tōhar āsū calat bā?
'So he asks (her), saying, "Why are your tears flowing?"'
ta nagar bhar hallā bhai gail bōlē ōkē sapwā kāt lēl
'So the news spread all over town that the snake bit her'

When the main clause contains a psychic predicate, *eg* **know**, **think**, etc. and the evidential noun clause does not give actual reported discourse the 'pure' complemetizers **ki** and **jē** are used instead of **bōlē**, as in:

ham jāṇīlā ki ōkar ranḍi calāk bā
***ham jāṇilā ki ōkar ranḍi calāk bā**
'I know that his wife is a schemer'

These examples show that **bōlē** has not been entirely freed from the quotative function peculiar to the verb **say**. When used as a complementizer before reported speech, it cannot be preceded by the verb.

However, Trinidad Bhojpuri has incorporated **se** from Trinidad Creole English **say**, where it is not used as a marker of reported discourse. This form is free to occur after the verb **bōl-** with a de-verbal complementizer function which is roughly equivalent to that of **bōlē**. Thus, **se** is apparently not identified with its semantic equivalent **bōl-**, as indicated in the example:

ta panḍit bōlē sē jō bētā hōwē ta āō hamār āgē
'So the pundit says, saying, "If you would be my son, then come before me"'

We can look at another case of grammaticalization which leads to an increase in referential power. It involves the use of **orait** [< English **alright**] as a sentence connective. Although its use in this function is mentioned by Dutton (1973), Mihalic (1971) and Laycock (1970), it has not received systematic study. Laycock (1970), for example, observes that the use of **orait** as a sentence connective is a characteristic feature of an emerging narrative style which is typically pidgin. Among the most notable elements of this style is the linking of sentences by repetition of the previous verb, often introduced by **orait**. He gives as an example, the text in [1]:

[1] **Orait, i go long raunwara, pukpuk i ken kisim em, na bikpela snek i stap long wara, em i ken kisim em. Orait, ol i kisim i kam, smokim pinis, em i ken kisim em**
'Well, they go to the pond, they can get crocodiles, and the big snakes that live by the water. They get them, smoke them, put them aside and go back'

We can now look in more detail at some examples I recorded in Papua New Guinea in 1986. Example [2] illustrates the use of **orait** in its root or prime sense, as used in English to signal agreement.

[2] **Mi tokim olsem. Nau ol kam tok: 'orait, yu stori long mipela na mipela harim**
'I said this to them. And they came and said: 'Alright you tell us some stories and we'll listen'

In this instance **orait** is part of a direct quotation and is the semantic equivalent of **alright** in the English translation.

The next text, however, illustrates some of the other connective functions of **orait**. The separate occurrences are labelled [a], [b] and [c] for ease of reference.

[3] **Mi tok gutnait, mi tok olsem. Tasol em i no bekim maus bilong mi. [a] Orait em sanap long hapsait na mi sanap long disla sait na mi bungim em pinis. [b] Orait na mi laik ranawe, tasol mi no inap long ranawe. Mi sanap tasol na em i kam long holim han bilong mi. Na taim em i holim disla han blomi disla han blomi mi ia kol nogut tru olsem disla. Na taim em holim disla han blomi em indai olgeta. [c] Orait em holim haphan blomi nau mi singaut**
'I said goodnight, I said, but he didn't answer me. He was standing on one side and I was on the other and I encountered him. Alright, then I wanted to run away, but I couldn't. I just stood there, and he came and got me by the hand. When he held my hand it got incredibly cold like this. When he held my hand it lost all feeling. Then he got me by the forearm and I screamed'

Example [3a] appears to be an introductory marker which does not advance the narrative. It is not clear that it is intended to be strictly temporally sequential to the previous proposition, although of course from the perspective of the internal text itself it is sequential in space or linear order. It merely sets the scene and gives additional information. It provides the background for the events which took place immediately before and after. In terms of its textual function it is a simple additive connective.

This use of **orait** is in contrast to the next one [3b], which is more properly sequential, as is the last occurrence in [3c]. It clearly has a temporal function, and follows the introductory event which involved the narrator saying goodnight and not receiving a reply. I am using the terms **internal** and **external** in the sense of Halliday and Hasan (1976:241). In the case of temporal markers, external temporal relations have to do with the sequence of events in real and narrative time, whereas internal relations have to do with the text itself and are created through the text itself via the sequencing of propositions in linear order.

In addition to its sequential function it also corresponds to English **right**, or **now** in marking the beginning of a new segment of discourse (*cf eg* Sinclair and Coulthard 1975:40), as in example [4] from Sankoff (1972:45–6):

[4] **Tok Pisin orait, disfela tok em bilong pepul**
'Tok Pisin, now this language, it belongs to the people'

The next text in [5] contains some more instances which illustrate yet more textual functions of **orait**.

[5] **Bifo long mipela em ol sa wokim olsem. Man i gat laik long yu na yu no laik. [a] Orait, em man. Em bai makim yu bai yu no laik long en bai em bai bagarapim yu disla kain olsem . . . Bifo taim bilong tumbuna em kilim meri indai. Em tu bai indai bifo. Nau lo i strong tru. [b] Orait bihainim lo tasol**
'Before our custom used to be like this. If a man liked you, and you didn't like him. He would mark you. If you didn't like him, then he'd ruin you like this. In the old days he would kill a woman and she would die then. Now however our laws are powerful and they just have to follow the law'

Example [5a] seems to express an adversative relation to the proposition which precedes it. That is, the meaning is 'however, or be that as it may', the fact remains that men are more powerful in these situations than women. Example [5b] combines a sequential temporal relation with a causal one. That is, the implication is that now that there are proper laws, people must follow them. The obeying of the laws follows both sequentially in time from the previous event and partly as a result of it. In other words, there is both internal and external cohesion.

Dutton also mentions (1973:236) the use of **orait na** as a sentence connective with causal implications, as in [6]:

[6] **Wanpela trak i pundaun long maunten. Orait na draiva i repotim dispela bagarap long plisman**
'A truck crashed on the mountain. So the driver reported the accident to the policeman' (Dutton 1973:237)

In this example **orait** appears to have the function of sequential temporal connective with causal implications as in the previous examples in [5b], and also [3b] and [3c].

Dutton (1973:133–6) also mentions the use of **orait** as a sentence connective in **if/then** clauses in combination with **sapos**, as in example [7]:

[7] **Sapos yutupela i wok strong, orait bai yutupela i kisim bikpela pe**
'If you two work well, then you'll get paid well' (Dutton 1973:33)

In such constructions the conditional clause usually comes first and the **then** clause is introduced by **orait**. Here there is a causal implication to the effect that good payment will follow as a consequence of hard work. As can be seen in example [5], hypothetical clauses in conditional constructions are not always overtly marked by **sapos**, *eg* **bai yu no laik long en, bai em bai bagarapim yu.**

Mühlhäusler (1985c:407) too notes the use of **orait** to express causal relationships as in [8]:

[8] **Mi no gat mani orait mi no kam asde**
'I had no money and therefore I did not come yesterday'

It is interesting too that the *Stail Buk* published by *Wantok* recommends the use of **orait** as a sentence connective in certain functions. Thus, (*Stail Buk*, *p* 9): 'After a direct quotation is finished, it is good to continue with some word that lets the listener know that the direct speech is ended, *eg* 'Em i tok, "Mi go nau." Orait nau em i kirap i go.'

In examples [1–8] we have seen that **orait** is used to express all of the major relations which Halliday and Hasan (1976) include in the textual component of grammar; namely, additive, adversative, causal and temporal. In their model of grammar they distinguish three functional components within the linguistic system: the ideational, the textual and the interpersonal. The ideational or propositional component has to do with the resources a language has for talking about something. It is the main locus for truth-conditional relations. The textual component contains the resources a language has for creating cohesive discourse. These include connectives like **but**, **therefore**, **because**, etc., items which can only be understood in terms of pragmatic discourse functions. The expressive or interpersonal component concerns the resources a language has for expressing personal attitudes to what is being talked about, to the text itself, and to others in the speech event or situation. These include items like the modals, **might, can**, etc., which express the speaker's assessment of possibility of occurrence of events and situations.

There is nothing in this kind of development which is specific to pidgin languages. Over time we would expect that all languages would renovate, restructure or increase their textual component either by grammaticalizing old forms in new functions or borrowing. Pidgin languages lack the full range of connectives found in natural languages such as English. A few items such as **na**, **tasol** and **orait** are pressed into service to express the full complement of semantic relations which comprise the textual component. During its expansion phase as Tok Pisin has come into renewed contact with English, connectives such as **bikos** are being borrowed from English. English too, of course, has relied on borrowing as a means of expanding its textual resources and enriching its pragmatic component. This is true not only in the case of connectives. At different times in its history English has had different resources for speech acting in general, and more specifically for reporting speech and thought (*cf eg* Dirven *et al* 1982).

Traugott (1982) has used this tripartite system as a kind of map of semantic space within which she has traced some general routes which chains of grammaticalization appear to follow. One of her hypotheses is that if a meaning shift occurs in the process of grammaticalization which involves a shift from one component to another, the shift is more likely to be from the propositional to textual to expressive than the reverse. However, if there is nothing unusual about the **kind** of change involved, it may be that the directionality is more typical of pidgins than natural languages. The case of **orait** poses a problem for Traugott's prediction about the directionality of shift. The original function of **orait** seems best characterized as interpersonal since it has to do with the speaker's attitude. Thus, in its new grammaticalized function of sentence connective we appear to be dealing with a case where a change has occurred from the interpersonal to textual component.

Given what we know about the functions of pidgin languages

this is not surprising. In the earliest stages of its formation a pidgin is a rudimentary code which is used in certain limited communicative contexts, *eg* trade. A pidgin represents a language which has been stripped of everything but the bare essentials necessary for communication. There are few, if any, stylistic options. The emphasis is on the communicative or referential rather than the expressive function of language. Only when a pidgin expands does it develop a pragmatic component and expressive functions. In first language acquisition however, Halliday (1974) stresses the fact that the interpersonal functions of language precede the referential. In a pidgin language the referential functions precede the interpersonal.

An obvious question to ask in the case of **orait** is whether its function as a discourse connective reflects substratum influence. In other words, are we dealing with a case where substratum semantics is being mapped onto a lexical item which has its origin in the superstrate? This is by no means an easy question to answer. Laycock (1970) seems to assume that the use of **orait** in linking sentences in Tok Pisin derives from the sentence medial verbs of Austronesian languages. Elsewhere, he (1966) and Sankoff (1972) say that this use of **orait** is transferred into vernacular discourse with an apparently identical function (*cf eg* Ross 1985:552–3). Sankoff (1972:48) observes that **orait** is used in Buang utterances in place of the Buang conjunctions **olo ba** or **olo ga**. The replacement is stylistic and serves to emphasize the utterance.

There are other cases of grammaticalization in Tok Pisin, which show the same direction of change, namely, from expressive to textual. For example, **tasol** [< English **that's all**] can be used more or less as in English to mark the end of something, as in **em tasol** – 'That's it/all'. However, in this particular case, it has lost its bimorphemic or clause level status which the expression 'that's all' has for English speakers. In the sentence **em tasol, tasol** functions as a single item. It can also be used as an emphasizer, as in [9]. It is unclear whether it makes sense to call it a noun or pronoun in these examples. In Tok Pisin **tasol** also has a function as a sentence connective meaning 'but' or 'however', as in [10]. In media Tok Pisin, it often appears clause initially, as in [11]:

[9] **Mi tokim yu tasol** – 'I told you only'

[10] **Ol i bin kisim em i go long haus sik tasol em indai long rot** (*Wantok* 3: May 1986)
'They took him to the hospital, but he died on the way'

[11] **Nau tasol, Mista Kaiku na ol wokman long Nesenel Musium i amamas tru bikos em i namba wan taim tru long wanpela viles i bungim samting tumbuna na salim fri i kam long musium.** (*Wantok* 3 May 1986)
'Now, however, Mr Kaiku and the employees of the National Museum are very pleased because this is the first time that a village can collect artefacts and send them free to the museum'.

There are also cases in Tok Pisin which involve a shift from a temporal marker to a causal connective. This can be seen in the example of **baimbai** mentioned earlier. The extension from temporality to causality is a natural one in the sense that what is caused is later in time than the event or state that precedes it. An example of this use of **baimbai** occurred in [5a]:

Bai yu no laik long en, bai em bai bagarapim yu disla kain olsem.

Here both the antecedent or cause clause and the result are introduced by **bai**. As can be seen from the gloss given earlier, it is semantically equivalent to an **if/then** construction in English. Sato has noted a similar extension of **bambai** in Hawaii English Creole, as in [12] and [13]:

[12] **Mai fada dem wen kam ova hia. Bambai de wen muv tu Kawai**
'My father and the others came over here. Then they moved to Kauai'

[13] **No it dæt. Bambai yu kam sik**
'Don't eat that. Or you'll get sick'

Example [12] is purely temporal, while [13] is causal.

What creolists urgently need is a map of semantic space with a well-defined set of trajectories for tracking chains of grammaticalization. Trajectory space will be defined partially by the inventory and system of entities in a language and partially by what is available in universal grammar. Taking into account the evidence presented here on the creation of complementizers and developments in tense, mood and aspect (*cf* Ch. 7), I have sketched out the following small bit of semantactic space (*cf* Romaine 1984c:121–2). The tense–mood–aspect cycle refers to the fact that in diachronic change the routes from tense to modality (but not aspect to modality) and from aspect to tense (but not tense to aspect) have been attested in diverse language families. The connection between these two chains of grammati-

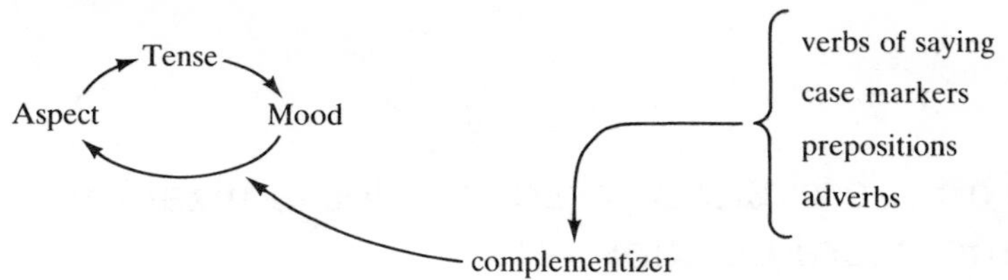

calization lies in the subroute from modality to complementizer. Further details of this kind of model are in Romaine (1983b).

Notes

1. The idea of life-cycle is not unique to pidgin and creole studies, as Hall seems to imply, but plays a prominent role in Neogrammarian thinking about language in the nineteenth century.
2. The use of the infinitive form of the German verb may be an indication that it was borrowed via the foreigner talk register of German (*cf* Clyne 1968:132).
3. The fact that Samoan Plantation Pidgin has a distinction between **as/dem** (object) and **mi/em** (subject) in the plural is mentioned by Mühlhäusler (1986:159) as a violation of a universal tendency for languages to make fewer distinctions in marked categories like the plural than in unmarked ones. Thus, in the singular we have forms like **mi/em** and **bilong mi/em**, but in the plural we get **mi ol/em ol** and **bilong as/bilong dem**.
4. One can compare the early borrowings from French into Middle English such as **cherries** (originally borrowed in the singular form from French **cerise**). Once the **-s** suffix had come to be the predominant indicator of plurality in English, the singular English form **cherry** was created by a process called back formation.
5. Another internal source is postulated by Dijkhoff (ms), namely that the function of **nan** as a plural is clearly derived from the independent use of **nan** as the third-person plural of the personal pronoun, the possessive pronoun and the reflexive. She does not, however, argue for a particular origin for these pronominal forms.
6. The text is transliterated into standard Tok Pisin orthography from Hall's phonemic transcription.

Chapter 5

The life-cycle of creoles: decreolization and recreolization

5.1 Creolization

Creolization can occur at any stage in the developmental continuum from jargon to expanded pidgin. Here Mühlhäusler (1980:32) proposes a different view from Bickerton (1974:126), who says that creolization after stabilization of a pidgin is rare. More specifically, Bickerton says that in the majority of situations pidgins have creolized while they were still highly unstable, very poorly developed and still without any underlying structure of their own. Alleyne (1971) has noted that the Caribbean creoles may have lacked a stable pidgin stage. This is true of Hawaii English Creole too; but from that case Bickerton then generalizes the claim to include all plantation creoles, and finally, to the point where he argues that creolization must take place before a pidgin has had time to stabilize. This route is only one of the three which Mühlhäusler distinguishes, as can be seen in the diagram in Figure 5.1.

Mühlhäusler's diagram shows that the pidgin input to a creole varies considerably. Depending on the developmental stage at which creolization occurs, different types of repair are necessary before the language can become an adequate first language for a speech community. In Type 1, where we have a creolized jargon, repair is needed at all levels. That is, there is a need for a natural phonological, syntactic, semantic and pragmatic system. In Type 2, the case of a creolized stable pidgin, additional derivational depth to existing structures is required, and pragmatic rules need to be developed. In the case of Type 3, creolized expanded pidgins, repairs are needed mainly to enrich its stylistic and pragmatic potential. Here the transition between the pidgin and creole is gradual rather than abrupt. Mühlhäusler adds that

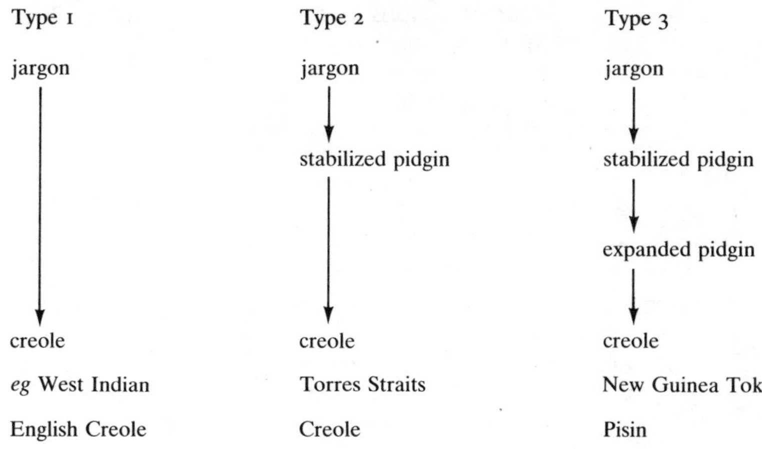

FIGURE 5.1 Three types of creolization

of the cases of creolization which can be observed *in situ* today most belong to Type 3, *eg* Tok Pisin, New Hebridean Bichelamar and West African Pidgin English. A smaller number belong to Type 2, *eg* North Australian Creoles, Torres Strait Creoles. There are no known instances of Type 1 presently undergoing creolization. These cases turn out to be the most interesting from the perspective of Bickerton's bioprogram hypothesis to be discussed in Chapter 7. A possible exception, however, is Hawaii Pidgin English and Unserdeutsch (*cf* Volker 1982).

It is apparent that the structural differences between an expanded pidgin and an incipient creole will be minimal. The same applies to functional differences, which emphasize the problem in using the criterion of native speakers as the defining feature of creoles to distinguish them from pidgins.

Mühlhäusler (1980:22) uses the term **development** or **expansion** to refer to an increase in overall referential and non-referential power of a language. Restructuring, on the other hand, is a process of change due to language contact which does not affect the overall power of a linguistic system. He outlines the types of change which characterize each kind of continuum, some of which have been seen to be operative in the expansion of a pidgin, as discussed in Chapter 4:

(i) Developmental continuum

(a) gradual introduction of redundancy

(b) development of a word formation component
(c) increase in derivational depth
(d) development of grammatical devices for non-referential purposes, *eg* focalizing rules
(e) gradual increase in morphological naturalness

(ii) Restructuring continuum
(a) language mixing leading to unnatural developments
(b) hypercorrection
(c) increase in variation, weakening of linguistic norms

In addition, there are three features which are common to both continua:
(a) the changes are by and large implicationally ordered
(b) both are determined by complex conditions involving various levels of grammar and pragmatics
(c) both result in new systems

Mühlhäusler also identifies three sources of structural expansion: substratum languages, superstratum languages and universal grammar. Creolized jargons depend mostly on universals, which is why they are singled out for special treatment by Bickerton. Stabilized and expanded pidgins can draw heavily on substratum and superstratum languages. Mühlhäusler's distinction between restructuring and development is useful because it allows us to recognize that both kinds of changes can take place in both pidgin and creole continua. Restructuring need not imply expansion.

Before looking at post-creole development, it can be noted that a further complication arises in distinguishing between pidgins and creoles and first and second languages. First language creoles can become either partially or totally repidginized. Mühlhäusler (1986) cites as an example of partial repidginization of a creole the case of plantation creoles, where first generation creole speakers are supplemented with raw recruits from elsewhere. Mortality was so high on the plantations of Surinam during the first hundred years of the existence of the Sranan language (an English- and Portuguese-derived creole) that the majority of plantation workers had to be recruited from overseas. Thus, creole speakers of Sranan were outnumbered by second language speakers. The result was partial repidginization. Mühlhäusler also reports a case of total repidginization of Tok Pisin on Rambutyo Island in the Admiralties. There a group of plantation workers from different parts of New Guinea founded a new village where children began to speak creolized Tok Pisin within a generation. However, because of the very limited usefulness of the language, the second generation grew up speaking Rambutyo as their first and Tok Pisin as their second language. Hawaii English Creole may also have been partially repidginized by new Filipino recruits on the plantations. An existing creole community may receive reinforcement whenever new waves of immigrants come in. For example, now in Hawaii there are groups of Koreans who are learning the creole rather than standard English (*cf eg* Klein 1986).

DeCamp (1971b:349) draws attention to the other end of the creole life-cycle in acknowledging that what happens in the final stages is not well known. However, he says that the alternatives seem clear enough. These are:

(i) A creole may continue without substantial change, as Haitian Creole seems to be doing.
(ii) It may become extinct as Negerhollands and Gullah are doing.
(iii) It may further evolve into a normal language.
(iv) It may gradually merge with the corresponding standard language as is happening in Jamaica.

On closer examination, these alternative routes seem far from clear and distinct. Creolists generally refer to the fourth one as decreolization. If this process of change eventually results in a merger with the superstrate language, then surely this is equivalent to the third alternative. In some sense we may then wish to speak of the creole dying, although this is not the sense in which DeCamp offers Negerhollands as an example of a creole which is becoming extinct. As I will show in 5.4 some linguists have argued that Black English in the United States represents a case where extensive and nearly complete decreolization has obscured the creole origins of the language. However, it would not be correct to say that a merger had taken place between it and standard English. Neither is it clear what DeCamp means by citing Haitian Creole as a case where there has been no substantial change. Presumably he means that the changes which are taking place in the language have not brought it any closer to French. There French and Haitian Creole are coexistent systems. Because a clear division remains between the majority of the population and an urban post-colonial elite the systems show few signs of merging or being linked by a linguistic continuum. There is still a further route which may be possible, which I will discuss in 5.7, namely recreolization, whereby a creole becomes further removed from its superstrate.

5.2 Decreolization and the notion of post-creole continuum

Bickerton (1980:109) describes decreolization as a process which occurs whenever a creole language is in direct contact with its superstrate. A characteristic feature of this process is the emergence of a linguistic continuum of varieties between the creole language and the standard language which was the main contributor to the creole's formation, *eg* the Guyanese post-creole continuum, as shown in Figure 5.2.

FIGURE 5.2 The Guyanese post-creole continuum

The creole language is usually referred to as the **basilect**, and its corresponding standard as the **acrolect**. The varieties in between these two endpoints are referred to as the **mesolect**. The mesolect is transitional, mediating between the polar opposites of basilect and acrolect. It is important to remember, as O'Donnell and Todd (1980:52) point out, that at the ends of the continuum, we are not dealing with two distinct systems, but 'an unbroken spectrum between the pidgin or creole, on the one hand, and the prestigious standard on the other. There is no point of the continuum where we find a sharp break between the varieties.' They illustrate this point from Guyana, where they record the following eighteen alternatives along the Guyanese post-creole continuum ranging from the basilectal to acrolectal:

Guyanese creole **mi gii am**
mi bin gii am
mi bin gii ii
mi bin gi ii
mi di gii ii
mi di gi hii
a di gi ii
a di gii ii
a did gi ii
a did giv ii
a did giv hii
a giv ii
a giv im

	a giv him
	a geev ii
	a geev im
	a geev him
English	**I gave him**

Allsopp (1958b) was the first to show how the variety of forms found in the Guyanese creole continuum could be arranged hierarchically on a scale ranging from those which were nearest to English to those furthest from it. He also argued that the scale corresponded to social stratification. However, as we will see in 5.6, this is somewhat of a simplification of a complicated situation (*cf eg* the discussion in Bickerton 1975a:Ch. 1).

Robertson (1978) gives Berbice Dutch as an example of a case where the superstrate language has been replaced by another language. Dutch has been superseded by English for nearly two hundred years. Other creoles in a similar position include Sranan, St. Lucia French and Papiamentu. However, Berbice is becoming extinct. It speakers number less than one hundred and are all over fifty years old. It is gradually being relexified into English. The transition from Dutch to English is nevertheless gradual rather than abrupt (*cf* 3.3), with Dutch and English items used side by side within the same utterance, as in the example:

eke duz pi eni pis pis-kiba kiba – 'I used to give them a piece'

Robertson argues that the transition to the new superstrate language is no more abrupt than it would be if the basilect were of the same lexical base. Thus, the notion of a continuum is still valid (*cf* however, Mühlhäusler 1986).

Similar continua may exist in other situations where two languages, neither of which is a creole, are in contact. Considerable evidence has emerged over the past two decades which supports the theory that Black English in the United States is an example of a creole English which is in the last stages of decreolization. When a creole has been exposed to its standard language or acrolect for a long period of time, it may eventually merge into it, and become virtually indistinguishable from it. Uncovering the creole ancestry of such a variety may be difficult (*cf eg* Baugh 1980).

O'Donnell and Todd (1980:53) also cite a similar continuum of varieties in parts of northern Ireland among speakers whose mother tongue was originally Gaelic. They cite the following utterances as typical of the range of varieties which might be heard in use by Catholic speakers:

Yiz is buyin' bread that biz kyoch
Yiz is buyin' bread that diz be kyoch
Yiz is buyin' bread that biz raw in the middle
Yiz is buyin' bread that diz be raw in the middle
Yiz is buyin' bread that biz raw in the middle
Yiz are buyin' bread that does be raw in the middle
Youse are buyin' bread that does be raw in the middle
You're buyin' bread that's usually uncooked in the middle

The term **creoloid** has been applied to varieties such as Singapore English by Platt (1975) and others to indicate that some of the same processes involved in creolization can take place in a multilingual society like Singapore, where English acts as a superstrate language and a continuum of varieties develops between it and and more 'basilectal' varieties which reflect influence from the speakers' mother-tongue(s). Corne (in Baker and Corne 1982:60) has also used this term to designate Reunion Creole, which has remained structurally close to French. On Mauritius the situation was different. During a long period of British colonial rule French was withdrawn as a target language. Thus, the creole could develop in isolation from its lexifier language.

The kinds of changes which can occur along the post-creole continuum are referred to as 'targeted' in the sense intended by Bickerton (1980:109–10):

> In decreolization, speakers progressively change the basilectal grammar so that its output gradually comes to resemble the output of an acrolectal grammar. The word 'gradually' needs a gloss here. The degree of closeness to the acrolect attainable at any degree may be constrained, first, by the fact that the speaker's perceptions of his ultimate target may be inaccurate, and second, because it would appear that, for a grammar of one kind to become a grammar of another kind, it may have to follow a line that is far from straight.

The type of targeted language change has been studied primarily in the English-based creoles of Jamaica (*cf* DeCamp 1971b), Guyana (*cf* Bickerton 1975a; Rickford 1979) and Costa Rica (*cf* Hertzfeld 1978). Valdman (1973) discusses decreolization in Haitian Creole, a French-based creole. Other cases are not so clear-out. For example, Bickerton (1975b) suggests that a post-creole continuum is developing in Tok Pisin. Silva argues that the situation in Capeverdean Criulo is best described as a post-creole continuum, though not everyone would agree with these assessments of the situation. I will examine some of the reasons why the concept of the creole continuum has aroused controversy in 5.6.

5.3 The structure of the creole continuum

One of the main problems faced by those working on creoles in the 1960s and 1970s was how to account for their variability within existing models of linguistic description which were designed primarily for the analysis of static homogeneous systems. The notion of linguistic continuum is not exclusive to creole studies, nor is it a novel one. It is implicit, for example, in the writings of Schuchardt (1882:800) (*cf* Le Page 1980a). It was DeCamp (1971b), who was the first to demonstrate that there were ordered patterns in what looked like a randomly variable set of systems. Using the technique of **implicational scaling** DeCamp showed that there were constraints on the occurrence of basilectal, acrolectal and mesolectal forms. DeCamp (1971b:355) took as an example the distribution of a set of acrolectal and basilectal forms in the Jamaican Creole continuum:

acrolectal features	basilectal features
+A **child**	−A **pikni**
+B **eat**	−B **nyam**
+C /θ/	−C /t/
+D /ð/	−D /d/
+E **granny**	−E **nana**
+F **didn't**	−F **no ben**

The feature [+A] indicates the habitual use of the word **child**; [−A] indicates the use of **pikni** or **pikini** in equivalent contexts. [+B] indicates the habitual use of **eat** rather than **nyam**, [−B]. [+C] indicates a phonological contrast in the final consonants of pairs such as **both** and **boat**, while [−C] indicates its absence. [+D] indicates a contrast in the initial consonants of pairs such as **den** and **then**, and [−D] indicates a lack of it. [+E] indicates the use of the word **granny** rather than **nana**, [−E]. Finally, [+F] indicates the use of **didn't** in negative past tense constructions, and [−F] the use of various alternatives such as **no ben**, **no did**, etc. The six features are among those which DeCamp found to define the Jamaican post-creole continuum.

It we were to combine the features randomly we could come

up with a number of possible systems ranging from, *eg* [+A,+B,+C,+D,+E,+F] to [−A,−B,−C,−D,−E,−F]. The first of these systems would be used by a consistent acrolectal speaker, and the second by a consistent basilectal speaker. DeCamp found, however, that only seven of the possible combinations could be observed in the speech of his seven informants. Thus, the following systems were identified:

Speakers	Features					
1.	+A	+B	+C	−D	+E	+F
2.	−A	+B	−C	−D	+E	+F
3.	−A	+B	−C	−D	−E	−F
4.	−A	−B	−C	−D	−E	−F
5.	+A	+B	+C	+D	+E	+F
6.	+A	+B	−C	−D	+E	+F
7.	−A	+B	−C	−D	+E	−F

DeCamp then examined the co-occurrence of features within each idiolect, and came up with the arrangement shown in Figure 5.3 (1971b:355). In doing so he observed (1971b:357) that:

> . . . if all the **n** varieties of a speech community are thus arranged in an ordered series such that the difference between any variety and its neighbours is minimal, the result is a significant spectrum.

Feature Speakers	B	E	F	A	C	D
5	+	+	+	+	+	+
1.	+	+	+	+	+	−
6.	+	+	+	+	−	−
2.	+	+	+	−	−	−
3.	+	+	−	−	−	−
4.	−	−	−	−	−	−

FIGURE 5.3 Implicational scale for six features in the Jamaican Creole continuum.

Note that this procedure scales two phenomena: firstly, it orders the features in a scale from least acrolectal, *ie* B, to most acrolectal, *ie* D; and secondly, it scales the idiolects of the speakers into those which are most acrolectal, *ie* 5, and those least acrolectal, *ie* 4. The features are said to be implicationally ordered in that the presence of a plus for a feature implies that all features to its left will also have the value plus. Thus, if the value for feature [D] is [+D], all the features to the left of it will also have the value [+]. Therefore, the existence of a system which contained the values [−B, +E, −F, +A, +C, −D] would be among those ruled out, or not predicted because the value [+] for the features [A] and [C] and [E] imply that the features [B] and [F] should also be [+]. In other words, in practice, the prediction is that we are not likely to find a speaker in Jamaica who uses the basilectal forms **nyam**, **no ben** and **den** (for **then**), and the acrolectal forms **granny**, **child**, and **both** (instead of **boat**) within the context of the same speech event.

From a more technical perspective we can say that the working assumption behind implicational scaling as used by DeCamp, Bickerton and other creolists is that the scale consists of a series of ranked **isolects** (*ie* systems of individual speakers), or **lects**. Each (iso)lect is the output of a grammar (which is part of a **polylectal grammar**), is invariant, and differs from the one immediately next to it with respect to a single feature or rule in the **panlectal grid**. The panlectal grid consists of the totality of possible sets of rules for an arbitrarily limited area in space and/or time. The results of the implicational scale are used as a means of checking data against various predictions, *eg* Bailey's (1973) wave model of change. The assumption is that if the data scale to an acceptable degree, then they do so by virtue of the fact that a succession (or wave) of rule changes has spread evenly through the grammar of a speech community. The model predicts that as a change moves through the grammar it will progress stepwise affecting one lect at a time according to the implicational sequence of features/rules. In other words, since isolects are located in both time and space in such a model, they participate differentially (*ie* earlier or later) in an incipient rule change which is introduced at any given point in the spatio-temporal continuum. Bailey (1973) makes certain predictions about the direction of rule spread and rate of change. For example, he claims that the farther a rule travels from its origins, the fewer will be the environments above it on an implicational scale. Change begins in the most heavily weighted environment and works its way through the grammar by spreading through successively less heavily weighted environments. The weighting is determined by universal principles of markedness. This pattern of spread has the consequence that rules generalize in time, but seem to become less general in space because the temporally earlier changes move farther than the later ones.

DeCamp (1971b:357) says that for every variable feature which is part of the continuum in Jamaica there is clear consensus on its position (*cf* Rickford 1979:332–3 for a discussion of the use of informants' intuitions about the level of features). There are however variables which cannot be located on the continuum, but most of such variables are geographically determined. The amount of variation in Jamaica which is neither a part of the continuum or a matter of geographical variation is, according to DeCamp, surprisingly small. Relatively few features vary with age, sex, occupation, ethnic group, etc., except to the extent that these variables are themselves a part of the linear continuum. Thus, the very old and the very young tend to be closer to the creole continuum than young adults.

Here we see the major difference between a dialect continuum and a post-creole continuum, *ie* any division of the continuum would be linguistically arbitrary, and would not correlate neatly with external social factors. We also see here one motivation for the use of the implicational scaling technique rather than the kinds of analyses of variation used by sociolinguists such as Labov (1966) to describe variation in urban dialects. For example, in his study of the New York speech community Labov identified a number of linguistic variables which correlated systematically with extralinguistic factors such as age, sex, social class, style, etc. These dimensions were later incorporated as constraints on the operation of variable rules in the community grammar. Thus, one could use these variable rules to make predictions such as, for example, that in New York City, younger middle-class women when speaking in their most formal styles are likely to use the highest percentage of post-vocalic /r/. Post-vocalic /r/ is a prestige pronunciation which is being introduced into the community, and younger middle-class women appear to be in the vanguard of the change. Similarly, drawing on a knowledge of the way in which external variables interact, *eg* social class, sex differentiation and style, one could also predict that working-class men when speaking in their most casual style would be the most likely to use the least percentage of post-vocalic /r/. Thus, one can build up a picture of the New York speech community as consisting of groups of speakers, defined in terms of social characteristics such as age, sex, and social class, whose linguistic usage can be regularly described in terms of variable use of certain shared features.

Bickerton (1975a) and others have argued that variable rule analysis will not work well in the case of creoles because there are no single items on which all informants show variable behaviour. Variable rules would obscure the considerable amount of invariant patterning in the creole situation. According to Bickerton (1975a:18) there do not seem to be any unambiguous social lines which divide variable from invariant speakers in Guyana. To take any one group as a unit of study for a given feature would lose sight of those speakers who were invariant on that particular feature. Similarly, to divide the continuum into co-existent systems on linguistic grounds would obscure the on-going processes of change in the Guyanese continuum. Labov assumes that the same variables are shared by the community and that what distinguishes one social group from another is the lesser or greater use of a particular variable. Variation in a creole community, however, results from 'the juxtaposition of several different isolects or lects, each at a different state of linguistic development' (Rickford 1979:47).

We can see too the connection between variation and change. To put this in Bickerton's (1975a:16) words: 'linguistic variation is the synchronic aspect of linguistic change, and linguistic change is the diachronic aspect of linguistic variation.' This connection has interesting implications when seen in terms of a creole continuum. Bickerton (1975a:17) observes that:

> . . . a synchronic cut across the Guyanese community is indistinguishable from a diachronic cut across a century and a half of linguistic development . . . therefore a grammar of the whole Guyanese continuum should be indistinguishable from the diachronic grammar that *could* have been written if *all* Guyanese had moved as close to standard English as *some* of them have. Thus the Guyanese continuum, far from being a quagmire of anomalies designed to bedevil the descriptivist, reveals itself as an unusual, though perhaps not unique, case of the preservation of diachronic changes in a synchronic state, and therefore an unrivalled laboratory for the study of linguistic change processes which can normally only be inferred from written materials.

A number of creolists have pointed to the fact that the evolutionary pace of creoles is more rapid than that of other language types. Markey (1982:173), for example, estimates that thirty years in the life-cycle of a creole might well be equivalent to three centuries in the life-cycle of a non-creole. Bickerton believes that there is a constant succession of restructurings of the original system across the continuum. This yields a very gradual transmission in terms of surface forms between the two extremes, such as I have illustrated above. Not all are agreed on the extent to which this process of development shows discontinuities. Some of these stages can be now be illustrated by reference to the study of a number of features of creole grammar. There are now many studies which describe the copula, pronominal systems, and tense and aspect in various creoles. As I will show in Chapter 7, the emergence of verbal categories and the way in which they are encoded in creole grammars plays a major role in Bickerton's theory of creole origins.

5.4 The distribution of the copula in the creole continuum

Bickerton (1975a) uses the implicational model to describe three points on the Guyanese creole continuum: the basilect, the mesolect and the acrolect, and then presents sets of rules indicating how changes take place between different points on the continuum. I have already noted that absence of copula is a characteristic feature of pidgins and creoles (2.9). Bickerton's (1973; 1975a) analyses of the distribution of the copula in the Guyanese creole continuum support the view that speakers start with zero (ø) forms and introduce the copula later, *ie* in the mesolect. Thus, only in the mesolect does it make sense to speak of 'copula deletion'.

In the implicational scale which Bickerton (1972) presents for the distribution of copula forms in the mesolect (shown in Figure 5.4), the 'true' copula enters the system in isolect E, where **iz/waz** forms are present. Zero forms are thus 'created' in the mesolect through the addition of an opposition which did not exist before in the system. The jump from the basilect into the acrolect or upper mesolect occurs when **iz/waz** are introduced into the grammar in isolect D; zero forms enter into contrast with **iz/waz**.

We can see that the environments and lects are implicationally ordered. Environment 1, the continuative verbal refers to the presence or absence of forms of the copula in constructions such as **mi livin a sevntiwan** – 'I was living in Seventy-one (village)' (Bickerton 1972:29). Environment 2 refers to locative and existential constructions such as **Shi mekin gud tu**, **shi daun at di ool leedi** – 'She's doing well too, she's down at the old lady's' (Bickerton 1972:33). The third environment refers to the use of the copula before a predicate adjective as in **wen i soba i wan lik yu dong** – 'When he's sober he wants to knock you down' (Bickerton 1972:30). The fourth environment refers to the forms of the copula which occur before a nominal in a sentence like **dooz pleesiz terribol rapidz** – 'Those places are terrible rapids' (Bickerton 1972:33).

The copula may be realized in a number of ways, *eg* as zero as in the examples given to illustrate the four environments. If it is present, it may appear as **iz** or **waz**, *eg* **if di ool man waz hia hi kuda giv you a laf** – 'If the old man was here he could have

	Environment				
Isolects	1	2	3	4	Speakers
A	1	1	1	13	98
B	1	1	1	23	27, 99
C	1	1	1	3	11, 17, 119
D	1	1	13 *	3	15, 105
E	1	12	13	3	13, 160
F	13	12	13	23	41
G	13	123	13	3	43, 125, 192, 236
H	13	13	13	23	196
I	13	3	13	23	122, 157
J	13		3	23	117
K	3	23	3	3	19

Col. 1 = continuative verbal
Col. 2 = locative and existential
Col. 3 = 'predicate adjective'
Col. 4 = nominal
1 = *Ving* without aux. in Col. 1; *de* in Col. 2; V(+ att) (or, ø + Adj.) in Col. 3; *a* in Col. 4
2 = ø
3 = *iz/waz*
* = point from which copula variability disseminates

FIGURE 5.4 The spread of zero

made you laugh' (Bickerton 1972:33). The copula may also be realized as **a**, which marks continuative and iterative verb phrases, *eg* **mi a kom back haptanuun** – 'I'm coming back in the afternoon' (Bickerton 1975a:34). In some of its functions, it is equivalent to English **be + ing**.[1] The copula diffuses throughout the system affecting different speakers/lects and different environments at different stages. Zero forms cannot spread to nominal environments until movement from the creole to a more English-like system is already far advanced. Other changes which remain to be implemented to make the system even more English-like are relatively minor ones. They include the complete elimination of **de** from the system and the introduction of variable copula before continuative verbs.

Bickerton (1972:33) observes that the net result of the changes which apply to the basilect bring a clearly creole system to a 'position where it is virtually indistinguishable from the Black English system described by Labov 1969'. However, he goes on to say (1972:34) that he had no intention of demonstrating similarities between Black English (BEV) and Guyanese Creole. They emerged simply as a by-product of his attempt to write a polylectal grammar for Guyanese creole. He cites the analysis as support for the view that a synchronic polylectal grammar is equivalent to a diachronic grammar of language change. Moreover, he suggests that there may be a 'universal decreolization process, or at least one applying to all English-based creoles in contact with English'. In order to assess the validity of this claim I will look at some more evidence from the copula in other English creoles.

The case of variation in the copula in BEV sparked a controversy between those who claimed that it demonstrated the creole ancestry of this variety, and those who claimed that it was a 'dialect' of English. One of the early analyses of the copula in BEV which gave support to the latter claim was that of Labov (1969), in which it was argued that contraction and deletion were two separate but similar rules which applied in the order of contraction followed by deletion. By **contraction** Labov means the process which is responsible for contracting full forms of the copula in certain environments, *eg* **I am** > **I'm**, **you are** > **you're**, etc.

Labov's claim that there were two separate rules involved which led to the surface zero forms of the copula was based on two aspects of the variable constraints which affected the application of the rules. Firstly, he observed that the effect of the preceding phonological environment (*ie* whether there was a consonant or a vowel) operated differently in the case of contraction and deletion, so that a preceding consonant favoured deletion and a preceding vowel favoured contraction. Labov argued that this pattern clearly demonstrated that both contraction and deletion were phonological (rather than grammatical) processes. Secondly, he found that the constraints for the following syntactic environment applied to both contraction and deletion, but were ordered identically so that deletion was the result of a more exaggerated or 'double' operation of the constraints on contraction. The syntactic constraints are similar to those discussed above in the analysis of the copula in Guyanese Creole by Bickerton, *eg* whether the copula is followed by a predicate adjective or a noun, whether the construction is locative, whether there is a continuative or progressive verb form (*ie* V + **ing**). In addition, Labov looked at contraction and deletion in the presence of verb forms with **going** + **to**, *eg* **She's going to get a job**. The verb form **going to** can be contracted to **gonna** or **gon**.

Labov (1969) concluded from his analysis that both black and white speakers shared the same rules and underlying forms, but just used the rules to a greater or lesser extent. It is significant that it was in this paper that Labov elaborated the notion of variable rule. Labov (1969:722) described the relationship between BEV and standard English as follows: 'Wherever SE [Standard English SR] can contract BEV can delete the copula, and vice versa: wherever SE cannot contract, BEV cannot delete and vice versa.' A more recent study of black and white speech in east central Texas (*cf* Bailey and Maynor forthcoming) argues that both varieties make use of the present tense forms of **be** in the same way, and that the syntactic constraints on the copula are much the same.

Some took Labov's evidence to indicate that BEV did not have a prior Creole ancestry. Dillard (1968; 1970) and Stewart (1968) were among those who argued that this approach was misguided. Bailey (1965) and Stewart (1969) both proposed that BEV had a zero copula, and stressed the importance of looking at the African and West Indian creole roots of contemporary BEV. Holm (1984) claims that the zero forms have their origins in African substratum, and that BEV preserves an African pattern inherited by creoles in which the following predicate determines the form of the copula. In considering whether BEV was a separate system, Labov (1972a:36) queried whether one could regard it as a mixture of two different systems or one of the intermediate stages in a system which encompassed both BEV and standard English. He stresses (1972:37) that:

> To say that BEV is a system completely different from other English systems is of course absurd. The great majority of the rules of BEV are the same as the rules of other English dialects. But within that overall similarity, there may be subsets of rules which are not easily integrated into other English grammars, and some of these subsets may be located at strategic points, close to the grammatical core.

Fasold (1972a), however, took a more moderate view in saying that accepting Labov's analysis of synchronic BEV was not tantamount to a denial of the Creole origin hypothesis, but simply a recognition that BEV had reached a late stage of decreolization. Similarities between white and black English do not demonstrate anything about the origin of the forms in question, since the common features may be the result of common origin or later parallel development, or convergence through intensive contact. It may also be the case that superficial identity of form camouflages underlying divergence (*cf eg* Spears 1982 and Harris J. 1984). Since that time more analyses of the copula (*cf eg* Baugh 1980) and other features of BEV in relation to white varieties of Southern English (*cf eg* the discussion of tense and aspect in Fasold 1972b, 1981; Wolfram 1974 and Rickford 1986b) have been carried out.

There have also been more detailed historical investigations of various documents (*cf eg* Dayton 1984; Brewer 1974, 1979). Fasold (1976), for example, examined the *Slaves Narrative Collection* (a set of 2,000 interviews with ex-slaves between the ages of 70 and 100 collected between 1936–38 as part of the Federal Writers' Project, *cf eg* the part collection assembled in Botkin 1945). He found that contraction was weaker in BEV 100 years ago. This makes it unlikely that a deletion rule operated on the output of a contraction rule, as suggested in Labov's analysis (*cf* also Romaine 1982:8.1 for further arguments of a different kind against this ordering).

In his re-examination of Labov's data on contraction and deletion, Baugh (1980) paid special attention to the following syntactic environments. He found that following adjectives overwhelmingly favoured deletion, but that locatives did not. In Labov's analysis this difference had been obscured by the fact that he had not looked at the effects of predicate adjectives separately from those of locative environments. Baugh (1980:100) concludes that deletion must have predated the emergence of contracted forms in this environment. This suggests that perhaps the original form of the copula was zero and that there was no copula before adjectives. He then claims (1980:103) that this establishes the creole ancestry of contemporary BEV beyond any doubt. Baugh also compared his analysis to Bailey's analysis of the copula in Jamaican Creole, where the same environment shows structural similarities.

It was the predicate adjective environment which was significant in Bickerton's analysis as the locus for the diffusion of variability in the copula. Bickerton argued that in the most basilectal forms of Guyanese Creole zero precedes adjectives, **de** precedes locatives, **a** precedes a nominal. At the mesolectal stage zero alternates with the **iz/waz** copula, so that zero is characteristic not of the creole basilect but of a mesolect in the process of decreolization. The system is then complicated (rather than simplified) through the addition of the **iz/waz** forms preceding adjectives, which then alternate with zero forms. In still later stages of development of the copula in Guyanese creole **iz/waz** is acquired in all syntactic environments and a full set of English inflections is introduced. It is not until these inflections have been extended to all environments that contraction occurs. At this stage there may be a switchover from syntactic constraints to phonological ones governing the processes of contraction and deletion. In other words, the dependency relations in creoles hold between the copula and its following predicate rather than between the copula and its subject as in other varieties of English. Decreolization thus involves a shift from one type of dependency relation to another. (This may be a more general characteristic of a developing system undergoing expansion as opposed to a relatively stable system, *cf* the discussion of relativization in 6.10 for a similar switchover in contraints.)

Bickerton's analysis differs from that of Fasold, who argues that in Black English **da** is first relexified as the acrolectal form **is**. Variability then spreads to the copula preceding a noun phrase. Zero is the result of deletion that occurs after relexification. In Bickerton's view zero is a reflection of variation which results when a basilectal form is dropped and a mesolectal one acquired. Zero arises from a process of acquisition for Bickerton, but from deletion for Fasold. Dayton (1984), however, argues that the **was** form of the copula in Black English today cannot be the result of the deletion of a contracted form because **was** does not contract in either Black English or Standard English.

Further support for the acquisition hypothesis comes from Alleyne's (1980:209) account of the emergence of the present tense paradigm in Caribbean creoles. He writes:

> . . . the most plausible way to account for the forms of [Black English SR] is to begin . . . with forms without copula; the copula is later added first as a form (is) which does not undergo suppletion change for person or number (the process of mastery of the rules of person and number concord of standard English involves the coexistence of **am**, **is**, and zero) until the later distribution of **am**, **is**, **are** for number and person is achieved.

There seems to be some consensus now on the nature and origin of BEV. Most linguists seem convinced that it had its origins in an earlier creole and that it has been decreolizing for some time. Many of the differences between BEV and standard English are due to the persistence of creole features. In his discussion of the famous 'Black English Trial' at Ann Arbor Labov (1982:192) put forward four points about BEV which seem to be agreed upon:

(i) BEV is a subsystem of English with a distinct set of phono-

logical and syntactic rules that are now aligned in many ways with the rules of other dialects.
(ii) It incorporates many features of southern phonology, morphology and syntax; blacks in turn have exerted influence on the dialects of southern whites where they have lived.
(iii) It shows evidence of derivation from an earlier creole that was closer to the present-day creoles of the Caribbean.
(iv) It has a highly developed aspect system, quite different from other dialects of English, which shows continuing development of its semantic structure.

In his most recent work Labov has argued that in urban areas Black English is becoming more unlike white English. This linguistic divergence reflects fundamental social and racial divisions between the two speech communities. One consequence of the migration of blacks from the rural south into northern urban cities has been the formation of separate black communities which have only marginal interaction with white ones.[2] Studies by Bailey and Maynor in east central Texas (1985) support the view that BEV is becoming less and not more like white varieties of English. Some of the most significant differences between black and white speech are the result of grammatical changes in progress rather than due to the persistence of creole features. I will discuss in 5.6 and 5.7 the kinds of changes involved in decreolization and recreolization which have the effect of making the creole more unlike its superstrate.

In his analysis of variability in the copula in Hawaii English Creole, Day (1972:113) says that one aspect of decreolization can be seen in the gradual acquisition of the standard English copula. The stages in this process are implicationally governed. There are some important differences between the copula in Hawaii English Creole and BEV. For one thing, overt forms of the copula are used much less frequently in Hawaii English Creole, and there is little support for contraction. In some environments the zero copula alternates wtih **stei**. Thus, the following exist as alternatives:

mai mada $\left\{ \begin{matrix} \text{stei} \\ \emptyset \end{matrix} \right\}$ **in da haus** 'My mother is in the house'

Day suggests (1972:80) that in present-day Hawaii English Creole we may have the same situation which preceded present BEV, *ie* optional insertion of the copula. He (1972:99) grouped his 23 speakers into five lects based on the distribution of the copula across four syntactic environments studied by Labov, as shown in Figure 5.5.

Lects	Syntactic environments			
	–NP	–Pred. Adj.	–Loc	–V +ing
5	X	X	X	X
4	X	X	X	0
3	X	X	0	0
2	X	0	0	0
1	0	0	0	0

FIGURE 5.5 Variability in the copula in Hawaii English Creole

In Figure 5.5 an X indicates that there is at least one occurrence of a present tense copula, and indicates the absence of the copula. According to this implicational scale, if a speaker lacks a form of the present tense copula before an adjective, then he will not have any forms of the copula in the environments to the right, *ie* before a locative and a progressive form of the verb. The environments are ranked according to the likelihood of promoting the presence of the copula. Thus the least likely category for the appearance of the copula is before a progressive, and the most likely is before a noun. Day also observes that there is no correlation between the lects and social status. In other words decreolization cuts across the whole social spectrum.

I have shown that there is some support for Bickerton's view that the process of decreolization occurs similarly across English creoles, although there are some differences between the cases we have considered. I will now look briefly at how decreolization affects the distribution of tense and aspect across the creole continuum.

5.5 Tense and aspect across the creole continuum

I explained in Chapter 3 (*cf* Table 3.1) that the similarities in the markers used for tense and aspect across the Caribbean, Surinam and other creoles were cited by Thompson (1961:110) in support of the relexification theory. We can also track developments in these systems across the decreolization continuum.

In his analysis of tense and aspect in Guyanese creole Bickerton (1975a) takes as his point of departure Voorhoeve's (1957) analysis of the Sranan verbal system.[3] Beginning with the basilect he divides the verbal system into two subsystems: the **realis** and **irrealis** (or factual vs. counterfactual). The realis refers to states and actions which have occurred or are in the process of taking place. The irrealis includes all states and actions which have not actually occurred, whether these are expressed by future or conditional tenses or by modals (Bickerton 1975a:42). The realis system consists of the stem or unmarked form of the verb whose function is dependent on its semantic status as stative or non-stative. There are four markers of tense and aspect in the realis system:

(i) **a**, a non-punctual marker indicating the continuative and iterative
(ii) **bin**, an anterior marker indicating the simple past with stative, verbs, *eg* **dem bin gat wan lil haus** – 'They had a little house' (Bickerton 1975a:35), and 'past before past' with non-stative verbs, *eg* **dem bin gatu get we and kom dis said**. . . – 'They had to get away and come over here' (Bickerton 1975a:36); the latter interpretation is not always unambiguous.
(iii) **bina**, a combination of **a** + **bin**, which functions as a past continuative and past iterative, *eg* **wan blakman an i waif bina liv abak** – 'A Negro and his wife used to live inland' (Bickerton 1975a:37);
(iv) **don**, a completive aspect marker indicating a past state of affairs as being either a necessary preliminary to a succeeding state, or as persisting unchanged into the present, *eg* **wen dem don plau, dem chip** – 'When they've finished ploughing, they harrow'.

Bickerton's tense system is based on the opposition between [± anterior]. However, it applies only to the realis system because in his view the irrealis is less structured. The irrealis consists mainly of two features. There are two basilectal forms, **go** and **sa**, which function as future tense markers and as modals. In addition, there are also modals such as **kyan** – 'can', **mos** – 'must', etc. The multifunctionality of **go** and **sa** is to be expected given that forms which are used to refer to the future may also have modal implications. This is a natural consequence of the fact that statements made about future occurrences are based on the speaker's beliefs and predictions about the hypothetical rather than on knowledge of fact (*cf eg* Lyons 1968:310 and 7.3).

The anterior tense system is dependent on the distinction between stative and non-stative. This means that for stative verbs [-anterior] means 'now', *ie* the state of liking, knowing, etc., which is in existence at the moment even though it may have begun in the past. By contrast, [+anterior] for stative verbs indicates 'not now', *ie* a terminated state (*cf* Bickerton 1975a:461). In linguistic terms this distinction is encoded in the choice between zero and **bin**. Bickerton claims that it is a general characteristic of creole languages that the zero form marks simple past for action verbs and non-past for state verbs. This has the interesting consequence that unlike English, which has a morphologically marked past tense and an unmarked non-past, basilectal Guyanese creole has a morphologically unmarked past and a marked non-past in certain cases (*cf* Bickerton 1975a:28). A similar distribution is corroborated for Capeverdean Crioulo by Silva (1985:144–5), where [-anterior] is encoded by the zero form for stative and non-stative verbs, and the anterior by the post-verbal suffix-**ba**. Thus, **lob' temba past'** – 'The wolf had food', where the combination of V + **ba** with a stative verb is interpreted as the simple past (*cf* Silva 1985:153).

The basic aspectual distinction in the basilectal system is between punctual and non-punctual. Combining the two parameters of tense and aspect in relation to the semantic opposition between stative and non-stative verbs we can diagram the system as in Figure 5.6, following Bickerton (1975a:47). We can note a four-fold merger of past and non-past, continuous and iterative in **a**. In addition, the same forms ø and **bin** have different functions when used with statives and non-statives.

Stative			Non-stative
ø	[−anterior]	+past	ø
		−past	**a**
bin	[+anterior]	+past	**bin**
		−past	**bina**

FIGURE 5.6 Tense and aspect in Guyanese creole: the basilect

Bickerton (1975a:47) argues that it would not be correct to consider the basilectal Guyanese creole system as a simplification of the English tense system. Distinctions such as stative vs. non-stative play no overt part in the English system, and no single English tense or group of tenses has a distinct Guyanese equivalent. Bickerton (1975a:48–9) compares the Guyanese system with the tense/aspect system of Krio, as discussed by Jones (1968:87), where the following paradigm is proposed for the realis:

a bin rait – 'I wrote'
a de rait – 'I am writing'
a bin de rait – 'I was writing'
a don rait – 'I have written'
a bin don rait – 'I had written'
a bin don de rait – 'I had been writing'

Bickerton points out the similarity between the forms of the pre-verbal markers in Krio and Guyanese Creole. He is suspicious, however, of the close correspondence between the Guyanese forms and their English translations. Agheyisi's (1971:133) analysis of West African Pidgin English however coincides with Bickerton's as far as the different functions of **bin** are concerned, as well as the use of the unmarked forms of action verbs to express the past. The system proposed by Voorhoeve (1957:383) for Sranan is also similar.

Bickerton (1975a:60–1) summarizes the changes which take place in the development from basilect to mesolect as follows:

> **doz** develops from a marginal to a central position in the grammar, acquiring a more precise function as it does so; the characteristic basilectal markers disappear and are replaced by other forms; **-ing** forms make their appearance, but with only sporadic accompanying **be**; **go** as irrealis marker is replaced by **gon** which develops as a pure future, with modals fulfilling conditional-type functions; extensive changes take place in verbal negation; English past morphemes begin to appear at first in sharply limited environments.

Bickerton (1975a:69–70) singles out one characteristic strategy of the decreolization process, namely, the replacement of non-standard looking morphemes by others which look more like morphemes of standard English. However, these English-looking morphemes are often simply slotted into place in structures which are still essentially creole in terms of their syntax and semantics. The replacement of **bin** by **did** is a case in point. Although **did** probably derives from English **did** (as **doz** derives from English **does**) the phonological resemblance is the extent of their similarity. Similarly, with regard to the appearance of **gon**, Bickerton (1975a:87) says that it might at first sight look like a reduced form of **going**; this may of course be in a sense its 'derivation'. However, it would not make sense to argue that its grammatical derivation is via an underlying form **going**, which morphophonemically reduces to **gon**. I have discussed in detail the consequences of this strategy of argumentation in looking at the copula in creoles. If **gon** were a reduced form of **go** + **ing** we would expect it to appear about the same time as V + **ing** structures. Although this is the case for many speakers, there are some who have acquired **gon** but not V + **ing**. If we look at the functions of **gon**, it is apparent that they have nothing to do with those of **going to** in English (*cf* Bickerton 1975a:88–90 for further discussion).

I have already mentioned the disjunction between basilectal creole and English with regard to the morphological marking of verb forms in relation to the semantic opposition of past vs. non-past. Bickerton (1975a:102) emphasizes that one of the most striking differences between the basilectal and acrolectal grammars lies in their functions for the verb-stem form of non-statives. The unmarked verb is unambiguously associated with past events in the basilect and with non-past events in the acrolect. Thus, past referents are marked in the acrolect and non-past ones are marked in the basilect and mesolect with **a**, **doz** or both. Only slowly does the underlying semantic system shift in the general direction of English. Bickerton (1975a:162–3;166) concludes that the Guyanese continuum may be described as a system or unbroken chain by virtue of the fact that variation can be handled as the result of a series of rule changes which link the various developmental stages from basilect to acrolect.

5.6 Some criticisms of the notion of creole continuum

While the notion of creole continuum has proved a powerful analytical device in coping with the variability inherent in such situations, a number of linguists have expressed dissatisfaction with it. Rickford (1986a) provides a lucid summary of the synchronic and diachronic issues surrounding the concept of the continuum, which have been the source of controversy among linguists. He identifies three synchronic issues.

The first of these he characterizes as the fundamental continuum question; namely, whether the variation between a creole and its related superstrate is relatively discrete, *ie* diglossic or continuous, that is, involving a spectrum of varieties between basilectal creole and acrolect. This issue is ultimately a question about the degree of discreteness between linguistic systems. Ferguson (1959) originally used the term **diglossia** to refer to a situation in which two language varieties co-exist and are specialized according to function. Where languages stand in a diglossic relation there is a simple one-to-one relationship between language choice and social context so that each variety can be seen as having a distinct place or function in the local speech repertoire.

As early as 1961 Cassidy had rejected the idea that there were discrete varieties of Jamaican speech. He remarked (1961:2) that it exists in two main forms which can be imagined as lying at opposite ends of a scale, with 'every sort of variation in between, but each variant inclining in some degree toward the right or left'. DeCamp's rejection of a discrete diglossic model for Jamaica is even more explicit. He says (1971b:350;354):

> . . . there is no sharp cleavage between creole and standard. Rather there is a linguistic continuum . . . Many Jamaicans persist in the myth that there are only two varieties: the patois and the standard. But one speaker's attempt at the broad patois may be closer to the standard end of the continuum than is another's attempt at the standard . . . By calling it a continuum I mean that given two samples of Jamaican speech which differ substantially from one another, it is usually possible to find a third intermediate level in an additional sample. Thus it is not practicable to describe the system in terms of two or three or six or any other manageable number of discrete social dialects.

It is of course possible to maintain a discrete interpretation of the Jamaican and other similar situations by recognizing intermediate varieties as essentially acrolectal or standard with interference or mixing from the creole, or vice versa. However, as Bickerton (1973:641) has pointed out, this suggests that a continuum is simply produced by the random, mutual interference of two discrete and self-consistent grammars.

Despite DeCamp's demonstration that there were implicational relationships between the ordering of features along the Jamaican creole continuum as shown in 5.3, a number of linguists have argued for an analysis in terms of two or three discrete systems. Among them have been native speakers of the creoles concerned, (*cf eg* Tsuzaki 1971 for Hawaii Creole and Gibson 1982 for Guyanese Creole). Gibson (1982), for instance, draws a discrete line between the acrolect and all other varieties in the continuum, thus minimizing the continuous differences between the basilectal and mesolectal varieties, which are all classified as 'creole'. Gibson observes that the local term 'Creolese' is used by its speakers to refer to all varieties short of the acrolect. They also regard as non-standard both mesolectal and basilectal features. An additional linguistic argument for the discreteness of the two basic systems is provided by the fact that different mesolectal and basilectal surface forms often represent common underlying syntactic and semantic categories. Gibson claims that the differences between the basilect and mesolect are purely lexical and not grammatical. This is however disputed by Rickford (1986a), who shows that there are differences between these varieties which cannot be reduced to alternate realizations of common underlying subcategories. Bickerton (1980) also shows this in relation to some lexical items. Alleyne (1980:196–7) argues that it is only when one reaches the intermediate stages of the continuum that English-like passives occur, *eg* **di trii get kot** – 'The tree got cut'.

There are also difficulties relating to the possible combinations of elements from one system with those from another, as Bickerton (1975a:12–4) shows by discussing the difficulties in manipulating Allsopp's (1958a) possible realizations of **I told him** into discrete co-existing systems. Rickford's (1986a) view is that the continuum model is a better representation of the gradient creole/standard relation in places such as Guyana or Jamaica, while a discrete co-existent systems analysis is better suited to places such as Haiti, where there is a sharper boundary between creole and standard (*cf* also Shilling 1980 on Bahamian English).

As I will argue, however, in 5.7, where I discuss the phenomenon of recreolization, Rickford's attempt to separate the synchronic and diachronic aspects of the continuum problem is in some respects misguided. One could argue that in the transportation of varieties of Jamaican speech to the United Kingdom what was essentially a continuum type of situation has become transformed into a more diglossic one. As Hymes (1971:423) has noted: 'In some areas of research it may appear possible to separate the linguistic from the socio-cultural, the synchronic from the diachronic or historical. Certainly it is not possible to do so in the study of pidgin and creole languages.'

A second related synchronic issue which Rickford (1986a) identifies as controversial for creolists is whether variation in the creole speech community is multi- or uni-dimensional. In other words, the question is whether all or most of the variants and varieties of speech can be ordered in terms of a single linear dimension such as creoleness or standardness. The continuum model assumes that varieties can be ordered along a single dimension. Similarly, the technique of implicational scaling is appropriate only for variables which can be unidimensionally or linearly ordered. If that were not so, then implicational relations would break down.

This can best be illustrated in terms of the diagram in Figure 5.7, where the horizontal axis represents the basic continuum model. We can assume that the relevant dimension is creoleness vs. standardness, and that varieties are ordered from Vi to Vn according to their degree of closeness to one or the other end. The vertical axis however introduces another dimension into the model. I will assume for the sake of the argument that it is a dimension such as rural vs. urban or ethnicity (*cf eg* Devonish 1983 and Edwards 1975). The assumption here in adding another dimension to the continuum is that urban variants are not characteristically less creole and rural variants not necessarily more creole. That is, there would be varieties such as V2 which would need to be classified with respect to two dimensions, [+urban +creole], in order to distinguish them from varieties such as V2', which is equally creole, but rural. In Belize Escure (1983) notes the divergence between actual practice and the stereotypical view that rural varieties are the most conservative and urban varieties the most decreolized. She finds that some morphosyntactic features are shared by both urban and rural Creoles as well as rural Caribs.

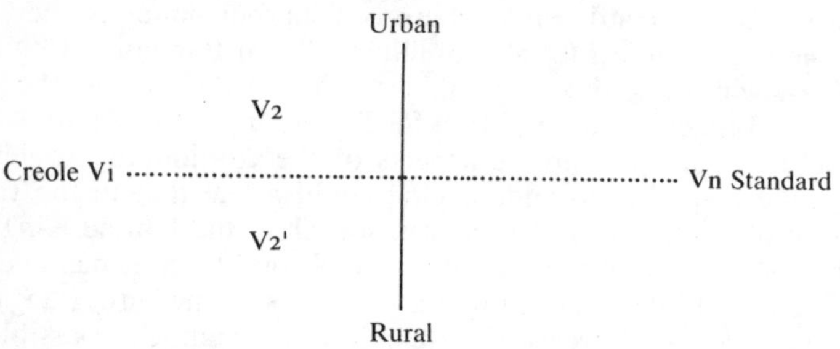

FIGURE 5.7 A multidimensional model of a creole continuum

The problem of dimensionality in relation to the creole continuum was raised in early treatments of Jamaican and Guyanese Creole (*cf* DeCamp 1971b and Bickerton 1973 respectively). De Camp (1971b:352–4) for example, observed that there were localisms and regionalisms which were incompatible with the continuum model, but that they were not difficult to sort out as they were almost entirely lexical. More critical and detailed analyses arguing the need for a multidimensional model were put forward by Washabaugh (1977) and Le Page (1980b).[4] Washabaugh (1977), for example, argued that variation in Providence Island Creole was both vertical and horizontal. In the case of the complementizer speakers varied between basilectal **fi** and acrolectal **tu**. However, basilectal speakers alternated between **fi** in careful speech and another variant **fe** in more casual styles. Acrolectal speakers also had a more casual variant, **te**. There was also a rule which deleted complementizer **fi**. Deletion is neither more or less basilectal than **fi**. Only the rule involving a change from **fi** to **tu** represents a move towards the acrolect.

At the moment Le Page's work represents the most comprehensive example of multidimensional analysis (*cf* especially Le Page and Tabouret-Keller 1985). His criticisms of unidimensional models are based on data from creole-speaking communities in Belize and St Lucia, where a number of different varieties and dimensions are brought into play, *eg* Carib, Spanish, French, English, and are more far-reaching. In speaking of the language of three female informants from St Cayo District in Belize, who regard themselves as creole speakers, he observes (1980a: 126–8):

> Neither the linguistic description of such speakers nor of the collective corpus of texts culled from their utterances, is scalable in the way Bickerton has claimed for his Guyanese verb phrases, because there is no two-dimensional linear progression from basilect to acrolect. One can only characterize their behaviour in terms of coordinates referring in a relational way to neighbouring cultures or internal models. The neighbouring cultures, such as Guatemalen Spanish or Coastal Carib or Belize City Creole or teacher's English are again in their turn related to other cultural models such as Castilian Spanish or Island Carib or West Indian Creoles or West Indian Educated Standards. Each of the three in their linguistic behaviour exhibits the effects of both individual and communal acts of identity, and in doing so they position themselves in . . . multidimensional space.

In order to deal with the continuity and non-discreteness of the linguistic variability of informants in this situation Le Page has used cluster analysis (*cf* however McEntegart and Le Page 1982 for a critical appraisal of this technique). For example, in analysing the speech of schoolchildren in St Lucia he notes (1980:135) that 'All of the children make some use of nearly all the [nine SR] features – thus they share the same repertoire . . . Nevertheless they can also be clustered into groups of similar behaviour according to the **extent** to which they use each component of the repertoire.'

A third synchronic issue to do with the notion of linguistic continuum, which is mentioned by Rickford (1986a), is whether social and stylistic considerations should be taken into account. Some have criticized creolists such as DeCamp and Bickerton for concentrating primarily on the internal linguistic constraints which affect implicational relationships in the creole continuum. In criticizing Bickerton's analysis of the Guyanese Creole continuum Le Page (1978:6), for example, says that 'a continuum of lects is described, but not how a speaker is motivated to move across the continuum'. Le Page is pointing here to the need to take into account the kinds of socio-psychological factors which condition linguistic variability. Bickerton however has argued that the basis for the distribution of lectal features is purely linguistic. He does not believe that the addition of a social component to implicational scales can add anything to our knowledge of the patterning of linguistic structure or to an explanation of change.

Escure (1983) stresses the fact that decreolization is affected by context. Any single speaker may have different target languages or varieties which are relevant in different situations or at different times in his life. This is in line with Le Page's view that speakers model their linguistic behaviour on various models to which they have access depending on their ability to identify these and modify their speech accordingly.

Rickford (1986a) treats a further two controversial issues relating to the notion of continuum, which he labels diachronic. The first of these is whether it is still valid to maintain DeCamp's view of the continuum as a simple extension of Bloomfield's (1933) and Hall's (1966) life-cycle model. As I indicated in Chapter 3, this refers to the view that a pidgin arising from interlingual contact may become a creole if used as a native language, and then a creole continuum develops as the creole continues to co-exist with its lexically related standard. DeCamp (1971b) assumed that the post-creole continuum reflected diachronic evolution from an earlier situation in which only the standard and the creole existed. In other words, intermediate or mesolectal varieties are regarded as younger and more recent than either the creole or standard. They arise to fill in the linguistic space between the two ends of the continuum, just as the social space between the highest and lowest social classes of post-colonial society is also filled in.

Although there is some diachronic textual data in support of this, evidence on the prior pidgin stages of many creoles is lacking (*cf eg* Cassidy's 1971 attempt to trace the pidgin element in Jamaican Creole). Moreover, it is not altogether clear in the case of many of the Caribbean creoles, for example, that there was a prior pidgin stage (*cf* 5.1). Alleyne (1980) has suggested that the full spectrum of varieties along the Atlantic seaboard may have existed from the beginnings of African–European contact. Guyanese Creole texts from the beginning of the 19th century show that basilectal and mesolectal features were in use among the slave and free-coloured population at approximately the same time as more pidgin-like varieties attested in texts at the end of the eighteenth century. This suggests that decreolization does not necessarily entail the creation of mesolectal varieties but rather involves an increase in the adoption of already existing ones.

As Rickford (1986a) points out, the idea of monogenesis is implicit in these discussions, *ie* that the varieties between the basilect and acrolect are created at only one point in time. Under this scenario at some stage the first slaves or group of immigrants with sufficient opportunity and motivation to increase their competence from basilect towards the acrolect do so by creating an inter-language continuum. Once the continuum has been delimited in this way, other speakers at later points in time decreolize by adopting the available intermediate varieties in a relatively passive fashion rather than actively creating them anew. Rickford (1979:411–13) however, suggests a polygenetic view of decreolization in which the restructuring which produced the continuum in the past continues actively in the present. Speakers of the present generation are seen not merely as the passive recipients of intermediate varieties created by their predecessors but as the active reshapers and restructurers themselves. Evidence from research on second language acquisition (*cf* Ch. 6) indicates that Rickford's view is plausible. Native speakers learning a second language independently of each other and without exposure to pre-existing intermediate varieties used by other learners may nevertheless follow similar developmental stages in their acquisitional route. This is presumably due to universals which constrain the language learning process.

Markey's (1982:173) model of a developmental continuum tries to accommodate the synchronic and diachronic dimensions of the creole continuum by incorporating both a horizontal and a vertical axis, as shown in Figure 5.8. At any point along the horizontal continuum a vertical slice could be made and variation observed between and among speakers classed as basilectal, mesolectal or acrolectal (depending on where along the horizontal axis the slice was made).

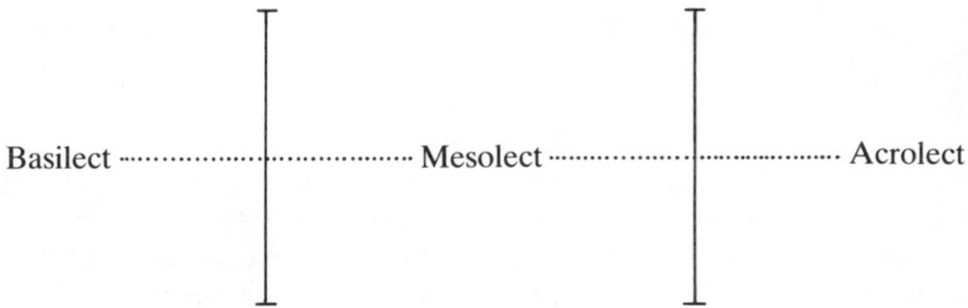

FIGURE 5.8 A model of a developmental continuum

The second diachronic question posed by Rickford (1986a) is whether linguistic variation in creole speech communities represents decreolization, *ie* movement away from creole norms and towards the norms of their lexically related standards. Markey's model, like the other continuum models we have looked at, assumes that overall movement in time is in the direction of the acrolect. This issue cannot of course be separated from the previous question of whether a uni-dimensional model can accommodate the facts of variability in creole communities. If change is assumed to be decreolization, then it is essentially seen as unilinear. Haynes, a Caribbean linguist, has reacted to this view by saying (1973:1) that the continuum is 'an abstract concept which places people in the Caribbean on their hillsides, rolling the stones of phonological, syntactic and lexical mastery to a European summit, getting there, but never quite'.

Hancock (1985, 1987) points out that decreolization has been used as a catch-all mechanism to explain varying approximations of creoles to each other, as well as to English (or other superstrates), as well as to explain variation in creoles. He observes (1987) that the term 'decreolization' is a questionable one since it implies the reversal of the same process as that which initially produced the creole, whereas progression toward the lexifier language is change that moves ahead, not backward.

It has become increasingly clear than not all changes in creole communities are in the direction of the acrolect; nor do all instances of variation result in true change over time. Escure (1983) found that Black Caribs in Belize seem to be aiming towards creole rather than standard English with respect to their use of certain features. The distribution of tense/aspect and the copula in the speech of urban and rural Creoles and Caribs indicates that the varieties used cannot be placed on a uni-directional axis of development converging towards English. There are linguistic targets other than Creole or English. Escure found that any mesolectal variety which excludes basilectal variants and a high frequency of acrolectal forms can constitute a desirable mode of expression in some situations and cannot be construed as an approximation to the acrolect. For Creole and Carib speakers the Belizean basilect constitutes the target language in most informal inter-ethnic and intra-ethnic encounters. Escure attributes this to the increasing prestige of the creole. Young Black Caribs become proficient in the creole at an early age and use it to achieve peer solidarity with young creoles (*cf* also Hewitt 1983 on white creole users in London).

The kind of data needed to assess this issue of the directionality of change must be drawn from longitudinal studies of communities, examination of textual evidence from earlier time periods, where available, and comparison of age distributions of features (*ie* age-grading, *cf* Labov 1966 on the distinction between change in real vs. apparent time).

Rickford (1986a), for example, offers some observations based on age distribution. He says he has encountered many cases of grandparents in Guyana controlling basilectal features which their grandchildren do not, but none in which the parents control upper mesolectal varieties while the children are restricted in terms of competence to the basilect. In some cases the younger generations are using more of the creole forms in casual speech. However, Rickford believes that this is a performance display. In terms of competence the repertoires of the younger people are broader and include more of the standard than do the repertoires of the older people. Escure (1983:8) underlines this point in saying that the younger generation's greater allegiance to creole does not imply that their ability to speak English is lesser. On the contrary, the lowest age group has the widest repertoire and the best control of all the varieties ranging over the continuum. This adds another dimension to decreolization; namely, repertoire extension rather than simple replacement.

Le Page's perspective on change is particularly valuable since he has longitudinal real-time data. He compares the language of informants he interviewed in childhood and eight to twelve years later. He found that some of the conservative Creole speakers appear to be using more standard English now that they are older and more upwardly mobile. In other areas however there had not been much change, *eg* among those who had settled down as agricultural workers. In Spanish areas, some are turning more towards creole (*cf* Le Page and Tabouret-Keller 1985).

Rickford's observations on the problems with the notion of the continuum and related analytical issues are not however exhaustive. Le Page has pointed to an even more fundamental problem with the continuum model; namely, the identity of the linguistic units to be analyzed. For example, McEntegart and LePage (1982:109) ask how one decides whether one end of a diglossic system or a linguistic continuum shares the same semantic distinctions as the other. To what extent can one say that Creole /wok/ and Standard English **work** are the 'same word' and that both are possible loci for looking at the incidence of postvocalic /r/? If the creole system is treated as separate, then there is no locus for the variable. If it is treated as part of a composite system, there may or may not be a locus depending on whether one regards the underlying system as that represented by the spelling or that represented by some external standard, *eg* r-less Received Pronunciation of Britain or r-ful Standard American English.

For instance, Akers (1981) in trying to account for the behaviour of consonant clusters in Jamaican Creole assumes that both English and creole share a rule of final consonant deletion. He postulates this as a single line of historical development involving successive generalizations of the class of permitted clusters. Clearly Akers is trying to maintain the idealization of the creole continuum by postulating a common grammar with one rule, but it is a rule which conflates data from speakers who delete consonants from underlying forms in which they are present and from those who insert them in forms where they are not present in the underlying structure. From a theoretical point of view we should require that inputs be the same before we assume rule sharing across lects with superficially identical outputs.

Furthermore, there are a number of problems with implicational scaling (*cf* Romaine 1982:177–82 for a more detailed treatment). The technique was introduced into linguistics from sociology. Guttman (1944), who developed the scale, suggests that in practice those which are 85 per cent or better in terms of their scalability can serve as efficient approximations to perfect scales. Some creolists, however, have put forward scales with much lower indices of scalability. This depends on what one counts as a deviation and to what extent the rows and columns (*ie* speakers' lects and linguistic features) are manipulated. For example, if empty cells (*ie* those for which there is no data) do not count as deviations, and full freedom is given to manipulate rows and columns, then virtually any set of data is scalable to an acceptable level, possibly as high as 90 per cent.

In Bickerton's data for Guyanese Creole empty cells very often do not count as deviations. If speakers who produce very little data are then moved up or down the scale, a high degree of scalability can be reached. To take a concrete illustration (discussed in more detail in Romaine 1982:177), in one case Bickerton offers a level of 95 per cent scalability for a scale showing copula distribution (Bickerton 1973:Table 2), but he has not counted empty cells. However, there are a total of 234 cells (*ie* 26 speakers and nine environments), and only 29 per cent of the cells are filled. What this means is that we are being asked to accept that scalability is as high as 95 per cent when we have no idea what happened to the copula in nearly three quarters of the cases where it could have occurred. The implicit assumption is that had more data been available they would have filled out the continuum in a predictable way. Bickerton (1975a:148) in fact admits that if strict implications are observed, then only 51.4 per cent of his data are scalable.

It is rarely made clear what the thresholds of significance are for any particular type of implicational scale; nor is it generally mentioned how the index of scalability is to be calculated. I have discussed three ways in which this seems to have been done, all of which have different results depending on sample size (Romaine 1982). Another uncertainty about implicational scales is that very often there is no indication of what numbers stand behind each filled cell about which a claim is made.

Since the claims one wants to make about the directionality of change will hinge on the ordering of speakers and environments, there should be some explicit constraints on how these may be manipulated. Otherwise, the device is far too powerful. A number of the explanations for particular orderings seem somewhat *ad hoc*. While it seems reasonable to suppose that a great many linguistic phenomena are governed by implicational relationships, the crucial question is what do implicational relationships imply (*cf* DeCamp 1973). In other words, what is their explanation?

Markey (1982:194–6), for instance, tries to explain what happens to the copula in decreolization by appealing to semantic factors. The reason why the continuative or progressive is the last environment to be affected by the introduction of the full English copula is that it is least accessible or most marked in terms of its semantic value. The nominal environments on the other hand are the least marked. These two extremes define the parameters of the system. Thus, there is a semantic implicational relationship between the environments in the scale such that progressive implies location and location implies existence, *ie* the values for features to the left impose on those to the right. Progression, for example, both implies and derives from location. In many languages there is a widespread parallel between progressive aspect and locative expressions referring to the place where something is located. Although the construction **working** in English does not show any formal affinity with locative expressions such as **to be at work**, it is clear that in some sense **to be at work** is equivalent to **to be working**. A dialectal variant of this shows its locative origins more clearly; namely, so-called **a**-prefixing as in Appalachian English described by Wolfram and Christian (1976): **he's been a-working all day** [where **a-working** = **at working**]. In other languages, in order to produce the equivalent of the English progressive locative forms are used. Bickerton, on the other hand, says simply that the V + ing environment is the last to give way to standard English because there is already a verb present. Therefore, the copula is unnecessary.

5.7 Recreolization

In Chapter 4 I mentioned the notion of repidginization as a possible stage in the life-cycle of a pidgin. I will now turn to a similar process in the life-cycle of a creole, namely, recreolization. Thanks to recent research by Edwards, Le Page and Sebba, we are in a position to give a reasonably detailed picture of this process as it is currently taking place in the speech of young black Britons who are descended from West Indian immigrants. The interface between varieties of British English in urban areas such as London and Birmingham with Caribbean Creoles such as Jamaican Creole is one of the more exciting linguistic developments taking place in Britain. It is giving rise to new varieties of language such as London Jamaican (*cf eg* Sebba 1984).

Research on these new varieties of language is still very much in the initial stages as it is only very recently that the languages of the different groups of people who came to Britain in the post-war period have begun to be studied (*cf eg The Linguistic Minorities Project* 1985). For some time observers have noted that many young black Britons who show no sign of creole usage in their early years start to 'talk Black' around the ages of 14–15. In fact, the *Select Committee on Race Relations and Immigration* (1976) records this observation and accounts for it as an assertion of identity:

> It is often pointed out to us that sometime during their early teens at secondary school many West Indian pupils who up till then have used the language of the neighbourhood, begin to use creole dialect . . . its use is a deliberate social and psychological protest, an assertion of identity.

It is this increase in the use of creole forms which some have called **recreolization** (*cf eg* Wright 1984:36). It is clear that in recreolizing black adolescents are not simply adopting the language of their parents. Adolescents whose parents or grandparents come from Caribbean islands other than Jamaica, such as St Kitts or Barbados, appear to be adopting forms which are typical of Jamaican creole rather than those of other Caribbean creoles. Le Page (1981), for example, observes that:

> The community which is emerging among London adolescents has a linguistic system, insofar as it can be detected by those who

> observe it, which is an abstraction from the originally diffuse behaviour of the children of immigrants from various parts of the Caribbean who now tend to identify with one another under the general name of **Jamaican**: but this diffuse system is being focused by close daily interaction in London schools and by the influence of the Rastafari movement.

The notions of **focusing** and **diffusion** used by Le Page in his characterization of the recreolization process are key concepts in his theory of language use, which I will return to below. An even more striking report of the convergence on Jamaican by British blacks can be found in Tate's (1984) study of a group of Rastafarians in Bradford, who are of Dominican French creole-speaking background. According to Tate, who is Jamaican, Jamaican creole is used as a language of in-group identity, and is spoken so authentically that these speakers could have passed for Jamaicans in Jamaica.

There was a rapid migration of British citizens from the New Commonwealth countries during the post-war period. Up until the 1950s the traditional destination for West Indians had been the United States, until immigration restrictions were imposed. Thereafter the United Kingdom became the obvious place for migration due to job opportunities and ease of access. Between 1955 and 1961 some 200,000 people arrived in Britain. The prospect of restrictions on immigration, eventually imposed in the 1960s, for a time accelerated the rate of migration. In 1971 the West Indian population in Britain was estimated at just over 1 per cent of the population, or 543,000 (*cf* Edwards 1986).

One effect of the imposition of more severe immigration controls was the emergence of distinctively British black as opposed to West Indian communities. The first children of post-war immigrants were born in Britain in the late 1950s. The proportion of British-born black children increased throughout the 1970s. Since 1970 virtually all children of West Indian immigrants have been born in Britain. Following Edwards (1986:20) and others, I will be using the term **British Black** to refer to these individuals. Edwards says that this label is a far more accurate description than the term **West Indian** because the experience of this generation who have grown up and been educated in Britain is very different from that of their Caribbean-born parents.[5] There are of course common values, traditions and experiences shared by both generations. Edwards (1986:10) also adopts the term **patois** for the language of British Blacks in accordance with the community's designation of it. What is of interest here is the issue of language transmission and what has happened to the

Caribbean creoles which were transplanted to the United Kingdom.

In the 1960s and 1970s a small number of studies were undertaken which investigated the influence of patois on the production and comprehension of black children. Edwards (1979) provides a good summary of the state of research and is the first systematic treatment of the linguistic and educational issues surrounding the use of language in the British Black community. Many of the early studies focused on the notion of interference in response to findings that West Indian children were seriously underachieving in school. The first official recognition that language might be playing a role in their poor performance is in the publication of the *Select Committee on Race Relations and Immigration* report on Education in 1973. It recommended that more attention be paid to the teaching of English (*cf* Edwards 1986:4). In the early 1980s, by contrast, it seems to have been taken for granted that the majority of children appear to be able to speak a form of English which is largely indistinguishable from that of their white peers. Two recent studies have, however, found varying degrees of influence on the language of British Black children. Lander (1979) found the written language of 10–12-year-olds to be further removed from standard English than that of children from Asian background. Wright (1984) found influence from Creole patterns of passivization on the comprehension and production of English passives by black male adolescents. She emphasizes (1984:43) the fact that black adolescents are rejecting standard English as a target language at the very time they require it most, in order to pass public examinations such as GCSE, and to enhance their job prospects.

The most recent treatment of some of these issues to appear at the time of writing is that of Gibson (1986), who maintains that language differences account for many of the problems West Indian pupils face at school. Gibson claims that the variety of English spoken by these pupils is a mixture of Creole and English and should be treated virtually as a foreign language.

I noted earlier in this chapter that it was the study of the Caribbean Creoles, in particular, Jamaican Creole, which led many researchers to the idea of a continuum model to account for the variation in speech patterns ranging from broad creole to standard English. Even though there are a number of problems with this model, it is clear from the work of DeCamp and Bickerton that an accurate picture of the Jamaican or Guyanese creole situation cannot be obtained by looking at the relative proportions of acrolectal vs. basilectal speech forms in the usage of an individual or a group of speakers. There are intermediate or mesolectal forms, which cannot be assigned to either pole of the continuum. In the British situation it is significant that support has emerged from at least three recent studies (Sutcliffe 1982; Sebba 1984; Edwards 1986) for the recognition of two separate but co-existent systems, English and patois. Sebba (1984) for example, refers to Afro–Caribbean London English and London Jamaican as two discrete varieties. Although individuals switch between them, their use is strongly polarized. Edwards (1986) and Sebba (1984) compare the situation to that of a bilingual community, such as the Puerto Rican community of New York City described by Poplack (1980), where code-switching between Spanish and English has become a style of speaking which serves as a marker of in-group identity.

Sutcliffe says (1982) that in spite of the existence of a phonological continuum linking the two varieties, at the morpho-syntactic level the varieties he calls British Black English and English are best treated as two separate systems. Edwards (1986:49), however, says that in Jamaica basilectal and acrolectal phonology differ in only a small number of areas. In Britain there are not only two distinct phonological systems, but distinct voice sets for the different varieties. Because the background features of speech such as pitch, tempo, loudness and timbre are quite different, Edwards says that there can seldom be any doubt as to whether a person is using patois or English on phonetic criteria. Local, Wells and Sebba's (1984) study of the use of prosodic markers for signalling turn-taking conventions adds further support. More work needs to be done to determine the extent to which accent plays a role in the distinctiveness of British Black English. In investigations carried out by Sebba (1984) it emerged that school pupils in an ethnically mixed class were considerably less accurate in identifying the race of pre-adolescent black speakers than adolescent ones. Sebba suggests that an identifiably 'black accent' may be first acquired in adolescence. This would be interesting to investigate further in relation to claims about the critical period hypothesis for language acquisition (*cf* 6.5).

In the data so far collected on British Black English then, it appears that intermediate forms are less common. The preferred patois forms are, according to Edwards, most often basilectal features. In the Caribbean context we would expect to find a whole range of alternative forms. Thus, in addition to basilectal **im a guo** and acrolectal **he's going**, we would also encounter intermediate forms like **im going** and **he going**.

Edwards (1986:48–9) accounts for the lack of a continuum in

terms of the differing socio-political conditions in Britain and the West Indies which have given rise to different outcomes. She points out that in the West Indies black people form the majority of the population, and despite a strong correlation between skin colour and social status, blacks are represented at all levels in the social hierarchy. With increasing opportunities for social mobility, larger number of speakers have gained access to standard English, and thus the necessary conditions for a continuum were created. In Britain, however, blacks are a minority, and for the most part belong to the working class, partly because they were expected to occupy low-status jobs and have been denied access to positions for which they were qualified by virtue of previous education or training. Thus, the conditions which would give rise to a continuum situation are largely absent in Britain. As we will see however, part of the reason has to do with the conscious choice of young people to focus their speech on what they perceive to the most basilectal or black or Jamaican, or in general on those features which are the most different from the speech of the white majority. It is this refocusing of norms in the direction of basilectal speech that I will call recreolization. I discussed in 5.6 some of the difficulties in assuming that the Jamaican situation was once polarized in this fashion, *ie* in the original stages of the formation of Jamaican Creole, and that under decreolization the continuum was filled. Recreolization in a sense recreates this gap.

Wright (1984:37–41) has illustrated this focusing on the basilect by comparing the performance styles of Malcolm, a British boy recorded by Sutcliffe (1982), and Tania, a Jamaican girl, whom she recorded in Kingston. An extract from each is given for comparison. Malcolm's story was told in two versions. The one given here illustrates that Sutcliffe's informants had notions of what constituted a basilectal or more Jamaican sounding utterance. Malcolm, after having told a story in a mesolectal variety, told Sutcliffe he could make it 'more Jamaican' (Sutcliffe 1982:37):[6]

Malcolm

Tri breda went a dakta, go a dakta . . . an di dakta tel dem se . . . wel wan a dem woz . . . dem a big ed, di ada wan a big beli an di ada wan a kenge fut. So dakta tel big ed se ef im shiek im hed im hed wi drap aaf . . . dakta tel big beli se him laaf him beli we bos, an im tel kenge fut se ef im ron, graastraa wi kot aaf im fut . . . so neks die big ed go klaim apl tri an en nyam di apl-dem an mm . . . big bel aas im fi . . . apl an big ed shiek im ed an se 'no' an im ed drap aaf . . . an big beli sit . . . stanop doun de a laaf an im bel bos, an kenge fut a ron go tel dakta an graastraa kotaaf im fut.

> Three brothers went to the doctor and the doctor told them that . . . well one of them was Big Head, the other one was Big Belly and the other was Kenge (puny) Legs. So the doctor told Big Head that if he shook his head his head would fall off, and he told Big Belly that if he laughed, his belly would burst, and he told Kenge Legs that if he ran the grass would cut his legs off. So the next day Big Head went and climbed an apple tree and ate the apples and Big Belly asked him for an apple. Big Head shook his head and said 'no' and his head fell off. And Big Belly stood down there laughing and his belly burst. And Kenge Legs was running to tell the doctor and the grass cut his legs off.

> Tania
> **Wantaim Anansi di wie im did so liezi im neva waan fi guo fi im puos leta. So Sniek waz paasim bai an im se Mista Sniek yu kyan du mi a fieva?**
> **Mista Sniek se wot is it?**
> **Yu kyan gib mi a fieva laik am now laik ow yu is a man that laik blod.**
> **Yes.**
> **Now man yu kyan go fi mi puos fi mi?**
> **Wot are yuu peying me enithing?**
> **Yessa mi a guo pie yu som blod.**
> **Blud ah ha wen wil ai get this blud?**
> **Wel wen yu gib mi mi puos in di diez wen mi sliipin in di nait yu kyan kom mi wi liiv di dour open Yu kyan kom bait mi an mi hed okie?**
> **Arait so the tuu frenz agriid.**
> **Lieta dat nait Anansi left di duor open.**
> **Sniek keim in an bit im an im hed . . .**

> Once upon a time Anansi was so lazy that he didn't want to go to collect his mail. So, Snake was passing by and Anansi said, 'Mr Snake, can you do me a favour?' Mr Snake said, 'What is it?' 'You can do me a favour, like you are a man who likes blood.' 'Yes.' 'Now, man you can go for my mail for me.' 'What, are you going to pay me anything?' 'Yes, sir, I'm going to pay you some blood.' 'Blood. Ah ha! When will I get this blood?' 'Well, days when you give me my mail, when I'm sleeping at night you can come. I'll leave the door open. You can come and bite me on the head, o.k.?' Alright, so the two friends agreed. Later that night Anansi left the door open. Snake came in and bit him on his head . . .

Tania's Anansi story shows a greater range of forms than Malcolm's story. Wright points out that Tania portrays Anansi's changes of mood by varying the speed and volume of delivery. She differentiates the two characters in the story by opting for basilectal forms to represent Anansi's dialogue and more acrolectal speech for the snake. In comparing the two performances

Wright says that while Malcolm focuses on the basilect, Tania's narrative is more diffuse. It draws on a wide range of lects for dramatic effect. Anansi's predominantly basilectal speech and Snake's acrolectal style are linked by the forms used by Tania as the narrator, which are mainly mesolectal.

Wright also showed the two narratives to Jamaican-born informants in England and Jamaica. She reports (1984:81) that the consensus of opinion about Tania's narrative is that the range of lects displayed in the narrative is typical of the Jamaican speech community. By comparison, however, many people said that Malcolm's speech would be unusual for a Jamaican because it lacked the usual mixing of forms. Malcolm 'corrects' himself when he uses the Standard English verbs **went** and **was**, and substitutes the Jamaican creole forms **go** and **a** respectively. They felt that the use of Jamaican Creole features in Malcolm's speech was stereotypical and not 'real Jamaican'. On the whole, they viewed it negatively. As characterized by Wright, the target language of recreolization is an abstraction of Jamaican Creole. It focuses on those features which are most distinct from standard English. A similar situation appears to be in the making in urban areas of South Africa, where the enforced move of many traditional black urban dwellers into black ghetto townships like Soweto has resulted in a shift away from Afrikaans in the direction of local Bantu languages. Janson (1983) reports that this new language, called Taal or Tsotsi Taal is popular because it is not understandable to white Afrikaaners.

Edwards (1986:36) says that there is considerable confusion over who uses patois in what situations. Her study of 45 young black people born in Britian of Jamaican parents between the ages of 16 and 23 in Dudley, West Midlands aimed at investigating the frequency of patois usage, competence in patois and patterns of language choice. I will now look in more detail at some of her findings.

She identified a number of social factors which influenced speakers' choice of patois vs. English in a range of situations. Among these were sex, social network relations, educational achievements and aspirations and their attitudes towards mainstream white society. Speakers were recorded in five situations which differed in terms of their formality and the ethnicity of the speakers involved in the conversation. Table 5.1 (from Edwards 1986:Table 10) shows the patterns of language choice which obtained in these situations. Situation 1 consisted of a formal interview between a black speaker and a white interviewer. Situation 2 was similar in formality, except that the interviewer and the speaker were black. In Situation 3 there was informal conversation between black and white interlocutors. In Situation 4 black peers conversed among themselves. Situation 5 consisted of an informal conversation between black speakers and the interviewer.

TABLE 5.1 Patterns of language use for young black speakers in Dudley

		Situations				
No. speakers		1	3	2	5	4
Pattern 1	5	English	English	English	English	Patois
Pattern 2	14	English	English	English	Patois	Patois
Pattern 3	13	English	English	Patois	Patois	Patois
Pattern 4	4	English	Patois	Patois	Patois	Patois
Pattern 5	6	Patois	Patois	Patois	Patois	Patois

It can be seen that the five patterns which Edwards found are ordered in an implicational hierarchy according to the extent to which the speaker uses patois vs. English. The situation in which black peers conversed (4) constituted a domain for patois usage for all the speakers. By contrast there was no one situation uniquely reserved for the use of English by all speakers, although the majority of the speakers use it in Situation 1. A situation marked for patois usage is one in which there is code-switching between patois and English rather than one in which exclusively patois variants are used.

Edwards (1986:115–16) established correlations between patterns of language choice and other social characteristics of the speakers in the case of Patterns 1, 4 and 5. Pattern 1 speakers are likely to have a limited competence in patois and overall use patois features infrequently. They are also likely to be female, to perform well in school, and have high educational aspirations. Pattern 4 and 5 speakers are likely to be competent and frequent patois users. They are also likely to be male and educational underachievers. Edwards found at least one important attitudinal factor which distinguished Pattern 4 and 5 speakers. Pattern 5 speakers had a more negative attitude towards mainstream white society. Thus, the greater the degree of criticalness of the speaker to white society, the more likely he is to be a frequent user of patois. Others had of course linked the use of talking black with black youth culture, Rastafarianism, reggae, etc., as indicated earlier. Patois is used as a symbol of black identity and defiance in opposition to mainstream society which stigmatizes blackness. Particularly when used in formal situations it constitutes what Halliday (1978:164) has called an 'anti-language'. 'Talking Jamaican' is one aspect of an alternative strategy to survival developed by a threatened group, *eg* hustling rather than 'Uncle Tomming', because they are denied access to the mainstream system.

The correlation between age and language choice is salient, given what we now know from a variety of sociolinguistic studies about the ways in which peer groups can exert powerful pressures to conform with group norms which are often at odds with those expressed by family and school (*cf eg* the discussion in Romaine 1984a:6.3). Contrary to what many believed earlier, we know now too that children do not simply acquire language by internalizing and reconstructing the input they receive from their parents (*cf* Halle 1962 for discussion of this model). Labov (1972b), for example, found that the parents of the Black boys he studied disapproved of their choice of friends and membership in clubs and street gangs. The social organization of groups such as the Jets and Thunderbirds is a tightly knit one, which has persisted for years with extraordinary stability. Grammar is just one of the elements of the social pattern which was transmitted. The group's influence extended to school-related areas such as level of acceptable academic achievement and reading ability. Labov found a regular relationship between peer group membership and status within the group and reading failure. When he compared the levels of reading ability for group and non-group members, he found that on the whole, group members had lower scores. The majority were three to four years below the level expected for their age.

Labov however emphasized the fact that the lower scores of the members do not reflect a deficiency in verbal skills, as had been argued by some educators. Edwards (1979) documents the same line of argumentation in the British context with reference to black pupils. The boys who fail in reading are the same ones who gain their prestige and status in the group by displaying their skill in telling narratives and other verbal genres. Some of the competitive speech events engaged in by the boys have analogues throughout the pan-Afro–Caribbean community (*cf eg* Kochman 1972; Abrahams 1972). Neither does Labov believe that the depressed reading scores are indicative of structural interference between Black English Vernacular and the standard English of the school. Labov's explanation is that the school and peer group embody conflicting sets of values and ideology. What makes one successful in school; *eg* reading well, is irrelevant to prestige within the group. The focal concerns of the peer group are toughness, smartness, trouble, excitement, etc. Those who were more integrated into the peer group and street culture rejected the ethos of the school and the values of white middle-class society. Other black students who were outside the street culture (either because they reject it or are rejected by it) accept the norms of the school, but at the expense of becoming 'lames'. Labov uses the term **lame** to describe a boy who does not know the rules for participating in street culture. The lames not only did better in school (as measured in terms of the school's criteria) but did not show the same degree of use of the linguistic features of BEV, *eg* copula deletion. Labov (1972b:255) concludes that the 'consistency of certain grammatical rules is a finely grained index of membership in the street culture and that patterns of social interaction may influence grammar in subtle and unsuspected ways'.

Edwards too found that it was those who were most closely integrated into the black community, as measured by factors such as residence, socialization patterns at work and in leisure, who were the heaviest and most competent users of patois. Since males on the whole had higher network scores, *ie* were more closely linked to the black community, than females, they were more frequent users of patois. Edwards (1986:86) cites a number of examples which indicate the strong pressure some speakers exerted on others to use patois in certain situations. She gives the following example from an interaction between Don and Tommy, who are two of the heaviest patois users (*ie* Pattern 5) in Situation 1, where they are interacting with a white interviewer. When Tommy is being interviewed, Don says: 'You watch how he talk English, how he sound daft. Im sound daft, you know.' Don replies: 'Hear di difference dough when me talking, hear di difference now. A true blackman dis, you know. True blackman, dis . . . You should coulda talk as nice as me dough.' At a later stage in the interview when Don uses the English word **hit** instead of patois **lick** Tommy corrects him:

Don: Unless hard time hit him.
Tommy: Talk patois, man, you sound daft. 'Unless hard time hit him.'
Don: Di man can't understand we – he can't understand we.

Speakers who don't use patois when expected are subject to ridicule or accusations of snobbery, as is evident from Julie's remark (Edwards 1986:98): 'When my friend – dem say – my coloured friends that used to talk to me – "Wa happen to you, you can't speak Patois?" I said, "Yeah, I know." Especially the black boys down our road when they say, "You alright, sis?" Me say, "Oh, I'm fine" . . . "Wa happen to you? You can't talk Patois. Wa happen? You tink you a white?"' Although she is a competent patois speaker, she downplays her abilities in certain situations.

At the other end of the range Edwards found speakers like Darleen, who only uses patois when with her friends; even then most of her speech is unambiguously English. Her social network includes both blacks and whites. She lives on a council estate where there are many white people. In commenting on her own language use Darleen seems to align herself with the expectations of the white community. She says (Edwards 1986:92): 'Tell the truth, we'm [Black country dialect form SR] very up on our English. We talk slang sometime in patois. If I was in Jamaica now I'd be brought up to talk like that, but it's a white community.'

Edwards adds considerable refinement to Labov's idea that certain grammatical rules or features can be finely grained indices of patterns of social interaction in her establishment of a hierarchy of patois features. Edwards (1986:103, Figure 7) found that the features she looked at clustered into five groups, as shown in Figure 5.9.

Group 1 dentals /o/ uninflected 3rd p.sg/ pl./ simple past **mi**
Group 2 **im dem do** + neg adjectival verbs continuatives
Group 3 focus questions infinitives patois pronouns
Group 4 locating verb plural **dem** psychic state transitives
Group 5 equating verb past markers

FIGURE 5.9 Acquisitional hierarchy of patois features

The implicational relationship which holds here is such that the presence of the features in Group 5 implies the presence of those in Group 4 etc. We have already seen examples of some of these features, *eg* the uninflected forms for the third person singular, past tense and plural. The patois plural uses **dem**. The patois pronouns, unmarked for either case or gender, **mi** – 'I, me, my', **im** – 'he, him, his, she, her', and **dem** – 'they, them, their' occurred often. Other pronouns such as **unu** – 'you/your (plural)' are characteristic of speakers who also know a range of other patois forms.

There were two phonological features, one consonantal and one vocalic. We have already seen the use of stops instead of dental fricatives in Jamaican Creole in words like **then** and **thin**. The feature /o/ refers to the use of a Jamaican rather than West Midlands English vowel in certain contexts (*cf* Edwards 1986:137–8). The feature **do** + neg refers to the use of the auxiliary **do** in the negation of positive sentences, such as **she doesn't go back home tomorrow**. In patois the forms **no** and **naa** (**no** + progressive **a**) are used: **Dem no have di answer** – 'They don't have the answer', and **im naa guo a yaad** – 'He isn't going home' (compare the positive form with the continuative marker **im a guo a yaad** – 'He's going home'). Edwards (1986:144) says that it is possible that the patois preference for **no** and **naa** reflects an overgeneralization of basilectal Jamaican Creole negation patterns (*cf eg* Bailey 1966).

The feature adjectival verb refers to the use of what would be adjectival forms in standard English as verbs, as discussed in 2.9, *eg* **John ready** – 'John is ready'. Cases such as these have tended to be treated in the literature as instances of copula deletion (*cf* 5.4), but a more appropriate analysis would seem to be one which recognizes them as a subcategory of stative verb (*cf eg* Edwards 1986:145 and the discussion in Wright 1984:48–58; 65–9).[7] Before nominals there is an equating verb **a**, as in **Di first one a me woman** – 'The first one is my woman'. There is a locative verb **deh** which is followed by a locative complement, *eg* **When me deh at school, di whole a dem hate me** – 'When I was at school, they all hated me'. The equating and locative verb are found only in the speech of a small number of speakers (Edwards 1986:145).

Focus in patois is indicated by moving the focused element to sentence initial position and adjoining **a**, *eg* **a di bwai Mieri hit** – 'It was the boy that Mary hit'. In standard English focus can be marked by cleft constructions, as in the translation of the previous patois form, and by stress and intonation. I have already shown in 2.9 that in pidgins and creoles questions are usually marked by intonation, and there is a lack of inversion. Compare the following patois forms: **Di man see im sister?** – 'Did the man see his/her sister?' and **Who di man see?** – 'Whom did the man see?' In patois infinitives are preceded by **fi**, as in **Mi no know where fi put dis one** – 'I don't know where to put this one' (Edwards 1986:144).

Finally, there is the feature referred to as psychic state transitive verbs. This involves the use of **seh** to introduce a clause which functions as the object of verbs like **hear**, **feel**, **mean**,

know, **believe**, which refer to the psychic state of the subject, *eg* **You feel seh you can chat patois like me**? – 'Do you think you can talk patois like me?' Cassidy (1961) traces the origin of **seh** to West African languages such as Akan, in which the verb 'say' follows a verb of telling or commanding and acts as a complementizer (*cf* also Cassidy and Le Page 1967:396 and the discussion in 4.5). Sebba (1984) also reports the use of **seh** as a feature of London Jamaican as well as Afro–Caribbean London English. He notes, however, that it has a different set of semantic and syntactic restrictions from those which apply to the English complementizer **that**. Unlike Edwards, who locates it at a relatively late stage of the acquisitional hierarchy of patois features (namely, Block 4), Sebba found the use of **seh** widespread among black speakers in London, even in conversation with white speakers.

Edwards (1986:95) concludes from her study that any assessment of speakers' competence in patois must be based on a measure of how large a proportion of the phonology and grammar an individual commands rather than how frequently he uses patois forms. Failure to use patois forms may indicate simply lack of opportunity to do so, and/or choice not to rather than inability. The degree of integration into black peer networks appears to be the most crucial factor affecting competence. In the case of the observations noted earlier to the effect that children who previously showed no signs of patois usage in their early years suddenly start using patois forms in adolescence, it may be that children have a working knowledge of patois which they do not use, or that they acquire it later through contact with other speakers. Edwards (1986:100) found that just over a third of the speakers were very fluent and used the full range of patois features. This group has a clear notion of what constitutes basilectal patois. Edwards (1986:132) observes that roughly the same percentage of her sample could be described as patois speakers if the baseline for comparison were the full range of Jamaican Creole forms. However, if patois is defined so as to include speakers who use a narrower range of features to mark certain situations as patois, then all of the young people could be described as patois speakers. Edwards prefers the latter conclusion, largely on the basis of the correlations she found between the use of certain features in the five situations we looked at earlier. Sebba too notes that speakers who would not be regarded as fluent by the usual linguistic criteria are nevertheless regarded by others as Jamaican speakers through their use of a few features. For these speakers however, Sebba suggests that London Jamaican is not a separate system, but is parasitic on the structures of London English with a few London Jamaican features added.

Edwards (1986:110) found that a small set of features (*ie* dentals, /o/, third-person singular verbs and plurals) appear to function as indicators for the Dudley speakers. The term **indicator** is used by sociolinguists such as Labov (1966) to refer to linguistic variables whose use differs from social group to social group but remains largely stable from one situation to another. In other words, they show little variation in response to situational or stylistic constraints. They occur even in the most formal styles of a large number of speakers. Other patois features however served as markers, *eg* **do** + neg, copula, adjectives, first-person singular pronoun, third-person singular and plural pronoun and infinitives. Markers are variables which show sharp stratification with respect to both social groups and styles. Edwards found that these features tended not to be used in situations which included a white participant, except by speakers who consistently used high proportions of patois forms throughout all five situations. She says (1986:111) that the use of this set of features represents a conscious marking of patois and functions as a means of asserting ethnic identity and solidarity. However, different ranges of patois features can serve the same marking function for different speakers.

Sebba (1984) also found that certain features were used by London speakers to evoke a London Jamaican stereotype. On the whole, however, Sebba believes that the norms for London Jamaican are more like those for London English than Jamaican Creole, even for the most fluent speakers. London Jamaican, unlike Jamaican Creole, has some inflectional morphology. It is also more complex with regard to the number of options which exist at various points in the system, due to contact with London English. Sebba, for example, discusses the restructuring of the pronoun system in London Jamaican. A female referent may be referred to as **im** (the classical Jamaican form) or **shi**. The latter is not unknown in the Caribbean, but its use in London Jamaican probably derives from English influence. The use of the form **shi** paves the way for a gender distinction to enter the London Jamaican pronoun system, where Jamaican Creole has none.

Much more research needs to be done to elaborate the details of this recreolization process. Of particular interest is the extent to which there are distinct regional varieties, *eg* Birmingham vs. London Jamaican, which are the result of contact between regional varieties of English and creole. Does Birmingham

Jamaican, for example, use **her**, instead of **shi** as a pronominal form in line with local West Midlands usage? There is also the question of the process of transmission and acquisition, and the extent to which West Indian influence, particularly in the form of Jamaican input, is being renewed in each generation of British Black speakers.

Le Page and Tabouret-Keller (1985) account for the kinds of processes I have been describing here under the heading of recreolization as a refocusing of linguistic norms. Although it was originally the study of linguistic behavior in creole speech communites which led Le Page (1978) to formulate the notions of projection, focusing and diffusion, they are part of a more general theory of language, which treats linguistic behaviour as a series of acts of identity in which people reveal both their personal identity and their search for social roles through the linguistic choices they make. Le Page and Tabouret Keller (1985:14–5) make the link between creole and other communities in saying that:

> We do not see evolutionary linguistic processes taking place within such [creole SR] communities as being describable in terms of a linear progression from a broad dialect towards a model language, nor even from one dialect towards another; but rather as the evolution of newly focused norms with each group of each generation and within each political entity according to their needs for various identities. Moreover, we see these processes not as peculiar to new communities, though more easily observable there, but as the common processes through which mankind has evolved its languages and its sense of linguistic identity.

With regard to the emergence of London Jamaican, Le Page and Tabouret-Keller (1985:180) write that it is more a set of norms to be aimed at than an internally coherent and consistent system. Speakers behave as if there were a language called 'Jamaican', but often all they do or perhaps know how to do is make a few gestures in the direction of certain tokens associated with Jamaican Creole which have a stereotypical value.

More generally, Le Page (1978) views each speech act as a projection of the speaker's identity. Speakers bring into play the variable linguistic resources available to them in a community as a means of identifying with certain groups, subject to certain constraints: (i) the speaker must be able to identify the groups; (ii) he must have both adequate access to the groups and the ability to analyse their behavioural patterns; (iii) he must have a sufficiently powerful motivation to join the groups; this will be reinforced or reversed by feedback from the groups; (iv) he must have the ability to modify his behaviour. To the extent that a speaker receives reinforcement, his behaviour may become more focused. Among tightly-knit, focused communities there may be considerable sharing and regularity of rules. Other speakers whose networks and patterns of interaction are more open and broadly-based, *eg* the lames in Labov's study, are in Le Page's terms, more diffuse in their language behaviour. The continuing process of realignment of linguistic norms is an on-going source of change in individual and community ways of speaking. When codes and variables lose their symbolic function as markers of various social identities, the way for linguistic change is paved.

Notes:

1. Bailey (1966:46) treats **a** in Jamaican creole as the equivalent of **be + ing**. It may also be realized as **de**, a locative verb, *eg* **hi en de a wok man** – 'He hasn't been at work, man'. (Bickerton 1972:33). This **a** is cognate with **da, de** in some other creoles (*cf* Bickerton 1972:*n*9, who suggests that **a**, **da**, **de** may all have a common pidgin ancestry in a form which combined the meanings of continuative and location).
2. A similar case of divergence from standard English has been observed by Milroy (1980) among white urban working-class communities in Belfast. There the existence of dense networks has fostered the maintenance of vernacular speech.
3. It is believed that the Surinam creoles such as Sranan and Saramaccan represent an earlier stage of Guyanese creole.
4. A number of sociolinguists have recognized the limitations of unidimensional models of variation without reference to data from creole communities, *cf eg* the notion of variety space and multidimensional modelling used in the Tyneside Linguistic Survey of Pellowe *et al.* (1972).
5. It is interesting that the label West Indian has emerged in the British context. Edwards (1986:52) quotes the novelist Salkey as saying that 'The blanket term West Indian doesn't exist in the West Indies; it does in London, has to for protection's sake'.
6. The transcription system employed here is that of Cassidy and Le Page (1967).
7. Corne (1981) cites evidence from Isle de France Creole to support the underlying unity of verbs and adjectives. They share five features in common: (i) they undergo the same vowel deletion rule; (ii) they share the same interpretation in progressive constructions, *ie* durative for non-statives and inchoative for statives; (iii) they have the same pattern of distribution and interpretation after the completive marker **fin**; (iv) they undergo the same passive vs. active alternation rules; and (v) they have the same distribution after the inchoative marker **gaȳ**.

Chapter 6

Language acquisition and the study of pidgins and creoles

It has been claimed that pidgins and/or creoles share a number of features in common with first and second language acquisition. The comparisons which have been made relate both to similarities in particular linguistic structures found in child and pidgin/creole grammars, and to similarities in process, *eg* developmental stages which characterize acquisitional phases or strategies which learners apply to construct rules and grammars. Perhaps one of the most explicit parallels at the process level is Bickerton's claim (1977a:49, 54–5):

> Existing theories about the process of pidginization have either all implied or directly stated that it is a process somehow distinct from other processes of language acquisition, whether these involve a first or second language. Theories of creolization, while much fewer and vaguer, have similarly suggested something unique about the process . . . However, . . . there is nothing at all mysterious or unique about either process: that pidginization is second language learning with restricted input and creolization is first language learning with restricted input.

If one takes a broad view of acquisition, it is not difficult to see why it is attractive to compare child language, pidgins and creoles and second language acquisition. One could argue simply that in so far as all cases of language acquisition have to do with changes in developing systems in real time, there must be some similarities. And the parallelisms have, not surprisingly, been extended to include historical change too (*cf eg* Slobin 1977 and Givón 1979a). The crucial question, however, is what the significance of such similarities is – and, indeed, whether the differences outweigh the similarities. Again, it is perhaps Bickerton (1981a), who has made the strongest claims in arguing that there seems to be only one way of building a language. In child language acquisition and creolization (but not in pidginization), we see innate language universals at work. This hypothesis is examined more carefully in Chapter 7.

Nevertheless, there are many problems which arise in making sweeping comparisons (for discussion see Aitchison 1983a:57). Perhaps the most serious one is how to define the phenomena which are being compared. I have said in Chapter 1 *et passim* that the terms **pidgin** and **creole** and **pidginization** and **creolization** are used to refer to a disparate range of entities and processes. I noted that one special difficulty lay in identifying a set of formal structural characteristics which are uniquely associated with either a pidgin or creole. In particular, given the fact that creolization can take place at various stages in the life-cycle of a pidgin (*cf* Ch 5), there is bound to be some overlap in the structural characteristics of an incipient creole and an expanded pidgin.

Apart from these problems in defining the relevant entities to be compared, there is the additional issue as to whether pidgins and creoles should be compared to second and first language acquisition respectively. As Aitchison (1983a:7) points out, this depends on the status of the claim that there is a 'critical period' for acquiring language – a claim which is open to question (*cf* Krashen 1973–4). Briefly, the critical hypothesis states that the ability to learn language atrophies before adulthood. I will examine it more carefully in 6.5.

In this chapter I will discuss some of the parallels between the processes of first and second language acquisition and pidginization and creolization. I will look first at the field of second language acquisition, where there has been a debate between the role of universals vs. transfer in the development of learner varieties. In later sections of this chapter I will give a more detailed comparison of the similarities and differences between first and second language acquisition and pidgins and creoles in one area of grammar, namely, relativization.

The relative clause is an interesting construction to choose in order to see whether there are parallels between first and second language acquisition and pidginization and creolization. There are at least two reasons why this is so. Firstly, relative clauses have received extensive discussion in the psycholinguistic and child development literature. Secondly, the finding that relative clauses develop in the later stages of acquisition is paralleled by the finding that they are generally lacking in pidgins. They are also comparatively late diachronic developments in the history of some languages. Claims about relativization also figure in Bickerton's creole prototype, as seen in 2.9.

6.1 Transfer vs. universals

From the increasing body of literature on second language acquisition it is possible to cite a number of studies which support the view that learning is constrained by universal principles. That is, there is a tendency for interlanguage development to proceed along lines that are common to all language learners, regardless of native language background. However, there is also evidence in support of what has been called transfer theory; that is, the tendency for interlanguage to be shaped by features of the learner's first language. I will consider some of the evidence from second language acquisition in relation to the role of universals vs. substratum in the processes of pidginization and creolization.

Before I look at specific studies, I will discuss some of the basic concepts which have emerged in the context of the study of transfer and interlanguage. Up until the late 1960s and early 1970s the prevailing account of the process of second language acquisition relied on the notion of **transfer** and **contrastive analysis**. It was assumed that most of the difficulties facing the learner of a second language were the result of interference from his native language. Where there were differences between the L1 and L2, the learner's knowledge would interfere with the L2. Where the L1 and L2 were similar, knowledge of L1 would aid L2 learning. This is the essence of the notion of transfer. The concept was originally formulated within the context of behaviourist psychology, which treated learning as a result of habit formation by reinforcement. Where there are similarities, transfer is positive; where there are differences, transfer is negative. Errors will result from negative but not positive transfer. For example, the use of the Spanish plural markers **-s** and **-es** on English nouns should yield a correct English noun, *eg* **girls** and **dresses**, if positive transfer takes place.

Contrastive analysis was developed as a means of comparing two languages in order to pinpoint the areas of difference and similarity. Such analyses in conjunction with so-called error analysis (*ie* an analysis of the actual errors produced by particular learners) were then used to predict and/or account for the problems and errors likely to result in the learning of a particular language by a learner with a given language background (*cf* James 1980 for a survey of the field). Essentially transfer theory predicts that learners with different L1 backgrounds will learn a second language in different ways due to the differing effects of positive and negative transfer. In this view the process of learning a second language consists in replacing the features of L1 that interfere with the acquisition of those of L2, and thus approximating the structures of the L2.

In the early 1970s these ideas were questioned as evidence accumulated which indicated that L2 errors were not the result of L1 interference and contrastive analysis was not a good predictor of learner errors. It was found, for example, that learners may not always transfer L1 rules, but avoid using rules in L2 which are not matched by corresponding ones in their own language (*cf eg* Schachter 1974). Dulay and Burt's (1974) research, in which four types of errors were identified, was a serious challenge to contrastive analysis:

(i) interference-like errors, which reflect native language structures and are not found in first language acquisition data,
(ii) first language developmental errors, which do not reflect native language structures but are found in the speech of first language learners,
(iii) ambiguous errors, which cannot be classified as interference or developmental errors,
(iv) unique errors, which do not reflect either first language structure and are not found in the first language acquisition data.

In a study of the frequency of these error types in the speech of Spanish children learning English, Dulay and Burt (1973) found that after eliminating ambiguous errors, 85 per cent were developmental, and only 3 per cent were due to interference. Although other studies have not replicated such a high proportion of developmental errors, there is now a great deal of research to support the idea that L1 interference is not the prime cause of learner errors. Part of the problem in interpreting the results lies in the difficulty of distinguishing interference from developmental errors. The presence of the same error in the speech of learners with a variety of first language backgrounds cannot be taken as proof that an error is developmental because all the languages may contrast with the target language with respect to a particular structure.

In a study of Spanish learners' acquisition of English Cazden *et al.* (1975) found that the same developmental route was followed by all learners. The first negatives consisted of **no** + V, *eg* **I no go** instead of **I am not going**. This could be explained as an error resulting from L1 transfer since Spanish has an identical pattern. However, **no** + V structures can be found in the speech of both native English speaking children in the early stages and second language learners of English whose first language does not have this pattern. Cazden *et al.* found that the **no** + V pattern remained longer in the speech of the Spanish learners than in that of learners who did not have this pattern in their native language. This seems to be an example of an error which is 'doubly determined' by factors such as naturalness and L1 interference (*cf* Hatch 1983).

The field of second language acquisition gained renewed impetus from the increasing attention being given to first language acquisition in the 1960s. Studies by Brown (1973) and others showed that children learning English as their first language followed a highly predictable sequence of stages in the acquisition of structures such as negatives and interrogatives, and of grammatical morphemes, such as plural, past tense, possessive and progressive marking, etc.

Once the role of interference was downplayed as the major source of learner errors, it seemed reasonable to hypothesize that both first and second language development followed predictable routes. Second language acquisition, like first language acquisition, followed a 'natural sequence of development', and all learners acquired the grammar of L2 in a fixed order regardless of their L1 background. In connection with research into the question of whether there was a universal order to second language acquisition, a related issue emerged, namely, the so-called **L1=L2 hypothesis**. This refers to the idea that the processes of first and second language acquisition are the same, or are characterized by the same sequence of development. The latter is a consequence of the fact that learners employ a common set of strategies which are part of the human language faculty.

Longitudinal studies of the acquisition of negatives, interrogative and relative clauses provided strong evidence for a natural or universal route of second language development, as well as for the L1=L2 hypothesis. A number of researchers have compared the order of acquisition in first and second language acquisition with mixed results. Cazden's (1972) findings on the order of development of interrogatives in first language development are very similar to those found in second language acquisition. She lists the following stages:

(i) one word utterances used as questions
(ii) intonation is used to mark questions, and some WH-questions are learned as ready-made chunks
(iii) productive WH-questions without inversion occur

(iv) inversion occurs in yes/no, but not WH-questions
(v) inversion occurs in WH-questions
(vi) embedded WH-questions emerge

There is, however, another aspect to claims about the ordering of morphemes and structures in first and second language acquisition, which is based on frequency of input. Larsen-Freeman (1976) and others have found that the frequency of occurrence of particular morphemes in native speaker speech is the principle determinant of the production order of second language learners. The question of input is a crucial one in both second language acquisition and pidginization and creolization.

Universalist claims for a fixed order of development are based on a very different idea about how learning takes place, in which emphasis is placed on factors internal to the learner. This view is often referred to as mentalism to contrast it with behaviourism (though this is an oversimplistic dichotomy), and is associated with Chomsky's ideas about universal grammar. Chomsky postulates the existence of a **Language Acquisition Device** (LAD), a human-specific and independent faculty of the mind, which determines the unfolding of innate language capabilities. This consists of a set of principles of syntactic organization, so-called **universal grammar**, which determine language acquisition. Chomsky (1980) has more recently compared the growth of the language faculty in the human mind to the growth of a physical organ in the body. In order for the LAD to work, the learner requires access to primary linguistic data, or input which triggers acquisition. Acquisition proceeds by means of a kind of hypothesis testing in which the child matches the principles of his universal grammar against the structures of the language he is acquiring. This view of acquisition is very different from the behaviourist one in which learning is seen as imitation and reinforcement. Child language researchers emphasized that the kinds of utterances produced by children were unique, and therefore were not imitations of adult models (*cf* 3.1).

6.2 Interlanguage

Second language researchers such as Selinker argued that adults also make use of the language acquisition device in acquiring a second language. It was also Selinker (1972) who introduced the notion of **interlanguage**. This concept refers to the structured system which the language learner constructs at any given stage in his development. This system is assumed to be independent of L1 and L2, and each system is part of a series of approximative systems which forms an **interlanguage continuum**. We can see of course in this idea the analogy with a creole continuum (*cf* 5.3). Corder (1967) invoked the notion of hypothesis testing to explain how the L2 learner progressed along the continuum, in much the same way as the child acquired the adult system of his native language by progressing through a series of interim developmental stages in the acquisition of rules and structures. Corder argued that the L1 and L2 learner used some of the same strategies. In particular, both made errors, which Corder took to be evidence of processing. Corder (1975) also interpreted interference as a learner strategy. When learners experienced difficulty, they may resort to their native language.

This accounts for the finding that transfer seems to be more in evidence in the earlier rather than later stages of acquisition when a learner has more target language resources to rely on. I noted earlier that substratum influence was more likely in the earliest stages of pidgin formation rather than in later stages of development (*cf* 3.5, 4.4 and also 7.5). There is also evidence from Meisel (1983a:30*ff*) to indicate that there are some general principles involved in what can be transferrred in second language acquisition. He found that bound morphology is never transferred. Syntactic transfer is likely to occur in areas where syntax and semantics are interwoven, *eg* in cases where the relative ordering of a category and its modifier, such as adjective-noun sequences, are involved. Omission of normally obligatory elements such as articles cannot be explained solely by transfer. Interference was one of five processes which Selinker claimed were operative in interlanguage development. Not all learners acquire proficiency in the target language. They stop learning at a stage when their interlanguage still contains some rules which are different from those of the target. Selinker refers to this as **fossilization**. I will be looking later at some explanations for the fact that second language learning is less successful than first.

My overview of some of the key issues and concepts in the field of second language research has been brief and oversimplistic in many respects (*cf* Klein 1986 and Ellis 1985 for comprehensive surveys of the field). However, more can be said about some of these issues and concepts by illustrating them.

6.3 Foreigner talk and second language acquisition

In discussing the foreigner talk theory of pidgin origin in 3.1, some similarities between the position of foreign workers in

Germany and pidgin speakers were noted. I will now look in more detail at the extent to which the acquisition of German in such situations can be regarded as a case of pidginization, or rather as governed by the same processes which apply to produce pidgins.

Gilbert and Orlovic examined the acquisition of the definite article in German by foreign workers of different language backgrounds. This feature was chosen because in the authors' view the absence of it constitutes an important indicator of pidginization. The syntactic slot for the definite article is almost always filled in the surface structure of all non-pidginized forms of German. The only instances in which native German speakers omit the article is in the foreigner talk register. However, in all Germanic and Romance-based pidgins categorical or variable deletion of articles is almost universal. In the process of decreolization the definite article may come to appear categorically in syntactic slots corresponding to usage in the standard language, but without markings for gender, number and case (compare the use of indeclinable **die** in Afrikaans, *cf* Markey 1982).

Four of the six source languages possess definite articles (*ie* Spanish, Greek, Italian and Portuguese) in syntactic environments which correspond to those of German. If it is true that it is much easier to learn equivalent filler morphemes in a second language for categories that already exist in one's native language, rather than to create whole new categories, the absence of definite articles in the German of these speakers could be attributed to pidginization rather than transfer. In other words, such a finding would lend support to the universalist hypothesis for second language acquisition advocated by Schumann and others. Table 6.1 shows the result of their study (Gilbert 1983:173):

TABLE 6.1 Frequency of occurrence of the definite article in the German of different first language speakers

Nationality	*Per cent of occurrence of definite article*
Turkish	15
Yugoslav	19
Portuguese	35
Italian	69
Greek	75
Spanish	87

It can be seen that speakers of languages with definite articles make more use of definite articles in German. Gilbert takes this as evidence for the transfer hypothesis. The differences between the groups are partly due to period of residence. Assuming there is greater progression towards the target, exposure to correction and that social constraints such as segregation do not block acquisition, then one would predict that those with longer residence would produce more definite articles. This was the case.

With regard to the morphological forms used, we might predict that if transfer were operative, then the speakers of those source languages having inflectional categories most similar to German (*ie* with six distinct definite articles inflected for case, number and gender) would tend to use a greater variety of marked forms (even if incorrectly distributed) rather than the invariant form **die**. Gilbert found instead that Italian speakers used **die** categorically, even though the Italian definite article shows a two-way gender and number distinction. In terms of its occurrence in native speaker German the form **die** is more often heard than the other five forms combined. Gilbert (1983:174) estimates its frequency of input as over 50 per cent. He also found that length of residence made little difference; all groups continued to use a high percentage of unmarked **die** forms. Gilbert says that for this feature there has been insufficient exposure to correction, but that overall the study supports the idea that there are universal operating principles of simplification and pidginization as well as positive and negative transfer in syntax.

There are of course a number of differences in the position of foreign workers in Germany and that of pidgin speakers. It has been argued that the preconditions for the formation of a true pidgin are lacking in the German case. The ratio of learners to native speakers is too small, and the segregation of these workers is not strong enough to encourage the persistence of this kind of pidginized German once the economic conditions that produced it have disappeared. Industrial societies provide different kinds of social environments and different conditions for linguistic assimilation than the plantation economies which gave rise to pidgins such as Hawaii Pidgin English and Tok Pisin.

6.4 The pidginization hypothesis and second language acquisition

The most detailed exposition of what has come to be called the **pidginization hypothesis** of second language learning can be found in Schumann (1978). Schumann's model is based primarily on a study of the longitudinal linguistic development of the untutored acquisition of English by six native speakers of Spanish (two children, two adolescents and two adults). Of particular importance is the case of a 33-year-old Costa Rican man, Alberto, who acquired a very limited proficiency in English. The research focused on the pattern of acquisition for a number of features of English. After establishing a series of developmental stages in the acquisition, which I will look at in more detail below, Schumann found that Alberto remained in the early stages of development with regard to all of these. He attributes Alberto's acquisition pattern to the process of pidginization. That is, Alberto uses a simplified and restricted variety of English. More specifically, he identified six features which are shared with pidgin languages (1978:75):

(i) use of the uniform negator **no** for most negative utterances placed external to the verb, *eg* **I no see**.
(ii) lack of question inversion, *eg* **where the paper is?**
(iii) lack of auxiliaries, *eg* **she crying** (only four auxiliaries appear, **is**, **am**, **are** – all forms of the copula, and **can**, but are not all acquired at the level of 80 per cent production rate).
(iv) lack of inflection for possessives, *eg* **the king food, a piece of chicken**.
(v) use of the unmarked form of the verb for past tense, *eg* **Yesterday I talk with one friend**.
(vi) deletion of subject pronouns, *eg* **no have holidays**

Schumann also looked at noun plurals and the progressive (in addition to the possessive and past tense) since bound morphemes tend to be absent in pidgins.

I will now take a look at the developmental stages in the acquisition of some of these features. Schumann found (1978:12–13) a sequence of four stages in the acquisition of the English negative:

(i) **no** + verb, *eg* **I no understand**.
(ii) **don't** + verb, *eg* **He don't like it**. **Don't** appears to be a variant of **no** rather than **do** + neg. This is used either simultaneously with Stage (i) or shortly thereafter.
(iii) auxiliary + negative, *eg* **You can't tell her**. The negative particle (*not* or the contracted form **n't**) in these constructions was placed after the auxiliary. **Is** and **can** were the first auxiliaries to be used in this way.
(iv) use of the analysed forms of **don't**, *ie* **do not**, **doesn't**, **does not**, **didn't**, **did not**, *eg* **We didn't have a study period**

Alberto showed less development than any of the other subjects. He used mainly **no** + verb, and to a lesser extent **don't** + verb constructions, throughout. Thus, he did not progress much beyond the initial stage of development.

As far as the acquisition of interrogatives was concerned, Schumann (1978:23) identified two main stages, the first with a series of steps:

(i) Stage I Undifferentiation: The learner does not distinguish between simple and embedded WH-questions.
 (a) uninverted: Both simple and embedded WH-questions are uninverted, eg. **What this is?/I know where is the book**.
 (b) variable inversion: simple WH-questions are sometimes inverted.
 (c) generalization: increasing inversion in WH-questions with inversion being extended to embedded questions.

(ii) Stage II Differentiation: Learner distinguishes between simple and embedded WH-questions.

The criterion for Stage II is set at 80 per cent inversion for simple WH-questions. Again, Alberto showed less development than the other learners. He remained in stage Ia, and inverted only 5 per cent of the time.

By comparison with the other learners Alberto showed very little development in the other features investigated. I have summarized the findings of Schumann's study in Table 6.2, where the level of attainment reached by Alberto is compared with that of the other subjects for the first three features. The figures for the four morphemes, *ie* possessive, past, plural and progressive indicate the percentage marked. Schumann does not give the levels for the other learners.

TABLE 6.2 Acquisition of seven features of English by Schumann's six Spanish speakers

Feature	*Alberto*	*Cheo*	*Jorge*	*Marta*	*Dolores*	*Juan*
% of inversion	5	19	37	43	55	56
no. of auxiliaries	4	4	12	9	17	18
negative (stage)	i	iii–iv	iii–iv	iii–iv	full	full
% possessives	26					
% past regular	33					
% past irregular	65					
% plural	85					
% progressive	58					

We can see that as far as the marking of categories like the past, etc. is concerned, Alberto fails to reach a high level except for plural marking. Although Alberto supplies plural forms 85 per cent of the time, he did not master the use of the correct allomorphs, which is phonologically conditioned, *ie* {**-s**, **-z**, **-iz**} as in **cats**, **bags**, **buses**. Even though the possessive morpheme in English is identical to one of the plural allomorphs, Alberto has practically no grasp of possessive marking. Schumann (1978:44) says that Alberto's better performance on the plural is probably due to positive transfer from Spanish. While English and Spanish plurals are similar, there are differences in the way in which the possessive is constructed in the two languages. It is interesting that children acquiring English as their first language acquire the plural before the possessive. With regard to past tense marking we can see that Alberto's performance is somewhat better for irregular verbs such as **go** than for regular verbs such as **walk**, which take the suffix **-ed** (the correct allomorph is again phonologically conditioned, *ie* {**-d, -t, -id**}, as in **dragged, walked** and **started**). In first language acquisition it has been found that children acquire the irregular forms first, probably as whole lexical items, rather than as analyzed forms.

Schumann considers a variety of factors which might account for Alberto's low level of attainment: ability, age, and social-psychological distance. On the basis of tests administered to all the learners Schumann concluded that Alberto had no cognitive defects which would impair his ability as a language learner. The question of how much Alberto's age affected his progress is more difficult to assess, because it hinges on whether or not there is a critical period for language acquisition. It is well known that native-like competence, particularly in the area of pronunciation, is difficult to achieve after puberty (*cf eg* Ioup 1979).

6.5 The critical period hypothesis

The idea of a critical period for language learning was first suggested in the work of Penfield and Roberts (1950). They argued that adults have difficulty in learning second languages because after puberty cortical lateralization is complete. This means that the language function becomes localized in the left hemisphere and the plasticity of the brain atrophies. Lenneberg (1967:142) examined evidence from the language abilities of the mentally retarded and aphasics to support his claim that 'the primary acquisition of language is predicated upon a certain developmental stage which is quickly outgrown at puberty'. It seems that retarded children appear to learn language in the same sequence as normal children, although at a slower rate. However, if the child's acquisition is not complete at puberty, it does not develop further beyond that period. In looking at the differential course of recovery from various kinds of aphasias incurred at different ages, Lenneberg found that in cases where the left hemisphere was removed or damaged before the teenage years, language functions could still be transferred to the right hemisphere. Adults do not seem to be able to transfer their language functions completely after hemispherectomies.

There has been considerable debate over Lenneberg's interpretation of the evidence and more research has been devoted to the critical period hypothesis. There is a great deal of agreement among neuropsychologists that processing functions are lateralized. Kinsbourne (1981) in fact, goes so far as to say that there is no dispute about the universals of lateralization. Geschwind (1980:314), however, stresses that it is functions which are lateralized, not skills as a whole, such as language. He adds that it should not be assumed that the lateralization of function is necessarily equivalent to lateralization of language.

Part of the problem in evaluating the evidence of neurological studies in terms of its linguistic implications is that the results are often obtained from pathological cases, such as Lenneberg studied, or from populations of a different nature from those normally investigated by second language researchers. This is why the findings appear so contradictory, with some studies claiming to have found negative effects, and other positive ones. Moreover, most of the evidence comes from dichotic listening tests (in which subjects receive different auditory stimuli in each ear), which are arguably not the best and most reliable measures of language lateralization. Krashen (1973–4), for example, has challenged the biological argument as a barrier to second language learning by findings which indicate that lateralization is complete much earlier. This leads him to suspect that it might however mark a critical period in first language acquisition, which is largely complete by the age of five or six.

There is a great deal of evidence to indicate that cerebral specialization exists in the processing of information from birth and increases up until puberty. Molfese and Molfese (1979) substantiate this view with the finding that neonates show an early propensity for left hemispheric processing for specific types of acoustic information. It may be that the process of lateralization is the functional correlate of a genetically determined asymmetry in neurological form which is unique to humans.

There are of course other measures of neurological maturation which bear on the acquisition of another language. Scovel (1981), for example, discusses myelinization, and intrahemispheric localization in addition to interhemispheric specialization (*ie* lateralization). Myelinization refers to the process whereby nerve cell axons in the central nervous system are coated with myelin. This improves the efficiency and speed of interneuronal communication. It has been shown that this stage is one of the first critical neurological events of significance for language acquisition because there can be no development in the aural–oral channel without myelinization.[1] It is essential for the production of speech sounds and the processing of acoustic signals. Scovel (1981:35), however, emphasizes that the onset, development and completion of myelinization is not firmly bound to chronological age. Marshall (1980:25, 132) points out the weakness of the traditional correlation between axonal myelinization and structural maturity. He observes that although myelinization of posthalmic pathways to the auditory cortex is relatively late, small babies hear rather well. This argues against the previously held view that myelinization in newborn infants was insufficiently advanced to permit learning.

With regard to the evidence for interhemispheric specialization, Scovel says (1981:37) that it 'has not vitiated the basic hypothesis that there is a neurologically determined critical period for the acquisition of a non-primary phonology and that the neurological age of this process is best measured in terms of the time at which interhemispheric specialization is complete'. Lenneberg (1967) pointed out that it was not lateralization *per se* which inhibited the acquisition of accent-free speech but rather the loss of brain plasticity. This entails a loss of flexibility in the neurophysiological programming of neuromuscular coordination mechanisms. There is no direct correspondence between neurological and chronological age for this process. The exact age at which it is complete varies from 8 to 14.

Hence both Krashen's view that its completion corresponds to a critical period for first language learning, and Lenneberg's that it coincides with puberty and is therefore a critical milestone for second language acquisition, can be accommodated within this continuum of variability. There are individuals who are strongly lateralized for language at a fairly early age, possibly before eight years, and others who have established little or no lateralization for language, even in adulthood. The idea that there is a continuum for lateralization was put forward by Shankweiler and Studdert-Kennedy (1975), and later taken up by Seliger (1978), who suggests that there are multiple critical periods for the acquisition of language which extend well into adulthood. The latter has suggested that variation in intra-hemispheric localization may reflect varying levels of brain plasticity, which correlate with degree of success in language acquisition.

Nevertheless, Krashen says that there is a critical period for second language acquisition, even if not biologically determined by neurological maturation in the strict sense. The notion of critical period can be considered independently of lateralization. The effects of the critical period remain: namely, that language acquisition ability declines. The critical period could apply only to phonology. Much of the discussion of the critical period hypothesis has to do with the alleged differences between children vs. adults as language learners. From a cognitive point of view this period may be linked to the onset of the formal operations stage, the highest stage of development in the Piagetian model (*cf eg* Inhelder and Piaget 1958).[2] At this stage the learner is capable of abstract thinking and this may force him to construct a conscious grammar.[3]

A number of studies have demonstrated that adults and children follow the same procedures in acquiring another language. This can mean either of two things: one is that they apply the same strategies, or what Slobin would call operating principles (*cf* 7.4), and another is that there is a universal hierarchy of difficulty involved in the acquisition of features which is related to the way in which a language encodes a particular category. The latter would then determine a natural order of emergence of features. If either is true, then it would appear that there are no maturationally-determined differences which affect the way children and adults learn. This finding does not however contradict the predictions of the critical period hypothesis which makes no claims about developmental progression, but simply the maximum level of achievement. As Seliger (1981:50) points out, it would probably be surprising if there were real qualitative differences between the strategies used by children and adults. More research needs to be done to determine which aspects of a second language are acquirable by all learners and which are dependent on retained plasticity.

After examining some cases of non-primary language acquisition by Downs' Syndrome patients (a congenital disease resulting in severe deficit in cognitive capacities as well as anatomical and behavioral abnormalities), Scovel (1981:40) concluded that if there was a limit on the intellectual or cognitive ability necessary for acquisition, it is so low as to be non-existent.

So far I have focused attention on neurological and cognitive development and haven't considered their interrelationship with the social context in which acquisition takes place. There are also affective factors which change after puberty. These socially or environmentally-determined aspects of acquisition are of particular importance since they are amenable to change. In other words, if factors which promoted the successful acquisition of language could be identified, they can be controlled, unlike cognitive and biological factors.

As part of the process of maturation the individual undergoes social and psychological changes which create distance between the learner and the group whose language he wants to acquire (*cf eg* Herman 1968). Lambert (1972) and his colleagues have undertaken detailed studies of the motivational and attitudinal factors which promote or hinder second language learning. Among the most important is the presence of an integrative rather than instrumental orientation towards the target language and culture. That is, learning is more successful if the learner has a positive orientation towards the language and group who speak it. It is less successful when the learner's primary reason for acquiring the language was out of necessity, *eg* for business, rather than out of a desire to become integrated in the target group.

Schumann considers the factor of social and psychological distance to be the key one in accounting for Alberto's lack of progress. He says that in general the speech of the learner will be restricted to the communicative function if the learner is socially or psychologically distant from the speakers of the target language. Or in other words, the restriction in function results from distance between the learner and the target group. Schumann compares Alberto's reduced language with pidgin languages which are also restricted in function. He says that since pidgins are always second languages the integrative and expressive functions are maintained by the speakers' native languages. Thus, Schumann claims that Alberto's speech is pidginized as a result of his social and psychological distance from English speakers. Moreover, he argues that pidginization may be a universal first stage in second language acquisition, which results initially from cognitive constraints and then persists due to social and psychological ones.

Bickerton (1977a:55) says much the same in observing that the 'difference between arriving at a pidgin and arriving at a reasonably accurate version of a standard language lies mainly in the availability of target models and the amount of interaction with speakers of the target language'.

6.6 Comparison of some linguistic features in second language acquisition and pidginization

Andersen (1981) has made a detailed comparison of the characteristics of Alberto's speech with those of Bickerton's 24 Hawaii Pidgin English speakers (*cf* Bickerton and Odo 1976), to see to what extent both Schumann and Bickerton are observing the same process when they describe their subjects' output as the result of pidginization. Bickerton's view is that pidginization and second language acquisition take place via a gradual relexification and restructuring of the learner's native language. More specifically, Bickerton (1977, 1981a) believes that pidginization is a process which begins with the speaker using his own language and relexifying a few key words. In the earliest stages the few superstrate words which appear will be rephonologized in line with the substrate phonology. At a later stage more superstrate lexicon will be added, but the items will be rephonologized to varying degrees. For the most part, these words will be slotted into syntactic surface structures which have their origin in the substrate. Even when relexification is complete down to grammatical items, elements from substrate syntax will be retained to some degree and will alternate with structures borrowed from the superstrate.

This gradual replacement of parts of the original grammar by rules of the superstrate system resulting in a common system is, according to Bickerton, not the result of simplification or direct access to linguistic universals. He found considerable mother tongue influence in the Pidgin English of Japanese speakers, but to a lesser extent in Filipino speakers. I indicated in 4.3 how Japanese pidgin speakers sometimes follow an SOV word order, as required in Japanese syntax rather than the canonical SVO word order of English. We can take another example here for comparison with a Filipino speaker:

> **samtaim gud rod get, samtaim, olsem ben get, enguru get, no? enikain sem. olsem hyumen laif. olsem gud rodu get, enguru get, mauntin get-no?**
> 'Sometimes there's a good road, sometimes, there's something like a bend, an angle, right? Everything's like that. Human life is the same. There are good roads, there are angles, there are mountains, right?' (66-year-old Japanese male speaker, *cf* Bickerton and Odo 1976:274)

Filipinos tend to place the predicate first following the verb initial word order of Tagalog; however, on the whole deviant word ordering is more common for the speakers of Japanese background. In their speech verb final sentences amount to over 60 per cent (Bickerton and Odo 1976:173), whereas among the Filipinos there is only one speaker for whom deviant word order constructions rise above 20 per cent. The verb initial syntax of the following example serves to mark the ethnic background of the Filipino speaker:

wok had dis pepl
'These people work hard' (Bickerton 1981a:11)

There are a number of examples of positive transfer of Spanish word orderings in Alberto's English which we can compare. Schumann (1978:55) gives three examples of deviations attributable to Spanish influence. These are cases where the subject was moved to the end of the sentence, following a possible Spanish word order, as in the following example:

For me is better the beer.
[*compare Spanish:* **Para mi es mejor la cerveza.**]

Andersen (1981:178) also notes the deletion of subject pronouns in Alberto's speech as due to influence from Spanish syntax.
There is also evidence of positive transfer in Alberto's marking of the possessive in English. Schumann (1978:36–7) found that Alberto consistently marked the possessive construction with either **'s** (*eg* **animal's big neck**) or **of** (*eg* **daughter of the mother**) only 26 per cent of the time. In these cases where a marker was present, most often it was **of** (*ie* 17 per cent). Andersen (1981:173) attributes this to Spanish influence interacting with Alberto's perception of the English constructions as being of the type Noun **of** Noun, as in **the school of your wife** [compare Spanish: **la escuela de su esposa** – 'your wife's school'], or the same construction without **of**, as in **food king** – 'food of the king/the king's food' [compare Spanish: **la comida del rey**]. Andersen found that 43 per cent of Alberto's possessive constructions consisted of two juxtaposed nouns with the Spanish rather than English ordering.

Andersen (1981:190) summarizes Alberto's use of possessive constructions, as in Table 6.3 (adapted from Schumann 1978:36–7; head noun italicized).

Although Bickerton does not discuss the possessive noun construction in Hawaii Pidgin English, Andersen (1981:189) says that seven out of the total nine constructions are of the juxtaposed N + N type (possessor + possessed), without the standard English **-s** marker. Thus, most of Alberto's possessives resemble

TABLE 6.3 Alberto's possessive constructions

	Type	*No.*	*Example*
Spanish order	*N* N	20	**food king**
English order	N *N*	4	**the king food**
	N	9	**this fat man** [= fat man's]
	Ns N	4	**animal's big neck**
	N **of** N	8	**school of your wife**
	N **de** N	1	**the brother de Kennedy**

those of Bickerton's Hawaii Pidgin English speakers in that both use the juxtaposition of two nouns as the preferred strategy of possessive construction. The Hawaii Pidgin English speakers maintain the English word order in at least seven of the nine examples, *eg* **hauli haus** – 'a white man's house', while Alberto does so only in 8 out of 37 examples. Andersen (1981:191) concludes that while Alberto seems to process English input in much the same way as Bickerton's pidgin speakers in that both use word order rather than inflections, this word order reflects native language transfer. Alberto also differs from the pidgin speakers in his extensive use of the **-s** plural, which as noted already, seems to be due to transfer from Spanish. Andersen interestingly points out the differential effects of positive and negative transfer from different language backgrounds. Even though we can identify common features in the speech of both the Hawaii Pidgin English speakers and Alberto, which appear to be the result of transfer, in some cases positive transfer from Spanish has the effect of making Alberto's speech appear less pidginized, *eg* the case of plural marking.

Andersen also compares patterns of negation in Alberto's speech and that of the Hawaii Pidgin English speakers. He notes (1981:178) that the earliest stage in the formation of negative sentences in pidgin English seems to be identical to Alberto's first stage, where negation consists of the use of **no** + V, Bickerton and Odo (1976:236) identify **no** + V as 'the basic pattern of Hawaiian Pidgin', *eg* **Yu no go hom pilipin ailen**? – 'Didn't you go home to the Philippines?' In Bickerton's study the percentage of use of this type of negation ranged from 100 per cent to 43 per cent. Since Alberto's use of the **no** +V pattern averaged about 60 per cent, he can be compared to the more depidginized speakers in Bickerton's sample.

Bickerton ranks his Hawaii Pidgin English speakers in an implicational scale according to their use of different patterns of negation. The speakers can be grouped into six lects (*cf* Bickerton and Odo 1976:Table 3.20). The most basilectal or pidginized consists of the **no** + V pattern, with some speakers occasionally using **neva** as a simple past negator, *eg* **ai neva go da taim** – 'I didn't go then'. The second lect contains those speakers who also use **nat** as a negator in sentences which are either verbless or would in standard English require a copula, *eg* **nat tu mach dispren bisayan æn tagalog** – 'Bisayan and Tagalog aren't very different'. These speakers also occasionally use **kænat** – 'cannot', *eg* **ai kænat tawk tagalog** – 'I can't speak Tagalog'. However **kænat** is on the whole a sporadic and rare variant. Most pidgin speakers use **no kæn**. Some of the speakers also use **don**, *eg* **sam da ada feirans, dei don advaiz gud da silren** – 'Some of the other parents don't give their children good advice'.

The other remaining pattern of negation to emerge during depidginization is neg + Aux. Bickerton does not give examples, but only two of his speakers use it; and there are only a total of seven instances in the sample. The final stage in the depidginization of negation occurs when the negative forms of the copula or modals appear, *eg* **won't**, **isn't**, etc. Only two of the speakers come close to reaching this stage. (see Table 6.4, below)

In placing Alberto in Lect V of Bickerton's six lect depidginization continuum, Andersen (1981:182) observes that this lect is identifiable not because of the percentage of use of the pidgin pattern **no** + V, but by the implicational matrix it is a part of. Alberto also uses **don't** V or **don't** before **can**, but not neg + Aux. In Bickerton's depidginization continuum there is no natural break between the most pidginized speakers, *ie* the two who only use the **no** + V pattern, and the most depidginized speakers, *ie* the two who use **nat**, **neva**, **kaenat**, **don** and neg + Aux. This implicational scale is presented in simplified form by Andersen (1981:183, Table 10), as in Table 6.4.

TABLE 6.4 Depidginization continuum for negation: Alberto compared with Hawaii Pidgin English speakers

Lect	*No. speakers*	*no*	*nat*	*neva*	*kaenat*	*don*	*neg + aux*
I	4	+	–	–	–	–	–
II	7	+	+	–	–	–	–
III	5	+	+	+	–	–	–
IV	3	+	+	+	+	–	–
V	3	+	+	+	+	+	–
VI	2	+	+	+	+	+	+

Andersen then goes on to compare Alberto with some of Bickerton's older and younger creole speakers. He says (1981:182) as a potential creole speaker Alberto ranks in the mid to upper half of the lectal continuum for older creole speakers (*cf* Bickerton 1977:Table 2.20), and about mid way in the lectal continuum for younger creole speakers (*cf* Bickerton 1977*b*:Table 3.19). This puts him in Lect II in each case (see Table 6.5). Andersen's conclusion is that as a second language learner Alberto is a pidginized negator as much as Bickerton's depidginizing and decreolizing speakers are of standard Hawaiian English. His comparison is summarized in Table 6.5 (from Andersen 1981:184, Table 11):

TABLE 6.5 Alberto compared with pidgin and creole negators

		no + V	**don't** V	Aux + neg	**don't**
Alberto		+	+	−	−
Pidgin speakers					
Lect	No. speakers	**no**	**don**	neg + aux	
I-IV	19	+	−	−	
V	3	+	+	−	
VI	2	+	+	+	
Creole speakers (older)					
		no	**don** copula/	neg copula/ modal	**didn**
I	1	+	−	−	−
II	3	+	+	−	−
III	2	+	+	+	−
IV	2	+	+	+	+
Creole speakers (younger)					
I	5	+	−	−	−
II	2	+	+	−	−
III	1	+	+	+	−
IV	3	+	+	+	+

It is interesting to look too at verbal morphology in Alberto's speech compared with Bickerton's Hawaii Pidgin English speakers. We saw earlier that Schumann cites the absence of past tense marking as a hallmark of pidginization in Alberto's speech. Overall, Alberto fails to mark past tense forms nearly half the time. In Bickerton's data 78 per cent of the verb forms used by Japanese speakers are unmarked, that is, they are not preceded by any of the five, pre-verbal free morpheme markers of tense and aspect (*ie* **bin, stei, go, baimbai, pau**). The percentage of unmarked forms ranges from 62 to 100. Only two speakers use **bin**, four **stei** and four **go**. Although Filipino speakers use tense–aspect markers more frequently than the Japanese, Bickerton does not give information on the total number of unmarked verb forms. As will be seen in Chapter 7, Bickerton is concerned with the emergence of tense–aspect markers because they seem to originate among pidgin speakers as pre-verbal markers without consistent meaning. During creolization they acquire their function as tense–aspect markers. He notes (Bickerton and Odo 1976:147):

> It has generally been reported of pidgins that they use markers of tense and aspect sparingly if at all. This certainly seems to be true of the Japanese pidgin speakers. In the creole system . . . there is a wide variety of tense and aspect markers, including **bin**, an anterior marker, **stei**, a nonpunctual marker and **go**, an irrealis marker. These markers may also be combined in several ways. Japanese pidgin speakers. however, have no combined forms of these particles and indeed very few single occurrences of the particles themselves.

The most that can be said without a more detailed analysis of Alberto's verb forms with regard to the marking of the categories of both tense and aspect is that both Alberto and Bickerton's Hawaii Pidgin English speakers use verb forms which are mainly unmarked for tense and aspect. Bickerton did however look at cases in which pidgin speakers used the standard English verbal morphology, *eg* the third-person singular present tense with **-s** (**he walks**), the use of regular and irregular past tense verb forms, past participles, forms of the copula (**is/was**) and the progressive. He proposes an acquisitional order, which is similar to that of some of the same morphemes used by Alberto. Andersen (1981:188) says that Alberto's performance places him among the eight most depidginized speakers. Alberto uses a rather high frequency of **is** by comparison with the pidgin speakers, but this is probably due to positive transfer. However, both **iz** and **-ing** are acquired fairly early even by the pidgin speakers. Andersen also suggests a positive transfer effect is responsible for Alberto's marking of the progressive. Spanish, like English, has a verb-final progressive marker – **ndo** (*eg* **jugando** – 'playing'), and it is acquired earlier by native Spanish speakers than most other bound morphemes.

Andersen (1981:189) also compares Alberto's use of plural marking with Bickerton's pidgin speakers. Bickerton and Odo (1976:225) consider the zero plural, *ie* no plural marking, to be the typical pidgin plural. Even the pidgin speakers who do mark plurals never do so more than 45 per cent of the time. By comparison, Alberto almost always marks plural forms, *ie* 85 per cent of the time, and therefore he marks more plural forms than even the most depidginized speaker. His high score for this feature was explained by Schumann as positive transfer.

As a final point of comparison I will look at question formation. Although Bickerton and Odo did not examine question formation in pidgin syntax, Andersen (1981:184) reports that none of the questions in their data have subject–auxiliary inversion, *eg* **wea yu go**? – 'Where are you going?' It is also the case that the pidgin speakers and Alberto do not distinguish between embedded and simple questions, *eg* **mai patna hi tel**, **hi gat telefon**? – 'My friend asked if he had a telephone'. Both are uninverted. Alberto's very low use of inversion (*ie* 5 per cent) puts his performance in much the same category as the pidgin speakers. Sokolik (1986), however, found a significant amount of inversion in experimentally-created German and Farsi pidgins.

In summarizing the results of his comparison between Alberto and Bickerton's Hawaii English pidgin speakers, Andersen (1981:191) says that Alberto's speech exhibits some of the same characteristics of pidginization and depidginization as the Hawaiian speakers. He cites the following: reliance on word order rather than inflections for expressing grammatical relations, native language transfer in word order as well as the use of English word order, the sporadic emergence of pre-verbal markers which come from lexical verbs promoted to auxiliary status, a basic pidgin negation that becomes eroded by depidginization towards standard English negation, lack of inversion in questions, and a preponderance of unmarked verb forms together with varying degrees of depidginization towards the standard English tense–aspect system. Alberto differed from the pidgin speakers mainly in his frequent use of the plural **-s**. Schumann (1981:196–7) records another parallel between Alberto's speech and that of the pidgin speakers with regard to the use of relative clauses. Neither Alberto nor the most pidginized speakers in Hawaii use relative pronouns. Bickerton's most pidginized speakers either produced no relative clauses or marked the few they did produce with either zero or pronominal relativizers (*cf* 6.10).

Andersen (1981:193) concludes that both Schumann and Bickerton are correct. Schumann is right in characterizing Alberto's speech as pidginized, and Bickerton is right in characterizing pidginization as second language acquisition with restricted input.

Researchers in the fields of pidgins and creoles and second language acquisition are really studying the same phenomenon from a different perspective. Andersen proposes a model of second language acquisition in which nativization and denativization are co-existent but opposing forces. He defines nativization as language acquisition towards an internal norm, *eg* pidginization in pidgin speakers and in early second language acquisition. Denativization is acquisition towards an external norm, *eg* depidginization in pidgin speakers and normal successful second language acquisition towards the target language. He sketches out these processes, as in Figure 6.1:

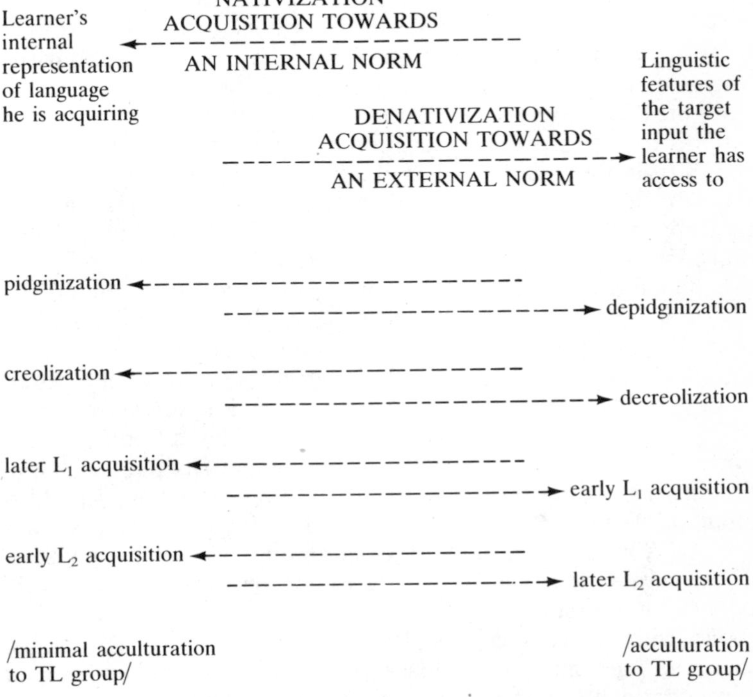

FIGURE 6.1 Nativization and denativization in language acquisition

I said earlier that Bickerton does not admit the existence of universals of pidginization which are independent of transfer from the first language. One possible exception to this is negation (*cf* Bickerton 1977a:66,*n*7). In order to find evidence against

Bickerton's hypothesis that the only strategy involved in pidgnization is transfer and piecemeal relexification, we would need to identify positively defined features which are shared by pidgins and are unrelated to either the first or target language. As seen in Chapter 2, pidgins have tended to be defined negatively, *eg* restricted lexicon, absence of gender, absence of true tenses, absence of inflectional morphology, absence of relative clauses, etc. Approximately 50 per cent of Alberto's output can be accounted for by transfer, *eg* word order. Another 35 per cent can be characterized as developmental errors. That is to say that they are errors which can be found in the speech of first language learners, *eg* unmarked verb forms, unmarked plurals, lack of **do** support, absence of copula and articles, etc. For example, the **no** + V pattern occurs as a stage in the acquisition of Spanish and English by children. Thus, nothing can be concluded about the origin of this pattern in Alberto's case or for that matter in the case of Bickerton's Hawaii Pidgin English speakers. Possible support for this pattern of negation as a universal of pidginization comes from the pidgin English of Japanese bargirls and American servicemen, where negation follows neither the Japanese nor the English pattern but consists of invariant **no** immediately preceding the negated predicate (*cf* Howell 1975).

Schumann (1981:199) does not agree with Bickerton on the issues of relexification and transfer since he claims that Alberto showed no evidence of relexification, and only 50 per cent of his speech could be accounted for by transfer. He points out too that even for Bickerton's speakers the case for relexification is stronger for Japanese than for Filipinos. The difference may, however, be due to the nature of the contact situations. Hawaii Pidgin English developed under a situation of **tertiary hybridization** (*cf* Whinnom 1971), in which the pidginized English was used as a means of communication among non-native speakers. Thus, community features of the pidgin had a chance to form. Alberto however rarely used English and when he did so he spoke with native speakers. Bickerton (1981b:203) too emphasizes the fact that the feedback received by the pidgin speaker is predominantly non-native. It is this factor which allows pidgins to stabilize in a form which is virtually unintelligible to native speakers of the base language. In second language development the learner's system cannot develop in such a way so as to become unintelligible to the native speaker. For Bickerton acquisitional changes are targeted. That is, the model for first or second language acquisition, depidginization or decreolization is the native adult version of the target language. (Historical changes by contrast, are for Bickerton untargeted in that there is no pre-existing model for them.) As far as Bickerton is concerned, pidginization seems to be a special case of second language acquisition which results in a unique system by virtue of using a transfer strategy throughout. Next I will undertake a more detailed comparison of the similarities between first and second language acquisition of relative clauses and the emergence of these structures in creoles.

6.7 Relativization and first language acquisition

The late development of relatives in child language has been attributed to the alleged processing difficulties posed by their syntactic complexity.There is some evidence which suggests that there are substantial cross-linguistic differences in rate of acquisition which have to do with the way in which the construction is encoded in particular languages. Slobin (forthcoming), for example, has shown that there are considerable differences in the rate of acquisition of relative clauses in Turkish and English. Not only are relative clauses used more frequently by English-speaking children (and adults) overall, but their development shows a much more accelerated growth curve. A major spurt takes place at around 3.6 for English speakers, while the mastery of Turkish relative clauses takes place later than the age of 4.8. Slobin attributes these differences to two general psycholinguistic processing problems which Turkish relative clauses present to the learner: (i) they are not easily isolable as clauses; and (ii) they are not constructed in a uniform way across different types of relativization. They are thus less transparently encoded in the syntactic structure of Turkish than English.

This brings us to the difficult problem of defining what is meant by a relative clause and the syntactic process of relativization. It is difficult to give an inclusive, unique and universal set of defining properties shared by all the types of constructions which syntacticians have discussed under the heading of 'relative clause'. Keenan and Comrie (1977:63–4), for example, define it as follows:

> We consider any syntactic object to be a relative clause if it specifies a set of objects . . . in two steps: a larger step is specified, called the **domain** of relativization, and then restricted to some subset of which a certain sentence is true. The domain of relativization is expressed in the surface structure by the head NP, and the restricting sentence by the restricting clause.

In defining a relative clause in terms of its semantic consequences, *ie* restriction of the domain of reference, Keenan and Comrie are following the practice of most typologists by beginning with a definition of the semantic/pragmatic function of the structure in question and then looking for its syntactic correlates.

Lehmann (1983) takes a more detailed starting point in identifying three constituent operations, which may be present to differing degrees and combined in different ways to construct different types of relative clauses: (i) subordination (nominalization); (ii) attribution; (iii) creation of an empty slot in the relative clause. He sees each of these operations as scalar, *ie* as varying along a continuum. As far as subordination or nominalization is concerned, the scale may range from a subordinate sentence to a noun, *ie* the transformation of a predicative construction into the category of nominal. For Lehmann subordination includes embedding and conjunction: nominalization implies the possibility of embedding and embedding implies subordination.

Although subordination is taken to be a prerequisite for relativization, the operation of having a subordinate clause function as a nominal of the matrix sentence means different things in different languages. In English, for example, a relative clause is embedded as modifer in an NP, where the embedded and matrix sentences share an identical nominal constituent, which is realized in the embedded sentence as a relative marker or pronoun (*eg* **that**, **who**, **which**, etc.). Subordination may or may not be marked. If it is not marked, the resulting construction may not be recognizable as a relative. If subordination is marked, it may be through the use of a particle or pronoun, which fills the empty slot created via the process of relativization. The extent to which a relative clause fulfills any of these three criteria reflects the degree to which that particular function is grammaticalized. Some languages may have devices which accomplish all these functions, but with no combination of the three being grammaticalized: in this case, the language would have no relative clauses.

As far as the evolution of relative clauses in language history and pidgins and creoles is concerned, there are a number of possible ways in which languages can come to have relative clauses. In some languages, as far as we can tell, there have always been relative clauses. One can identify constructions in the modern language which are continuations or renewals in some sense of constructions which existed in earlier stages. A language may 'create' a relative clauses from a related construction; that is, an old form may come to serve a new function. Through expansion a simple participle or attributive adjective may increasingly gain sentence status. Another route to relativization may be via the grammaticalization of an anaphoric relationship between two independent successive sentences, so that either the first or the second becomes subordinate. I will argue here that it is the exploitation of this route of grammaticalization which the child's acquisition of relative clauses has in common with the development of relative clauses in pidgins and creoles. I will look first at the process of children's acquisition of relatives.

6.8 Children's acquisition of relative clauses in English

Most of what I will say about children's acquisition of relative clauses will be based on studies of English-speaking children; and most of the data which I will discuss in detail come from an earlier investigation of schoolchildren in Edinburgh (*cf eg* the discussion in Romaine 1984a:Ch. 3).

For the moment, I will define relativization as a syntactic process whereby a sentence becomes embedded as a modifier in an NP, where the embedded sentence and the matrix sentence share an identical nominal constituent, which is realized as a relative marker or pronoun (*eg* **that**, **who**, **which**, etc.). I will argue later that a number of relative-like constructions cannot be easily accommodated within purely formal structural accounts of relativization. The following example, taken from my study of Edinburgh schoolchildren, was produced by a ten-year-old boy:

[1] The lassie was remembering about things [**that had happened**].

The matrix sentence, or main clause, is **the lassie was remembering about things,** and the relative clause, enclosed in brackets, is **that had happened**. The relative clause is considered to be a modifier of, or embedded within the NP headed by **things**, which is coreferential with the relative marker **that**. I will refer to **that** as a marker to distinguish it from what traditional grammarians call **relative pronouns**, *eg* **who**, **whom**, **whose**, **which**. The choice among the latter in English relative clauses is roughly determined by whether or not the antecedent or coreferential NP in the matrix sentence is human, and by the function of the relative pronoun in the relative clause, *eg* subject, object, etc. The marker **that**, by contrast, is invariant, and not sensitive to these features of the antecedent.[4] In addition to the option of relativization by means of the **WH**-pronouns and **that**, there is also the possibility of relativization by deletion, or the so-called **zero relative**, as in

the film [Ø I saw yesterday]. Thus, there is a tripartite division of relativization strategies in English: **WH, that** and ø.[5]

Returning to example [1], we can identify two factors which have been cited as contributory to the complexity of these constructions: **embeddedness** and **focus** (*cf* De Villiers *et al.* 1979). Embeddness varies according to the function in the matrix sentence of the antecedent NP modified by the relative clause, while the focus varies according to the function in the relative clause itself of the relativized element. Examples [1] to [4] from the Edinburgh data illustrate the four major types of relative clause resulting from different combinations of values for these two variables (where **NP_a** is the antecedent NP, **NP_r** is the relativized NP, **S** stands for subject and **O** for object of the verb or preposition):

		TYPE
[1]	**The lassie was remembering about things** NP_a:O **[that had happened]** NP_r:S	OS
[2]	**That person** NP_a:S **[that hasnae scored] goes out** NP_r:S	SS
[3]	**Ken they carties** NP_a:O **[that you pull behind you]?** NP_r:O	OO
[4]	**The one** NP_a:S **[that I like best] is kick the can** NP_r:O	SO

I will speak of constructions like [2] and [4], where the antecedent NP is subject as **subject-embedded relatives**, and of those like [1] and [3], where it is object, as **object-embedded relatives**; and similarly, of constructions like [1] and [2], where the relativized NP is subject as **subject-focus relatives**, and of those like [3] and [4], where it is object as **object-focus relatives**.

It has been proposed that there is a relation between ease of processing and the order in which children acquire these four types of relative clause. It is not hard to imagine why researchers have claimed that object-embedded relativization is easier than subject-embedded relativization, for the latter involves the insertion of one sentence within the other (*ie* centre-embedding), whereas in the former the relative clause simply follows the matrix sentence (*ie* right-branching). We should expect then to find that children are able to process the OO and OS types earlier and with greater accuracy than the SS and SO types. This would follow from the hypothesis that children are using a parsing strategy of the type proposed by Slobin, where sequences of NVN are interpreted as subject verb object (SVO).

This strategy would yield the correct interpretation for an OS relative clause, but not for the other types. The problem posed by subject-embedded relative clauses is that the relative clause interrupts the linear processing of constituents, *ie* it is embedded is a sequence like NP_1 [NP_3 V NP_4] V NP_2, where either NP_3 or NP_4 is the position relativized within the relative clause.

A number of experiments have been conducted to test children's ability to understand relative clauses. In most of these, children were asked either to repeat various types of relative clauses or to manipulate toys. For example, Tavakolian (1977) and De Villiers *et al.* (1979) asked children to make toys act out the sequence of events described in sentences such as [5]:

> [5] The dog stands on the horse [**that the giraffe jumps over**] OO

In order to score a correct interpretation the child must be able to comprehend the roles of agent and patient correctly.

The experimental literature has produced conflicting findings. The results of some of the major investigations are summarized in Table 6.6 (*cf* Romaine 1984b for further discussion). I have included in the table the results for the production of relative clauses by three age groups of the Edinburgh schoolchildren. The last line shows the hierarchy obtained without regard to age group. It can be seen, however, that this overall trend is not operative within the individual age groups. The marking of OO and OS and is reversed for the 10- and 8-year-olds, and the marking of SS and SO for the 6-year-olds. The factor of embeddedness is clearly the one which carries the most weight, with object-embedded relative clauses being greatly preferred over

TABLE 6.6 Hierarchies for relative clause types

Perception experiments:								
Sheldon		SS	>	OO	>	OS	>	SO
Tavakolian		SS	>	OO	>	OS	>	SO
De Villiers *et al.*		OS	>	SS	>	OO	>	SO
Production:								
Edinburgh children	Age 10	OS	>	OO	>	SS	>	SO
	8	OS	>	OO	>	SS	>	SO
	6	OO	>	OS	>	SO	>	SS
	Average	OO	>	OS	>	SS	>	SO

subject-embedded ones. The effect of focus, which is a much weaker factor, results in fewer clauses being produced by relativization of NPs which serve as object. The effects of focus and embeddedness can be seen for age group in Table 6.7. The interaction between age and focus is statistically significant. As far as the factor of embeddedness is concerned, however, age is not significant.

TABLE 6.7 Effects of focus and embeddedness on relative clause production

	FOCUS: S > O				EMBEDDEDNESS: O > S			
	Subject-focus (SS+OS)		Object-focus (SO+OO)		Subject-embedded (SS+SO)		Object-embedded (OS+OO)	
Age	N	%	N	%	N	%	N	%
10	41	22	30	16	20	11	51	28
8	27	15	22	12	9	5	40	22
6	26	14	37	20	24	13	39	21
SUM	94	51	39	49	53	29	130	71

I will consider now the extent to which the production data shed light on children's operating principles, and in particular, what answer they suggest to the question why there should be differences between the age groups. I will argue that the data show the evolution of relative clause formation rules. In order to trace the development from the child to the adult system, I will need to take a brief look at adult relative clause formation strategies.

6.9 Relative clauses and universal grammar

The most detailed work in this area comes from cross-linguistic research done by Keenan and Comrie (1977, 1979). They have made some interesting predictions about the types of relative clause formation strategies possible in languages. After examining a wide cross-section of different types of languages, they found that they did not vary randomly with respect to the syntactic positions of the NPs which could be relativized. They postulated the existence of an **accessibility hierarchy** which predicted constraints on the positions in which relative clauses could appear, as given below:

Keenan-Comrie accessibility hierarchy

Subject > Direct Object > Indirect Object > Oblique > Genitive > Object of Comparison

The two most important predictions made by Keenan and Comrie to be considered here are:

(i) The frequency with which NPs in certain syntactic positions are relativized in a language is in accordance with their ordering in the accessibility hierarchy; that is, subject NPs are most frequently relativized and objects of comparison least frequently.
(ii) the order of grammatical relations in the accessibility hierarchy is correlated with ease of relativization; that is, subject is the easiest position to relativize.

The first of Keenan and Comrie's predictions about accessibility relates to my previous discussion of the factor of focus, *ie* the position occupied by the relative in the relative clause. According to Keenan and Comrie's hypothesis, subject–focus relatives (OS and SS) should be more frequent than object–focus relatives (OO and SO) (*cf* the results of De Villiers *et al.* 1979). This prediction is supported when we consider the total number of relative clauses produced by the Edinburgh children, as can be seen in Table 6.8.

TABLE 6.8 Number of relative clauses in relation to the case hierarchy

Subject	Object	Oblique	Locative	Temporal	Genitive
94	73	16	9	8	1

A few comments are necessary. There were no relative clauses with indirect object focus in the sample – no examples like **the man that I gave the book to/the man to whom I gave the book**, etc. The term **oblique** is used to refer to relatives in whose underlying structure the coreferential NP functions as the object of a preposition, as in:

[6] **the house that he lived in**
[7] **the house which he lived in**
[8] **the house in which he lived**

There are two types of oblique focus construction: 'stranded' and 'shifted'. These terms refer to the placement of the preposition in relation to its object. In the stranded construction, the preposition is separated from its relative marker or pronoun, as in [6] and [7]. In the shifted construction the preposition has been shifted or fronted along with coreferential NP to the beginning of the relative clause, as in [8]. Oblique-focus relatives marked by that cannot undergo shifting. Examples like [9] are ungrammatical:

[9] ***the house in that he lived**

The behaviour of **that** in these kinds of constructions constitutes an argument to treat **that** as a non-pronominal relativizer. If **that** had the same syntactic status as the **WH**-pronouns, we would expect them to behave similarly. I will give further evidence of the different nature of **that** later.

The categories of temporal and locative have been included in Table 6.8, even though they are not strictly speaking syntactic positions on a par with the others in the accessibility hierarchy. There seems to be no general agreement among syntacticians with regard to the status of adverbs of time and place when used in a relativizing function. Examples of what I will refer to as **locative focus** and **temporal focus** relatives are given in [10] and [11] respectively:

[10] **I've watched a horror film [where there's a big giant].**
[11] **The first time [that I tried it] I liked it.**

I have included clauses of this type in the category of relative clauses because they participate in a pattern of variation similar to the other types of relative clause. That is to say, they may be introduced by **WH**-forms like **where** or **when**, by **that** or by no marker at all. Only cases in which there is a nominal element which can be understood as coreferential with the temporal or locative marker are included here. In some cases locative-focus relatives can be thought of as having some similarity to oblique focus relatives, as in [12]:

[12] **That's the place [where I got my fishtank frae].**

Locative and temporal focus relatives are also sometimes paraphrasable by oblique-focus relatives. Compare [13] and [14], for example, with [15]:

[13] **I like the one [what Tom plays a trick on Jerry].**
[14] **I like the one [where Tom plays a trick on Jerry].**
[15] **I like the one [in which Tom plays a trick on Jerry].**

There was only one example of a genitive focus relative in the Edinburgh data, produced by a 10-year-old boy:

[16] **the person [that's foot is touched].**

In modern standard English the only permissible construction in this case would be **whose**, which is marked for genitive case. The fact that Scots uses a form of **that** to mark relativization on a genitive NP reflects its historical development (*cf* Romaine 1982). Scots possesses the option of using **whose** to relativize genitive NPs, but it tends to favour the alternative strategy of using **that**'s (**that** is invariant in other varieties of English); or it uses a pronoun-retaining strategy, as in [17]:

[17] **the person [that his foot is touched]**

These two alternative strategies permit case-marking on the lower positions of the case hierarchy. In general, the use of **WH**-pronouns as relativizers is very infrequent in Scots; most commonly **that** is used and often no marker appears at all. I have already noted some of the constraints which affect the choice of relatives according to features of the antecedent in particular syntactic positions (*cf* Quirk *et al.* 1972:867 for further details).

The Edinburgh schoolchildren tend to use **that** and ø roughly equally in preference to **WH**, although there are some important developmental trends in evidence here. Limber (1973), who studied the development of complex sentences in pre-school children, found that the first relative clauses involve no relative marker or pronoun; later **that** is used. As far as the use of **WH** relatives is concerned, only the subject form **who** is used; the inflected forms **whom** and **whose** never appear. We can see a clear progression from the 6- to the 10-year-olds, which is characterized by increasingly less reliance on the ø strategy, a correspondingly greater increase in the use of **WH** and **that**. Overall, however, even in the 10-year-old group, the **WH** strategy is not very frequent; **that** is the preferred relativizer. These findings are well in line with the local adult norms (*cf* Romaine 1982).

We can say then that part of the process of the acquisition of relative clauses does not involve a wholesale qualitative shift from one strategy to another. In other words, it isn't the case that children lose a 'primitive' rule or strategy which juxtaposes clauses without any formal mark of their relation. English, unlike French, for example, allows relativization by deletion, and the deletion strategy is commonly used by adults. Acquiring English relative clauses involves adding other strategies, *ie* **WH** and **that**. This involves some decrease in the frequency with which the ø strategy is employed, but not its loss, not even in subject position.

There are some further comments to make about the kinds of relative clause formation strategies used by these Edinburgh schoolchildren. Examples like [18] do not fit neatly into the typology established so far.

[18] **Things [what you sit on] they go**

Earlier I defined relativization as a process of embedding in which a relative clause is embedded in a matrix clause and there is a relation of coreference between an NP in a matrix clause and an NP in the relative clause. In [18], however, the relationship between the two clauses is not quite the same as in the other examples I have cited so far. The use of the pronoun **they** to mark the subject slot is in a sense redundant because **things** already serves this functions. The NPs **things** and **they** are coreferential, just as the relative marker **what** is also coreferential with **things**. The terms '**resumptive**', '**shadow**' or '**copy**' **pronoun** are used to refer to a pronoun like **they**. Example [17] (although it did not actually occur in these data) illustrates a similar phenomenon. This time the resumptive pronoun is marked for genitive or possessive case since this is the function it serves in the relative clause. Furthermore, it sometimes happens that the resumptive element is a full NP and not a pronoun, as in [19], from a 10-year-old boy:

[19] **Then whoever the person [that's he] catches first that person's he in the next game.**

In this sentence **that person** is coreferential with the NP **the person**, as is the relative marker **that**. There were fifteen instances in which shadows or resumptives were used by the Edinburgh schoolchildren. Most (twelve) of these cases were like [18], where a resumptive pronoun occurs in subject position of the matrix clause immediately following a relative cause in subject position. Of the remaining three, one was [19]; the others were [20], from an 8-year-old boy, and [21], from a 6-year-old girl:

[20] **but the ones [ø you can put pounds and notes on it]**
[21] **That man [who Mickey Mouse was putting] – Mickey Mouse [who was putting him upside down]**

In both these the shadow appears within the relative clause itself to mark the position of the relativized NP. In [20] the shadow pronoun is the object of a preposition, appearing in the slot which would have been occupied by a relative pronoun or marker. The prototypical relative clause in this syntactic position would have been either [22], [23] or [24]:

[22] **but the ones [on which you can put pounds and notes]**
[23] **but the ones [which you can put pounds and notes on]**
[24] **but the ones [that you can put pounds and notes on]**

Since the child has used a zero strategy of relativization in which there is no overt relativizer to indicate the case relation of the relativized NP, and the pronoun **it** marks its slot. Example [21] is slightly more complicated. The girl appears to be hesitating between two constructions: **The man [who Mickey Mouse was putting upside down]** . . . and **Mickey Mouse was putting the man upside down**. What results is a conflation of the two with a shadow pronoun appearing in direct object slot, which is the syntactic position she was trying to relativize initially.

These two additional types of relative clauses can be thought of as alternative strategies to the ones I have already discussed. It remains to be seen, however, what role they play in the child's syntactic development, and what implications they have when seen in terms of the Keenan–Comrie accessibility hierarchy and the perceptual hierarchy based on focus and embeddedness.

There is evidence from a variety of sources which can be used to argue that these alternative strategies serve an important syntactic and pragmatic function and represent intermediate developmental stages in the child's acquisition of the fully syntacticized adult prototype construction. Children seem to be using these alternatives in cases which involve some degree of perceptual difficulty. For example, in the instance where resumptive pronouns mark the case relation of relativized genitive and oblique NPs in the relative clause, I would argue that they help make the case of the relativized NP recoverable, particularly when a zero strategy of relativization is used. Resumptive proouns aid the relativization of NPs which are in less accessible positions of the Keenan–Comrie hierarchy.

From a universal perspective Keenan and Comrie (1979) have noted a tendency for languages to use pronoun-retaining strategies on the lower positions of the hierarchy. The use of these alternative strategies is no doubt also connected with the fact that these children do not seem to use the pronominalizing or case-coding **WH** strategy very frequently. The alternative strategies take up the slack in the system, particularly at the lower end of the hierarchy. One could also argue that perceptual difficulties are at work in the other type of alternative relativization strategy in which the copy appears in the matrix clause. In this case, the syntactic position is easily accessible to relativization; that is, most of these resumptive pronouns appear in subject position. However, as we have seen, object-focus relatives on subject antecedents interrupt the matrix clause, and in terms of deep structure, the two NPs are maximally distant. Here the copying of the subject after the relative clause may serve to minimize the effects of interruption and act as a place holder for the referent introduced initially by the speaker.

Although perceptual factors probably go a long way towards accounting for the appearance of these two types of resumptive pronoun strategies, they do not completely explain the developmental changes. For one thing, adults use these alternative strategies too (*cf* Romaine 1980). It may be that children are not exposed to the fully syntacticized strategies in any great frequency until they reach school. Thus, the difference between these two modes of relativization reflects in part a dichotomy between written and spoken language on the one hand, and between formal and informal registers on the other. Secondly, resumptive pronouns can occur when the relativized NP occupies one of the more accessible syntactic positions in the case hierarchy, *eg* subject and direct object. There were no examples of these in the Edinburgh children's data. Wald (1982), however, who studied relativization in the discourse of 11–12-year-olds in Los Angeles, found cases, such as [25] in which subject shadows appeared:

[25] **It was about some lady that she was asleep and that they told her to read the Bible**.

In fact, Wald reports that subject shadows were more common that shadows in other case relations in embedded clauses. This appears to be at odds with what we would expect the case hierarchy to predict if perceptual factors were the most important;

namely, that the least accessible positions would be most likely to retain pronouns. His results indicate a need for examining more carefully the functions relative clauses serve in discourse. From a functional perspective, relative clauses do the work of providing further information about an NP which has been introduced into discourse. In this respect, they are like comments on topics. For example, in [26] from an 8-year-old boy, the relative clause identifies the NP **that lassie** as one of a potential group of lassies and singles one particular one out for further comment:

[26] **that lassie [ø I go to school with]**

Along with various other syntactic devices, *eg* indefiniteness (*cf* Bates and MacWhinney 1979 for a list of devices which act as topics or comments), it provides some necessary background information which the listener may not be assumed by the speaker to have. One reason why I found that children produced more object- than subject-embedded relative clauses (*cf* Table 6.7) is that new information nouns tend to be located in object position. Thus, the high percentage of object-embedded relatives may merely reflect this fact. During the course of acquisition it may be that speakers switch from a primarily discourse-oriented system to a more purely syntactically motivated system (*cf* the discussion in 5.4 of a similar constraint switch-over in the case of the copula).

6.10 Relative clauses in pidgins and creoles

It is at this stage that some important links between the child's acquisition of relative clauses and the development of these structures in pidgins and creoles can be seen. I have already noted in Chapters 2 and 4 that pidgin syntax tends to be shallow. Pidgins lack rules for embedding and subordination of clauses. They tend to use no formal marking to indicate that one part of an utterance is subordinate to another. Distinctive marking of relative clauses comes later in the stabilization or expansion phase of the pidgin life cycle, or arises in the process of creolization.

Bickerton (1977b), for example, found in Hawaii English Creole, where relativization is being introduced as a new syntactic construction where none existed previously, that object-focus relatives were more frequent than subject-focus ones. In the data from the Edinburgh children, we can see an indication of this switch from object- to subject-focus relatives between the ages of six and eight. This is apparent in Table 6.7, where subject-focus relatives do not become more frequent than object-focus relatives before the child is eight.

Another parallel can be drawn from Bickerton's work on the development of relative clauses in Hawaii English Creole. He gives the following example:

[27] **Da boi jas wawk aut from hia, hiz a fishamæn.**
'The boy [who] just walked out of here [he's] a fisherman'

Bickerton argues that we can see the beginnings of a rudimentary strategy of relativization here. In the earliest stages of the development of this construction it is difficult to tell whether 'true' embedding or merely a conjoining process has taken place. The surface marker which eventually becomes used in a relativizing function is not a specialized relative pronoun like **who** in English, but a personal pronoun. Bickerton (1977b:274) suggests that the use of personal pronouns represents an intermediate stage between zero forms and the full range of English relative pronouns. Thus, the route to fully syntacticized relativization in Hawaii English Creole can be illustrated in sentences [28] to [30]:

[28] **You fain Hawaiians [ø spik English].** [zero strategy]
'You found Hawaiians who could speak English'
[29] **Sam [dei drink] meik chabrol.** [personal pronoun strategy]
'Some who drink make trouble'
[30] **Evri filipino [hu kud aford it] bai wan.** [English relative pronoun]
'Every Filippino who could afford it bought one'

The fully syntacticized stage is reached when zero marking in subject position gives way to overt relativization (either by **WH** pronominalization or **that**) and the copy pronoun in the subject slot of the matrix following the relative clause is deleted.

A similar progression can be traced in children's acquisition of relative clauses. In the earliest stages of syntactic development children do not use embedded sentences at all; and indeed, even in the casual spoken language of adults simple conjunction of clauses or the use of independent sentences may be a preferred discourse alternative to relativization. We can see the close relationship between these alternatives in examples like [31], from an 8-year-old boy, where two independent clauses occur side by side with no formal mark of connection (either subordination or coordination) between them:

[31] **He met 'Toothless'. That was this big lion.**

Another possible way of presenting the same information or

introducing the referent 'Toothless' would be by means of a fully syntacticized relative clause, as in [32]:

[32] **He met 'Toothless', who was a big lion.**

Another example attesting the close relationship between relative clauses and conjoined sentences is given in [33], from an 8-year-old girl:

[33] **There's a big alarm bell and that goes off.**

A possible alternative again would be a relative clause, as in:

[34] **There's a big alarm bell [that goes off].**

The existence of sentences like [31] and [33] as possible alternatives to relativization and their earlier emergence than relatives suggests that in the initial stages of syntactic development children do not possess strategies for the syntactic incorporation of one clause within another. Two propositions simply occur side by side or in a coordinate construction as shown in the diagram in Figure 6.2. Only later do they acquire the syntactic means for making the relation between propositions and clauses explicit. In the case of OS relatives there is little in the way of formal marking to distinguish them from two independent clauses which occur side by side; and it is therefore not surprising that these are among the first types to be perceived and produced by children. Later, the child is able to produce true embedded constructions. In Stage I the interpretation of such a construction as relative as opposed to two distinct clauses with no connector is largely a pragmatic and prosodic matter. The transition from Stage I to Stage II illustrates a changeover from discourse–pragmatic to grammatical–syntactic constraints on relativization. In this way loose paratactic structures become condensed or syntacticized into tight hypotactic structures.

Wurm (1970), Dutton (1973) and Sankoff and Brown (1976) note the importance of intonation in the bracketing of relative clauses in Tok Pisin. On the basis of data from Churchill (1911), Sankoff and Brown say that relativization in the early period of Tok Pisin's development appears to have involved no markers in the matrix S and equi NP deletion rule in the embedded S (*cf* Ch. 3 *n*3). Hearers probably deduced the embeddedness from word order and juxtaposition of elements with the aid of prosodic features like stress and intonation.

The standard relative clause types discussed in grammars of Tok Pisin, such as those of Wurm and Dutton, use no special marker of subordination. The third-person pronoun functions as

Stage I: Conjunction of independent clauses

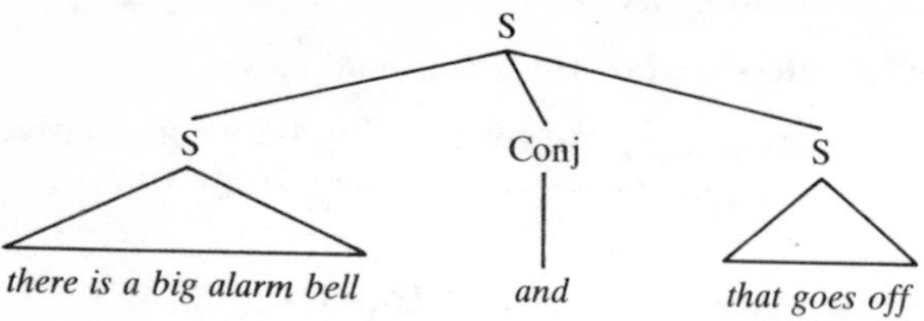

Stage II: Embedding

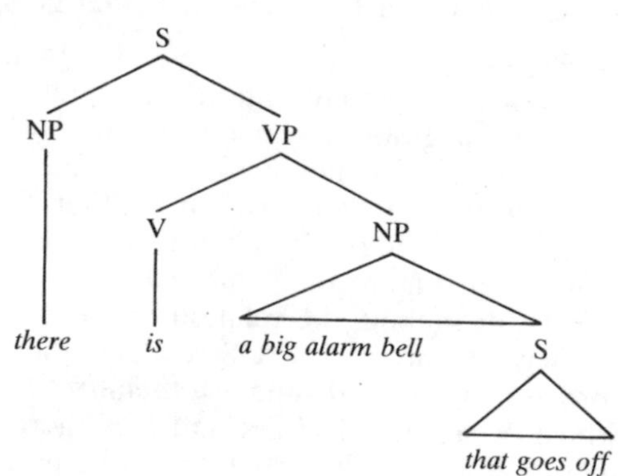

FIGURE 6.2. Stages in the acquisition of relative clauses

a type of relative marker. For instance, Dutton (1973:95–6) cites [35] and [36] as possibilities for combining the two sentences **Mi lukim dok** – 'I saw the dog' and **Dok i ranim pik bilong mi** – 'The dog chased my pig' in a relative construction:

[35] **Mi lukim dok [em i ranim pik bilong mi].**
'I saw the dog that chased my pig'

[36] **Dok mi lukim em [em i ranim pik bilong mi].**
'The dog I saw chased my pig'

Dutton says that the second type is less common than the first. Although there is no case or gender marking in the pronoun, there is a plural form, **ol**, which is used with plural antecedents. In oblique-focus relatives, however, case marking does turn up: **em** becomes **en** after **long**, **bilong**, etc.

Prepositions cannot be stranded; the relativized NP always appears as a pronoun and is never deleted, as in [37] and [38], from Dutton (1973:120, 138), and [39], from Sankoff and Brown (1976:214):

[37] **Pikinini [yu givim mani longen] em i stap long hap.**
'The child you gave the money to is over there'

[38] **Mi save dispela ples [yu go longen].**
'I know where you're going'

[39] **Yu lukim dispela ia [kon ia wantaim i sanap longen ia].**
'Did you see this one that has corn and cassowaries on it?'

In subject- and object-focus relatives there is alternation between deletion and pronominalisation of the coreferential NP, but never full copying of the NP, according to Sankoff and Brown (1976; reprinted in Sankoff 1980:214). Subject-focus relatives show the greatest variation in surface marking of the coreferential NP. Sankoff and Brown found that there was a tendency towards deletion rather than pronominalization. This is not the case for Aitchison's (1983b:6) study of six young women in Lae. She reports that four of the five subject-focus relatives and five of the 15 object-focus relatives in her data had introductory markers.

Since Aitchison does not discuss her results in terms of the factor of embeddedness, and Sankoff and Brown do not discuss theirs in terms of the factor of focus, it is not possible to make exact comparisons. Nevertheless, it can be seen that some interesting similarities, but also some differences, exist between the findings of my own study of children's relatives and those of studies of Tok Pisin speakers' relatives. Sankoff and Brown (1976:216) found that 67 per cent of subject-embedded, *ie* SO and SS, clauses were subject focus, *ie* SS. This is paralleled by my finding that for the Edinburgh children 58 per cent (31 out of 53) of subject-embedded relatives were subject focus, although object-focus relatives were overall more frequent than subject-focus ones. The difference is, however, not as great as in Aitchison's data, where three quarters of the relatives were object focus. In the Edinburgh data just over one half (51 per cent) of the relatives were subject focus. We can also note a few more findings from other studies of children's acquisition of relatives. Menyuk (1969) found that 87 per cent of children between the ages of three and seven used object-focus relatives, while 40 per cent used subject-focus relatives. Slobin (forthcoming) also found that for both English- and Turkish-speaking children and adults overall more relative clauses had non-subject focus. He concludes that if a language provides equivalent means for relativizing various positions of the accessibility hierarchy, the advantage to subject-focus relatives is not demonstrated.

There are also some points of comparison with Bickerton's data on relativization in Hawaii English Creole. Bickerton and Odo (1976:274–9) have observed that the few Hawaii Pidgin English speakers who produce relative clauses, relativize on the object NP of the matrix sentence far more often than on the subject NP. This is in agreement with my finding that the Edinburgh children produce more than twice as many object-embedded clauses as they do subject-embedded ones (130 as against 53). In Sankoff and Brown's data the difference is less, although still in the direction of favouring object- over subject-embedded relatives (52 as against 38).

Bickerton (1977b:284) also found that in Hawaii English Creole markers were present at least twice as often in subject-focus relatives as in object-focus ones. Although this is paralleled by Aitchison's and my findings that deletion is less frequent in subject position, Sankoff and Brown (1976; reprinted in Sankoff 1980:215) report that the tendency for Tok Pisin speakers was to delete in a ratio of two to one.

As far as pidgins and creoles are concerned, I have discussed the use of strategies of relativization involving deletion or marking. However, I have not said much about the different possibilities for marking relative clauses. I have already shown that Tok Pisin and Hawaii English Creole use third-person personal pronouns. Sankoff and Brown discuss the creation of a new relativizer **ia** (from the place adverbial meaning 'here') in Tok Pisin via its extension as a demonstrative or generalized deictic particle in discourse, as in [40]:

[40] **Meri ia** [**em i yangpela meri**, **draipela meri ia**] **em harim i stap.**
'This girl, who was a young girl, big girl, was listening'

Here the particle **ia** is used to bracket an embedded clause from a matrix sentence by virtue of its placement after both the head noun and the embedded clause. Sankoff and Brown (1976:239) found that most sentences used some form of **ia**-bracketing, and that the highest frequency of **ia** was in oblique-focus relatives.

Aitchison (1983b:7) found no instances of **ia**-bracketed relative clauses. She did, however, observe the use of **we** in seven out of 20 of the clauses, as in [41]:

[41] **Klostu em laik paitim dispela sista ia, sista** [**we wok**].
'She almost hit this nursing sister, the sister who was on duty'

This example does, however, arguably show the rudimentary traces of a **ia**-bracketed relative clause, since **ia** occurs here as a post-posed deictic. See Sankoff's 1980: 244–5 discussion of the constraints on **ia**-bracketing).

In my study of young children's creolized Tok Pisin in Lae, there are examples of double-bracketed **ia** clauses (*cf* Romaine and Wright 1986). The one in [42] was produced by a first grade girl in spontaneous play with two other girls, who were also first language Tok Pisin speakers.

[42] **Narapela ia [em i em draivim ka ia] mi no save nem bilong en.**
'The other one [she's the one who drives the car] I don't know her name'

Aitchison, however, found, that the use of **we** as a relativizer is confined to a group of three young women who were related to each other and whose families lived near Goroka. According to Sankoff (1979:38) **we** is a 'low frequency relativizer for some current speakers'. Woolford (1979:121) notes that it is used by a very small percentage of Tok Pisin speakers. Siegel (1981) cites the use of **we** as a relativizer as a feature of creolized Tok Pisin. Mühlhäusler (personal communication) also says that **we** is very frequent in many parts of the country, especially Manus. It is also found in combination with **em**, as in **man we em i kam**. The use of **we** as a relativizer also occurs in West African Pidgin English, Krio, Torres Strait Broken and other English-based pidgins and creoles.

There are a number of examples of **we** used as a relativizer by children who use Tok Pisin as a first and second language (*cf* Romaine and Wright 1986). The example in [43] is from an 11-year-old Lae boy:

[43] **Em la go antap long hul [we ol pasim long tupela ain].**
'He wanted to go on top into the hole [where they shut (him) behind two iron bars]

Here **we** is used in a locative relative construction. From there it has spread so that it can now be used in cases where the relative marks a subject as in Aitchison's example in [41]. Mühlhäusler (1986:189–90) suggests that there is an implicational hierarchy governing the introduction of **we** as a relative marker so that its use begins first in locative environments. From there it spreads to temporal ones, followed by subjects and then direct objects. He does not provide documentation for this process. If it proved to be correct, then the spread of **we** to direct object be subject relatives would be a violation of the Keenan–Comrie hierarchy.

Even more characteristic of written Tok Pisin, however, is the emergence of the relativizer **husat** (interrogative 'who'), which does not normally occur in the spoken language. Siegel records (1981:31) the first usage in **Wantok** (April/May 1979), and says that it also occurs in media broadcasts. As an example he cites (1981:31) [44]:

[44] **Mi laik autim wari bilong mi i go long ol manmeri [husat i save baim samting long maket]**
'I'd like to bring out my worry to the people who buy things at the market'

It will be interesting to see whether the use of **husat** spreads into colloquial usage. Those who speak urban varieties of the language, which are heavily anglicized, will be more likely to use **husat**. Example [45] is from a young educated man who works at the technological university in Lae.

[45] **Em man [husat i drawim] em i go lapun tru na em i dai pinis.**
'The man [who drew (it)] got very old and died'

As far as typology is concerned, Lehmann may be right when he says (1983:251) that the occurrence of a relative pronoun is evidently independent of language type. Furthermore, in talking about the morphological form of subordinators which function as relativizers, he suggests (1983:165) that there is no reason why a relativizer should have morpho-semantic connections to any other morphemes. This might be the conclusion one would draw from treating grammars as structural entities in isolation from their communicative functions. Bickerton (1981a) argues that **ia** relatives in Tok Pisin have their origin in substratum influence and does not consider the fact that common discursive practices may provide the route for the grammaticalization of syntactic constructions.

Once one rejects a strictly syntactic view of relativization in favour of a functional one, it can be seen that so-called natural languages create relativizers in similar ways to pidgins and creoles. There are certain kinds of linguistic categories which can become relativizers, and thus come to perform the work of separating an NP from an embedded sentence. Among these are deictics such as demonstrative pronouns and place adverbials, and interrogatives. Further support for the view that parallel independent development rather than substratum influence is at work in this process of grammaticalization can be found in the fact that similar strategies emerge in widely separated English-based creoles as well as in French-based creoles.

Posner (1985:180–82) has discussed the use of **la** to demarcate relative clauses in certain French-based creoles. **La** is the definite NP marker derived from the French locative particle **la** – 'there' (*cf* also Valdman 1977a:163). It can be used as a post-posed deictic like Tok Pisin **ia**. Compare Tok Pisin **dispela meri ia** – 'this woman' and Haitian Creole: **fãm blãʃ la** – 'the white woman'. From what Posner says, it may be that the French-based creoles represent various stages in the grammaticalization of this construction. It appears to be unknown in Louisiana and the Indian Ocean Creoles. It is optional in Martinique and Guadeloupe, but general in Haitian Creole. The latter also possesses another strategy of relativization by means of **ki/ke** (*cf* French **qui/que**). Lefebvre claims that **la** is obligatory in restrictive relative clauses in Haitian Creole. An example is given in [46] from Lefebvre (1982:37):

[46] **tab la [m te aste a]**
[table determiner I tense buy determiner]
'The table that I bought'

It is interesting that this development has apparently progressed furthest in Haitian, since it has less contact with superstrate varieties of French than other French-based creoles. Thus, there would be less pressure to counteract natural developmental tendencies.

The common unity of these linguistic elements which come to serve as relativizers is probably best accommodated within a deictic theory of discourse reference. That is to say, that they can all be used to alert the listener to a referent. Such a theory is outlined by Lyons (1975), who argues that the grammatical structure and interpretation of referring expressions can be accounted for through the deictic function of demonstrative pronouns and adverbs. He observes (1975:61) that the definite article and the personal pronouns in English and other languages are weak demonstratives, and that their anaphoric use is derived from deixis. It is well known that the definite article, demonstratives and third-person pronouns are diachronically related. On the grounds of their semantic and syntactic similarity some have argued that they should all be synchronically relatable, at least in the grammar of English. Possibly the same is true of French.

There is support for this view not only from diachrony and child language but also from pidgins and creoles. Dreyfuss (1977) compared the relative clause formation strategies used in four creoles: Haitian Creole, Tok Pisin, Sango and Sranan. Three of these languages used a deictic marker as a relativizer. According to Dreyfuss (1977:150) the choice of a deictic in a relativizing function is an independent innovation; that is, the languages have not borrowed them from their respective superstrates. The fact that the languages are creoles does not seem to have influenced the kind of marker. None uses 'true' relative pronouns that vary with case, animacy or other characteristics of their antecedents.

Resumptive pronouns occur in all four languages, but there are differences in the positions in which they occur. All the languages, however, use them in oblique and genitive-focus relatives. Dreyfuss (1977:170) suggests that this may be evidence that pronominalization is the most favoured mechanism of the three possible choices available for marking the case of a coreferential NP. The other possibilities would be marking the case on the relative pronoun (*ie* the Rel-S strategy of Maxwell 1979) or deletion (the 'WO-S strategy'). Where the relativized NP is a subject or direct object, however, the languages use a variety of means of encoding case. I have summarized these in Table 6.9 (from Dreyfuss 1977:170), including modern English for comparison.[6] If we just consider the **WH** relatives, then English can be thought of as using only the first two strategies, namely either by marking case on the pronoun or by deletion. I have put parentheses around the deletion strategy to indicate that it is not always possible to delete relatives in subject, genitive and oblique positions in modern English.

TABLE 6.9 Case marking in four creoles

	Haitian	Tok Pisin	Sango	Sranan	English
Subject	1	2/3	2/3	2	1/(2)
Direct Object	2	2/3	2/3	2	1/2
Oblique/Genitive	3	3	3	3	1/(2)

[where 1 = coding on relativizer; 2 = deletion;
3 = pronominalization]

As I have already noted, the use of resumptive pronouns in standard English is somewhat limited. We might expect further changes to take place in the newer creoles, *ie* Tok Pisin and Sango, as they come to be more widely spoken. One thing that may happen is that the use of resumptive pronouns in subject and object position would decrease or disappear. There might also be more constraints on deletion. Before summarizing the results of this comparison, I will look briefly at some studies of relativization in second language acquisition.

6.11 Relative clauses in second language acquisition

In a study of 17 adult learners of English with various native language backgrounds Gass (1983) has shown that the acquisition of relative clauses was primarily governed by universal principles, but that language-specific effects contributed to the overall developmental progression. Learners followed the constraints of the Keenan–Comrie accessibility hierarchy regardless of their language background. The native languages of the learners varied in terms of the positions in the hierarchy which were relativizable in their own languages as well as in terms of the kinds of markers used as relativizers (*eg* variant vs. invariant). The kind of marker used was not a factor in the prediction of difficulty of acquisition. Speakers of all languages, regardless of the positions which their own languages allowed to be relativized, produced more correct responses to subject than to direct object relatives, etc. in accordance with the frequency effects predictable from the hierarchy. The factor of embeddedness appeared to have no effect. That is, there were no differences between sentences in which the head was a subject vs. object in the matrix sentence (*cf* also Gass and Ard 1984:46). Where the learners deviated from the intended structure the resulting relative clause was one which was formed on a higher position, *ie* more accessible position, in the hierarchy. In Keenan and Comrie's terms this is an instance of promotion. Gass and Ard (1984:47) interpret this as an avoidance strategy. There were more examples of this on the lower end of the hierarchy than the upper end, indicating the greater difficulty of the lower positions.

There was however at least one phenomenon which they attributed to specifics of the native language of the learner. I have already mentioned Keenan and Comrie's finding that pronoun-retaining strategies are favoured in the lower positions of the hierarchy. Gass and Ard found that all speakers in their study tended to retain pronouns in relative clauses formed in the lower positions of the hierarchy regardless of whether their languages had pronoun-retaining strategies. Gass (1980), however found that there were significant differences between speakers of languages with and without pronoun-retaining strategies in relative clauses on the higher positions of the hierarchy.

In other words, a transfer effect seems to be operative at the higher, but not the lower end of the hierarchy. This indicates that the difficulties found in relativizing on the lower end of the hierarchy may be common to all language learners, and therefore universally constrained. However, it is not possible to determine whether the speakers of languages with pronoun-retaining strategies in the lower positions are simply following patterns of their own first languages, or whether they are relying on the 'same', *ie* universal principles, used by the speakers whose languages do not have pronoun-retaining strategies. This argues against frequency in input as an primary factor in this case. One of the hierarchy effects entails that relativization on the higher positions of the hierarchy is more frequent than on the lower positions. One might expect that frequency of target models in the input might work against pronoun retention in the case of those speakers whose native languages have this kind of relativization strategy.

Other studies have produced evidence in line with the transfer hypothesis as well as the universals one. Cook (1973), for example, tested the comprehension of English relative clauses by adult learners of different language backgrounds and compared the results with those of children acquiring English as their first language. There was little native language effect for the adults; most of the errors were similar to those made by children (*cf* also Ioup and Kruse 1977 for a similar conclusion). Schachter (1974), however, claimed that avoidance of relative clauses was correlated with native language background. However, all these studies used different methods of elicitation. A more relevant comparison is what happens in so called undirected language acquisition, but I do not know of any studies which have looked at this.

6.12 Chains of grammaticalization

I have argued that we can identify some common developmental principles which govern the process of relativization across different contexts of language acquisition, *eg* child language, pidgins and creoles, once we recognize that a key part of the semantic–pragmatic function of the relative clause is the assignment of a referent to an empty NP slot. Although there has often been more interest in the formal properties of grammatical rules so that their expressive function has been neglected, in both child language acquisition and creolization we can see the evolution of structure and function. Sankoff and Brown (1976) explicitly make the link between expansion of discourse function and the emergence of the relative clause in Tok Pisin. A bracketed relative clause is in some respects better suited to the needs of autonomous and non-interactive discourse situations, where meaning is conveyed largely by syntax rather than negotiated in face-to-face interaction (*cf* also the discussion in Deuchar 1983).

One could carry this argument a bit further and say that at some levels a language with relative clauses is in some respects 'better' than one without them, at least with respect to the efficiency with which it can perform certain discourse functions. But what can one say about the qualitative differences between natural languages which do have relative clauses? The Keenan–Comrie hierarchy suggests some basic inequalities with respect to both the kinds of strategies different languages make available to their speakers, and the extent to which these strategies permit relativization in various positions of the hierarchy. There is also the interesting fact that in many languages which have more than one type of relative clause, the different strategies are correlated with social and stylistic levels (*cf* Romaine 1980 and 1982 for discussion).

What are the consequences of such syntactic variation when seen in terms of logical structure and expressivity? Is there a difference in logical expressive power between languages which have certain types of relativization strategies and not others? And is there a connection between the type of relativization strategy a language has and the depth to which it penetrates the hierarchy? In a cross-linguistic survey Keenan (1975) observed that languages which had pronoun-retaining strategies to mark the NP position relativized generally permitted the formation of relative clauses in a greater variety of environments than those which did not have such a strategy. To the extent that a language can express a logical structure which another language cannot, then the former may be said to be logically more expressive than the latter in that respect. Keenan proposes what he calls the **Principle of Conservation of Logical Structure**: a construction which presents more of its logical structure (*ie* is logically more perspicacious) will have a wider distribution than one which does not, and there will be fewer restrictions on its syntactic functions (*cf* also Fodor 1981).

One can also query whether there is any difference in expressivity between a language which has a weakly grammaticalized version of some syntactic operation like relativization, and one which has a strongly grammaticalized one. If we look at the relative clause as one possible solution to the communicative problem of locating and specifying referents in discourse, then it is not hard to see why one path of development leading to the creation of relativizers is the grammaticalization of an anaphoric relation through the re-interpretation of what are basically deictic categories situated in the context of utterance. We can think of anaphora as a cline, as in Figure 6.3 (from Romaine 1984b:278), which may be encoded by various syntactic means ranging from explicit to implicit. '[+Pro] languages', *ie* pronoun-retaining ones, encode anaphora more explicitly than '[-Pro] languages'. The former are thus more transparent in their marking of semantic information. Since strong grammaticalization is characterized by semantic bleaching, this process operates at the expense of the expressive capacity of the language.

Chains of grammaticalization repeat themselves developmentally and diachronically. Certain seemingly arbitrary syntactic structures may have their origins in a few basic communicative functions, such as deixis and anaphora. A number of emergent solutions may compete for accomplishing the same discourse functions. Some may eventually become grammaticalized, and as such serve as highly conventionalized, and often very efficient strategies for dealing with recurrent communicative problems.

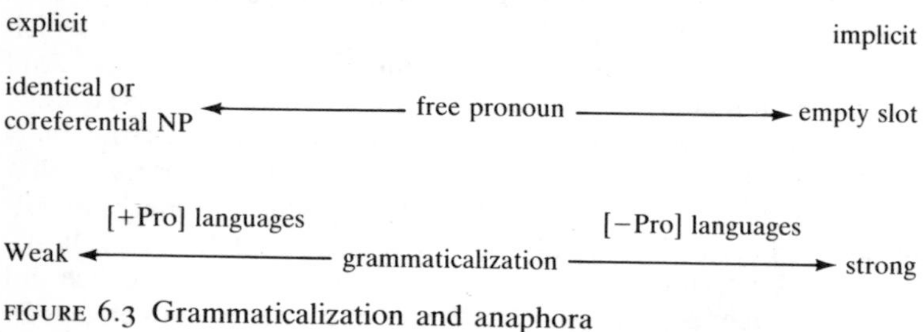

FIGURE 6.3 Grammaticalization and anaphora

Notes

1. It is not clear what implications this has for acquisition of language by the congenitally deaf.
2. The Piagetians divide cognitive development into three primary age periods: 2–7 years, the pre-operational period; 7–11 years, concrete operational period; and 11–14, formal operational period. The limits of each stage and its defining characteristics are debated, but it is assumed that the stages are universal.
3. It is not immediately clear why this should be a barrier to acquisition since both children and adults must extrapolate patterns on the basis of the input they receive (*cf* Klein W.'s 1986 notion of 'critical rule').

4. There has been no general consensus among grammarians about the status of **that** (*cf* the discussion in Romaine 1982:58, 214*ff*). Jespersen (1909–49) was among the first to argue that modern English **that** in relative clauses is not a true pronoun (*cf* more recently, Lightfoot 1979:314, who cites six arguments in favour of this position, and Van der Auwera 1985, for a comprehensive survey of the debate and arguments for the pronominal status of **that**). If one accepts complementizer status for **that**, then my earlier definition of relativization is problematic, since **that** would not be introduced via the process of pronominalization.
5. Generative treatments of relativization have tended to be based on the derivation of both **WH**- and **that**-constructions from the same underlying source. Within the Extended Standard Theory, for example, they are generated under the node COMP, which can then be deleted in situ, thus allowing for the derivation of zero clauses; or it could be filled by **WH** or optionally realized as **that** by deletion of **WH** and **that** insertion (*cf* the analyses in Bresnan 1977 and Chomsky 1977 respectively). I have argued from a socio-historical perspective that the English relativization system is best viewed in terms of an opposition between the **WH** and the **that** strategy (*cf* Romaine 1982).
6. Dreyfuss does not consider the **la** relativizer in Haitian creole.

Chapter 7

Language universals and pidgins and creoles

In this chapter I will discuss a number of issues relating to language universals, and pidgins and creoles. I noted in Chapter 1 that the study of pidgins and creoles has been recognized as an important testing ground for universals, but only recently have serious proposals been put forward. In particular, the work of Bickerton has aroused a great deal of excitement and controversy in the field of pidgin and creole studies. That is especially the case with his book *Roots of Language* (1981a) and a later paper (1984a) elaborating the 'bioprogram hypothesis'. These two works represent Bickerton's most complete statements about a theory which he has discussed in piecemeal fashion for a number of years in various articles under the heading of 'natural semantax', blueprint for language, etc. (*cf eg* Bickerton 1977a). I will use some of these ideas as the point of departure for the discussion of how significant the process of creolization is for the study of human language. I will also contrast Bickerton's approach to universals with that of Chomsky.

7.1 The bioprogram hypothesis

The essence of Bickerton's (1981a) claims is that the 'roots' of language are to be explained by a unified theory which answers three questions:

(i) How did creole languages originate? (*ie* the development of new languages)
(ii) How do children acquire language? (*ie* development in the individual)
(iii) How did human language originate? (*ie* original development of language).

Bickerton is of course not the first to see the links between acquisition and pidgin and creole languages. Jespersen, as we have seen in 1.1, for example, says (1922:225) that the similarities arise via imperfect acquisition (*cf* also Schuchardt 1889 and Samarin 1971:126).

What Bickerton calls the bioprogram consists partly of species-specific structures of cognition and partly of processes inherent in the linear expansion of language. It ensures that people will have a particular type of grammar in much the same way as a 'physical bioprogram' ensures that they will have a particular skeletal structure. A creole language is the realization of the instructions of the bioprogram with minimal cultural admixture. The contents of the bioprogram reflect Bickerton's belief that the semantic distinctions whose neural-infrastructure was laid down first in the course of mammalian development will be the first to be lexicalized/grammaticalized in the course of human language development. He hypothesizes that if a creole-like language were the end product of a long period of biological evolution, then the overall capacity to produce languages of this type must have formed part of the genetic inheritance of every individual member of the species. It would thus unfold as part of the normal growth development of every child. In most cases, however, it would be quickly overlaid by the local cultural language. Bickerton's case rests largely on a comparison of evidence from creole grammars and studies of child language acquisition. He claims that the incorrect hypotheses which children make in the process of acquiring their first language are similar to the structures which emerge in creole grammar. In other words, the features which children learn early and effortlessly turn out to be the features which the children of first generation creole speakers learn in the absence of direct evidence (*ie* without input from the speech of others in the community). Thus, the more we strip creoles of their recent developments, the greater the similarities; and hence there appears to be only one way (with minor variations) of building a language. I will now consider his hypothesis in relation to the evidence.

It is well known that creolization can take place at any point in the life-cycle of a pidgin, as indicated in 5.1. The notion of life-cycles in pidgins was discussed in Chapter 4. Mühlhäusler's distinction between developmental and restructuring continua was also noted. Bickerton is aware of the qualitatively different contact situations which have given rise to various creoles. However, he admits as evidence for the bioprogram only those creoles which meet two criteria:

(i) they must have arisen out of pidgins which had not existed for more than a generation; and
(ii) not more than 20 per cent of the population could be speakers of the dominant language, and 80 per cent should have been composed of diverse language groups.

According to Bickerton these conditions are necessary to ensure that the pidgin model is highly impoverished (i), and that no single other language could serve as a significant model for the regrammaticalization of the developing creole. These restrictions rule out just about all 'creoles' except Hawaii English Creole and Guyanese Creole; and even in these cases, the conditions are not ideal for observing the bioprogram. It must be remembered that when Bickerton makes claims which allegedly hold for all creoles, he in fact refers to only a very small number. As I will show in 7.3 and 7.4, there are a number of problems with Bickerton's interpretation of the data even for those creoles which meet his criteria. Moreover, as I have already briefly indicated in 2.9, there are a number of cases which show close overlap with the bioprogram features. These too require explanation.

In a more recent paper, Bickerton (1984a) relaxes the demographic requirement (ii), largely on the basis of some excellent socio-historical reconstruction of Isle de France Creole (Baker and Corne 1982), in which it is argued that pidginization took place *in situ* in Indian Ocean Creoles and that there is no evidence for the importation of a West-African-based pidgin. In particular, Baker and Corne compared Reunion Creole with other Indian Ocean Creoles (*eg* Seychelles and Mauritius Creole) and found that it was very different. It arose in a situation where there were many more native speakers of French than there were in any other settings where French Creoles were produced, *eg* Haiti. The result was that Reunion Creole is creole-like, but is not as close to the prototypical creole as other Indian Ocean creoles. It is also much more like French than any of the other creoles.

Bickerton is no doubt right to abandon this rigid criterion. Sankoff (1980:140) is of the view that whether a language becomes the target in multilingual encounters depends on the nature of the contacts. Under this heading come two factors. The first concerns who has the power, and the second has to do with whether or not the speakers are on the 'home territory' of one of the languages. A third factor, which is of lesser importance to Sankoff, concerns numerical superiority of speakers. Although he recognizes the factor of 'home territory' as important, Bickerton (1984a:178) attaches more significance to numbers, since he argues that it is the ratio between numbers of substrate and superstrate speakers which determines the quality of input and exposure to the target language. It is this which will affect the degree of impoverishment in the pidgin which has to be repaired by subsequent generations. The longer the period between the point at which substrate and superstrate population achieved numerical parity, the richer the second language version that would be transmitted to the first influx of immigrants. Samarin (1984:207) adds that one has to take into account also the frequency and nature of contact among speakers. He says that there is no reason why a few persons could not have had an impact disproportionate to their numbers. He believes that this is what has more typically happened. We know that this is what happened on Pitcairn Island (*cf* 2.9), where a handful of Englishmen imposed their language under conditions which were very different from those of the plantations.

However, without the demographic criterion there is no longer any overt recognition of the social factors which constrain pidginization and creolization as processes. This, of course, has considerable implications for 'input'. Bickerton's criteria still rule out Tok Pisin from the category of 'true creole', because the degree of complexity it attained prior to creolization/nativization made it susceptible to substratum influence. Another factor which Bickerton neglects is the extent of similarity or degree of linguistic distance between the languages in contact. Bickerton restricts his evidence to creoles with major colonial languages as the lexifiers, *eg* English. Mufwene (1984:203) observes that creoles which arose from the contact of genetically and typologically related languages (*eg* Lingala and Kikongo-Kituba) show fewer drastic structural simplifications than other creoles. Chinook Jargon is another case in point. Many syntactic and phonological features which from a universal perspective would be considered marked have survived in the Jargon presumably because they are widely shared by the Indian languages which provided the input. Thomason (1983:824) has argued that these features of Chinook Jargon do not represent the lowest common denominator of the languages in contact.

7.2 The contents of the bioprogram

Bickerton admits that there is much more work to be done on specifying the contents of the bioprogram. As it is put forward in his book, it contains four semantic distinctions which have various syntactic consequences:

(i) specific/non-specific
(ii) state/process
(iii) punctual/non-punctual
(iv) causative/non-causative.

The fact that the bioprogram is seen as essentially semantic (rather than syntactic, as in Chomsky's notions of 'core grammar' and LAD, *ie* 'language acquisition device') indicates the significance which Bickerton attaches to what he calls 'natural semantax'. Chomsky's language acquisition device contains a set of universal categories and constraints which together sharply limit the theoretically possible types of language that the child may be expected to learn. The child's learning task is to select from a range of possible grammars. There are also certain open parameters which are fixed in accordance with language specific input (*cf eg* Chomsky 1981). I will now discuss the specific/non-specific and causative/non-causative distinctions.The second and third concern tense and aspect and are the topic of 7.3.

The distinction specific/non-specific affects noun phrases and marks whether their references are specific or non-specific. Compare English **a man** vs. **the man**. We can take some examples from Hawaii Pidgin and Creole English. In the pidgin articles appear sporadically and unpredictably. Bickerton (1981a:22–3), for example, contrasts the case of Japanese speakers, who tend to use very few definite articles in the contexts where English would require them and Filipino speakers who overgeneralize the use of the article to environments where they would not occur in English. An example of the latter is:

hi get da hawaian waif – 'He has a Hawaiian wife'

Creole speakers however use the definite article **da** for all and only specific reference NPs, *ie* those that can be assumed to be known to the listener, as in:

æfta da boi, da wan wen jink dæt milk, awl da maut soa – 'Afterward, the mouth of the boy who had drunk that milk was all sore'

Creole speakers also use the indefinite article **wan** for all and only specific-reference NPs that can be assumed to be unknown to the listener. Typically these are used for first mention, *eg*:

hi get wan blæk buk – 'He has a black book'

No articles or markers of plurality are used with other NPs, *eg*:

yang fela dei no du dæt – 'Young fellows don't do that'
bat nobadi gon get jab – 'But nobody will get a job'
hu go daun frs iz luza – 'The one who goes down first is the loser'

In English some of these forms which are not marked in creole would be marked by **the** and others by **a**. In other words Hawaii Creole English seems to unite in one category cases which English would treat as separate categories. English has an obligatory number distinction, but the creole does not. Bickerton (1981a:25) says that the origin of this system cannot be accounted for by substratum or superstrate influence. Of the substratum languages involved many do not have articles at all. Of those that do, none shows the same distribution of unmarked forms as the creole does, *eg* Hawaiian and Portugese. Neither can the system be traced to Hawaii Pidgin English, where each individual seems to transfer his native language system. Bickerton's conclusion is that the zero marking of specifics was an invention introduced by creole speakers.

He then goes on to say (1981a:56) that virtually all creoles have a system which is identical to Hawaii Creole English. A definite article is used to mark presupposed-specific NPs, an indefinite article for asserted-specific NPs and zero for non-specific NPs. He gives some additional examples from Guyanese creole:

Jan bai di buk [presupposed-specific NP] – 'John bought the book'
Jan bai wan book [asserted-specific NP] – 'John bought a (particular) book'
Jan bai buk [non-specific NP] – 'John bought books'

The contrast between the two systems can be summarized in the following diagram.

		Non-specific	Specific: Indefinite	Specific: Definite
ENGLISH				
count nouns	sg.	**a book**	**a book**	**the book**
	pl.	**books**	**books**	**the books**
uncountables		**money**	**money**	**the money**
HAWAII ENGLISH CREOLE				
count nouns	sg.	**buk**	**wan buk**	**da buk**
	pl.	**buk**	**buk(s)**	**da buk(s)**
uncountables		**mani**	**mani**	**da mani**

I will look now at the causative/non-causative distinction. Languages possess many different ways of marking the distinction between causatives and non-causatives. Typically, it may be marked on the subject (as in so-called ergative languages) or on the verb. English relies on verb marking to express the distinction. The simplest way of indicating the causal as a verbal category is to use the same verb. In one case, however, the subject will be the causative agent, the verb will be transitive and there will be a direct object. In the other, the subject will be a patient or experiencer, and the verb will be intransitive and have no direct object, as in the examples:

Bill opened the door [causative and transitive]
The door opened [non-causative and intransitive]

There are other cases in English where the same verb is used, but where the non-causative must be a passive, as in:

John planted the tree
The tree was planted [by John] [*cf* ***The tree planted**]

In other cases, however, a different verb is used for causative and non-causative meanings, as in:

The sheep ate [non-causative]
John ate the sheep [John caused the sheep to eat]
John fed the sheep [causative]

In still others there is no lexical pair. The causative alternative must be formed by means of a periphrastic construction such as **to make/cause X to**, as in:

Mary suffered [non-causative]
John suffered Mary [John caused Mary to suffer]
John made Mary suffer [causative]

In other languages such as Turkish, the same lexical verb is used for both causative and non-causative meanings, but different suffixes differentiate them. In ergative languages the same lexical verb is generally used, but causative subjects are marked with a special ergative suffix and subjects of non-causatives are marked with the accusative, like the objects of causatives. Creoles, however, avoid what Bickerton (1981a:199) calls 'bound morphology solutions' to the problem of marking the causative/non-causative distinction (or for that matter any category). Out of all the possible strategies for marking the distinction creoles use a simple transitive/intransitive verb alternation. As examples, Bickerton (1981a:72) gives the following sentences from Guyanese Creole and Hawaii English Creole:

GC: **dem a ponish abi**
'They are making us suffer'
GC: **Abi a ponish**
'We are suffering/being made to suffer'
HCE: **dei wen teik foa boad**
'They took four [surf] boards'
HCE: **foa boad wen teik**
'Four [surf] boards were taken'

The use of the same verb form for transitive and intransitive meanings is also a feature of some pidgins, as in the examples from Pidgin and Standard Fijian (Moag 1978:83):

SF: **ā mate na vuaka** [past die the pig]
PF: **na vuaka sa mate** [the pig predicate die]
'The pig died' (intransitive)
SF: **ā vaka-mate-a-na tamata koyā** [past cause-die-it the pig the man demonstrative]
PF: **oqo na tamata sa mate na vuaka** [demonstrative the man predicate die the pig]
'The man killed the pig' (transitive).

When a verb is transitive in Standard Fijian it takes a verbal prefix and suffix, *eg* **vaka-mate-a**, while in Pidgin Fijian it is invariant. Other pidgins, however, such as Tok Pisin, have a more complex system of indicating the distinction between causative and non-causative (*cf eg* Mühlhäusler 1985c for a discussion of Tok Pisin).

The verbal system of Pidgin Fijian is in general reduced by comparison with that of Standard Fijian in the sense that distinctions which are marked in the standard are not marked in the pidgin. Where Standard Fijian has a variety of markers indicating tense and aspect, as shown in Table 7.1, Pidgin Fijian has only a generalized predicate marker **sā** (*cf* Moag 1978:82). Time relations are indicated by context or through the use of the temporal adverbs which occur sentence-initially or before the marker **sā** (*cf* Siegel 1983).

TABLE 7.1 Convergences in tense and aspect in Pidgin Fijian

Standard Fijian		Pidgin Fijian
Aspect	Tense	
sā	**na** (future)	
	ø	
	ā (past)	**sā**

7.3 Tense, mood and aspect

The categories of tense, mood and aspect are generally regarded as verbal (*cf eg* Lyons 1968) because they are usually, though not exclusively, marked by means of verbal inflection. Tense, as indicated in 5.5, has to do with the relationship between the moment of speaking and the situation or event. This is what Comrie calls absolute time reference. It forms the core of any tense system. In his (1985:14) terms tense is the grammaticalized expression of location in time. In a sentence like **John played tennis**, we assume that the action to which the speaker refers at the moment of speaking occurred in the past. Aspect on the other hand has to do with the internal structure of the event or situation (*cf eg* Comrie 1976). In a sentence like **I was playing tennis**, it is understood that the action of playing was continuous over a period of time in the past, rather than abrupt. Aspect may be marked by means of verbal morphology or adverbial expressions, or it may be part of the inherent semantics of a particular verb form. Thus, in English the verb **roll** is inherently durative because it describes a situation which lasts over a certain period of time. There is a connection between tense and aspect. An event that is on-going at the speech moment has not been completed. Hence there is a correlation between present tense and incompletive (imperfective or progressive) aspect, and by implication between past tense and completive (perfective or non-progressive) aspect. A consequence of these correlations is that temporal distinctions may be expressed by morpho-syntactic categories that have wider modal or aspectual functions.

Modality refers to the speaker's assessment of the event in terms of its likelihood or probability, as in **John might come**, where the form **might** indicates there is some doubt. There is much more to tense, mood and aspect that just indicated. In a way it is unfortunate that some of the most substantial claims regarding creolization and child language have been made in relation to categories over which there is such little terminological agreement among linguists. As I will show, this makes a number of Bickerton's hypotheses more difficult to test than might at first appear. However, these brief definitions will suffice until I have discussed Bickerton's claims relating to this area of creole grammar.

There are a number of similarities in the emergent tense systems of creole grammars, which have been discussed in detail by Bickerton (1981a). Some of these have been mentioned in connection with Guyanese Creole in 5.5. A basic characteristic of creole tense systems is for the present to be unmarked in contrast to the past and future. (This, however, is also true of the English so-called present tense.) Bickerton (1975a) proposes that the creole verb expresses one tense opposition [± anterior], one aspectual opposition, [± punctual], and one modality distinction [± irrealis]. Bickerton's explanation for the emergence of these categories and their semantic content is that they are part of the bioprogram. The categories express basic semantic primitives. Their emergence and subsequent ordering as tense, mood and aspect in pre-verbal position reflects the order in which their neural infrastructure was wired in during the course of the evolution of the human brain. In short then, Bickerton is arguing that the creole tense, mood and aspect system (TMA) is a human universal linguistic prototype.

Bickerton (and Givón 1982) posit three functions which are central to the communicative event:

(i) knowing the temporal order of the occurrence of past events
(ii) being able to distinguish between sensory input and one's own imagination.
(iii) being able to tell whether an event occurred once or is protracted.

Note, however, that both argue in a circular fashion. In other words, they claim that the features represent basic distinctions because they are present in creoles. These is no independent evidence that they are more basic in any other sense by comparison to other distinctions which human languages routinely make. If, however, there is some doubt about their presence in creole grammars (*cf* 7.4), then their case is considerably weakened.

Bickerton argues that all known creole TMA systems exhibit the same three member inventory of pre-verbal elements marking the same semantic (and pragmatic) functions. The zero form of the verb encodes the simple past for verbs of action, and the non-past for state verbs. In the case of Hawaii Creole English, for example, the markers are **bin** [anterior], **go** [irrealis] and **stei** [punctual]. Givón (1982:119) notes that this opposition coincides with the discourse–pragmatic functions of backgrounding/foregrounding. The zero verb forms are used to carry the backbone of the action narrative (as opposed to the background). The main line of the story is given in the same temporal sequence as it occurred, marked by the zero form of the verb. Digressions, flashbacks, parenthetical interjections are handled by anterior markers (*eg* **bin** in Hawaii English Creole).

The ordering in-sequence of the main-line action clauses is characteristic of the use of the zero form, as is additionally, the continuation of the same subject–topic. The semantic–pragmatic function of the anterior is to mark out of sequence clauses in the narrative, particularly those which look back and relate events that occurred earlier than the preceding clause in the narrative.[1] To this it can be added that non-punctual aspect tends to occur in the background rather than main-line events of the narrative, and thus it shares a similar discourse–pragmatic function to the anterior. Bickerton says that the creole verb has a marker of non-punctual aspect (*eg* **stei** in Hawaii English Creole), which indicates durative or iterative aspect for action verbs, and is indifferent to the past/non-past distinction. As far as modality in creoles is concerned, it is the realis mode which carries the background of the story's action line. The distribution of realis/irrealis modalities in discourse coincides to a large extent with narrative vs. quoted speech, according to Givón (1982:123).

Thus, it appears that the unmarked member of these three oppositions, T, M, A (which in creole grammar is the unmarked form) is always used to relate clauses that are foregrounding in terms of their discourse–pragmatic function, and which form the backbone of a narrative. The marked members by contrast are used largely in clauses which break narrative continuity, present background material or otherwise digress in some way from the narrative mainline. Moreover, as I have already noted, Bickerton ascribes great significance to the rigidity of ordering of these markers, viz.:

(Anterior) (Modal) (Non-punctual) V

Givón (1982:127) suggests that the relative ordering of these markers corresponds to a scope gradation. The non-punctual aspect has only the verb under its semantic scope. The modal operator has the larger proposition/sentence scope, while anterior has the widest, discourse scope. Thus, there is a one-to-one mapping of semantic–pragmatic and syntactic scope. Givón (1982:126) states that it is hard to find a human language in which these three basic semantic–pragmatic oppositions found in creoles do not form part of the TMA system. This suggests that these are loci to which particular semantic notions tend to gravitate. The background is more elaborate in terms of temporal grammatical marking than the foreground because the marking load of the background is greater. Creoles represent, however, a particularly interesting case to examine because, as Givón puts it, they have no diachronic, only ontogenetic history. Therefore, they show the most transparent one-to-one correlation between semantic–pragmatic scope and morpho-syntactic coding (*cf* however, the discussion of interlanguage in 7.5).

In general, arguments about the basicness of certain structures make appeals to such factors as frequency in languages of the world and early emergence in child language (*cf* 7.4 on the latter). Some evidence from typology can be used to bolster claims about the primacy of aspect. Bybee (1985)) surveyed a sample of 50 languages in order to examine the distribution of verbal categories. She found that aspect conditioned changes in the verb stem more frequently than any other inflectional category. She therefore argues that aspect is the category most directly relevant to the verb. In all the languages in the sample aspect morphology was the second most frequent after valence-changing morphology, *ie* distinctions such as transitivity, causativity, etc. The latter would also offer some support for Bickerton's inclusion of the causative/non-causative distinction in the bioprogram. Bybee predicts that if a language has any morphology at all, it has valence-changing morphology. This is operative in Tok Pisin, where the first verbal morphology, apart from the predicative marker, is the transitive marker **-im**, which has developed into a causative suffix. Tok Pisin shows the development of aspect and number marking too, as I have shown in 4.4, but these markers are not bound to the verb. Only the valence morphology is bound to the verb.

Bybee also found a tendency in some of the languages for aspect to occur closer to the stem than tense or mood markers. There were no languages in the sample in which the mood marker occurred closer to the stem than the aspect marker. She proposes a diagrammatic relationship (*cf* 2.4) between the meanings and their expression, which is similar to Givón's principle of scope: the closer or more relevant the meaning of the inflectional morpheme is to the meaning of the verb, the closer the expression unit must occur to the verb stem.

I noted some general problems with typology in 2.9, the main one being that it is static rather than dynamic. When applied to predictions about the creole prototype, it is easy to argue that change has taken place, or that other factors have obscured the evolution of the bioprogram. This is Bickerton's strategy of argumentation in the face of counter evidence. More generally however, Bickerton (1981a:155–60) discounts typological arguments. Whether a feature is frequent in languages of the world is irrelevant. The features which are innate are there from the beginning and not because of their universality in the synchronic structures of natural languages. Thus, the bioprogram specifies features which may or may not turn out to be frequent in the world's languages. Typology provides a selective view of structures which survive largely by accident because the languages are used in successful speech communities, and not because they are universal. This distinguishes Bickerton's view of universals very sharply from that of Chomsky. The latter assumes that what is universal in language can be uncovered by examining one language in depth. However, from Bickerton's perspective highly evolved cultural languages like English are likely to reveal little of the biological origins of language.

Now I will consider the extent to which Bickerton is justified in his claim that this type of verb system is the so-called creole prototype, and furthermore that this creole prototype is the basis of all human languages.

Muysken (1981a) is critical of Bickerton's explanation of tense, mood and aspect in creoles for several reasons (*cf* Bickerton 1981a:73–8 for comments on Muysken's analysis). One is that it does not explain why only these three semantic features should be required. Bickerton's account is circular in the absence of neurological and other evidence. A second reason is that it does not explain why these features should be realized as particles in pre-verbal position ordered in this particular way, unless we accept Givón's explanation based on pragmatic scope as sufficient. I have stressed at several stages the tendency for pidgins and creoles to opt for greater analyticity and transparency of encoding, *ie* one form – one meaning (*cf* 2.3 and 2.4). Given the semantic–pragmatic and syntactic isomorphism of the creole prototype, one could argue that it is in some respects better suited to basic communicative needs. However, as I pointed out in 5.1, there does not appear to be a case for arguing that the referential power of the grammar is increased by the grammaticalization of the categories of TMA. Likewise, it is not clear that one can easily argue that just because semantic distinctions such as irrealis, etc., are not obligatorily and overtly marked, they are not expressed or capable of being expressed. Similarly, morphological boundness is not in itself a necessary criterion in deciding whether a given category is grammaticalized (*cf* Comrie 1985). So what then is the advantage of the grammaticalized creole prototype over the pre-creole system of marking time relations by adverbs and discourse rules which indicate the scope of adverbs and regulate the ordering of clauses? Furthermore, if such a system is advantageous, why should languages diverge from the prototype and develop semantic and pragmatic elaborations which interact with the prototype features in different ways?

Labov (1970/1977:36) says that there is no basis for arguing that tense markers express the concepts of temporal relations more clearly than adverbs of time. The advantage of a highly grammaticalized tense system is therefore purely stylistic. Probably all languages have a marker of sequence and successive event, such as the adverb **then**.

In the experimental Farsi pidgin referred to in 2.4, markers of temporality were created from the deictic/demonstrative particles **inja** – 'here/this' and **anja** – 'there/that'. The former was used to indicate present time, and the latter past time reference. Various other words like **gerd** – 'year' and **vaqt** – 'time' were used in combination with **anja**. The Farsi word for 'follow' – **dombal**, was used as a future marker. There are numerous parallels for this in natural pidgins, *cf* Hawaii Pidgin English **bipo** – 'before', or **smol boi taim** ['small boy time'] as a marker of past time. Markers of spatial location are frequently grammaticalized in other functions. In the German pidgin one of the subjects used **rücken** – 'back' either for past or future tense. In this case 'before' and 'after' are apparently being construed as located 'in front or in back of' another event in space/time (*cf* Cassidy 1985). The property which tense markers possess which adverbs of time do not is stylistic flexibility. Without more studies addressed to the question of the referential and stylistic adequacy of creoles, it is difficult to go beyond this point in the argument (*cf* however, Rickford 1986c).

Muysken (1981a) furthermore argues that within each semantic category of tense/mood/aspect there is a hierarchy of distinctions governed by a theory of markedness. This theory would be used to predict that in the early stages of development of TMA systems only the unmarked distinctions appear and that the complex distinctions appear only later. He then tries to show how this markedness hierarchy might work for the categories of tense and aspect.[2]

His hierarchy of distinctions in the tense system draws on Hornstein's (1977) model, which in turn is based on Reichenbach's (1947) system, where tense is viewed in terms of combinations of S, E, and R, where S = moment of speech, E = moment of the event, and R = a theoretical entity, the reference point. Where S, R and E coincide we have the simple present, or unmarked case; this is so because the moment of speaking, the event and the reference point are all temporally coincident in a simple present form like **I play**. By assuming that dissociations, *ie* the separations between two moments, is marked, and associations are unmarked, he draws up a markedness index, shown in Table 7.2 (Muysken 1981a:191).

TABLE 7.2 Markedness hierarchy for tense

tense	*dissociation*	*1*	*2*	*S_E*	*markedness index*
simple past	(E,R_S)	u	m	u	1
past perfect	(E_R_S)	m	m	u	2
simple present	(S,R,E)	u	u	u	0
present perfect	(E_S,R)	m	u	u	1
simple future	(S_R,E)	m	u	m	2
future perfect	(S_E_R)	m	m	m	3

This means that the simple past would be the next in the hierarchy because there is a dissociation between the event and the moment of speaking in a form like **I played**; thus, E, R_S. The future perfect would be the most marked form because there are two dissociations, *ie* S_E_R_. In a form like **I will have played**, the event is posterior to the moment of speech, but anterior to the reference point. Muysken furthermore assumes that all cases where the moment of the event is posterior to the moment of speech, *ie* where S_E obtains, are marked. This means that the future perfect has a value of three because there are two dissociations and the moment of speaking is anterior to the event. Hence Muysken claims that the emergence of the feature anterior as the prime tense category in early creole systems would be predicted from markedness values. The universal grammar which the children of pidgin-speaking parents presumably have to draw on in creating the creole will represent the unmarked case for all parameters.

Muysken also draws up a markedness hierarchy for aspectual distinctions based on Woitsetschlaeger (1977). In this system nine aspectual categories are distinguished in terms of six binary features, *eg* reference to sequential information, which is marked. Forms requiring no reference to sequential information are unmarked. As it happens in this system, two aspectual categories are unmarked: imperfective and perfective. The category of imperfective corresponds roughly to Bickerton's feature non-punctual, and is prominent in creoles.

This sort of analysis might at first glance seem promising. However, I do not think universal hierarchies of markedness will yield much insight into the study of tense and aspect, since the meanings conveyed by these categories depend on the categories available within a particular system and the relationships among them. In other words, forms have certain combinatory potential within particular systems. What the perfective means in any particular language will depend on what other aspectual oppositions are encoded in that system (*cf* also Bickerton 1981a:177). For example, the semantic space circumscribed by an explicitly marked future form will not necessarily be the same cross-linguistically. That will depend on whether the language is primarily retrospective or prospective in terms of its marking of time relations. A language is retrospective if the present tense may mark past or if the past may be unmarked. A language is prospective if the present tense may be used to mark a future or if the future is unmarked. For prospective systems the opposition between past and non-past is primary, while for retrospective systems the future vs. non-future is primary (*cf* Ultan 1978:88–9). Degree of markedness will also depend on the relative division of labour and degree of fusion of tense, mood and aspect. This means that we cannot assume, as Muysken does, that all cases where the event is posterior to the moment of speech are universally marked. Such cases may be more or less marked relative to the distinctions within a particular system. Moreover, what Bickerton and Muysken neglect is the fact that the meaning of any tense form depends on the occurrence of that form in a particular context. In discourse it is possible for the speaker to set up a relative time frame in which any situation can be located relative to the time of some situation other than the moment of speaking.

In Gibson and Levy's (ms.) analysis of Guyanese and Jamaican Creole there is evidence for two aspectual oppositions of [±imperfective] and [±punctual] as well as a tense opposition of [±non-present]. The distinction [±imperfective] depends on the syntactic classification of verbs, while [±punctual] depends on the inherent aspectual properties of the predicate phrase. The [±non-present] tense system relies on the relationship between a speaker and events in the sense of whether it is 'now' or 'not now' *ie* non-present. The formally unmarked present, past and future denote things in the deictic here and now.

These semantic categories are different from the ones used by Bickerton. Moreover, Gibson (1982) has argued that the same semantic system does not hold over the Guyanese post-creole continuum. Her analysis assumes unity between the basilect and mesolect, but discontinuity between them and the acrolect.

Gibson argues that Bickerton's aspectual system applies only to non-statives. He claims that it makes no sense to ask whether stative verbs are [±punctual] because all states by definition have an extended duration. Gibson, however, says it is meaningful to ask this question for non-statives in Jamaican Creole. Although statives imply an extended duration, they can combine with progressive and habitual to indicate the continuity of state or that the continuity is characteristic of a long period. Thus, both [±statives] can combine with progressives and habituals. Bickerton's anterior tense system does not include the future, although uninflected and inflected verbs can have past, present and future meanings. Bickerton discusses only those which have past and present meanings. Even in the case of Hawaii English Creole it is not generally agreed that the TMA system operates with the meanings Bickerton proposes.

Sato (1978) has done a detailed analysis of the **go** + verb construction in 13 pidgin and 13 creole speakers from Bickerton's sample. Its distribution is skewed towards outer islanders (*ie* those from Hawaii and Kauai, which are the least decreolized areas) and Filipino pidgin speakers. She says (1978:35) that this distribution suggests that **go** + verb was more common during the late pidgin and basilectal creole period in roughly the late 1920s and 1930s.

Following Bickerton and Odo's (1976) analysis she grouped the instances of the construction according to the semantic contexts in which it could occur. These are as follows with examples (Sato 1978:41–2):

(i) completed past [–habitual +realis +past]

Ai mub ai- go mub nada sai – 'I moved – I went and moved to another place'

(ii) habitual past [+habitual +realis +past]

So ere nau æn den de go fid om wid kandens milk – 'So every now and then they used to feed him with condensed milk'

(iii) habitual non-past [+habitual +realis −past]

Evritai ai go chek mai chikin neks yaw haus, æ? – 'I frequently go and check my chickens next to your house, don't I?'

(iv) irrealis conditional [+habitual −realis]

If da baga no meik wan gud mada dag, den ai go yuz om fo hanting – 'If the bugger isn't a good mother dog, then I'll use her for hunting'

(v) irrealis future [−habitual −realis]

Bambai til tumaro he go teli telifon – 'Later by tomorrow, he'll call'

Table 7.3 (adapted from Sato 1978:51) shows the distribution of the **go** + verb forms according to these semantic environments.

TABLE 7.3 Distribution of go + verb forms

semantic context	*% of forms*		
completed past	37.4		
habitual past	20.5	habitual	37.7
habitual non-past	17.2		
irrealis conditional	8.8	irrealis	24.8
irrealis future	16.0		

On the basis of the fact that four out of six of the pidgin speakers used **go** primarily in the completed past and habitual contexts, Bickerton concluded that these were the earlier environments and that from there **go** spread to irrealis contexts later. Sato's analysis, however, showed that there was not much support for the idea that **go** + verb use is closely related to year of arrival or birth of the speaker. The distinction adopted for categorizing a person as a pidgin vs. creole speaker is based on birth. Only those who were born and raised in Hawaii were classified as creole speakers.

It is not always possible to isolate instances where **go** functions solely as a verb of motion from those where it contributes aspectual and tense meaning. It is not hard to see how the spatial meanings of **go** become transferred to the domain of futurity. Going to a place where the speaker will perform an action implies movement towards the time when one will do it. In this case we are dealing essentially with an analogical or metaphorical extension from spatial to temporal movement. In other words physical movement in space becomes translated into movement in time. There is also a connection between futurity and modality because events in the future by definition are hypothetical, and thus there is some uncertainty about them. The process by which **go** is used as a marker of tense, aspect and modality is another case of grammaticalization, which involves a shift from referential to grammatical meanings (*cf* 4.5). Verbs of motion like **come** and **go** have frequently been the source of tense and aspect markers in other languages. Sato (1978:60) also found instances where **go** seemed to be a semantically empty discourse marker, as in:

so wi wen go cheinj ar yuniformz tu dem
'So we changed our uniforms to them [the other clothing]'

In these cases, tense and aspect were indicated by discourse context or adverbials etc.

When Sato (1978:84) looked at the distribution of meanings for the **go** + verb constructions, she found that the majority (45 per cent) of cases involved motion. Irrealis meanings accounted for 12 per cent and habitualness for 9 per cent. There was a tendency for the creole speakers to use more irrealis meanings for **go** than pidgin speakers. The creole speakers also had more cases where **go** was used redundantly. Her conclusion was that **go** played a very minor role in marking irrealis.

Sato (1978:45) comments that the picture is complicated by the fact that many of the pidgin speakers are Filipinos who emigrated late and are the contemporaries of creole speakers. They represent a late stage of pidginization, and thus can be expected to use some creole features. She found evidence that the irrealis use of **go** is of basilectal creole rather than pidgin origin since the use of **go** in that context is twice as great for creole as for pidgin speakers. Pidgin speakers use **go** twice as much in completed past contexts as do the creole speakers. Sato says that in order to establish any clear diachronic shift from the use of **go** in past tense contexts to its irrealis use, one would have to examine the usage of speakers from the early period of pidginization, *ie* Portuguese, Chinese and Japanese. More decreolized speakers have access to other irrealis markers, *eg* **gon**, **gonna** and **will**. The first of these forms are mesolectal and the latter acrolectal.

Both Bickerton's and Sato's studies used the same data corpus although the analyses were undertaken separately. They illustrate the difficulties in testing some of the hypotheses related to the bioprogram. Two investigators using the same material can come to different conclusions because their analyses depend on their interpretations of the speakers' intended meaning. As I will show next, the problem is even greater when children's language is being analyzed. This, however, is a good example of what Bickerton (1981a:83) has called the First Law of Creole Studies: 'Every creolist's analysis can be directly contradicted by the creolist's own texts and citations.'

7.4 Some evidence from child language acquisition

I already indicated that there is nothing new in the idea that ontogeny recapitulates phylogeny. Bickerton relies heavily on the work of Lamendella (1976), who suggests that developments in the evolution of human language were hard-wired into the genotype in such a way so that the ontogeny of language in the child recapitulates to a large extent the phylogenetic development of language over time. But to what extent are the evolution of language, creolization and first language acquisition really comparable? Surely, the starting point is not quite the same in each case. Bickerton's claim (1981a:213) that the original human language was not learned through acquisition strategies, inductive learning procedures or hypothesis formation, and therefore must have been invented, will probably not meet with much resistance. Chomsky (1979:55), however, seems to discount the possibility of evolutionary development in language when he asserts that 'stone age man spoke languages like ours'. The extent to which Bickerton is justified in claiming that creole speakers 'invent' creoles and child speakers 'create' their own language is more contentious. Although language acquisition is a creative and on-going process, there is a sense in which it is generally acknowledged that children do not create their own language, but step into a more or less ready-made one, which they reproduce and transform.

Bickerton believes that children can learn language only because they already know one, namely, the bioprogram (*cf* also Fodor 1975:63–4). It is interesting to note at this point the similarity between Bickerton's reasoning and that of Chomsky: both assume that the child's exposure to degenerate or impoverished input leads to the conclusion that there must be an innate language acquisition device, for how else could children learn language if they are not pre-programmed? One could however argue that it is instead Chomsky's and Bickerton's impoverished imaginations and highly restricted database rather than the allegedly meagre input which children are supposed to receive which brings them to argue 'how else?'.

Bickerton argues that the structures used by young children which violate the grammatical rules of the target language are consistent both with the rules hypothesized for the bioprogram and with the surface forms found in creoles. Where the bioprogram conflicts with the grammar of the target language one finds delayed learning and frequent errors. He relies heavily on a few studies of language acquisition which can be interpreted in accordance with the bioprogram predictions. Some of these studies have been cross-linguistic, and have shown that some devices for the grammaticalization of certain semantic categories are available to learners earlier than others. A number of such studies have been done by Slobin (1973), who sees first language acquisition as guided by a set of operating principles. These are general cognitive–perceptual strategies and processing limitations imposed by memory. They are in effect instructions to the child on how to analyse linguistic input rather than specific instructions for the construction of a grammar. Bickerton (1984a:185) claims that these fall out from the bioprogram. In other words, children acquire certain distinctions because they are part of the bioprogram and not because they are guided by features in the linguistic input. Slobin's Operating Principles are as follows:

(i) Pay attention to the ends of words.
(ii) The phonological forms of words can be systematically modified.
(iii) Pay attention to the order of words and morphemes.
(iv) Avoid interruption and re-arrangement of linguistic units.
(v) Underlying semantic relations should be marked overtly and clearly.
(vi) Avoid exceptions.
(vii) The use of grammatical markers should make semantic sense.

Research by Andersen and others has argued that a similar guiding principle behind second language acquisition is the preference for a one-to-one mapping of underlying form onto surface form. Andersen (1984), for example, subsumes iv to vii under the heading of what he calls the 1:1 Principle, which says that there should be a one-to-one relationship between form and meaning. Naro's (1978:340–41) factorization principle is also equivalent in that it states that each invariant element of meaning should be expressed by at least one phonologically separate and invariant stress bearing form. Seuren and Wekker (1986) also speak of semantic transparency as the organizing principle behind second language acquisition and creolization. For Bickerton it does not seem possible that children could create creole languages which are fundamentally different from pidgins, share a number of basic similarities and still be learned by means of a general knowledge acquisition device.

Operating principles are of little use with pidgin input, if Bickerton is right about its limitations. All acquisition models which are solely input driven will have trouble accounting for the origins of creoles. One could argue however that the operating principles reflect not so much innate tendencies as convergent solutions to other problems such as the linguistic one of encoding meanings onto a linear speech channel and the perceptual one of decoding and memory of forms in time. In other words, the issue is whether the bioprogram grammar is the output of a genetically coded program for language or whether it is the product of on-going cognitive processes.

Bickerton (1981a) catalogues a variety of evidence from child language acquisition studies which seems to support the predictions of the bioprogram; namely the hypothesis that the features which children learn effortlessly and early are key features of the bioprogram (and also creole languages). With regard to the creole system of specific/non-specific marking Bickerton relies on work done by Maratsos (1976), who has shown that specificity in the article system is mastered very early without error by English-speaking children as young as three years of age. An interesting fact about the acquisition of English however is that another distinction between definite and indefinite NPs is acquired much later. This is surprising because this distinction is marked, while the specific/non-specific distinction is not. Not all researchers, however, agree that these distinctions are mastered at such an early age. Karmiloff-Smith (1979), for example, states that the full control of all the functions of the article system isn't acquired until around age ten. The non-specific reference function is acquired relatively late.

Bickerton (1981a:147–8) gives some examples which show that the specific/non-specific distinction is not systematically marked:

If you're sick, you should see the doctor [non-specific]
Call the doctor who treated Marge [specific]
Dogs are mammals [non-specific]
The dog is a mammal [non-specific]
A dog is a mammal [non- specific]
A dog just bit me [specific]
Mary can't stand to have a dog in the room [specific]

From the point of view of the child learner the problem posed by the English system is that three articles, **the**, **a** and zero correspond to two sets of semantic distinctions: supposed-known to the listener/supposed-unknown to the listener and specific referent/no-specific referent. There is not a one-to-one mapping between form and meaning, as there is in the case of the plural, for example, where the plural morpheme **-s** uniquely marks the meaning of plural. Bickerton claims that it is highly unlikely that the child manages to arrive at the distinction between specific and non-specific on the basis of linguistic input. Maratsos (1976:94) comments that specific and non-specific reference are not connected in a clear way with external attributes or relations with perceived objects, by contrast, for example, with plural marking. Bickerton's (1981a:153) conclusion is that the child is able to learn the specific/non-specific distinction in the absence of direct evidence because he is programmed to do so. The child knows the distinction in advance and looks for evidence in the target language which marks it.

Bickerton relies on Slobin's evidence for the causative/non-causative distinction. Slobin (1978) conducted a cross-linguistic study in which he found that children learning different languages acquired the distinction between causative and non-causative with different facility and at different rates. The languages concerned were Turkish, Serbo-Croat, English and Italian. The Turkish causative suffix was learned and used productively and correctly by the age of two. Serbo-Croat speakers however did not reach this level until they were four or older. At this age the English and Italian speakers averaged between 60–80 per cent. Bickerton (1981a:198–9) interprets this difference in accordance with the bioprogram. The encoding of the causative/non-causative distinction in Turkish is regular and unique. In the other languages the relationship between form and meaning is less direct and hence more difficult to acquire.

Bickerton (1981a:200–1) also interprets the kinds of errors English-speaking children make in terms of bioprogram predictions. Because English-speaking children are unable to find a consistent way of expressing the causative/non-causative distinction on the basis of the input they receive, they generalize the simplest solution. This involves taking the same verb and using it both transitively and intransitively. Bowerman (1974) found that from the age of 2.3 children employed intransitive non-causative verbs in causative meanings, as in these examples:

I'm gonna fall this on her [= make this fall on her/drop this on her]
She came it over here [= made it come over here]
How would you flat it? [= make it flat, flatten it]

Bickerton (1981a:154–211) also interprets a number of studies of children's acquisition of tense and aspect as evidence in support of the bioprogram. He claims that the English progressive morpheme **-ing**, as in **singing**, is acquired early and errorlessly. This is what would be predicted since it involves a basic bioprogram distinction between state and process. Despite the fact that in the early stages children often generalize other morphological markers, such as the plural **-s** to items which do not take them (*eg* ***foots**), they do not overgeneralize **-ing** to stative verbs like **want** and **know** with which it does not combine, *eg* ***I am liking this book**. Maratsos and Chalkley (1980), however, point out that if a semantic category like the distinction between state and process operated in child language, then we would expect to find it generalized across categories. This would mean, among other things, that process adjectives like **noisy** would be assigned verbal endings, but errors such as ***I am noisy-ing** – 'I am making noise', are rare (*cf* also Aitchison 1983c:89).

Another piece of evidence which Bickerton interprets in favour of the bioprogram comes from children's acquisition of morphemes used for past tense marking in Turkish. The marker **-di** is used for direct experience events which are personally observed by the speaker; **-mıs** is used for indirect events reported to or inferred by the speaker. Slobin and Aksu (1982) found that these distinctions are acquired at age 1.9 and 2 respectively, but that they are used to differentiate between dynamic and stative events. Clear differentiation of the two forms according to their adult meanings is not stabilized until much later at around age 4.6. The child's earliest uses of the **-di** marker occur with completed processes without regard to the speaker's direct or indirect experience of the processes. The earliest references to the past all have this completive character and are, according to Slobin and Aksu (1982:191), more appropriately described in terms of aspect than tense. The use of **-di** is limited to change of state verbs with immediately perceptible results. The **-mıs** particle moves from its initial use with process and stative verbs for the description of resultant states to be used in a past tense function. Then, **-di** changes from being a completive aspectual marker to a more general past tense function.

They conclude that there seem to be good psychological grounds for positing a general development from completive and perfect aspect to tense. Historically, the **-mıs** marker had a perfective meaning. It then lost the characteristics of a perfect and took on the modal and tense distinctions which it now has. Thus, what was originally an aspect marker became a tense marker. This had the effect of limiting the other particle **-di** to the domain of direct experience. These has been a pragmatic extension to the effect that perception of a resultant state implies an antecedent process, but does not imply that it was directly observed.

The distinction evidential vs. non-evidential does not occur in the bioprogram. Bickerton (1981a:161) says that non-bioprogram distinctions that have emerged in natural languages are particularly vulnerable to re-interpretation in the course of acquisition so that they would be used initially to mark a bioprogram distinction.

He also cites evidence from the work of Bronckart and Sinclair (1973) and Antinucci and Miller (1976) that children use markers of past tense to mark the punctual/non-punctual distinction rather than past time reference. During the period when past tense markers are being acquired, some past reference verbs are marked and some are not. Bickerton (1981a:164–5) compares the acquisition of the English past tense by speakers of Hawaii English Creole and Guyanese Creole to first language acquisition. In the case of the two creoles he says that more past tense markers were inserted when the verb referred to a single punctual event than a habitual or iterative one. In all these cases punctuality rather than past tense was the semantic distinction being marked. Bronckart and Sinclair noted that when French-speaking children were asked to describe past events their choice of tense often seemed to be influenced by the nature of the event. They start out using the uninflected form of the verb for reference to all events, past or non-past, punctual or non-punctual, and realis or irrealis. If the event was one of some duration, *eg* **washing the car**, they chose the present tense. For a punctual event *eg* **kick the ball**, they chose the past. Bickerton's (1981a:166) interpretation is that when French children use different verb forms for different kinds of past events, they are doing the same thing as creole speakers, who always mark non-punctual events differently from punctual pasts. The past tense is associated with perfective events. Bronckart and Sinclair concluded that the temporal relation was less important than the distinction between perfective and imperfective until at least the age of six.

The fact that children acquire temporal reference gradually has been attributed to a number of factors, among them the syntactic and semantic complexity of the notions involved. A number of researchers have stressed the importance of cognitive factors. It has been found, for example, that children begin to use temporal adverbials well after they have begun to produce other adverbials and that relatively complex temporal expressions are not acquired until about five years (*cf eg* Cromer 1968; Ferreiro

1971). Generally, the explanation given for the finding that aspect marking precedes tense marking is based on Piaget's model of conceptual development. Piaget claims that during the pre-operational stage, which may according to some last up until the age of six, the young child lives in the present and assesses the past purely in terms of its results. The critical period for the development of tense and aspect falls within this period *ca.* 1.6–2 and 3.6–4 years of age. Acquisition of the full adult system requires the coordination of three times, *ie* speech time, reference time and event time. The child's initial tense system is limited to speech time and event time. The reference point is always fixed to speech time. It is through the grammaticalization of tense distinctions that the child is able to move out of the here and now, or, in Piagetian terms, to de-centre his frame of reference from his immediate surroundings.

Other studies of first language acquisition have not demonstrated the priority of aspectual over tense marking. In a replication of Bronckart and Sinclair's experiment Weist *et al.* (1984:348) tested what they call the defective tense hypothesis, which predicts that in the early stages of acquisition only inherent aspectual distinctions are encoded by verbal morphology and not tense or grammatical aspect. In other words, not only is aspect prior to tense, but emerging tense morphology is defective in its function since it does not encode deictic relations.

They found, however, in their study of Polish children that although the distinction between perfective and imperfective was basic, tense was not being used defectively (Weist *et al.* (1984:369–70). Children did not lack an abstract concept of time. However, they predicted that the speed at which conceptual breakthrough occurs will depend on how a particular language encodes tense morphology.

A study by Smith (1980) also disputes the findings of Bronckart and Sinclair (1973). She found that by age five children combined both the imperfective and perfective with past tense. She says (1980:273) that children at this age can but need not report events in the aspect that corresponds to their perfectivity. In her view the reason why French children used tense to express aspect is due to the complexity of French and not the cognitive inability to deal with temporal notions.

Further support comes from a longitudinal study of the acquisition of tense and aspect in bilingual French and German-speaking children done by Meisel (1985). He argues that the early verb forms used by French children do not mark either temporal or aspectual distinctions initially. Moreover, the use of verbal morphology to mark tense and aspect is preceded by the use of adverbials on the part of the German children. This is interesting in view of the fact that pidgins tend to use adverbial expressions placed sentence externally prior to developing tense marking as a verbal category (*cf* 2.9). A preference for the use of adverbs has also been found in adult second language acquisition (Meisel, forthcoming; Klein W. 1986:124–7). It disagrees, however, with the results of other studies of first language acquisition such as Smith's (1980) and those mentioned earlier, where it is claimed there that children use temporal adverbials later than other adverbials, and that they do not acquire relatively complex temporal expressions until about five years, *ie* after they have acquired the use of the verbal morphology of the tense system. Meisel, observed, however, that after completing an activity French children would comment on it by saying **voilà** – 'there it is' [*ie* the finished product]. German children used the particle **so** – 'thus', in apparently the equivalent function. Moreover, in French they used the past participle to express what looked like aspect, but not in German. Thus, a French-speaking child would use forms like **tombé** – 'fallen', and **cassé** – 'broken' to express completion. German-speaking children used adverbials or adjectives, *eg* **unten** – 'under' rather than **gefallen** (*cf* French **tombé**) and **kaputt** – 'broken' rather than **gebrochen** (*cf* French **cassé**). Meisel questions why this difference should occur if the children are cognitively at the same level. It is particularly significant that the children are using adverbials in one language (*ie* German) and verb forms in another (*ie* past participles in French) in an equivalent function, *ie* to describe qualities and attributes.

In evaluating the literature on child language acquisition it is important to bear in mind the context in which data is elicited. Bronckart and Sinclair's study was based on comprehension rather than production in a naturalistic setting. Meisel (1985) also points to a number of problems in interpreting the results of studies of children's acquisition of tense, mood and aspect. It is very difficult to tell when a child uses a particular form whether he is referring to the nature of the action (*ie* punctuality, as Bickerton would like to claim), or the result of an action (*ie* accomplishment). The categories of past and punctual overlap semantically. All pasts need not be punctual, but all punctuals must be past. In many cases Meisel says there is a fusion of three categories typically singled out by researchers, telic (*ie* goal-directed), punctual and accomplishment. It is not surprising that this confusion exists given the fact that the first morphological markers used by children occur with telic verbs which describe a punctual action. By their very nature these verbs describe things which can't be verbalized as acts except after their accomplishment or result, *eg* **break**. In a sentence like **He broke the window**, the verb form indicates that the action of breaking has taken place (resultative) and that the broken state is still in existence.

Most of the past participles used by the French children did not make reference to punctual actions. They were used instead to refer to the result of an action. At this stage then Meisel (1985:345) claims that the past participle corresponds to adverbs or adjectives in adult language. Their function has nothing to do with tense or aspect but rather is attributive. They serve to describe qualities of events and states. Antinucci and Miller (1976:171–3) also found that children used past participles as adjectives to describe the states of objects or the final state of a process. It is also possible to interpret the results of Bronckart and Sinclair's study in this way; namely, that the children were describing the final state of the actions of the experimenters rather than the punctuality of the actions referred to. Further support can be found in studies by Kielhöfer (1982) and Bronckart (1976).

It is difficult to isolate precise meanings in the domain of tense and aspect because notions like perfectivity subsume distinctions such as punctuality, completedness, resultativity and stativity (*cf eg* Comrie 1976:16–24). Thus, accomplishment is one aspect of perfectivity. There is also an inevitable overlap between tense and aspect since pastness and perfectivity overlap. Events that are completed, *ie* perfective, are by definition past. The interpretation of perfective aspect depends on the type of event. Perfective aspect implies completion for perfective events and termination for imperfective events. All these factors make the data difficult to interpret. The issue is further complicated by the tendency for children to use forms multifunctionally in the early stages of languages acquisition.

A further problem is the fuzziness of tense, aspect and modality as semantic categories. Wallace (1982:203), for example, notes in connection with the category of tense that:

> No reasonable person would deny that time is an important semantic property of the categories of tense. The moot point is whether or not it is a focal, central, nuclear property. One might in fact argue that the distinction between 'present' and 'past' 'tense' . . . is not so much temporal as it is modal: immediate-direct-certain – 'present' mode vs. remote-indirect-hesitant 'past' mode.

The terminology used by researchers who study tense, mood and aspect also varies a great deal. This makes studies difficult to compare. Bronckart and Sinclair, for example, did not make a distinction between the aspectual nature of an event represented by a particular verb and the aspect used in referring to it. In other words, they did not distinguish aspect from Aktionsart, or kinds of action. Aspectual contrasts such as punctual vs. non-punctual can be marked lexically rather than grammatically. Some verbs can have inherent aspect. For example, they can be inherently punctual, *eg* **hit** and **jump**, while others are inherently non-punctual, *eg* **push**. In other cases, however, verbs may indicate perfective or imperfective events depending on the types of context in which they occur. Thus, in a sentence like **Mary ran home** vs. **Mary ran in the park**, **run** indicates a perfective event in the first instance and a completive event in the second. Comrie (1976:7*n*) avoids the use of the term Aktionsart, while Meisel and others include only the grammaticalized distinction between perfective and imperfective as part of aspect. The distinction between durative and punctual would for them be part of Aktionsart.

The way in which aspectual distinctions are interpreted changes as the child matures. At first, Bickerton (1981a:171) claims that they observe the relative length of actions and do not pay attention to the inherent characteristics of different actions. For the French-speaking child this means that more events become available for past tense marking as the child semantically recategorizes the non-punctual category. According to Meisel (1985:354), however, children attend first to the inherent semantics of verb forms. As they get older, the use of grammatical marking of time progressively detaches itself from this pragmatic system.

One could also interpret some of the evidence from creoles as being consistent with the hypothesis that perfectivity or completion rather than punctuality is the first distinction to be grammaticalized. For example, in Isle de France Creole Corne (Baker and Corne 1982) reports that the completive marker is already present in the archaic creole. Later it is grammaticalized as **fin**. The completive marker has been in the language at least as long as the irrealis and punctual markers. The non-punctual marker isn't attested however until 1850. Bickerton however excludes Isle de France Creole from the category of true creole and says that the deviations from TMA can be accounted for by substratum influence.

Although the anterior tense emerges in all true creoles according to Bickerton, it does not seem to play a part in primary acquisition. He (1981a:281–6) suggests that this may be because it emerges quite late in the development of the bioprogram at a time when the child's auxiliary-verb system has already been slanted in the direction of the target language. In fact, there has been a great deal of dispute anong creolists over the presence vs. absence of the feature [anterior] in various creoles. Papiamentu, for example, has no marker of anterior. Moreover, its marker of punctuality is not zero, as Bickerton would predict. Papia Kristang, Palenquero and the Philippine Spanish Creoles, *eg* Chabacano, follow the Papiamentu system, although some of the precise details are different. Bickerton (1981a:85) says that the Papiamentu deviations reflect either heavy superstrate influence on the pidgin stage or subsequent decreolization.

Cape Verdean Creole and Guinea Bissau Krioulu, however, do have a zero punctual marker and an anterior marker. In Cape Verdean Crioulo, however, the marker of anteriority is a post-verbal suffix, **-ba**, rather than a pre-verbal particle. The completive marker is **dia**, which occurs clause-initially with pronominal subjects, but preverbally with full NPs. It can also occur in clause final position. According to Silva (1985) it plays a central role in the tense–aspect system.

Another deviation from the creole prototype mentioned by Silva (1985:159–60) is that the iterative/habitual and the irrealis are expressed by the same marker **ta**. The non-punctual **sta** expresses only the progressive/durative. In Bickerton's system (1981a:78) the non-punctual incorporates both the progressive/durative and the habitual/iterative. Thus, in some creoles, irrealis and iterative/habitual have distinct markers (*eg* in the French- and English-based creoles), while in others (*eg* Portuguese-based creoles) they do not.

Bickerton (1981a:80) says that the syntactic position of **-ba** in Capeverdean Crioulo is due to the persistence of pidgin-like features (*cf* also Bickerton 1975a:43–4 on post-verbal **don**). That must be the case in order for his claim to be true that the system of TMA marking which emerges in creoles has no source in any antecedent pidgin stage of the creoles. In the case of Hawaii English Creole, for example, **bambai** – 'then, later, afterward' [<English by-and-by], and **pau** [< Hawaiian 'finish'] are used to express temporal relations, as in the examples from Bickerton (1981a:78):

> **bambai mi waif hapai, bambai wan lil boi kam** – 'Then my wife got pregnant, and later a little boy was born'
> **pau wrk fraidei, go daun kauai** – 'After work on Friday, we went down to Kauai'

In accordance with the tendency I noted earlier in 2.9, Hawaii Pidgin English places these temporal adverbs sentence externally.

They may occur initially or finally. When Hawaii Creole English developed, neither **pau** or **bambai** underwent any change of meaning; nor were they incorporated into the auxiliary as was the case for Tok Pisin, which now has the pre-verbal future marker **bai**. This can be clearly traced to antecedent **baimbai**. The pidgin sequence markers **pau** and **bambai** remain as optional forms in Hawaii Creole English. The difference between the two outcomes lies in the fact that Tok Pisin had a longer time period in which to stabilize. The original sequence markers became firmly established in the language and began to take on more tense-like and modal-like functions through the operation of normal gradual change. The evidence from Tok Pisin is not as clear-cut as it might seem. It is obvious from Sankoff and Laberge's data (1973) that the change in the status of **bai** was well under way prior to the existence of a large number of native speakers. However, they claim that native speakers appear to be carrying further these tendencies. My findings dispute this. I have found that rural speakers are well ahead of those in some urban areas in implementing the shift from clause initial to pre-verbal **bai**. Thus there is no evidence to indicate that creolization and/or urbanization is associated with the incorporation of tense markers into the verb phrase (*cf* 2.9 and also Jourdan 1985 on Solomon Islands Pijin).

Bickerton does not really justify satisfactorily the exclusion of post-verbal markers of completion from the core TMA system. He notes that most creoles have an earlier form, which is derived from a verb meaning 'finish', *eg* Hawaii English Creole **pau** [< Hawaiian – 'finish'], Indian Ocean Creole **fini** [< French **fini** – 'finish'], Guyanese English Creole **don** [< English – 'done'], Portuguese creole **kaba** [< Portuguese **acabar** – 'finish']. This marker can become grammaticalized as the past, completive or anterior marker and incorporated into the auxiliary, but this is the exception rather than the rule.

Baxter (1983:147), for example, says that in Kristang (Malacca Creole Portuguese) the tense particle is not an anterior marker but rather just a simple past marker. There is however an additional marker, **sta**, which appears to mark anteriority for action verbs when it is preceded by the tense particle **ja**. The markers **kaba**, **logu** and **ja** can also occur within and outside the auxiliary, which suggests to Bickerton traces of pidgin origins. However, Baxter claims that the verb system as well as other areas of grammar in Kristang parallels closely that of Bazaar Malay, a pidgin form of Malay spoken in Malacca. There are no features of creole grammar common to Bazaar Malay that Kristang does not share. Contact between the two might have played a more important role in the formation of Kristang than bioprogram universals. However, the end result would have been the same. Thus, whatever pidgin traces remain in Kristang may be the result of convergence.

Another case which deserves more careful examination is Kriol, an English-based creole of the Northern Territory and Kimberley area of Western Australia. Here too the marking of TMA is split between pre-verbal and post-verbal position. The Kriol verb consists of a stem and three orders of suffixes, all marking either transitivity or aspect (Hudson 1983). Although this system is not in conformity with Bickerton's true creole prototype, it does not violate the predictions made by Bybee (*cf* 7.3) about the coding of verbal morphology. Valence-changing morphology is closest to the verb, and aspect is closer then tense because aspect is bound to the verb. The transitive marker **-im** is closest to the verb, *eg* **baitim** – 'to bite (someone)'. The progressive **-in** is also post-verbal, as is the marker of iterativity, **-bat**. Sometimes the two combine, as in the example from Hudson (1983:170):

Det boi bin jandap-ing-bat langa riba
'The boy was standing for a long time by the river'

There is also a pre-verbal marker **bin**, which indicates past time reference, as in this example from Hudson (1983:171):

Mela bin tjak-in-abat najing
'We were casting (our fishing lines) repeatedly for a long time without success'

Silva does not accept Bickerton's analysis for Capeverdean. However, the status of the language as pidgin or creole is not clear. She says (1985:164) that Bickerton appears to have confused the anterior with the completive marker. The so-called anterior forms which he refers to as the 'earlier' markers in pidgins are actually associated with the completive category and not the anterior. As examples she gives **don** and **bin** as the completive and anterior markers respectively in Guyanese Creole. In Seychelles Creole **fin** is the completive and **ti** the anterior marker. In Papiamentu **caba** is the completive marker and **tava** the anterior marker. Silva concludes that it is questionable whether the anterior marker **-ba** in Guinea Bissau and Capeverdean can be linked to Portuguese **acabar**, which is realized as the completive marker **caba** and **kaba** in Papiamentu and Sranan respectively.

As far as the completive marker in these Portuguese creoles is concerned (*ie* **dia**), Silva notes that it occurs finally in São Tomense and Guinea Bissau, but initially and pre-verbally as well in Capeverdean. This suggests to Silva that the three represent different stages in decreolization. In São Tomense and Guinea Bissau these markers are marginal and therefore these languages represent an earlier stage. The forms **caba** and **kaba** found in Papiamentu and Sranan may represent the earliest forms for the completive. They may not have been replaced with **dia** because they are no longer in contact with Portuguese.

Bickerton (1981a:86) predicts that in the original stages of Portuguese creoles one should find either **tava** or **taba** as the anterior marker. This claim is supported by the fact that anterior markers are often derived from a past copula form, *eg* French **été** yields French creole **ti/te**, and Portuguese **estava** yields Portuguese Creole **tava**. Silva (1985:167), however, says that a more plausible origin for **ba** in Capeverdean is that it represents the ending **-va** found in the third and first persons singular of the past imperfect of all Portuguese verbs terminating in **-ar**, including **estar**, from which **estava** is derived. She suspects that the forms **tava** and **taba** represent later developments in many of the Portuguese creoles and are not part of the original stage.

So far I have focused my discussion on formal aspects of child language acquisition in terms of their relation to the bioprogram and creoles. Now I will turn to another aspect of child language acquisition, where Bickerton has claimed a great contrast between children acquiring creoles and children acquiring 'normal' languages; namely, the context of acquisition. Bickerton says (1981a:139) that well-formed input from mothers cannot constitute even a necessary condition for children to acquire language; otherwise, creoles wouldn't exist. While he is right to query the assumption implicit in most existing theories of child acquisition to the effect that children are exposed to competent adults, who provide the necessary input in a referentially adequate language, he does not fully appreciate the qualitative differences which may exist in learning natural languages cross-culturally. Language acquisition for non-creole speaking children is not always and everywhere the same; this is pointed out by Hockett (1950). Language is acquired from whomever one comes into contact with. The fact that adults, in particular mothers, are not universally the primary caregivers has a number of consequences, which Bickerton has neglected.

Ochs (1982), for example, argues that the process of acquisition for Samoan children is strongly shaped by the social norms for using language and cultural attitudes and beliefs about communication between caregivers and children. These can be seen to affect the form and content of the child's grammar and the order of acquisition. In Samoan households there are a number of caregivers who differ in age and status; it is the lowest-ranking persons (generally older siblings) who bear the responsibility of satisfying children's needs.

Bickerton (1981a:198) cites Schieffelin's (1979) study of Kaluli children, who acquire ergative case marking quite early (*ie* 2.2 years) as an important piece of evidence for the inclusion of the causative/non-causative distinction in the bioprogram. His prediction is that since the syntactic marking of ergativity is salient and uniform (*ie* it consists of a causative suffix applied to agentive nouns), it is acquired early. Ochs, however, found that Samoan children acquired ergative case marking late (*ie* after four years of age). In her view (1982:78) the reason for this 'delayed acquisition' is social. Ergative case marking is not distributed equally thoughout the community: it is more typical of men's than women's speech. Furthermore, it rarely appears in the speech of family members within the household, where women and family members are the child's primary socializing agents. Ochs's findings certainly have far-reaching ramifications for developmental psycholinguistic studies which attempt to explain the order of acquisition of various structures in terms of purely cognitive and innate principles. Bickerton, like a number of others whose studies he cites in support of a link between complexity and order of emergence, has not taken account of the fact that social context is an important mediator in this process (*cf* the discussion in Romaine 1984a:Ch. 5 on the differential effects of home, school and peer group as contexts of socialization on the language of children). If Bickerton is right about the changing nature of the bioprogram over time, then order of exposure to certain kinds of data will affect the resultant grammar in different ways.

Ochs's study also indicates that Bickerton has exaggerated the similarity between the position of the 'bioprogram-activating child' *vis-à-vis* the target language and that of the creole speaker *vis à vis* the superstrate language. Bickerton says (1981a:191) that both adult and superstrate speaker believe that the child and creole speaker are speaking merely a 'broken' form of their language. This may be true for the middle-class Anglo caregiver: and hence we find that caregivers expand utterances which are seen as imperfect renditions of what the caregiver assumes the child intends to say. Ochs says that the Samoan caregiver 'sees the unclear utterance as nothing like adult language' and therefore doesn't expand it (1982:93). The child's imperfect output is ridiculed (if it is attended to at all) and treated as if it were literally a foreign language. By comparison, the society which Schieffelin studied is one in which caregivers assume the role of language teachers. Samoan caregivers do not. We needn't go to the South Pacific for examples of 'exotic cultures', where beliefs and expectations have an effect on the caretaker register and the child's input (*cf eg* Heath 1982 for a striking comparison of the differences in the norms of linguistic socialization between middle-class communities and lower-class black and white communities in the south-eastern United States). Indeed, Marshall (1984:201) points out that some children learning natural languages may be faced with a similar problem to that of the creole-speaking child, if we regard 'motherese' as deficient input. Despite the marked deviations which this register has by comparison with the full version of the target language, children who are exposed to it still manage to acquire the adult version (*cf* 3.1).

I have commented at length on the implications of Ochs's work in order to illustrate the fact that Bickerton has been highly selective in his coverage of child acquisition studies, citing those which can be re-interpreted to suit his own needs. (Granted, Ochs's paper appeared too recently for Bickerton to take it into account in 1981a; *cf* however, Bickerton 1984a:186, where it is cited but not discussed.) The fact remains, however, that there is a lot of evidence to be gathered before we can confidently compare 'creoles' and the process of creolization and child language acquisition as if there were only one route in each case. We do not have fully documented ethnographic accounts of the various social contexts in which children learn creoles. Studies of this type are urgently needed.

Bickerton exaggerates the non-existence of models for the creole-speaking child in saying (1981a:28) that the first generation of creole children produce rules for which they have no evidence in the previous generation's speech. He says that children born into multilingual communities where the language of inter-group communication is an inadequate pidgin do not acquire either the parents' language or the pidgin. According to Bickerton in the case of Hawaii Pidgin English there was too much variability and the language was too deficient to be worth learning.

As an example Bickerton (1984a:175) cites the variable word order of the pidgin. He says that although children elsewhere who are acquiring free word order languages, must cope with the same kind of variability, free word order languages (*eg* Warlpiri, an Australian Aboriginal language) have other mechanisms such as case inflections which unambiguously mark case roles. The pidgin had none of these. Instability of word order also meant that the pidgin had no unambiguous way of marking focus by constituent movement of the kind that developed later in the creole. Because the creole has a movement rule for use in focusing (*cf* 2.9), it has orderings which the pidgin does not permit and it also lacks orderings that the pidgin permits. The predominant word order of Japanese pidgin speakers is SOV, which is not permitted in the creole. Conversely, the creole has OV word ordering, which is not allowed in the pidgin. However, in the creole they are the result of a movement rule, as in:

> **difren bilifs dei get, sam gaiz** – 'Some guys have different beliefs'

In cases where both pidgin and creole share word orderings the source is different. For example, verb initial constructions are possible in both, but in the pidgin they are the result of native language influence. Filipino pidgin speakers often use verb initial constructions, but for creole speakers verb initial constructions are the result of a defocusing rule, as in (*cf eg* Perlman 1975):

> **waz had, da tes** – 'The test was hard'

In this sentence, **tes** is assumed to be background knowledge. Thus, the word ordering in the pidgin and creole have different explanations. The appearance of non-SVO word order in the pidgin is not of any discourse significance; it merely reflects first language background.

Another problem in the input was the lack of models for complex structures. Ferguson (1984:163) is critical of this view, which is untested. It underestimates the abilities of human children and ignores the fact that even in relatively homogeneous communities the input to children can be highly variable.

A counterexample to Bickerton's predictions comes from the acquisition of Turkish. Slobin (1984) reports that children acquiring Turkish have no difficulty in learning the use of inflectional case marking, along with pragmatic variations in word order. They never go through a stage of non-inflectional, word order marking of case relations, which is what he says would be predicted by the bioprogram. Slobin says that children are aided in their acquisition of case inflections if they are acoustically salient, easily segmentable and regular. English-speaking children similarly do not go through a stage where they use serial verb constructions instead of prepositions. Creoles typically use serial verbs to fulfil the functions that prepositions or case inflections perform in other languages. What is learned seemingly effortlessly and without error varies a great deal cross-linguistically. Meisel (1986:134) reports that as soon as subordinate clauses appear in children's German, the verb is correctly placed in final position (*cf* 2.2). Children do not overgeneralize main clause order. The placement of verbs in second position in main clauses, however, presents a major acquisitional difficulty. The difference in word order between the two clause types in German is a purely syntactic phenomenon without any pragmatic motivation. It is thus difficult to see why one should prove easier to learn than the other. This case also shows that we do not want to attribute all apparently arbitrary or difficult syntactic principles that are learned early and effortlessly to innate factors.

The claim that Hawaii English Creole is a completely *ex nihilo* creation rests largely on Bickerton's interpretation of the evidence. In his discussion of **ste**, for example, the Hawaii English Creole aspect marker of [−punctual], he cites seven instances in which **ste** precedes a verb, but claims that none of these are true auxiliaries. Upon closer examination, however, some of these are ambiguous cases, where two alternative analyses are possible. For example, the utterance: **ai ste kuk** could mean 'I was a cook', where **kuk** is a noun and not a verb. If, however, it was being used as a pre-verbal auxiliary marking non-punctual aspect, the meaning would be: **'I was/am cooking'**. In the example, **mi papa ste help**, Bickerton says we are dealing with a case of verb serialization rather than a true auxiliary, *ie* the meaning is 'I stayed and helped my father'/'I stayed to help my father'. Historical linguists are however accustomed to examining just these kinds of ambiguous cases in which alternative analyses are possible. It is often in these instances that we find syntactic restructuring.

In this case the interpretation is ambiguous between a structure of the type **N V N** and **N V V**. Moreover, Sato has pointed out that **ste** can be used as a completive marker by some speakers, so that an utterance like, **ai ste kuk da stu so go it**, can mean 'I have cooked the stew, so please have some'. The question is whether the development of the creole has been as abrupt as Bickerton claims, or whether we lack sufficient information about the intervening stages to see that change really took place by means of a series of gradual transitions. In fact, Bickerton has pointed out that locative **ste** replaced an earlier **stap**. Only one of the Hawaii Pidgin English speakers, a 92-year-old Japanese, used this form. In Nagara's (1972) study, however, all the older

Japanese speakers used this marker. Bickerton is no doubt right when he says that Nagara has incorrectly glossed some occurrences of **stap** as 'stop/finish', as in:

> **Or kanak stap** – 'All the Hawaiians stopped [working on the plantation]'

This sentence probably means: 'There were only Hawaiians on the plantation'.

This and other examples suggest that **stap** might have covered existential as well as locative meanings at an earlier stage. This would mean that Hawaii Pidgin English was more like the Sino–Pacific pidgins referred to by Clark (1979). That is, Clark claims that the use of **stop** as a locative marker is a feature found in China Coast Pidgin and most of the South Pacific pidgins, but was not shared by English-based pidgins and creoles elsewhere (*cf* 3.4).

Nevertheless, Bickerton says that the only significant difference between adult speakers of Hawaii Pidgin English and child speakers of Hawaii English Creole is that the first group encountered HPE as adults and the second as small children. Sato (1985), however, says that even though from a technical point of view we might describe the earliest Hawaiian-born children of pidgin-speaking immigrants as creole speakers, most of them tended to be bilingual in their ancestral tongues as well as in Hawaii Creole. They continued to receive considerable input from members of their own ethnic group. Bickerton (1984a:183) comments that all of the speakers born locally prior to 1905 whom he interviewed were bilingual, and some were trilingual. It was not until the mid 1930s or so, when there was a greater proportion of local-born than immigrant speakers, that Hawaii Creole English usage was at its peak. At this stage significantly more second and third generation children approached monolingualism in creole. These newer generations of creole speakers were probably passive bilinguals. Parents continued to speak the ancestral language and children used the creole. Sato (1985:261) points out that the fact that the earliest Hawaii English Creole speakers were bilingual provides evidence against a view that attributes creolization exclusively to children's innate language creation abilities. While the pidgin input they received from their parents was probably scanty, it is also likely that they relied heavily on their ancestral languages in developing the creole (*cf* also Bruner and Feldman 1982). A convergence of features from Hawaii Pidgin English, Hawaiian, English and various immigrant languages was systematized and elaborated by these new creole speakers, who produced innovations of their own. This is not to deny the role of universal tendencies in language development, particularly in relation to the TMA system. Some of the newly stabilized creole features were also adopted and incorporated by more recent immigrants, such as the Filipinos who arrived between 1907 and 1915, at a stage when Hawaii Pidgin English had been in use for some time. Although the variety of Hawaii Pidgin English spoken by these newcomers sounds distinctly Filipino, it contains many creole forms, and could therefore be considered to be repidginized (*cf* Sato 1985 and also 5.1).

There is much to be learned still about the differential learning abilities and cognitive constraints of children as opposed to adults. Bickerton has placed undue evidence on creoles (as opposed to pidgins) as the source of universal grammar. More work needs to be done on children's acquistion of creoles in places such as Papua New Guinea, where a variety of different contexts exist in which creolization is taking place. For example, in a study done by myself and Wright (Romaine and Wright 1986) of the Tok Pisin of urban and rural children in Morobe and Madang Provinces, the children came from a variety of language backgrounds. Some had parents who spoke the same language at home, and in some cases the children were also able to speak the language. Others came from homes where the parents did not speak the same language. Presumably in these situations children receive more input in Tok Pisin from their parents. A crucial question to examine is how elaborate the pidgin input is which the children receive in these cases.

There are further caveats to be noted in connection with the data from Hawaii Pidgin English. The reason why the evidence from this language is so crucial to the bioprogram hypothesis is that the creole emerged in the period between 1876–1920 and therefore Hawaii is the only place where it is still possible to study surviving speakers from that time. At the time of Bickerton's study in the the early 1970s the speakers were in their 70s or older. The data can be interpreted as evidence for what happened in the early decades of the twentieth century only if we assume that the language of these individuals had not changed much in adulthood.

Sato has begun an investigation of some of the changes which have taken place in the speech of some of the individuals who took part in Bickerton's study. She found that in the case of one individual there had been little development or change in phonology, but at the level of morphosyntax there had been decreolization or increasing convergence towards English. For example, instead of the usual Creole use of **wen/bin** as simple past marker, **hæd** was used. An example is given of each feature. The first two examples were recorded in 1973 as part of the project described in Bickerton (1977b), and the third was recorded by a colleague of Sato's in 1986:

> **a bin go si toni abaut go spansa da kidz** – 'I went to see Tony about sponsoring the kids'
> **læs yia dei hæd plei widaut no mo koch dei jas hæd go plei awn dei on** – 'Last year they had played without a coach. They just had to play on their own'
> **hæd pæs awredi omos wat, chri wiks no awredi, mo dæn chri wiks ai tingk awredi** – 'There had already passed, what, three weeks, no I think more than three weeks already'

Sato offers the comparison in Table 7.4 for past tense marking between the two time periods.

TABLE 7.4 Change in past tense marking between 1973 and 1986

	% of HCE past tense forms	*% of Standard English forms*
1973	79	21
1986	54	46

In the same individual she observed a similar shift from the creole marking of indefinite reference. In 1973 he made greater use of the creole markers **wan**/ø, while in 1986 his system was closer to the standard English system of using **a** (*cf* also Mufwene 1986 on this aspect of decreolization in Gullah). Sato says that one reason why the phonology and prosody remain relatively intact is that this area of the grammar provides a means of marking the speaker's social identity. Another reason may be the effect of the critical period hypothesis, which seems to hold more for phonology than grammar (*cf* 6.6).

In fact, Bickerton (1981a:2) says that he is primarily interested not in creoles *per se*, but in 'situations where the normal continuity of language transmission is most severely disrupted'. If that is the case, then he should have looked at studies on sign language acquisition in support of the bioprogram (*cf eg* Edwards and Ladd 1983; Deuchar 1984, 1986). In more recent work (*cf eg* Bickerton 1984b) he has acknowledged that research on sign language and other areas can provided support for the bioprogram hypothesis. I will look at some of these now.

7.5 Other areas of research relating to bioprogram grammar

There is a great deal of similarity across modality as far as acquisition of language is concerned. This means that evidence from sign language acquisition is similar in important respects to acquisition in the non-deaf child. Moreover, since about 90 per cent of deaf children are born to hearing parents and therefore learn sign language from their peers, sign languages are generally learned on the basis of limited input. Most deaf children first learn sign language at a residential school for the deaf. Deuchar (1986) says that in such schools in Britain it is common for teachers to be unable to sign and for the official mode of communication in the classroom to be spoken language (*cf* James (forthcoming) on the process of sign language acquisition in schools). Children thus 'invent' a sign language system with very little input from adult signers. Fisher (1978:329) says that American Sign Language may be 'recreolized' in each new generation. Woodward (1973) has demonstrated that the sign systems developed by children in the absence of linguistic input from proficient adults are qualitatively different from the systems used by those who had deaf parents and acquired the language before age six (*cf* Deuchar 1984:Ch. 7 for discussion of the data from British and American Sign Language in relation to the creolization hypothesis).

Deuchar (1986) considers five of the twelve characteristics of true creoles noted by Bickerton (*cf* 2.9) and discusses them in relation to sign language. These are: (i) the ordering of tense, mood and aspect in relation to the verb; (ii) existential and possessive constructions share the same lexical item; (iii) absence of copula; (iv) adjectives function as verbs; and (v) absence of passives.

With regard to the ordering of TMA, Deuchar (1986) says that sign languages cannot be analyzed in terms of purely linear order since they have a three-dimensional signing space. She assumes therefore that simultaneity with the verb involves the closest proximity, followed by temporal (or linear) adjacency, followed by some temporal separation from the verb. Of the four sign languages (British, American, French and Russian Sign Language) which Deuchar investigated she found that aspect marking is achieved by inflection on the verb itself, modality is marked by separate lexical items, either before or after the verb itself, and time is marked by an adverbial placed often at some distance from the verb. Thus, it appears that aspect is the category which is closest to the verb while mood and tense are further away (*cf* Bybee 1985). The modality markers are placed as close to the verb as possible without being an inflection, *ie* a modification of one of the formational components of the verbal sign, such as movement. Deuchar prefers to use the term **time** rather than **tense marking** in relation to sign language. By this distinction she means that time marking is done by means of adverbials placed sentence externally (*cf* 2.9) rather than by markers which are incorporated within the scope of the verb phrase proper. Deuchar suggests in view of the predominance of time rather than tense marking in sign language, that perhaps the latter might be considered early creoles where the development of tense marking is not yet complete.

With regard to the second feature Deuchar also found similarities between creoles and sign languages. Fisher (1978), for example, notes that Hawaii English Creole and American Sign Language have the same lexical items for existentials and possessives. Deuchar reports the same convergence of signs with these meanings in British and French Sign Language.

Creoles also share with sign languages a characteristic lack of the copula, as well as a concomitant feature that blurs the distinction between verbs and adjectives. Deuchar observes that some signs which might be translated as adjectives function grammatically more like verbs, *eg* in British Sign Language **good** takes negative inflection.

Deuchar also says that creoles and sign languages have in common the absence of a passive construction. Edwards and Ladd (1983) cite sentences such as **party postpone** – 'The party was postponed' in British Sign Language. Deuchar attributes the lack of passives to two specific factors. One is the apparent preference for topic–comment pragmatic order in informal communication situations and in emerging languages (*cf eg* Givón 1979b and Ochs 1979). The second is the lack of a grammatical subject in emerging languages (as well as in some others, *cf eg* Li and Thompson 1976). The grammatical category of subject is usually associated with the semantic–pragmatic notions of agency and topichood (*cf* Comrie 1981). The function of the passive in those languages which have subjects is to separate these two notions, *ie* to promote an NP which is not the subject to topic. Where the topic is not the agent, there is no special need for a passive construction.

Edwards and Ladd (1983) compare some additional features cited by Bickerton and compare them with British Sign Language. They note that British Sign Language follows the creole pattern of using the definite article for the presupposed specific NP, an indefinite article for the asserted-specific NP, and zero for the non-specific NP. They also cite the prototypical negative construction in British Sign Language as being in accord with the creole pattern of negation stated by Bickerton, in which non-definite subjects as well as non-definite VP constituents must be negated as well as the verb, *eg* **nobody all them not see nothing**. They also looked at question words. Bickerton maintains that no creole shows any difference in syntactic structure between questions and statements. Edwards and Ladd (1983) compare the use of intonation in spoken languages with eyebrow movement in British Sign Language to mark propositions such as **John eggs buy finish** – 'John has bought the eggs' as a question. Formally, there is no difference between questions and statements, although due to its basically topic–comment ordering, word order in British Sign Language is relatively free. Eyebrow movement rather than change in word order, is also used to mark WH-questions in British Sign Language, although the question word is placed after rather than before the declarative form of the sentence, *eg* **Mary come when**?

Edwards and Ladd suggest that two other features mentioned by Bickerton might have parallels in British Sign Language once more data are available. One of these is that in creoles the choice of complementizer is determined by the semantics of the verb. They were unable to find any examples in British Sign Language. The second feature is the absence of relative pronouns in subject position, which Bickerton says characterizes conservative creole dialects or can be found in restricted sentence types. Edwards and Ladd cite the absence of surface relativizers in British Sign Language constructions such as **Man dog kick me see** – 'I saw the man who kicked the dog'. They concluded from their comparison that British Sign Language did not follow the creole pattern in only four of Bickerton's twelve features. In one case, namely movement rules for focusing, the comparison is not applicable, given the difference in modality. A further area of overlap between the bioprogram and sign language has been reported by Goldin-Meadow and Mylander(1983:373*n*). Deaf children apparently spontaneously create ergative case systems in sign language, which do not reflect the case structures found in English.

Deuchar concludes on the basis of shared similarities in both structure and development that sign languages, like creoles, are emerging languages of the same kind. Sign languages will continue to be newly created languages in each generation as long as the chain of transmission from deaf adult to child is very weak. Deuchar points to new possibilities of explaining the similarities among sign languages which arise once it is accepted that sign languages are creoles. In particular, she observes that it makes similarities between historically unrelated sign languages, such as British and American Sign language, less difficult to account for. We have seen in relation to the study of pidgins and creoles how an approach based on universals opens the way for similar insights. However, just as in the case of children's acquisition of creoles, we do not know enough about the different contexts in which the child's acquisition of sign language takes place. In particular, we would need to examine the type of input received by the child, and also the possibility of transfer, and influence from the spoken language the child is exposed to in school.

Bickerton (1984b:143) has also recently noted another area of research which can provide support for the bioprogram. Some bioprogram features may emerge when languages undergo extreme forms of change such as from SOV to SVO word order. It is evident that a number of the processes observed in pidginization, creolization and the historical development of languages appear to have their own seemingly internally-targeted trajectories (*cf eg* Slobin 1977 for a discussion of some of the parallels). The fact that bioprogram-like features surface in other contact situations, which are qualitatively different from those which produce creoles, but give rise, nonetheless, to some of the same features of creolization, is evidence that the bioprogram does not self-destruct, as claimed in Bickerton (1981a). The convergence in Kupwar discussed in 3.1 is such a case. Seuren (1984:209) says that whatever is universal in creoles is also characteristic of contact languages of any kind that get turned into native languages. It would be wrong to attach too much importance to the process of creolization as the unique source of universal grammar.

Studies of language contact such as those of Dorian (1981) and Silva-Corvalán (1986) have shown that a proficiency continuum may develop between two languages in contact, which resembles in some respects a creole continuum. Individuals can be located at various points along it depending on their level of dominance and/or proficiency in one or other of the languages. Silva-Corvalán looked specifically at changes which were taking place in the verb morphology used to mark tense, mood and aspect in the speech of Spanish-English bilinguals in Los Angeles. She found a progressive simplification and loss of verbal morphemes marking tense, mood and aspect. In explaining these phenomena she drew on a number of factors, *eg* cognitive ones such as transparency, and universal grammar. In comparing the discourse of first and second generation immigrants, she found that first generation speakers followed the general Spanish rule of encoding in the preterite both narrative abstracts and orienting and evaluative clauses which refer to the narrative events as a whole. This tense in Spanish has perfective aspect. Other speakers violated this rule and substituted the imperfective. In general the imperfect is used in background clauses in narrative both in Spanish (*cf* Silva-Corvalán 1983) and other languages (*cf* Hopper 1979).

There were further differences separating the Spanish of first generation immigrants from the other speakers. Silva-Corvalán found either loss or simplification in the future, the preterite, the imperfect subjunctive and the pluperfect indicative and subjunctive. The preterite–imperfect opposition has become neutralized in a closed set of verbs, which appear with imperfect morphology in both perfective and imperfective contexts. She established a series of eight implicationally ordered stages in this progressive simplification. What is of particular relevance for the discussion here is her argument that these stages conformed to a predictable trend to develop a less grammaticalized system. There are five separate systems which represent a steady move towards a less grammaticalized system, which relies heavily on context.

Among the first distinctions to be lost are in the area of modality, *eg* the subjunctive and conditional. There are at least two factors involved here. One is the fact that these are categories which are not matched in English. English has only a vestigial subjunctive and modality is not marked by bound morphology. Another is the cognitive complexity of hypothetical discourse. Many informants switched to English to handle topics which involved speculation and various degrees of possibility. Inhelder and Piaget (1958:245) regard hypotheticality as an essential and the most distinctive feature of formal thought to emerge during children's development. Hypothetical discourse creates problems in linearization, conceptualization and encoding of matter which do not stem from perception and memory (*cf eg* Levelt 1979). Narration of past events is easier than hypothesizing.

The last distinction to disappear is the past with present relevance, or the present perfect. This category overlaps with Bickerton's anterior. Its pervasiveness might be taken as an indication of its basicness. However, this basicness could be taken to be the result of biological universals or more general principles of markedness, such as those indicated in Table 7.2. Muysken's hierarchy too would predict the loss of more marked tense forms like the future and past perfect, if we assume that contact involves a progressive unmarking. Silva-Corvalán, however, suggests that the pattern of change for the preterite and the imperfect may be an indication that the location of matter in time, *ie* tense, is more crucial than signalling, at least morphologically, certain aspectual distinctions. This would not appear to follow predictions about the primacy of aspect over tense. More work should address the question of whether the features which are closest to the bioprogram are the last to be lost (*cf* Jakobson 1972:60 on the principle of irreversible solidarity to the effect that the dissolution of the linguistic sound system in aphasia is an exact mirror-image of the phonological development in child language).

Another issue of relevance in this domain is that of universals vs. transfer or substratum at particular stages (*cf* 4.3). Dorian (1981), for example, says that most of the changes which are ongoing in East Sutherland Gaelic cannot be explained as interference from English. Similarly, Silva-Corvalán attaches more significance to universals than transfer. She observes, however, that transfer may play a role once certain forms have been lost. At this stage, and under pressure to communicate a particular message, bilinguals make use of the forms available to them in the recessive language, but tend to distribute them according to the syntactic and semantic rules of the dominant language.

Tense loss and simplification, according to Silva-Corvalán, do not affect the level of information communicated in those parts of the narrative which complicate the action, *ie* foregrounded clauses. The deviations affect the background information and evaluation. This might be expected, given the fact that most pidgins exist with a minimal or weakly grammaticalized tense system, and that grammaticalization of these distinctions does not necessarily increase the referential power of the language. Some languages do not have grammaticalized tense systems. Speakers can still rely on the pragmatic strategy of ordering clauses to indicate sequence of events. Silva-Corvalán and others such as Dorian have noted that simplification or loss often affects one of two alternate forms, so that the language suffers a reduction in its stylistic rather than referential potential. In other cases such as that of Ontarian French described by Mougeon, Beniak and Valois (1985) speakers are apparently unable to preserve the structural integrity of their language in the face of pressure from English, which is socially, and in parts of the province and country as a whole, numerically dominant.

Work to date on language loss and death suggests that the process of language loss is in some respects like a process of 'creolization in reverse'. Trudgill (1978), for example, has characterized the changes taking place in one situation of language death in these terms (*cf* also Dorian 1983 on some of the differences between dying languages and pidgins and creoles). In other words, a main source of developments in creolization is the grammaticalization of distinctions and the movement from a more pragmatic to a more syntactic mode of communication. In language death the reverse is true.

The distinction between pragmatic and syntactic modes of communication is drawn by Givón (1979a and b). The process of syntacticization involves a move away from a more transparent iconic mode of communication to a more abstract and less obviously iconic one. Givón claims that this process is a pervasive fact of language change, language ontogeny and language evolution. Bickerton (1984c) has elaborated the connection between ontogeny and evolution and the pragmatic mode by linking them with Chomsky's (1980) distinction between a conceptual and a computational component in the human language capacity.

The conceptual component is a more general cognitive domain, but the computational component is responsible for language-specific processing capacities. Bickerton argues that the conceptual component is linked to the pragmatic mode. (More precisely, his term is paralanguage.) Therefore it must have emerged first. He has also modified his model of evolution so as to bring it more in line with current views that it takes place in leaps and bounds. Earlier he proposed that there was a relatively gradual progression from a state of no language to paralanguage and then to syntactic language. Now he admits that a punctuated equilibrium model of the type outlined in Gould and Eldredge (1977) is more compelling. This is in fact suggested in my review of Bickerton (*cf* Romaine 1983b), but not noted by him. Now he believes that the gulf between paralanguage and syntactic language is too sharp ever to have been bridged gradually. The higher evolutionary mode is not entirely displaced however. It emerges in early pidginization.

Bickerton has also recently given thought to the question of whether the bioprogram steers second language acquisition. Both first and second language learners face a similar problem in that in the language they are expected to acquire the bioprogram distinctions may be partially or wholly overlaid by other language specific distinctions. Both need to modify their grammars in order to match the grammar of the community whose language they are trying to learn. The second language learner also has to contend with the additional problem of his first language. However, Bickerton (1984b:151) suggests that in at least one sense there may be no such thing as primary acquisition, at least if we accept his claim that the child already knows the bioprogram. In both cases a speaker moves from a known language to a new one. Both the child and adult may transfer rules from the grammar they already know to the one they are trying to acquire. In both cases acquisition proceeds in the first stages by transfer. He draws attention to one important difference. Primary acquisition draws its hypotheses from a base which is relatively simple by comparison to that faced by the second language learner. By this Bickerton means that the bioprogram grammar is simpler than the grammar of any natural language, which is the product of cultural as well as biological evolution. He suggests that movement from a simple system to a complex one is possibly easier than movement between two systems of equal but differing complexity.

Ferguson (1984:163), however, says that if we accept Bickerton's claim that children already know the bioprogram, then language could never have evolved historically. There must have been a time when individuals were between knowing a language and not knowing it. Ferguson, I think, misunderstands the various possible interpretations of the innatist position. The sense in which Fodor (1975), for example, believes that an already present language facilitates the acquisition of a primary language is that there is a cognitive structure which facilitates the representation of linguistic rules. Thus, for example, in the case of the bioprogram distinctions such as specific/non-specific, a child cannot know which members of an NP are specific and which are non-specific unless he knows what specific and non-specific mean. He cannot know these meanings unless he has some language in which these meanings are represented.

There is of course considerable disagreement as to whether the mind, brain (or some other mental organ) which underlies language is modular and functionally specialized (*cf eg* Chomsky 1980 and Fodor 1983), or whether there is no particular portion of the human cognitive apparatus which is specifically devoted to language. Bickerton's position is that there is a biological basis for the acquisition of language which is not part of some general learning procedures. He (1984a:187) characterizes his approach as compatible with that of Chomsky in that no general purpose mechanisms are invoked. For both there is a series of 'highly modular task-specific cognitive devices interacting with an equally modular and task-specific processing component which imposes a formal structure on the output of the former'. Children are programmed for both the cognitive relations and their formal realizations. Ferguson is right of course to draw attention to the fact that if language is controlled by neurological structures which are species-specific, they must have emerged at some stage, whether gradually or abruptly. He also objects to Bickerton's equation of the bioprogram with a grammar or language. Thus, just as a bioprogram for nest-building is not a nest, neither is a bioprogram for language the same as a language or grammar (*cf* Chomsky 1980 on the abstract relationship between a grammar and a language). He prefers (1984:165) to see it as a propensity or ability to make certain abstract distinctions.

Bickerton (1984b:149–50) says that it is highly questionable whether the original infrastructure of the bioprogram grammar survives intact into adulthood. If it did, he argues that these would be no need for people in a pidgin-speaking community to await the birth of the first locally-born generation in order to generate a fully viable human language. They would be capable of producing such a language themselves. Bickerton claims that the existence of pre-pidgin continua indicates that this is impossible for the adult, who is forced to tolerate an unstable and makeshift language. Moreover, once the creole is in existence he is incapable of learning it. He says that in Hawaii there are many immigrants whose speech is totally uninfluenced by Hawaii Creole English even though it has been in existence for some 70 years. Moreover, there are none who have completely mastered it. This seems an overly strong claim, and it ignores the language expansion abilities of adult pidgin speakers in elaborating post-pidgin continua such as exist in West Africa and Papua New Guinea. There is no reason why pidgin speakers should adopt the rules of the new creole-speaking generation. Thus, motivation is an additional factor to be considered. Ferguson (1984:164) also draws attention to the fact that the rules of the newly emergent creole grammar would represent only one of the possible targets for pidgin speakers. The one feature of bioprogram grammar which Bickerton says does seem to be accessible to second language learners, mature creole speakers, pidgin speakers and children is the rule of preverbal negation discussed in 2.9 and 6.7.

Bickerton also seems to ignore evidence to indicate that nativization does not necessarily alter the syntactic structure of a pidgin. I have presented some of the evidence from Tok Pisin. Another case is discussed by Goodman (1984), which involves Kinubi, the Arabic-based creole of an ethnic group in Uganda.

Kinubi is an offshoot of Juba Arabic, a pidgin spoken in southern Sudan. Kinubi and Juba Arabic split about a century ago when a group of Sudanese soldiers went to Uganda, and there has been very little contact between the languages since. The subsequent nativization of Kinubi has not resulted in any major syntactic differences between the two. Bickerton (1984c:213), however, argues that Juba Arabic is a creole since it has a substantial population of native speakers. The position of Juba is in fact similar to that of Tok Pisin. It exists in a number of varieties ranging from second to first language.

Bickerton rightly points out that even if it could be shown that both first and second language learners acquired the features of a particular target language in the same order, we would not be entitled to conclude that the paths of acquisition in both cases were identical or that acquisition was being steered by the same set of principles. The bioprogram does however make certain testable predictions about second language acquisition. If adults have access to the bioprogram we would predict rapid and errorless acquisition of those features acquired rapidly and errorlessly in primary acquisition. We would also expect to see evidence that the categories laid down in bioprogram grammar were being used along with if not in preference to the categories used in the native and target languages. Bickerton notes (1984b:155) that research in second language acquisition can only provide a positive test for the bioprogram hypothesis. It cannot provide a negative one (unlike primary acquisition) because the finding that the bioprogram played no part in non-primary acquisition would be consistent with the hypothesis that the bioprogram decayed after primary acquisition as well as with the hypothesis that it never existed in the first place.

Even positive evidence may not be conclusive. Bickerton (1984b:155) gives the example of a Spanish speaker trying to learn the use of the simple past tense in English. This tense refers to both protracted and repeated actions in the past. Thus, we can have all of the following:

He walked to school yesterday [+punctual]
The pilgrims walked from Jerusalem to Mecca [non-punctual]
John walked five miles a day until he was 65 [non-punctual]

If a Spanish speaker treated these as formally different, we might conclude that the bioprogram was guiding his acquisition of English, since in bioprogram grammar [punctual] is marked differently from [non-punctual]. However, there is a complicating factor in that Spanish has a similar, but not identical distinction encoded in the difference between the preterite [punctual] and imperfect [non-punctual], so we cannot assume that errors are uniquely due to the influence of the bioprogram. It may be due to first language transfer or to some mixture of the two.

A number of studies of second language acquisition have asserted that the primacy of aspect over tense is operative in both first and second language acquisition (*cf* 7.4). Kumpf (1982) claims that in the early stages of acquisition of English speakers of Japanese and Spanish use zero marking of the verb to indicate completive aspect. Flashner (1982) argues that Russian speakers of English transfer their native perfective/imperfective distinction to the past morphology of English. Both Flashner and Kumpf explain their findings in terms of Givón's (1982) view that the distinction between completive and non-completive is the natural outcome of the organization of discourse in terms of foreground and background (*cf* 7.3).

Flashner (1982), however, found the opposite system of marking to what Givón predicts. In narrative contexts mainline events were represented by the past forms of the verb, and background events by non-past forms. The English past forms showed perfective aspect (which is marked in Russian), and the non-past ones imperfective aspect. Flashner claims that it is the Russian system of aspect marking which is being transferred onto narrative structure. In Russian the perfective is used in the mainline and the imperfective in the background of a narrative. Flashner emphasizes, however, that what is important is the use of aspect to structure a narrative, not which marking system is more prototypical for second language learners, as well as the fact that learners are marking aspectual rather than tense distinctions in delineating the foreground from background. She argues for the existence of systems in interlanguage which reflect a form–function correspondence with the learner's native language.

In a study of the interlanguage system of a Japanese speaker of English Kumpf (1984:141) concluded that completed action in the foreground was expressed with the base verb form. In other words, there was no tensing of these verbs. There were many cases of marking in the background. Most verbs were marked for tense. Virtually all statives were tensed, while active verbs were marked for habitual and continuous aspect and irregularly for tense.

She points out that using an unmarked verb form to report completed actions is grammaticalized in some languages, *eg* Yoruba and Igbo. In these languages what is commonly called the past tense is not marked. The reference of these unmarked verb forms is not always exclusively to past time, but rather to completed aspect. Her conclusion is that aspect is primary to tense in the grammaticalization of temporal systems. This is reflected in the interlanguage system in which one broad distinction is made between completed and non-completed action. Kumpf's claim (1984:141) is that this kind of system does not correspond to either the native Japanese or to the newly acquired English system.

Andersen (1986) examined the validity of the defective tense hypothesis for second language learners of Spanish. He found that initially all verbs were uninflected. In the later stages, however, there was evidence that learners first used preterite forms primarily on Spanish verbs which were inherently punctual. Only later do they depart from using the inherent semantics of verbs to use the past tense and the perfective/imperfective distinction as native Spanish speakers do. In the earliest stages then the learner uses only one marking for each verb form, which Andersen suggests follows from the one form: one meaning principle. Only later do they adopt the native Spanish system whereby the aspectual distinction is marked at the same time as the tense distinction. Every past tense verb in Spanish, unlike English, has a preterite (perfective) and an imperfective form, *eg* **hizo** [preterite form of the verb **hacer** – 'to do, make'], and **hacia** [imperfect]. Andersen speculates whether the reason for this outcome lies in the fact that there is a universal prototype in the brain, or whether there is a distributional bias in the input which learners receive.

A similar finding emerged in a study of the acquisition of Portuguese by an English speaker (as reported by Schmidt and Frota 1985). The learner distributed the marking of perfect and imperfect according to the semantics of the verb, in this case according to whether the verb was stative or non-stative. Imperfect marking occurred with verbs that were stative, while perfect marking appeared with punctual verbs.

Clearly more work needs to be done before we can accept the conclusion that aspect is primary across different contexts of language acquisition. One problem which particularly needs to be addressed is the overlap between tense, mood and aspect referred to in 7.3. If the underlying organizational principle of the English system is not based on time grammaticalized in terms of tense distinctions, but is really more modal as Wallace (1982) suggests, then Kumpf's claim that Japanese interlanguage follows a non-English system in its marking of aspect is unwarranted. Pennington (forthcoming) argues that the meaning of the simple tenses in English is essentially modal rather than temporal. They encode the speaker's perspective on events and situations. According to her analysis the meaning of the simple present is 'unmarked within the speaker's frame of reference'. Past, on the other hand, encodes distance from the speaker's point of view. This contrasts, for example, with Comrie's (1985:20) view that past time reference is the basic meaning of the past tense. Interpreted in terms of Givón's and Kumpf's claims about the distribution of tense/aspect marking in relation to the discourse notions of foreground and background, we can say that the past tense is naturally backgrounded as compared to the present tense, which represents the speaker's conceptual point of reference. Thus, the present is foregrounded.

Bickerton (1984b) cites the case of the acquisition of English by Hindi speakers as one where native language influence overrides the bioprogram. Hindi learners frequently make mistakes such as ***I am liking it**. The use of non-punctuals with statives is a bioprogram violation. In Hindi, however, imperfective marking can be used with statives. This is a case where cultural evolution has affected the bioprogram. It also suggests that the tendencies of the bioprogram are overlaid by first language influence (*cf* also Huebner 1982 for further support from a study of the acquisition of the specific/non-specific distinction in English by a Hmong learner).

According to the bioprogram hypothesis it should be possible to rank all languages along a developmental hierarchy in terms of their closeness to or distance from the bioprogram. Bickerton (1984b:158) says that this should give us a measure of the distance between any two languages which are in contact in a learning situation. This should allow us to predict whether the learning of a particular language will be more difficult or easier for one set of learners as opposed to another. Among other things, this means that 'true' creoles, *ie* those which are close to the bioprogram, should be easiest to acquire. If that is so, then it is curious that adult pidgin speakers seem unable to acquire Hawaii English Creole. The reasons must be social rather than biological.

More work needs to be done on language change in general with a view to testing bioprogram predictions in this domain. One could ask, for instance, why is it that all natural languages do not gradually evolve towards creoles? Why aren't they gradually modified by the children of each new generation into a form that is closer to creoles? Bickerton would argue that the presence of a target would override the influence of the bioprogram. If so, then how is it that socially transmitted features of language can override biological universals? Apparently in some cases they do not. Bickerton (1984a:178), for example, says that Saramaccan Creole in Surinam is extremely close to the bioprogram, yet it is around 300 years old. If this is true, it would mean that cultural evolution had had virtually no effect on grammar. For Bickerton (1984a), however, it is the degree of influence from the superstrate language restricting access to the bioprogram at the time of creolization rather than subsequent decreolization that separates true creoles from others. This suggests an implausible scenario in which there is a creolization phase without contact followed by decreolization with contact.

Without more comparative evidence from the early stages of pidgin and creole formation it is hard to evaluate the case of Hawaii Creole English in relation to Bickerton's claims. It may have been the case that ethnic separateness on the plantations made it possible for transfer to have been a more viable strategy than elsewhere, where there was more inter-group contact and communication. These situations lead to tertiary hybridization and stabilization. More general or universal solutions become necessary in mixed groups.

Since the changes which occur in both pidginization and creolization are just like other cases of historical change (with or without contact), there is no need to posit a bioprogram to account for the majority of cases. Even where Bickerton has claimed that the bioprogram is involved, the details of the transmission of the language intergenerationally are not clear. Janson (1984) has argued that the Hawaii Creole article system can be accounted for in terms of ordinary change. The English indefinite article was lost, followed by the introduction of **wan** as a new marker for indefinite NPs. The definite article existed in the language throughout its development. This is not to say that change is not biologically limited. No doubt change is constrained by biological limits which specify what a human language can be like. There is more work to be done before claims can be substantiated as to which universals of languages are innate and which are by-products of the way in which humans are structured and function.

Notes

1. This bears some resemblance to the discourse function of alternation between the so-called conversational historical present, *ie* CHP and the preterite to mark shifts in scene, as discussed by Wolfson (1982).

2. There is not enough information on mood yet, so this is not discussed by Muysken.
3. This is interesting in the light of Wolfson's finding that the conversational historical present is more likely to occur in narratives where the listener shares some characteristics, *eg* age, sex, ethnicity, etc., solidarity or empathy with the narrator. On such occasions the speaker chooses to encode more verb forms in the present. This would follow from the meaning of the present, which realizes a perspective that is closer to the speaker (*cf* also Note 1.).

Chapter 8

Conclusion

My concluding remarks will be brief. Although there are a number of factors inhibiting progress in pidgin and creole studies, I will confine my comments here to just two of these. One is the lack of adequate theoretical models of language change and development. Another has been a failure to consider the social context of creolization. Let me begin with some observations on the second of these issues.

I indicated in my preface that more work remains to be done on the socio-historical context of pidginization and creolization, and on the sociolinguistic dimensions of pidgin and creole languages. The collection of papers by Woolford and Washabaugh (1983) is devoted to elucidating the social context of creolization. In particular, it addresses the question of whether social forces are the most crucial factor in the emergence of pidginization and creolization. In her introductory essay Woolford (1983:6) says that it is not yet clear whether social factors actually 'cause' the creolization of a pidgin or whether linguistic processes automatically 'induce' creolization unless prevented by social factors. I find it hard to imagine how linguistic processes could 'automatically induce' anything. That is not to deny that there are internal linguistic principles which govern the development of any language system of the kind identified in Chapters 6 and 7. These must be part of any model of language change. She suggests that the first step in developing an explanatory model is to correlate specific social factors with particular linguistic processes to enable us to predict the occurrence of language change.

That won't work for a variety of reasons (*cf* Romaine 1982; 1984d). It is clear from the evidence presented by the contributors to the volume that there does not seem to be a common set of socio-historical factors which give rise to creoles. The very different social circumstances surrounding pidginogenesis in the Atlantic and Pacific have of course been recognized by creolists. In particular, the effect of slave vs. migratory labour trade has been cited as contributory to the rate of creolization and the different character of the creole languages which have emerged in these circumstances. Washabaugh and Greenfield (1983:106), for example, note that the Atlantic creoles are developmentally and functionally related to the plantation as a social form. Although they define creolization narrowly as 'creole language genesis', they attempt to construct what one might call a socio-psychological model which explains the development of the Atlantic creoles in terms of the role played by language in the social life of the earliest creole speakers and in the expression of their psychological needs.

Washabaugh and Greenfield say that creole languages emerged as a consequence of large cultural-historical processes that combined political and economic forces in the creation of new and distinct social situations. Creoles developed to provide a world of meaning to enable their speakers to adapt to the constraints of the new situation. More specifically, they associate the expansion of the Portuguese state with the appearance of Portuguese creoles. The slaves on the island were set apart from the Europeans, and although expected to assimilate, were not accepted as full-fledged Portuguese. The linguistic result was creolization, *ie* the creation of a new language of self-reference and identification. There is nothing in this scenario, however, which is specific to creolization as opposed to the social processes which shape the development of *all* languages. Where is language *not* used as a major tool for the construction of a world view and an identity? As indicated in 5.7, Le Page and Tabouret-Keller (1985) see these forces as universal processes which operate in all communities.

It is interesting, and surely significant too, that the expansion of the Portuguese nation-state was also associated with the standardization of Portuguese. Similar factors are associated with the rise of almost all of the standard languages of the modern Western European states. Polomé (1983) cites with approval Schlieben-Lange's claim (1976:101) that there is a constant relation between historical situations and types of linguistic development. This is an oversimplification, given that both standardization and pidginization are processes of language development connected with the expansion of a nation-state. The fact that the former is often internal to its territorial borders and the latter external does not obscure the basic connection. As far as the more specifically linguistic consequences are concerned, the former more often involves elaboration and minimization of variability, while the latter involves reduction, simplification and maximization of variability. This particular example shows the importance of looking at situations which share many of the social factors associated with creolization, but in which creolization did not occur.

Some would argue that it is a bit too premature to be talking about theory in the field of pidgin and creole studies. Corne (1977b), for example, says that 'questions about the "genesis" of the creole languages, their genetic relations with each other and with their source language(s), the processes of creolization (and pidginization), cannot be approached seriously unless we know something about the object being talked about, and that we shall not know (in sufficient detail) until a lot more of the unglamourous drudgery of careful descriptive work has been completed'. Descriptive work, however, cannot be done in a theoretical vacuum.

I have tried to argue here for a developmentally-oriented theory of language which will fit all acquisition phenomena into a single model. In this connection I want to stress the importance of distinguishing between processes and their outcomes. The entities called 'pidgins' and 'creoles' are salient instances of the processes of pidginization and creolization respectively, although they are not in any sense to be regarded as completed outcomes of them. Furthermore, neither first or second language acquisition, nor pidginization and creolization is a uniform and predictable phenomenon. There does not appear to be one single way in which learners acquire a knowledge of either a first or second language. Both appear to be the product of a number of factors which pertain to the learner, the context in which acquisition takes place, and linguistic universals (*ie* properties of language itself). The importance of the contribution from the study of the latter seems self-evident. There are of course a number of different approaches to universals, among them the bioprogram, Chomskyan formal universals and typological universals. As indicated in Chapter 7, although there are many differences between Bickerton's and Chomsky's views on universals, there are some points in common too. Bickerton has increasingly tended to frame the bioprogram in terms of the unmarked parametric settings of Chomsky's universal grammar (*cf* also Macedo 1986).

There seems to me to be no reason to draw strict boundaries between diffusion, fusion, pidginization and creolization and other processes of change. Historical linguistics, which is more specifically concerned with the question of language change, has traditionally dealt with diffusion resulting in divergence rather than convergence. The task of synthesizing a model of language change which is adequate for progress in the study of pidgins and creoles (and for language in general) is not lessened by treating pidgins and creoles as special cases. Nor is it aided by trying to isolate a social context of creolization distinct from the more general forces which operate on all languages.

Appendix I

A survey of the pidgins and creoles of the world

(from Hancock 1971:507–23)

1. Hawaiian Pidgin English
2. Pitcairnese Creole English

3a. Chinook Jargon
 b. Pidgin Eskimo

4a. Pachuco or Pochismo (a Spanish–English contact language in waning use between Spanish and English speaking Americans, and used as an argot by some users of Mexican ancestry in Arizona and parts of Southern California
 b. Trader Navaho

5. Franco–Amerindian contact vernacular (extinct) between French and indigenous population around Montreal
6. Souriquoien (extinct) between French fisherman and local population of Nova Scotia

7a. New Jersey Amerindian trade pidgin (extinct) used between local population and visiting English and Dutch traders
 b. Mobilian, and Amerindian based pidgin derived mainly from Choctaw, used between tribes on Gulf coast
 c. General Amerindian Pidgin English

8. Gullah
9. Louisiana Creole French
10. Creole English of British Honduras

11a. Pidginized variety of various Caribbean Creole English dialects in use along coast of Nicaragua
 b. Creolized Nahuatl–Spanish (now probably extinct)

12. Papiamentu
13. Creole Spanish
14. Jamaican Creole
15. Haitian French Creole
16. Virgin Islands Dutch Creole

17. French Creole dialects of the Antilles
18. Sranan (Taki Taki) coastal creole of Suriname
19. 'Bush Negro' English based dialects of Suriname (Boni or Aluku and Djuka or Aucan)
20. French Creole of French Guiana
21a. English Creole of Trinidad
 b. English Creole of Antigua
22a. Guyana Creole English
 b. A Portuguese-based creole, near Brazilian border in Guyana
 c. Pidgin Dutch – on inland rivers in Guyana
23. 'Bush Negro' dialects of Surinam, *ie* Saramaccan and Matuwari
24 Brazilian Creole Portuguese
25. Lingoa Geral (or Ava'-nee), a rudimentary pidgin based on the Tupi–Guarani languages of central South America
26a. Cocoliche – Italianized Spanish
 b. Franco–Spanish contact language in Buenos Aires
 c. German–Portuguese contact language in Brazil
27. Russenorsk
27a. Anglo–Romani
 b. Sheldru/Shelta, Anglo–Irish pidgin
28. Ingles de Escalerilla – Spanish–English pidgin used in Mediterranean seaports
29. Pidgin French of North Africa
30. Sabir (extinct)
31. Portuguese derived creole of the Cape Verde Islands – two main dialects are Sotavento and Barlavento
32. Senegal Creole Portuguese, or Kryol
33. Creole English of Bathurst, The Gambia (aka Aku, Krio or Patois)
34. Guine Creole Portuguese or Crioulo. Used as lingua franca in Guinea, creolized in larger towns
35. Krio
36a. Liberian English
 b. Kru English, used by Liberian fisherman on West African coast
37. Pidgin French; Ivory Coast
38. Fernando Po Creole
39. The Gulf of Guinea Portuguese Creoles
40. Cameroons Pidgin English
41a. Ewondo Populaire – African based pidgin between inland tribes of different linguistic backgrounds
 b. Pidgin Hausa, or Barikanci

42a. Tekrur, or pidgin Arabic
 b. Sudan Arabic
 c. North Nigeria pidgin Arabic
 d. Galgaliya; a pidgin Arabic in NE Nigeria
43. Sango, pidgin Ngbandi
44. Several pidginized forms of indigenous African languages current in the Congo area, including Kituba, Ngbandi, Pidgin Chiluba, Bangala, etc.
45. Asmara Pidgin Italian
46. Swahili; various pidginized varieties, inc. 'kisetta' 'Settler Swahili' used between Europeans and Africans
47. Pidginized Afrikaans, used by Hottentots and Afrikaners in Namaland region
48. Afrikaans – a rudimentary creole, its formation involving only semi-creolization away from the metropolitan language
49a. Fanagalo; pidginized Zulu used by migrant African mine workers
 b. Town Bemba – simplification of an indigenous language
50. Reunion French Creole
51a. Mauritian French Creole
 b. A Swahili–Malagasy contact language
52. Rodrigues French Creole
53. Seychelles French Creole
54a. Creole Portuguese of Sri Lanka
 b. Now extinct semi-creolized Dutch in Sri Lanka
55. Goanese, Creole Portuguese of Goa, now probably extinct
56. Creole Portuguese of Diu and Daman
57a. Hobson–Jobson
 b. Indo-Aryan
58. Madras English Pidgin, or Butler English
59. Tay Boi, or Indo-French Pidgin, practically extinct
60. Makista or Macauenho, Portuguese based creole of Macao
61a. China Coast Pidgin English
 b. A pidginized Chinese in NW of Laos and Vietnam
 c. Sino-Russian
62. Korean Pidgin English, or Bamboo English
63a. Japanese Pidgin during nineteenth century
 b. Japanese Pidgin English, in Hamamatsu area during American occupation
 c. Pidgin English in Vietnam, shaped by 62 and 63b
64. Malacca Portuguese Creole, aka Papia Kristang
65. Singapore Portuguese Creole
66. Portuguese Creole of Jakarta
67. Pasa or Bazaar Malay, a pidginized variety of High Malay,

widespread throughout Malaysia and Indonesia

68. Caviteño and Ermitaño, Spanish creoles from the Manila area
69. Zamboangueño or Chabacano, spoken in Zamboanga City, influences from Tagalog and Cebuano
70. Davaueño or Abakay Spanish, spoken in Davao; an offshoot of 69 above
71. Ternateño: progenitor of the Philippine Creoles, developed from contact between Spanish/Mexican soldiers and local Portuguese Pidgin speaking community
72. New Guinea or Papuan Pidgin English
73a. Police Motu
  b. Pidginized Siassi, as lingua franca in Astrolabe Bay, New Guinea
74. Melanasian Pidgin English, aka Neo-Melanesian, Beach la Mar, Sandalwood English, etc.
75a. Solomon Island Pidgin English
  b. Now extinct English derived pidgin in Micronesian islands during nineteenth century
76. Bagot Creole English in Aboriginal Reserve near Darwin, N. Australia
77. Australian Pidgin English (from Neo Melanesian)
78. New Caledonia Pidgin French, aka Bichelamar
79. Norfolkese, an offshoot of Pitcairnese (2 above) spoken by descendants from *HMS Bounty* who settled on the island of Norfolk in the nineteenth century
80. Maori Pidgin English, no longer spoken. Similar to Neo-Melanesian

Repertory of pidgin and creole languages (from Hancock 1977)

(Bracketed figures following entries denote the listing numbers in Hancock's 1971 listing, see above. Entries IN CAPITAL LETTERS not in earlier listing.)

	Name of language	Section reference
1.	Hawaiian Creole English (1)	English
2.	Pitcairnese Creole English (2)	English
3.	Pidgin Eskimo (3b)	Amerindian
4.	Chinook Jargon (3a)	Amerindian
5.	Trader Navaho (4b)	Amerindian
6.	Pachuco (4a)	Spanish
7.	Mobilian (7b)	Amerindian
8.	Louisiana French Creole (9)	French

9.	Michif Creole French (5)	French
10.	Souriquoien (6)	French
11.	New Jersey Amerindian Pidgin (7a)	Amerindian
12.	Gullah (8)	English
13.	US BLACK ENGLISH	English
14.	General Amerindian Pidgin English (7c)	English
15.	BAHAMA & CAICOS ISLANDS CREOLE ENGLISH	English
16.	Jamaican Creole English (14)	English
17.	Haitian Creole French (15)	French
18.	CAPE SAMANA, DOMINICAN REPLUBLIC CREOLE	English
19.	Virgin Islands Dutch Creole (16)	Dutch
20.	Lesser Antilles Creole French (17)	French
21.	Lesser Antilles Creole English (21a, b)	English
22.	SAN ANDRES & PROVIDENCIA, COLOMBIA CREOLE	English
23.	Nahuatl-Spanish (11b)	Spanish
24.	Belize Creole English (10)	English
25.	Nicaragua's Mosquito Coast Creole (11a)	English
26.	Papiamentu Portuguese/Spanish Creole (12)	Portuguese
27.	VENEZUELAN PIDGIN SPANISH	Spanish
28.	PALENQUERO	Spanish
29.	Guyana Dutch Creole (22c)	Dutch
30.	Guyana Creole English (22a)	English
31.	Sranan Creole English (18)	English
32.	Guyana French Creole (20)	French
33.	Saramaccan (23)	Portuguese
34.	'Bush Negro' Creole English (19)	English
35.	Brazilian Portuguese Creoles (24,26c?)	Portuguese
36.	'ASHANTI'	African
37.	Lingoa Geral (25)	Amerindian
38.	FAZENDEIRO	Italian
39.	Cocoliche (26a)	Spanish
40.	ICELANDIC PIDGIN FRENCH	French
41.	Russenorsk (27)	misc. European
42.	PLAT LEEWAADERS	Dutch
43.	Romani-derived cants (27a, b)	misc. European
44.	YIDDISH	German

45.	LETTO-GERMAN PIDGIN	German
46.	GASTARBEITER GERMAN	German
47.	YUGOSLAVIAN GERMAN PIDGINS	German
48.	RUMANIAN-HUNGARIAN	Misc. European
49.	SLAVO–GERMAN	German
50.	VOLGA GERMAN	German
51.	Sabir (30)	Misc. European
52.	North African Pidgin French (29)	French
53.	KOURIYA	African
54.	Cape Verde Portuguese Creole (31)	Portuguese
55.	Senegal Creole Portuguese (32)	Portuguese
56.	Banjul Creole English (33)	English
57.	Guine Creole Portuguese (34)	Portuguese
58.	SEYOU, GUINE PIDGIN FRENCH	French
59.	KANGBE	African
60.	Krio (35)	English
61.	Liberian English (36a)	English
62.	Ivory Coast Pidgin French (37)	French
63.	COMMERCIAL DYULA	African
64.	WESTERN NIGERIAN PIDGIN	English
65.	FUL	African
66.	Fernando Po Creole (38)	English
67.	Cameroon Pidgin English (40)	English
68.	Ewondo Populaire (41a)	African
69.	Gulf of Guinea Portuguese Creoles (39)	Portuguese
70.	Barikanchi (41b)	African
71.	Galgaliya (42d)	Arabic
72.	Tekrur (42a)	Arabic
73.	Sango (43)	African
74.	Kituba (44)	African
75.	CONTACT PORTUGUESE	Portuguese
76.	ST HELENA PIDGIN ENGLISH	English
77.	Pidginized Afrikaans (47)	Dutch
78.	Afrikaans (48)	Dutch
79.	SOUTHERN AFRICAN PORTUGUESE PIDGINS	Portuguese
80.	LANZI	Italian
81.	Fanagalo (49a)	African
82.	Town Bemba (49b)	African
83.	CHIKUNDA	African

84.	Barracoon (51b)	African
85.	Ki-Setla (46)	African
86.	MBUGU	Swahili
87.	Sudan Arabic (42b)	African
88.	NUBI SUDAN ARABIC	African
89.	BOJUNI SWAHILI CREOLE	Swahili
90.	Asmara Pidgin Italian (45)	Italian
91.	CI-MIINI	African
92.	Seychelles French Creole (53)	French
93.	Mauritian Creole French (51a, 52)	French
94.	Reunion Creole French (50)	French
95.	Diu & Daman Creole Portuguese (56)	Portuguese
96.	Ceylon Creole Portuguese (54a)	Portuguese
97.	Hobson-Jobson (57a, 58)	English
98.	Hindi Pidgins (54b)	Hindi
99.	VEDDA	non-European
100.	PALIYAN	non-European
101.	NAGAMESE	non- European
102.	Pidginized Chinese (61b)	non-European
103.	Tay-Boi French Pidgin (59)	French
104.	Pasa Malay (67)	non-European
105.	Malacca Portuguese Creole (64)	Portuguese
106.	Jakarta Portuguese Creole (65, 66)	Portuguese
107.	Bagot Aboriginal Reserve Australian Creole English (76)	English
108.	NORTHERN TERRITORY PIDGIN	English
109.	NEO-NYUNGAR	English
110.	Australian Pidgin English (77)	English
111.	JARGON ENGLISH	English
112.	Maori Pidgin English (80)	English
113.	Norfolkese (79)	English
114.	New Caledonia Pidgin French (78)	French
115.	Melanesian Pidgin English (73, 74)	English
116.	Police Motu (73a)	non-European
117.	Micronesian Islands (75b)	English
118.	Ternateño (71)	Spanish
119.	Chabacano (68, 69, 70)	Spanish
120.	Makista Portuguese Creole (60)	Portuguese
121.	China Coast Pidgin English (61a)	English
122.	Korean Pidgin English (62, 63a)	English
123.	Japanese Pidgin English (63b)	English
124.	Japanese Pidgin (63c)	non-European

125. SINO-SLAVIC	non-European
126. Siassi Pidgin (73b)	non-European
127. PARAU TINITO	non-European

Notes on entries not in Hancock 1971 (ie entries above in capital letters)

English-based

13. US Black English, Afro-American. Dillard suggests the existence in the early USA of a creole distinct from the more intelligible Black English [sic].
15. Creole spoken throughout Bahama and Caicos Islands in various stages of approximation to US English.
18. Descendants of ex-US slaves who settled in Cape Samana, 1824.
22. Known locally as BENDE
64. West Nigerian Pidgin (Pidgin English varieties also reported in Ghana)
76. Pidgin English reported as once having been spoken on St Helena.
108. Used by Aborigines throughout north central Australia.
109. Neo-Nyungar or Aboriginal English is an English–Nyungar contact language used as the everyday speech of Aborigines in Southwestern Australia. A more anglicized version is used in communication with white Australians, WETJALA, and an intentionally disguised variety called YERAKA is used as a play-language with women.
111. Similar to New Guinea Pidgin, spoken in the islands between Cape York and the Papuan coast opposite Torres Straits.

French

40. E and W coasts of Iceland show traces of a French–Icelandic language arising from the long sojourn of the French fishermen there.
58. Use of a pidginized French structured on the local Portuguese creole was reported in Seyou, Guine.

Portuguese

75. ‘Broken Portuguese’ Pequeno Portugues, or ‘Blackigiese’ spoken in the larger towns in Angola.
79. Pidginized contact forms of Portuguese have been reported on S. African coast as well as on St Helena in nineteenth

century and survived into the twententh century in Cape Town.

Spanish

27. Used principally by two Amerindian tribes inhabiting western Venezuela in dealing with traders.
28. Afro- & Amerindian-influenced creolized forms of Spanish have been reported throughout NW South America and in Mexico.

Other European based pidgins and creoles

Dutch

42. Spoken by Jews in the Friesian capital of Ljouwert.

Italian

38. A rudimentary creole FAZENDEIRO exists in São Paolo, spoken by some Brazilians of mixed Italian and African descent.
80. Sixteenth-century German–Italian pidgin known as LANZI or LANZICHENECCHI

German

44. 'Yiddish appears to have some features of creolization such as simplified morphology and eclectic lexicon.'
45. Letto-German Pidgin, once spoken in Latvia with Yiddish and Plattdeutsch elements and a phonology heavily influenced by Latvian.
46. Gastarbeiter Deutsch, spoken by immigrant workers in Germany, showing features found in such earlier forms of German as those used in POW, concentration and displaced person camps. 'Appears to be more a foreigner talk than a stable pidgin'.
47. Two pidgins, one German and one Slavic derived, used in Bosnia-Zegovina (Yugoslavia) before WW1.
49. Slavo-German as it developed during the time of the Austro-Hungarian Empire showed features of pidginization.
50. A highly reduced and Slavicized offshoot of the Volga German dialects survises in Chkalov (Orenburg) Province in the eastern part of the USSR.

Slavic

125. A Sino-slavic contact language came into use in some northern Manchurian cities such as Harbin and A-szu-ho, where Russians, Poles and others settled at the beginning

of the twentieth century in connection with the construction of the Eastern Chinese Railway.

Misc. European

48. Rumanian–Hungarian: discussed by Schuchardt (see Hancock for ref.)

African

36. Surviving African languages (Ashanti, Koromanti, Yoruba, KiKongo etc.) containing heavy admixture from European languages have been reported in the Caribbean and the NW coast of South America from the Guineas to Brazil, many associated with religious cults.
53. 'A variety of mongrel Sudanese dialects now almost extinct, and known as KOURIYA is spoken by slaves and their descendants at Gourara near Touat'.
59. Over a wide area of Manding-speaking W. Africa, a vehicular dialect called Kangbe, *ie* clear language, is in use between speakers of various Manding languages such as Mandinka and Bambura.
63. Commercial Dyula, a pidiginized variety, is used in towns in the Ivory Coast.
65. A reduced FUL is spoken at various places in Cameroon and Nigeria.
83. Spoken by the descendants of a slave community on the lower Zambesi.
86. Some languages in the Tanzania–Kenya border region such as Mbugu and Beja appear to have a Bantu-based structure with a non-Bantu lexicon.
88. Pidginized military Sudan Arabic was carried into Uganda *c.* 1891 where it adopted further lexical items from Luo, Bari, Swahili and Lendu and became the mother tongue of a Muslim community called the Nubi.
89. A Swahili-derived and reportedly creolized language is spoken in the Bajuni Islands in the Somali-Kenya coastal border area.
91. A very similar language to Ki-Tiku. Spoken by a mixed and inbred population in Brava (Miini, Barawa) on the Somali coast. Its speakers believe it to be a mixture of Portuguese and Swahili.

Miscellaneous non-European

99. Vedda, spoken by about 400 speakers of an Austro-Mongoloid and Sinhalese creole in the Polonnaruwa and Dambulla districts of Sri Lanka.

100. The language of the Paliyans, a hill tribe in S. India. Tamil jargon.
101. Spoken throughout the entire state of Nagaland as a lingua franca (several miles NE of Garo territory).
127. Parau Tinito or Prao Tinto, pidginized Tahitian, spoken by older Chinese merchants in Papeete, Tahiti.

The following entries appear in Hancock 1971 but not in Hancock 1977

22b. A Portuguese-based creole near Brazilian border in Guyana.
26b. A Franco-Spanish contact language in Buenos Aires.
28. Ingles de Escalerilla – Spanish/English pidgin used in Mediterranean seaports.
54b. Now extinct semi-creolized Dutch in Sri Lanka.
55. Goanese, Creole Portuguese of Goa, now probably extinct.

References

ABRAHAMS, R. (1972) 'The training of the man of words in talking sweet', *Language in Society* **1**:15–30.

ADAMS, R. (1974) *Watership Down*. Harmondsworth: Penguin.

ADLER, M. K. (1977) *Pidgins, Creoles and Lingua Francas: A sociolinguistic study*. Hamburg: Helmut Buske Verlag.

AGHEYISI, R. N. (1971) 'West African Pidgin English: simplification and simplicity', PhD dissertation, Stanford University.

AIKIBA-REYNOLDS, K. (1983) 'Reconstruction of *nu- A hypothesis for the origin of Japanese', *Papers in Japanese Linguistics* **8**. Tokyo: Kaitakusha.

AITCHISON, J. (1983a) 'Pidgins, creoles and child language', *Working Papers of the London Psycholinguistics Research Group* **5**:5–16.

AITCHISON, J. (1983b) 'Social networks and urban New Guinea Pidgin (Tok Pisin)', *York Papers in Linguistics* **11** (Papers from the York Creole Conference).

AITCHISON, J. (1983c) 'Review of Derek Bickerton *Roots of Language*', *Language and Communication* **3**:83–97.

AKERS, G. (1981) 'Admissibility conditions on final consonant clusters in the Jamaican continuum', in Muysken, P. (ed.) *Generative Studies on Creole Languages*. Dordrecht: Foris. *pp* 1–25.

ALBERT, H. (1922) 'Mittelalterlicher English-Französischer Jargon', *Studien zur Englischen Philologie*, Heft LXIII. Halle: Max Niemeyer.

ALLEYNE, M. C. (1971) 'Acculturation and the cultural matrix of creolization', in Hymes, D. (ed.) *pp* 169–87.

ALLEYNE, M. C. (1980) *Comparative Afro-American*. Ann Arbor: Karoma.

ALLSOPP, R. (1958a) 'The English Language in British Guiana', *English Language Teaching* **12**:59–66.

ALLSOPP, A. (1958b) 'Pronominal forms in the dialect of English used in Georgetown (British Guiana) and its environs by persons engaged in nonclerical occupations', MA thesis, University of London.

ANDERSEN, R. (1981) 'Two perspectives on pidginization as second language acquisition', in Andersen, R. (ed.), *pp* 165–96.

ANDERSEN, R. (ed.) (1981) *New Dimensions in Second Language Acquisition Research*. Rowley, MA: Newbury House.

ANDERSEN, R. (ed.) (1983) *Pidginization and Creolization as Language Acquisition*. Rowley, MA: Newbury House.

ANDERSEN, R. (1984) 'The one to one principle of interlanguage construction', *Language Learning* **34**:77–95.

ANDERSEN, R. (1986) 'Interpreting data: second language acquisition of verbal aspect' (unpublished manuscript).

ANTINUCCI, F. and MILLER, R. (1976) 'How children talk about what happened', *Journal of Child Language* **3**:167–89.

BAILEY, B. L. (1965) 'Toward a new perspective in Negro English dialectology', *American Speech* **40**:171–7.

BAILEY, B. L. (1966) *Jamaican Creole Syntax*. London: Cambridge University Press.

BAILEY, C-J. (1973) *Variation and Linguistic Theory*. Washington, DC: Center for Applied Linguistics.

BAILEY, C-J. and MAROLDT, K. (1977) 'The French lineage of English', in Meisel, J. (ed.) *Pidgins-Creoles-Languages in Contact*. Tübingen: Narr. *pp* 21–53.

BAILEY, G. and MAYNOR, N. (1985) 'Decreolization?' Paper read at the International Linguistic Association, New York City, March 1985.

BAILEY, G. and MAYNOR, N. (forthcoming) 'The present tense of *be* in White folk speech of the Southern United States', *English World Wide*.

BAKER, P. (1972) *Kreol. A Description of Mauritian Creole*. London: C. Hurst and Co.

BAKER, P. and CORNE, C. (1982) *Isle de France Creole. Affinities and Origins*. Ann Arbor: Karoma.

BALINT, A. (1969) *English-Pidgin-French Phrase Book and Sports Dictionary. Inglis-Pisin-Frans tok save na spot diksineri*. Port Moresby: The author.

BATES, E. and MACWHINNEY, B. (1979) 'A functionalist approach to the acquisition of grammar', in Ochs, E. and Schieffelin, B. (eds) *Developmental Pragmatics*. New York: Academic Press *pp* 167–211.

BAUGH, J. (1980) 'A reexamination of the Black English Copula', In Labov, W. (ed.) *Locating Language in Time and Space*. New York: Academic Press *pp* 83–106.

BAXTER, A. (1983) 'Creole universals and Kristang (Malacca Creole Portuguese)', in *Papers in Pidgin and Creole Linguistics No. 3*. Pacific Linguistics A- **65**:143–60. Canberra: Australian National University.

BENDER, L. M. (1987) 'Some possible African creoles: a pilot study', in Gilbert, G. (ed.) *Pidgin and Creole Languages: Essays in Memory of John Reinecke*. Honolulu: University of Hawaii Press.

BENTOLILA, A. (1971) *Les systèmes verbaux créoles: Comparaisons avec les langues africaines*. Thèse de 3e cycle de l'Université de Paris V-René Descartes.

BEREITER, C. and ENGELMANN, S. (1966) *Teaching Disadvantaged Children in the Pre-school*. Englewood Cliffs, NJ: Prentice-Hall.

BERKO, J. (1961) 'The child's learning of English morphology', in Saporta, S. (ed.) *Psycholinguistics. A Book of Readings*. New York: Holt, Rinehart and Winston *pp* 359–75.

BERRENGER [no first name listed] (1811) *A Grammatical Arrangement on the method of learning the corrupted Portuguese as spoken in India* (2nd edn) didicated [sic] to the English Gentlemen in the Civil and Military Service on Ceylon. By their much obliged and most obedient servant, Berrenger. Colombo: Frans de Brun at the Government Press.

BERRY, J. and AIDOO, A. A. (1975) *An Introduction to Akan*. Evanston: Northwestern University.

BICKERTON, D. (1972) 'The structure of polylectal grammars', in Shuy, R. (ed.) *Sociolinguistics*. 23rd Annual Roundtable, Washington, DC: Georgetown University Press *pp* 17–43.

BICKERTON, D. (1973) 'On the nature of a creole continuum', *Language* **49**:641–69.

BICKERTON, D. (1974) 'Creolization, linguistic universals, natural semantax and the brain', *Working Papers in Linguistics* University of Hawaii **6**(3):125–41.

BICKERTON, D. (1975a) *Dynamics of a Creole System*. Cambridge: Cambridge University Press.

BICKERTON, D. (1975b) 'Can English and Tok Pisin be kept apart?', in McElhanon, K. A. (ed.) *pp* 21–8.

BICKERTON, D. (1977a) 'Pidginization and creolization: language acquisition and language universals', in Valdman, A. (ed.) (1977b) *pp* 49–69.

BICKERTON, D. (1977b) *Change and Variation in Hawaiian English*. Vol. 2: *Creole Syntax*. University of Hawaii: Social Sciences and Linguistics Institute.

BICKERTON, D. (1980) 'Decreolisation and the creole continuum', in Valdman, A. and Highfield, A. (eds) *pp* 109–29.

BICKERTON, D. (1981a) *Roots of Language*. Ann Arbor: Karoma.

BICKERTON, D. (1981b) 'Discussion of "Two perspectives on pidginization as language acquisition"', in Andersen, R. (ed.) *pp* 202–6.

BICKERTON, D. (1984a) 'The language bioprogram hypothesis', *The Behavioral and Brain Sciences* **7**:173–221.

BICKERTON, D. (1984b) 'The language bioprogram hypothesis and second language acquisition', in Rutherford, W. E. (ed.) *Language Universals and Second Language Acquisition*. Amsterdam: John Benjamins *pp* 141–61.

BICKERTON, D. (1984c) 'Creole is still king', *The Behavioral and Brain Sciences* **7**:212–18.

BICKERTON, D. (1984d) 'Evidence for a two-stage model of language from ontogeny and phylogeny', paper presented at the Workshop on Ontogeny and Human Development. Tel-Aviv University, Israel.

BICKERTON, D. and GIVÓN, T. (1978) 'Experimental creation of a natural language', (unpublished manuscript).

BICKERTON, D. and ODO, C. (1976) *Change and Variation in Hawaiian*

English. Vol. I: *General phonology and pidgin syntax*. University of Hawaii: Social Sciences and Linguistics Institute.

BLOOMFIELD, L. (1933) *Language*. New York: Henry Holt.

BOTKIN, B. A. (1945) *Lay my burden down: A folk history of slavery*. Chicago: University of Chicago Press.

BOWERMAN, M. (1974) 'Learning the structure of causative verbs: A study in the relationship of cognitive, semantic and syntactic development', *Stanford Papers and Reports on Child Language Development* **8**:142–78.

BRADSHAW, J. (1979) 'Serial causative constructions and word order change in Papua New Guinea', *Working Papers in Linguistics*, University of Hawaii. Vol. 11. No. **2**:13–34.

BRESNAN, J. (1977) 'Variables in the theory of transformations', in Culicover *et al*. (eds) *pp* 157–97.

BREWER, J. (1974) 'The verb "be" in early Black English: A study based on the WPA ex-slave narratives', PhD dissertation, University of North Carolina.

BREWER, J. (1979) 'Non-agreeing *am* and invariant *be* in Early Black English', *The SECOL Bulletin* **3**:81–100.

BRITO, A. DE PAULA (1887) 'Dialectos Crioulos-Portuguezes. Apontamentos para a Gramática do Crioulo que se Fala na Ilha de Santiago de Cabo Verde', *Boletim da Sociedade e Geografia de Lisboa* **7**:611–69.

BROCH, I. and JAHR, E. H. (1984) 'Russenorsk: a new look at the Russo-Norwegian pidgin in Northern Norway', in Ureland, P. S. and Clarkson, I. (eds) *Scandinavian Language Contacts*. Cambridge: Cambridge University Press *pp* 21–65.

BROCH, O. (1927) 'Russenorsk', *Archiv für Slavische Philologie* **41**:209–62.

BRONCKART, J-P. (1976) *Genèse et organisation des formes verbales chez l'enfant*. Bruxelles: Dessart et Mardaga.

BRONCKART, J-P. and SINCLAIR, H. (1973) 'Time, tense and aspect', *Cognition* **2**:107–30.

BROWN, R. (1958) *Words and Things. An Introduction to Language*. New York: The Free Press.

BROWN, R. (1973) *A First Language: The Early Stages*. Cambridge, Mass.: Harvard University Press.

BRUNER, J. and FELDMAN, C. (1982) 'Where does language come from?', *New York Review of Books* **29**(11):34–6.

BURT, M. and DULAY, H. (1980) 'On acquisition orders', in Felix, S. (ed.).

BYBEE, J. (1985) 'Diagrammatic iconicity in stem-inflection relations', in Haiman, J. (ed.) *Iconicity in Syntax*. Amsterdam: John Benjamins *pp* 11–49.

CASSIDY, F. G. (1961) *Jamaica Talk*. London: Macmillan.

CASSIDY, F. G. (1971) 'Tracing the pidgin element in Jamaican Creole', in Hymes, D. (ed.) *pp* 203–23.

CASSIDY, F. G. and LE PAGE, R. B. (1967) *Dictionary of Jamaican English*. Cambridge: Cambridge University Press.

CASSIDY, P. (1985) 'Going native and getting it across', unpublished manuscript. Department of English. UCLA.

CAZDEN, C. (1972) *Child Language and Education*. New York: Holt, Rinehart and Winston.

CAZDEN, C., CANCINO, H., ROSANSKY, H. and SCHUMANN, J. (1975) *Second Language Acquisition Sequences in Children, Adolescents and Adults*. Final report. United States Department of Health, Education and Welfare.

CHAMBERS, J. and TRUDGILL, P. (1980) *Dialectology*. Cambridge: Cambridge University Press.

CHARPENTIER, J. M. (1983) 'Le Pidgin Bichelamar avant et après l'Independence de Vanuatu', *York Papers in Linguistics* **11**.

CHOMSKY, N. (1977) 'On WH movement', in Culicover *et al.* (eds) *pp* 71–133.

CHOMSKY, N. (1979) *Language and Responsibility*. Cambridge, Mass.: MIT Press.

CHOMSKY, N. (1980) *Rules and Representations*. Oxford: Blackwell.

CHOMSKY, N. (1981) 'Principles and parameters in syntactic theory', in Hornstein, N. and Lightfoot, D. (eds) *Explanation in Linguistics. The Logical Problem of Language Acquisition*. London: Longman *pp* 32–76.

CHOMSKY, N. (1982) *Some concepts and consequences of the theory of government and binding. Linguistic Inquiry* Monograph 6. Cambridge, Mass.: MIT Press.

CHURCHILL, W. (1911) *Beach-la-Mar, the jargon or trade speech of the Western Pacific*. Washington, DC: Carnegie Institution (Publication No. 164).

CLARK, R. (1979) 'In search of Beach-la-Mar: towards a history of Pacific Pidgin English', *Te Reo* **22**:3–64.

CLYNE, M. (1968) 'Zum Pidgindeutsch der Gastarbeiter', *Zeitschrift für Mundartforschung* **35**:130–9.

CLYNE, M. (ed.) (1981) *Foreigner Talk. International Journal of the Sociology of Language* **28**.

COELHO, F. A. (1800–1886) 'Os Dialectos Românicos ou Neo-Latinos na Africa, Asia e América', *Boletim da Sociedade de Geografia de Lisboa*.

COHEN, J. M. and COHEN, M. J. (1971) *The Penguin Dictionary of Modern Quotations*. Harmondsworth: Penguin.

COLLINSON, C. W. (1929) *Cannibals and Coconuts*. London: George Philip & Son.

COMHAIRE-SYLVAIN, S. (1936) *Le créole haitien: morphologie et syntaxe*. Port-au-Prince and Wetteren: Imprimerie de Meester.

COMRIE, B. (1976) *Aspect*. Cambridge: Cambridge University Press.

COMRIE, B. (1981) *Language Universals and Linguistic Typology*. Oxford: Blackwell.

COMRIE, B. (1985) *Tense*. Cambridge: Cambridge University Press.

COOK, V. (1973) 'The comparison of language development in native children and foreign adults', *IRAL* **11**:13–28.

CORDER, S. P. (1967) 'The significance of learners' errors', *IRAL* **5**:161–9.

CORDER, S. P. (1975) 'Simple codes and the source of the second language learner's initial heuristic hypothesis', in Corder, S. P. and Roulet, E. (eds) *Linguistic Approaches in Applied Linguistics*. Paris: Didier.

CORDER, S. P. (1977) 'The language of Kehaar', *RELC Journal* **8**(1):1:1–12.

CORDER, S. P. (1978) 'Language distance and the magnitude of the learning task', *Studies in Second Language Acquisition* 2/1:

CORNE, C. (1974–5) 'Tense, aspect and the mysterious *i* in Seychelles and Reunion Creole', *Te Reo* **17–18**:53–93.

CORNE, C. (1977a) 'A note on passives in Indian Ocean Creole dialects', *Journal of Creole Studies* **1**:33–58.

CORNE, C. (1977b) *Seychelles Creole Grammar*. Tübingen: Narr.

CORNE, C. (1981) 'A reevaluation of the predicate in Ile de France Creole', in Muysken, P. (ed.) *pp* 103–24.

COSTA, J. V. B. and DUARTE, C. J. (1886) 'O Crioulo de Cabo Verde. Breves Estudos Sobre o Crioulo das Ilhas de Cabo Verde Oferecidos ao Dr. Hugo Schuchardt', *Boletim da Sociedade de Geografia de Lisboa* **6**:325–88.

CROMER, R. (1968) 'The development of temporal reference during the acquisition of language', PhD dissertation, Harvard University.

CROSS, T. (1977) 'Mothers' speech adjustments: the contribution of selected child-listener variables', in Snow, C. and Ferguson, C. F. (eds) *pp* 151–89.

CROWLEY, T. and RIGSBY, B. (1979) 'Cape York Creole', in Shopen, T. (ed.) *Languages and Their Status*. Cambridge, Mass.: Winthrop Publishers, Inc. *pp* 153–209.

CULICOVER, P., WASOW, T. and AKMAJIAN, A. (eds) (1977) *Formal Syntax*. New York: Academic Press.

DAA, L. K. (1870) *Skisser fra Lappland, Karelstranden og Finland*. Oslo.

DAIBER, A. (1902) *Eine Australien- und Südseefahrt*. Leipzig: Teubner.

DAY, R. (1972) 'Patterns of variation in copula and tense in the Hawaiian Post–Creole continuum', PhD dissertation, University of Hawaii.

DAY, R. (ed.) (1980) *Issues in English Creoles*. Heidelberg: Julius Groos Verlag.

DAYTON, E. (1984) 'The alternation between the "was" form of the zero copula, unstressed *been* and *was/were* in copula position in Black English: A reflection of creole origins', Paper given at NWAVE 13. University of Pennsylvania, Philadelphia, Pa.

DEBOSE, C. E. (1974) 'Papiamento plurals', *Studies in African Linguistics* **5**:67–73.

DECAMP, D. (1971a) 'The study of pidgin and creole languages', in Hymes, D. (ed.) *pp* 13–43.

DECAMP, D. (1971b) 'Towards a generative analysis of a post–creole continuum', in Hymes, D. (ed.) *pp* 349–70.

DECAMP, D. (1973) 'What do implicational scales imply?', in Bailey, C-J. and Shuy, R. (eds) *New Ways of Analyzing Variation in English*. Washington, DC: Georgetown University Press *pp* 141–9.

DECAMP, D. (1977) 'The development of pidgin and creole studies', in Valdman, A. (ed.) *pp* 3–20.

DECAMP, D. and HANCOCK, I. (eds) (1974) *Pidgins and Creoles: Current Trends and Prospects*. Washington, DC: Georgetown University Press.

DEUCHAR, M. (1983) 'Relative clauses and linguistic equality', paper presented at the Linguistics Association of Great Britain meeting. Newcastle-upon-Tyne.

DEUCHAR, M. (1984) *British Sign Language*. London: Routledge and Kegan Paul.

DEUCHAR, M. (1986) 'Sign languages as creoles and Chomsky's notion of universal grammar', in Modgil, S. and Modgil, C. (eds) *Noam Chomsky Consensus and Controversy*. Brighton: Falmer Press.

DE VILLIERS, J. G., FLUSBERG, T., HAKUTA, K. and CHEN, M. (1979) 'Children's comprehension of relative clauses', *JPsyR* **8**:499–518.

DEVONISH, H. (1983) 'Creole language standardization in Guyana: race, class and urban–rural factors', *York Papers in Linguistics* **11**.

DIJKOFF, M. (ms.) 'The suffix nan in Papiamentu', unpublished manuscript. The John Reinecke Collection, Sinclair Library University of Hawaii at Manoa, Honolulu, Hawaii.

DILLARD, J. L. (1968) 'Non-standard Negro dialects – convergence or divergence', *Florida FL Reporter* **6**:2.

DILLARD, J. L. (1970) 'Principles in the history of American English – Paradox, virginity and cafeteria', *Florida FL Reporter* **8**.

DIRVEN, R., GOOSENS, L., PUTSEYS, Y. and VORLAT, E. (1982) *The scene of linguistic action and its perspectivization by speak, talk, say and tell*. Pragmatics and Beyond III:6. Amsterdam: Benjamins.

DOI, T. (1984) 'On the hypothesis of the pidgin–creole origin of the Japanese language', MA thesis, Southern Illinois University.

DORIAN, N. C. (1981) *Language Death. The Life Cycle of a Scottish Gaelic Dialect*. Philadelphia: University of Pennsylvania Press.

DORIAN, N. C. (1983) 'Natural second language acquisition from the perspective of the study of language death', in Andersen, R. (ed.) *pp* 158–68.

DRECHSEL, E. J. and MAKUAKANE, T. H. (1982) 'Hawaiian loanwords in Chinook Jargon and Eskimo Jargon', *International Journal of American Linguistics* **48**:460–6.

DREYFUSS, G. (1977) 'Relative clause structure in four creole languages', PhD dissertation, University of Michigan.

DULAY, H. and BURT, M. (1973) 'Should we teach children syntax?' *Language Learning* **23**:245–58.

DULAY, H. and BURT, M. (1974) 'Natural sequences in child second language acquisition', *Language Learning* **24**:37–53.

DURAN, J. J. (1979) 'Non-standard forms of Swahili in west-central Kenya', in Hancock, I. (ed.) *pp* 129–53.

DUTTON, T. (1973) *Conversational New Guinea Pidgin*. Pacific Linguistics D-12. Canberra: Australian National University.

DUTTON, T. (1980) *Queensland Canefields English of the Late Nineteenth Century*. Pacific Linguistics D-29. Canberra: Australian National University.

DUTTON, T. (1983a) 'The origin and spread of Aboriginal Pidgin English in Queensland: A preliminary account', *Aboriginal History* **7**(1):90–122.

DUTTON, T. (1983b) 'Birds of a feather: a pair of rare pidgins from the Gulf of Papua', in Woolford, E. and Washabaugh, W. (eds) *pp* 77–105.

DUTTON, T. and MÜHLHÄUSLER, P. (1979) 'Papuan Pidgin English and Hiri Motu', in Wurm, S. A. (ed.) *New Guinea and Neighbouring Areas: A Sociolinguistic Laboratory*. The Hague: Mouton *pp* 225–42.

DYEN, I. (1975) *Linguistic Subgrouping and Lexicostatistics*. The Hague: Mouton.

EDWARDS, V. (1979) *The West Indian Language Issue in British Schools*. London: Routledge and Kegan Paul.

EDWARDS, V. (1986) *Language in a Black Community*. Clevedon, Avon: Multilingual Matters Ltd.

EDWARDS, V. and LADD, P. (1983) 'The linguistic status of British Sign Language', *York Papers in Linguistics* **11**.

EDWARDS, W. (1975) 'Sociolinguistic Behaviour in Rural and Urban Circumstances in Guyana'. DPhil. dissertation, University of York.

ELLIS, R. (1985) *Understanding Second Language Acquisition*. Oxford: Oxford University Press.

ERVIN, S. (1964) 'Imitation and structural change in children's language', in Lenneberg, E. (ed.) *New Directions in the Study of Language*. Cambridge, Mass.: MIT Press *pp* 163–91.

ESCURE, G. (1983) 'The acquisition of creole by urban and rural black Caribs in Belize', *York Papers in Linguistics* **11**.

EZE, S. N. (1980) *Nigerian Pidgin English Sentence Complexity*. Beiträge zur Afrikanistik. Band 8. Vienna: Institut für Afrikanistik und Ägyptologie der Universität Wien.

FAINE, J. (1936) *Philologie créole; études historiques et etymologiques sur la langue créole d'Haiti*. Port-au-Prince: Imprimerie de l'Etat.

FASOLD, R. (1972a) 'Decreolization and autonomous language change', *Florida FL Reporter* **10**:9–12; 51.

FASOLD, R. (1972b) *Tense Marking in Black English: A Linguisic and Social Analysis*. Arlington, Va: Center for Applied Linguistics.

FASOLD, R. (1976) 'One hundred years from syntax to phonology', Chicago Linguistic Society: University of Chicago.

FASOLD, R. (1981) 'The relation between Black and White speech in the South', *American Speech* 56:163–89.

FELIX, S. (ed.) (1980) *Second Language Development*. Tübingen: Narr.

FERGUSON, C. F. (1959) 'Diglossia', *Word* **15**:325–40.

FERGUSON, C. F. (1971) 'Absence of copula and the notion of simplicity: a study of normal speech, baby talk, foreigner talk and pidgins', in Hymes, D. (ed.) *pp* 141–5.

FERGUSON, C. F. (1975) 'Towards a characterization of English Foreigner Talk', *Anthropological Linguistics* **17**:1–14.

FERGUSON, C. F. (1977) 'Simplified registers, broken language, Gastarbeiter Deutsch', in Molony, C., Zobl, H. and Stölting, W. (eds) *Deutsch in Kontakt mit anderen Sprachen*. Kronberg/Ts. *pp* 25–39.

FERGUSON, C. F. (1984) 'Comments on the paper by Bickerton', in Rutherford, W. E. (ed.) *Language Universals and Second Language Acquisition*. Amsterdam: John Benjamins *pp* 162–5.

FERGUSON, C. F. and DEBOSE, C. (1977) 'Simplified registers, broken languages and pidginization', in Valdman, A. (ed.) *pp* 99–129.

FERRAZ, L. (1976) 'The origin and development of four creoles in the Gulf of Guinea', *African Studies* 33–8.

FERREIRO, E. (1971) *Les relations temporelles dans le language de l'enfant*. Geneva: Librairie Droz.

FISCHER, S. (1978) 'Sign language and creoles', in Siple, P. (ed.) *Understanding Language through Sign Language Research*. New York: Academic Press *pp* 309–30.

FISHMAN, J. (1972) *Language in sociocultural change: Essays by Joshua Fishman* ed. by A. S. Dil. Stanford, California: Stanford University Press.

FLASHNER, V. (1982) 'Transfer of aspect in the English oral narratives of native Russian speakers', unpublished manuscript, Dept. of Applied Linguistics, UCLA.

FODOR, J. A. (1975) *The Language of Thought*. Cambridge, Mass.: MIT Press.

FODOR, J. A. (1983) *The Modularity of Mind*. Cambridge, Mass.: MIT Press.

FODOR, J. D. (1981) 'Does performance shape competence?', *Philosophical Transactions of the Royal Society of London*, Series B **295**:285–95.

FOX, A. J. (1973) 'Russenorsk: A study in language adaptivity', unpublished manuscript, University of Chicago.

FRENCH, A. (1953) 'Pidgin English in New Guinea', *Australian Quarterly* **25**(4):57–60.

FRIEDERICI, P. G. (1911) 'Pidgin-English in Neuguinea', *Koloniale Rundschau* **2**:92–106.

GARDNER, R. C. and LAMBERT, W. E. (1972) *Attitudes and Motivation in Second Language Learning*. Rowley Mass.: Newbury House.

GASS, S. M. (1980) 'An investigation of syntactic transfer in adult L2 learners', in Scarcella, R. and Krashen, S. (eds) *Research in Second Language Acquisition*. Rowley Mass.: Newbury House.

GASS, S. M. (1983) 'Language transfer and universal grammatical relations', in Gass, S. and Selinker, L. (eds) *pp* 20–33.

GASS, S. M. and ARD, J. (1984) 'Second language acquisition and the ontology of language universals', in Rutherford, W. E. (ed.) *Language Universals and Second Language Acquisition*. Amsterdam: John Benjamins *pp* 33–67.

GASS, S. M. and SELINKER, L (eds) (1983) *Language Transfer in Language Learning*. Rowley, Mass.: Newbury House.

GESCHWIND, N. (1980) 'Some comments on the neurology of language', in Caplan, D. (ed.) *Biological Studies of Mental Processes*. Cambridge, Mass.: MIT Press.

GIBSON, A. [with J. Barrow] (1986) *The Unequal Struggle*. London: Centre for Caribbean Studies.

GIBSON, K. (1982) 'Tense and aspect in Guyanese Creole: a syntactic, semantic and pragmatic analysis', DPhil. dissertation, University of York.

GIBSON, K. and LEVY, C. (ms.) 'A semantic analysis of tense and aspect in Jamaican Creole', unpublished manuscript, University of the West Indies, Jamaica.

GILBERT, G. (1981) 'Discussion of Andersen "Two perspectives on pidginization as second language acquisition"', in Andersen, R. (ed.) *pp* 207–13.

GILBERT, G. (1983) 'Transfer in second language acquisition', in Andersen, R. (ed.) *pp* 168–81.

GILBERT, G. and MAKHUDU, D. (1984) 'The creole continuum in Afrikaans: A non-Eurocentric view', unpublished manuscript, Department of Linguistics, Southern Illinois University at Carbondale.

GILES, H., TAYLOR, D. M., LAMBERT, W. E and BOURHIS, R. Y. (1973) 'Towards a theory of interpersonal accommodation through language: some Canadian data', *Language in Society* **2**:177–92.

GILMAN, C. (1972) 'The comparative structure in French, English and Cameroonian Pidgin English: An exercise in linguistic comparison', PhD dissertation, Northwestern University.

GIVÓN. T. (1979a) *On Understanding Grammar*. New York: Academic Press.

GIVÓN, T. (1979b) 'From discourse to syntax: grammar as a processing strategy', in Givón, T. (ed.) *pp* 81–112.

GIVÓN, T. (ed.) (1979c) *Discourse and Syntax*. Vol. 12 Syntax and Semantics. New York: Academic Press.

GIVÓN, T. (1979d) 'Prolegomena to any sane creology', in Hancock, I., Polomé, E., Goodman, M. and Heine, B. (eds) *Readings in Creole Studies*. Ghent: E. Story-Scientia P.V.B.A. *pp* 3–37

GIVÓN, T. (1982) 'Tense–aspect–modality: the creole prototype and beyond', in Hopper, P. (ed.) *Tense–Aspect. Between Semantics and Pragmatics*. Amsterdam: John Benjamins *pp* 114–63.

GIVÓN, T. (1984) 'Universals of discourse structure and second language acquisition', in Rutherford, W. E. (ed.) *Language Universals and Second Language Acquisition*. Amsterdam: John Benjamins *pp* 109–36.

GOLDIN-MEADOW, S. and MYLANDER, C. (1983) 'Gestural communication in deaf children: Noneffect of parental input on language development', *Science* **221**:372–4.

GOODMAN, M. F. (1964) *A Comparative Study of Creole French Dialects*. The Hague: Mouton.

GOODMAN, M. F. (1984) 'Are creole structures innate?', *The Behavioral and Brain Sciences* **7**:193–4.

GOULD, S. J. and ELDREDGE, N. (1977) 'Punctuated equilibria: the temporal mode of evolution reconsidered', *Paleobiology* **3**(2):115–51.

GREEN, J. (1987) 'Romance creoles', in Harris, M. B. and Vincent, N. B. (eds) *The Romance Languages*. London: Croom Helm.

GREENBERG, J. (1963) 'Some universals of grammar with particular reference to the order of meaningful elements', in Greenberg, J. (ed.) *Universals of Language*. Cambridge, Mass.: MIT Press.

GUMPERZ, J. J. and WILSON, R. (1971) 'Convergence and creolization; a case from the Indo-Aryan/Dravidian border', in Hymes, D. (ed.) *pp* 151–69.

GUNTHER, W. (1973) *Das portugiesische Kreolisch der Ilha do Principe*. Marburg: The author.

GUTTMAN, L. (1944) 'A basis for scaling quantitative data', *American Sociological Review* **9**:139–50.

GUY, J. B. M. (1974) *Handbook of Bichelamar. Manuel de Bichelmar*. Pacific Linguistics C-34. Canberra: The Australian National University.

HAIMAN, J. (1980) 'The iconicity of grammar', *Language* **56**:515–40.

HAIMAN, J. (1985) *Natural Syntax. Iconicity and Erosion*. Cambridge: Cambridge University Press.

HALL, R. A. (1943) *Melanesian Pidgin English: Grammar, Texts, Vocabulary*. Baltimore, MD: Linguistic Society of America.

HALL, R. A. (1953) *Haitian Creole: Grammar, Texts, Vocabulary*. American Folklore Society Memoir No. 43.

HALL, R. A. (1955a) *Hands Off Pidgin English*. Sydney: Pacific Publications.

HALL, R. A. (1955b) *A Standard Orthography and List of Suggested Spellings for Neomelanesian*. Port Moresby: Department of Education.

HALL, R. A. (1956) 'Innovations in Melanesian Pidgin (Neo-Melanesian)', *Oceania* **26**:91–109.

HALL, R. A. (1958) 'Creole languages and genetic relationships', *Word* **14**:36–73.

HALL, R. A. (1959) 'Neo-melanesian and glottochronology', *IJAL* **25**:265–7.

HALL, R. A. (1961) 'How pidgin English has evolved', *New Scientist* **9**:413–5.

HALL, R. A. (1962) 'The life-cycle of pidgin languages', *Festschrift De Groot* (*Lingua* **11**) *pp* 151–6.

HALL, R. A. (1966) *Pidgin and Creole Languages*. Ithaca: Cornell University Press.

HALL, R. A. (1972) 'Pidgins and creoles as standard languages', in Pride, J. and Holmes, J. (eds) *Sociolinguistics*. Harmondsworth: Penguin *pp* 142–54.

HALLE, M. (1962) 'Phonology in a generative grammar', *Word* **18**:54–72.

HALLIDAY, M. A. K. (1974) *Learning How to Mean*. London: Edward Arnold.

HALLIDAY, M. A. K. and HASAN, R. (1976) *Cohesion in English*. London: Longman.

HALLIDAY, M. A. K. (1978) *Language as a Social Semiotic*. London: Edward Arnold.

HANCOCK, I. F. (1964) 'Krio', *The Linguist* May 1964.

HANCOCK, I. F. (1971) 'A survey of the pidgins and creoles of the world', in Hymes, D. (ed.) *pp* 509–25.

HANCOCK, I. F. (1976) 'Nautical sources of Krio vocabulary', *International Journal of the Sociology of Language* **7**:23–36.

HANCOCK, I. F. (1977) 'Appendix: Repertory of Pidgin and Creole Languages', in Valdman, A. (ed.) *pp* 277–94.

HANCOCK, I. (ed.) (1979a) *Readings in Creole Studies*. Ghent: E. Story-Scientia.

HANCOCK, I. (1979b) 'On the origins of the term pidgin', in Hancock, I. (ed.) *pp* 81–9.

HANCOCK, I. (ed.) (1985) *Diversity and Development in English-related Creoles*. Ann Arbor: Karoma.

HANCOCK, I. (1986) 'The domestic hypothesis, diffusion and componentiality: An account of Atlantic Anglophone Creole Origins', in Muysken, P. and Smith, N. (eds) *Substrata vs. Universals in Creole Genesis*. Amsterdam: John Benjamins *pp* 71–103.

HANCOCK, I. (1987) 'A preliminary classification of the Anglophone Atlantic Creoles', in Gilbert, G. (ed.) *Pidgin and Creole Languages: Essays in Memory of John Reinecke*. Honolulu: University of Hawaii Press.

HARRIS, J. (1984) 'Syntactic variation and dialect divergence', *Journal of Linguistics* **20**:303–27.

HARRIS, J. W. (1984) 'Language Contact, Pidgins and the Emergence of Kriol in the Northern Territory: Theoretical and Historical Perspectives', PhD dissertation, University of Queensland.

HARRISON, S. (1972) *The language of Norfolk Island*. B. A. Thesis. Macquarie University.

HATCH, E. (1983) *Psycholinguistics. A Second Language Perspective*. Rowley, Mass: Newbury House.

HAUGEN, E. (1950) 'The analysis of linguistic borrowing', *Language* **26**:210–32.

HAYNES, L. (1973) 'Language in Barbados and Guyana: Attitudes, behaviors and comparisons', PhD dissertation, Stanford University.

HEATH, J, (1978) *Linguistic Diffusion in Arnhem Land*. Canberra: Australian Institute of Aboriginal Studies.

HEATH, S. B. (1982) 'What no bedtime story means: narrative skills at home and school', *Language in Society* **11**:49–77.

HEINE, B. (1973) *Pidgin-Sprachen im Bantu-Bereich*. Berlin: Dietrich Riemer Verlag.

HEINE, B. (1979) 'Some linguistic characteristics of African-based pidgins', in Hancock, I. (ed.) *pp* 89–99.

HELLAND. A. (1899) *Norges land og folk. Topografisk-statistisk beskrevet. Tromso Amt*. **XIX**: Oslo.

HELLINGER, M. (1985) *Englisch-orientierte Pidgin- und Kreolsprachen*. Darmstadt: Wissenschaftliche Buchgesellschaft.

HELTON, E. C. N. (1943) *Pidgin English as used in the Mandated Territory of New Guinea*. Brisbane: Solo Publishing.

HENZELL-THOMAS. J. (1982) 'A study of English foreigner talk by non-native speakers', unpublished ms. University of Edinburgh.

HERMAN, S. (1968) 'Explorations in the social psychology of language choice', in Fishman, J. (ed.) *Readings in the Sociology of Language*. The Hague: Mouton *pp* 492–512.

HERSKOVITZ, M. J. and HERSKOVITZ, F. S. (1936) *Suriname Folklore*. New York: Columbia University Contributions to Anthropology. Vol. 27.

HERTZFELD, A. (1978) 'Tense and aspect in Limon Creole: A sociolinguistic view towards a creole continuum', PhD dissertation, University of Kansas.

HESSELING, D. C. (1897) 'Het Hollandsch in Zuid Afrika', *De Gids* **61**:138–62. [English translation 'Dutch in South Africa', in Markey, T. L. and Roberge, P. T. (eds and trans.) *pp* 1–23].

HESSELING, D. C. (1905) *Het Negerhollands der Deense Antillen. Bijdrage tot de Geschiedenis der Nederlandse Taal in Amerika*. Leiden: A. W. Sijthoff.

HESSELING, D. C. (1933) 'Hoe onstond de eigenaardige vorm van het Kreools?', *Neophilologus* **18**:209–15. [English translation 'How did creoles originate?', in Markey, T. L. and Roberge, P. T. (eds and trans.) *pp* 62–71.]

HESSE-WARTEGG, E. VON (1898) *Schantung und Deutsch-China*. Leipzig: Weber.

HESSE-WARTEGG, E. VON (1902) *Samoa, Bismarckarchipel und Neuguinea*. Leipzig: Weber.

HEWITT, R. (1983) 'White adolescent creole users and the politics of friendship', *Journal of Multilingual and Multicultural Development* **3**:217–32.

HIGHFIELD, A. and VALDMAN, A. (eds) (1981) *Historicity and Variation in Creole Studies*. Ann Arbor: Karoma.

HILL, K. C. (ed.) (1979) *The Genesis of Language*. Ann Arbor: Karoma.

HINNENKAMP, V. (1982) *Foreigner Talk und Tarzanisch*. Hamburg: Helmut Buske Verlag.

HINNENKAMP, V. (1983) 'Eye-witnessing pidginization? Structural and sociolinguistic aspects of German and Turkish Foreigner Talk', *York Papers in Linguistics* **11**.

HJELMSLEV, L. (1938) 'Relations de parenté dans les langues créoles', *Revue des Etudes Indo-Européennes* **1**:271–86.

HOCKETT, C. F. (1950) 'Age-grading and linguistic continuity', *Language* **26**:449–57.

HOCKETT, C. F. (1958) *A Course in Modern Linguistics*. New York: Macmillan.

HOENIGSWALD, H. M. (1971) 'Language history and creole studies', in Hymes, D. (ed.) *pp* 473–81.

HÖGSTRÖM, P. (1747) *Beskrifning öfwer de til Sweriges Krona lydande Lapmarker*. Stockholm [reprinted Umeå 1980].

HOLLYMAN, K. J. (1964) 'L'ancien pidgin français parlé en Nouvelle-Calédonie', *Journal de la Société des Océanistes* **20**:57–64.

HOLLYMAN, K. J. (1976) 'Les pidgins européens de la région calédonienne', *Te Reo* **19**:25–65.

HOLM, J. (1984a) 'Variability of the copula in Black English and its Creole Kin', *American Speech* **59**:291–309.

HOLM, J. (1984b) 'African features in white Bahamian English'. *English World Wide* **1**: 45–65.

HOPPER, P. (1979) 'Aspect and foregrounding in discourse', in Givón, T. (ed.) *pp* 213–41.

HORNSTEIN, N. (1977) 'Toward a theory of tense', *Linguistic Inquiry* **8**:521–77.

HOWELL, R. W. (1975) 'Bamboo English revisited', unpublished paper.

HUDSON, J. (1983) 'Transitivity and aspect in the Kriol verb', *Papers in Pidgin and Creole Linguistics* **3**. Pacific Linguistics A-65:161–76. Canberra: Australian National University.

HUDSON, R. A. (1980) *Sociolinguistics*. Cambridge: Cambridge University Press.

HUEBNER, T. (1982) 'From topic to subject dominance in the interlanguage of a Hmong speaker', PhD dissertation, University of Hawaii.

HUTTAR, G. L. (1972) 'A comparative word list for Djuka', in Grimes, J. E. (ed.) *Languages of the Guianas*. Norman, OK: Summer Institute of Linguistics of the University of Oklahoma *pp* 12–21.

HUTTAR, G. L. (1975) 'Sources of creole semantic structures', *Language* **51**:684–95.

HYAMS, N. (1983) 'The pro-drop parameter in child grammars', *Proceedings of the West Coast Conference on Formal Linguistics*. Department of Linguistics. Stanford University.

HYMES, D. (ed.) (1971) *Pidginization and Creolization of Languages*. Cambridge: Cambridge University Press.

INHELDER, B. and PIAGET, J. (1958) *Growth of Logical Thinking from Childhood to Adolescence: An Essay on the Construction of Formal Operational Structures*. New York: Basic Books.

IOUP, G. (1979) 'Is there a structural foreign accent?', paper presented at the 13th annual TESOL Convention, Boston.

IOUP, G. and KRUSE, A. (1977) 'Interference vs. structural complexity as a predictor of second language relative clause acquisition', in Henning, C. (ed.) *Proceedings of the Second Language Research Forum*. University of California. Los Angeles.

JAKOBSON, R. (1972) *Child Language, Aphasia and Phonological Universals*. The Hague: Mouton.

JAMES, C. (1980) *Contrastive Analysis*. London: Longman.

JAMES, H. (forthcoming) 'Pidgin sign English in the classroom', in Stokoe, W. and Volterre, E. (eds) *Proceeding of the Third International Symposium on Sign Language Research*. Silver Spring, MD: Linstock Press.

JANSEN, B., KOOPMAN, H. and MUYSKEN, P. (1978) 'Serial verbs in the creole languages', *Amsterdam Creole Studies* **II**:125–59

JANSON, T. (1983) 'A language of Sophiatown, Alexandra and Soweto', *York Papers in Linguistics* **11**.

JANSON, T. (1984) 'Articles and plural formation in creoles: change and universals', *Lingua* **64**:291–323.

JESPERSEN, O. (1909–49) *A Modern English Grammar on Historical Principles*. London: George Allen and Unwin.

JESPERSEN, O. (1922) *Language, its Nature, Development and Origin*. London: Allen and Unwin.

JESPERSEN, O. (1968) *Growth and Structure of the English Language*. New York: The Free Press.

JOHNSON, M. C. (1974) 'Two morpheme structure rules in an English proto-creole', in DeCamp, D. and Hancock, I. (eds) *pp* 118–29.

JOHNSON, S. V. (1975) 'Chinook Jargon Variation: Towards the compleat Chinooker', Paper given at the International Conference on Pidgins and Creoles, Honolulu, Hawaii.

JONES, E. (1968) 'Some tense, mode and aspect markers in Krio', *African Language Review* **7**:86–9.

JONES, F. (1983) 'English Derived Words In Sierra Leone Krio', PhD dissertation, Leeds University.

JOURDAN, C. (1985) 'Sapos iumi mitim iumi. Urbanization and creolization in the Solomon Islands', PhD dissertation, Australian National University.

KARMILOFF-SMITH, A. (1979) *A Functional Approach to Child Language*. Cambridge: Cambridge University Press.

KAY, P. and SANKOFF, G. (1974) 'A language universals approach to pidgins and creoles', in DeCamp, D. and Hancock, I. (eds) *pp* 61–72.

KEENAN, E. L. (1975) 'Logical expressive power and syntactic variation in natural language', in Keenan, E. L. (ed.) *Formal Semantics of Natural Language*. Cambridge: Cambridge University Press *pp* 406–21.

KEENAN, E. L. and COMRIE, B. (1977) 'Noun phrase accessibility and universal grammar', *Linguistic Inquiry* **8**:63–99.

KEENAN, E. L. and COMRIE. B. (1979) 'Data on the noun phrase accessibility hierarchy', *Language* **55**:332–52.

KEESING, R. (forthcoming) *Melanesian Pidgin and Oceanic Substrate*.

KIELHÖFER, B. (1982) 'Entwicklungssequenzen beim Erwerb der Vergangenheitstempora in der französichen Kindersprache', *Linguistische Berichte* **81**:83–103.

KIHM, A. (1983a) 'Is there anything like decreolization? Some ongoing changes in Bissau Creole', Paper presented at the York Creole Conference.

KIHM, A. (1983b) 'De l'intérêt d'étudier les creoles, ou qu'ont-ils d'espécial?', *Espace créole* **5**:75–100.

KINSBOURNE, M. (1981) 'The brain basis of consciousness and communication', Paper presented at the Symposium on The Neurological Basis of Signs in Communication Processes. Toronto Semiotic Circle. Victoria University.

KLEIN, E. (1986) 'Koreans in Seoul and Honolulu: Aiming for different targets', Paper given at the TESOL conference, Anaheim, California.

KLEIN, W. (1986) *Second Language Acquisition*. Cambridge: Cambridge University Press.

KLEIN, W. and DITTMAR, N. (1979) *Developing Grammars. The Acquisition of German Syntax by Foreign Workers*. Berlin: Springer Verlag.

KNOWLTON, E. (1967) 'Pidgin English and Portuguese', in Drake, F. S. (ed.) *Proceedings of the Symposium on Historical, Archaelogical and Linguistic Studies on Southern China, South-East Asia and the Hong Kong Region*. Hong Kong: University of Hong Kong Press *pp* 228–37.

KOCHMAN, T. (ed.) (1972) *Rappin' and Stylin' Out*. Chicago: University of Illinois Press.

KOEFOED, G. (1979) 'Some remarks on the baby talk theory and the relexification theory', in Hancock, I. (ed.) *pp* 37–54.

KOOPMAN, H. (1986) 'The genesis of Haitian: Implications of a comparison of some features of the syntax of Haitian, French and West African languages', in Muysken, P. and Smith, N. (eds) *Universals vs. Substrata in Creole Genesis*. Amsterdam: John Benjamins.

KOOPMAN, H. and LEFEBVRE, C. (1981) 'Haitian Creole *pu*', in Muysken, P. (ed.) *pp* 201–23.

KRAKOWIAN, B. and CORDER, S. P. (1978) 'Polish foreigner talk', *Work In Progress*. Department of Linguistics. University of Edinburgh No. **11**:78–87.

KRASHEN, S. D. (1973–4) 'Lateralization, language learning, and the critical period: some new evidence', *Language Learning* **22**:3–74.

KUMPF, L. (1982) 'A case study in temporal reference', Paper presented at the Fourth Annual Second Language Research Forum, UCLA.

KUMPF, L. (1984) 'Temporal systems and universality in interlanguage: A case study', in Eckman, F. R., Bell, L. H., and Nelson, D. (eds) *Universals of Second Language Acquisition*. Rowley, Mass.: Newbury House *pp* 132–43.

KURATH, H. *et al.* (1939–43) *Linguistic Atlas of New England*, 3 Vols, Providence: Brown University Press.

KURYLOWICZ, J. (1949) 'La nature des procés dits analogiques', *Acta Linguistica* **5**:17–34.

LABOV, W. (1966) *The Social Stratification of English in New York City*. Washington, DC: Center for Applied Linguistics.

LABOV, W. (1969) 'Contraction, deletion, and inherent variability of the English copula', *Language* **45**:715–62.

LABOV, W. (1970/1977) 'On the adequacy of natural languages: the development of tense', *Linguistic Agency University of Trier* Paper No. 23 Series B.

LABOV, W. (1971) 'Methodology', in Dingwall W. O. (ed.) *A Survey of Linguistic Science*. Linguistics Program: University of Maryland *pp* 412–97.

LABOV, W. (1980) 'Is there a creole speech community?', in Valdman and Hughfield (eds) *pp* 369–89.

LABOV, W. (1972a) 'Is Black English Vernacular a separate system?', in *Language in the Inner City*. Philadelphia: University of Pennsylvania Press *pp* 36–64.

LABOV, W. (1972b) 'Some sources of reading problems for speakers of the Black English Vernacular', in *Language in the Inner City*. Philadelphia: University of Pennsylvania Press *pp* 3–36.

LABOV, W. (1982) 'Objectivity and commitment in linguistic science: The case of the Black English Trial in Ann Arbor', *Language in Society* **11**:165–202.

LACROIX, P. F. (1959) 'Observations sur la "koiné" peule de Ngaoundéré', *Travaux de Linguistique* **4**.

LAMBERT, W. E. (1972) *Language, Culture and Personality: Essays by W. E. Lambert*. (A. S. Dil ed.) Stanford: Stanford University Press.

LAMENDELLA, J. (1976) 'Relations between ontogeny and phylogeny of language: a neo-recapitulationist view', in Harnard, S. R. *et al.* (eds) *Origins and Evolution of Language and Speech*. Annals of the New York Academy of Science, Vol. 5280.

LAMENDELLA, J. (1977) 'General principles of neurological organization and their manifestation in primary and non-primary acquisition', *Language Learning* **27**:155–96.

LANDER. S. (1979) 'Morpho-syntactic features in the writing of second generation West Indians', MA thesis, University of Sheffield.

LARSEN-FREEMAN, D. (1976) 'An explanation for the morpheme acquisition order of second language learners', *Language Learning* **26**:125–35.

LAYCOCK, D. (1966) 'Papuans and pidgin: aspects of bilingualism in New Guinea', *Te Reo* **9**:4–51.

LAYCOCK, D. (1970) *Materials in New Guinea Pidgin Coastal and Lowlands*). Pacific Linguistics D-5. Canberra: Australian National University.

LEFEBVRE, C. (1982) 'L'expansion d'une categorie grammaticale', in Lefebvre, C., Magloire-Holly, H. and Piou, N. (eds.) *Syntaxe de l'Haitien*. Ann Arbor: Karoma Press pp 21–63.

LEHMANN, C. (1983) *Der Relativsatz*. Tübingen: Narr.

LELAND, C. G. (1876) *Pidgin English Sing Song or Songs and Stories in the China-English Dialect*. (10th ed. 1924). London: Trübner.

LENNEBERG, E. (1967) *Biological Foundations of Language*. New York: John Wiley and Sons.

LE PAGE, R. B. (ed.) (1961) *Proceedings of the Conference on Creole Language Studies*. London: Macmillan.

LE PAGE, R. B. (1977) 'Processes of pidginization and creolization', in Valdman, A. (ed.) *pp* 222–59.

LE PAGE, R. B. (1978) 'Projection, focussing, diffusion or, steps towards a sociolinguistic theory of language, illustrated from the sociolinguistic survey of multilingual communities Stages I: Cayo District, Belize (formerly British Honduras) and II: St. Lucia, School of Education. St Augustine, Trinidad: Society for Caribbean Linguistics Occasional Paper No. 9.

LE PAGE, R. B. (1980a) 'Hugo Schuchardt's Creole studies and the problem of linguistic continua', in Lichem, K. and Simon, H. J. (eds) *Hugo Schuchardt: Schuchardt-Symposium 1977 in Graz, Vorträge und Aufsätze*. Vienna: Austrian Academy of the Sciences.

LE PAGE, R. B. (1980b) 'Theoretical aspects of sociolinguistic studies in pidgin and creole languages', in Valdman, A. and Highfield, A. (eds) *pp* 331–68.

LE PAGE, R. B. (1981) 'Social perspectives on language', unpublished manuscript of open lecture given at the University of York.

LE PAGE, R. B. and TABOURET-KELLER, A. (1985) *Acts of Identity*. Cambridge: Cambridge University Press.

LEVELT, W. J. M. (1979) 'Linearization in discourse', unpublished manuscript. Max-Planck-Institut für Psycholinguistik. Nijmegen, Netherlands.

LI, C. and THOMPSON, S. (1976) 'Subject and topic: a new typology of language', in Li, C. and Thompson, S. (eds) *Subject and Topic*. New York: Academic Press *pp* 457–89.

LIGHTFOOT, D. (1979) *Principles of Diachronic Syntax*. Cambridge: Cambridge University Press.

LIMBER, J. (1973) 'The genesis of complex sentences', in Moore, T. T. (ed.) *Cognitive Development and the Acquisition of Language*. New York: Academic Press.

LINGUISTIC MINORITIES PROJECT (1985) *The Other Languages of England*. London: Routledge and Kegan Paul.

LLOYD, [no first initial] (no date) *Kitchen-Kafir Grammar and Vocabulary*. John Reinecke Collection, Sinclair Library, University of Hawaii at Manoa. Honolulu, Hawaii.

LOCAL, J., WELLS, W. and SEBBA, M. (1984) 'Phonetic aspects of turn delimitation in London Jamaican', *York Papers in Linguistics* **11**.

LORD, C. (1976) 'Evidence for syntactic reanalysis: From verb to complementizer in Kwa', in Steever, S., Walker, C. Mufwene, S. (eds) *Papers from the Parasession on Diachronic Syntax*. Chicago: Chicago Linguistics Society *pp* 179–92.

LUND, N. (1842) *Reise igjennem Nordlandene og Vertfinmarken i Sommeren 1841*. Christiana (Oslo).

LUNDEN, S. S. (1973) 'Tracing the ancestry of Russenorsk', *Slavia Orientalis* **27**:213–17.

LYONS, J. (1968) *Introduction to Theoretical Linguistics*. Cambridge: Cambridge University Press.

LYONS, J. (1975) 'Deixis as the source of reference', in Keenan, E. L. (ed.) *pp* 61–83.

MACEDO, D. P. (1986) 'The role of core grammar in pidgin development', *Language Learning* **36**:65–75.

MCELHANON, K. A. (ed.) (1975) *Tok Pisin i go we*? Special Issue of *Kivung* 1. Ukarumpa: Linguistic Society of Papua New Guinea.

MCENTEGART, D. and LE PAGE, R. B. (1982) 'An appraisal of the statistical techniques used in the sociolinguistic survey of multilingual communities', in Romaine, S. (ed.) *Sociolinguistic Variation in Speech Communities*. London: Edward Arnold *pp* 105–124.

MAFENI, B. (1971) 'Nigerian Pidgin', in Spencer, J. (ed.) *The English Language in West Africa*. London: Longman *pp* 95–112.

MAGENS, J. M. (1770) *Grammatica over det Creolske sprog, som bruges pass de trende Danske Eilande, St. Croix, St. Thomas og St. Jans. i Amerika*. Copenhagen: Gerhard Giese Salikath.

MANESSY, G. (1977) 'Processes of pidginization in African languages', in Valdman, A. (ed.) *pp* 129–55.

MARATSOS, M. P. (1976) *The Use of Definite and Indefinite Reference in Young Children*. Cambridge: Cambridge University Press.

MARATSOS, M. P. and CHALKLEY, M. A. (1980) 'The internal language of childrens' syntax: the ontogenesis and representation of syntactic categories', in Nelson, K. (ed.) *Children's Language*. Vol. 2. New York: Gardner Press.

MARKEY, T. L. (1981) 'Diffusion, fusion and creolization: A field guide to developmental linguistics', *Papiere zur Linguistik* **24**:3–37.

MARKEY, T. L. (1982) 'Afrikaans: Creole or Non-Creole?', *Zeitschrift für Dialektologie und Linguistik* **IL**:169–207.

MARKEY, T. L. and FODALE, P. (1983) 'Lexical diathesis, focal shifts and passivization: the creole voice', *English World Wide* **4**:69–85.

MARKEY, T. L. and ROBERGE, P. T. (eds and trans.) (1979) *On the Origin and Formation of Creoles: A Miscellany of Articles by D. C. Hesseling*. Ann Arbor: Karoma.

MARSHALL, J. (1980) 'Biology of language acquisition', in Caplan, D. (ed.) *Biological Studies of Mental Processes*. Cambridge, Mass.: MIT Press.

MARSHALL, J. (1984) 'Pidgins are everywhere', *The Behavioral and Brain Sciences* **7**:201.

MASTER, P. (1986) 'Noun compounding in an experimental Farsi pidgin', Department of Applied Linguistics. UCLA.

MATTHEWS, W. (1935) 'Sailors' pronunciation in the second half of the seventeenth century', *Anglia* **47**:192–251.

MAXWELL, D. (1979) 'Strategies of relativization and NP accessibility', *Language* **52**:352–72.

MAYERTHALER, W. (1981) *Morphologische Natürlichkeit*. Wiesbaden: Akademische Verlagsgesellschaft Athenaion.

MEILLET, A. (1912/1958) 'L'évolution des formes grammaticales', *Scientia* **12**. [Also in *Linguistique historique et linguistique générale*. Paris: Campion *pp* 130–49.].

MEILLET, A. and COHEN (1978) *Les Langues du Monde*. (Cited in Hancock (ed.) (1979)).

MEISEL, J. (1983a) 'Transfer as a second language strategy', *Language and Communication* **3**:11–46.

MEISEL, J. (1983b) 'A linguistic encounter of the third kind or, Will the non-real interfere with what the learner does? Reply to discussants', in Andersen, R. (ed.) *pp* 196–209.

MEISEL, J. (1985) 'Les phases initiales du développement de notions temporelles, aspectuelles et de modes d'action', *Lingua*. **66**:321–74.

MEISEL, J. (1986) 'Word order and case marking in early child language. Evidence from simultaneous acquisition of two first languages: French and German', *Linguistics* **24**:123–83.

MEISEL, J. (forthcoming) 'Reference to past events and actions in the development of natural second language acquisition', in Pfaff, C. (ed.) *Cross-Linguistic Studies of Language Acquisition*. Rowley, Mass.: Newbury House.

MENYUK, P. (1969) *Sentences Children Use*. Cambridge, Mass.: MIT Press.

MIHALIC, F. (1957) *Grammar and dictionary of neo-Melanesian*. Westmead, New South Wales: Mission Press.

MIHALIC, F. (1969) *An Introduction to New Guinea Pidgin*. Milton,

Queensland: Jacaranda Press.

MIHALIC, F. (1971) *The Jacaranda Dictionary and Grammar of Melanesian Pidgin*. Brisbane: Jacaranda Press.

MILROY, L. (1980) *Language and Social Networks*. Oxford: Blackwell.

MOAG, R. F. (1978) 'Standardization in Pidgin Fijian: Implications for the theory of pidginization' in Schütz, A. (ed.) *Fijian Language Studies; Borrowing and Pidginization*. Bulletin of the Fiji Museum No. **4**:68–98. Suva, Fiji.

MOHAN, P. (1978) 'Non-lexical *say* and language universals', Papers from the Conference of the Society for Caribbean Linguistics. University of the West Indies at Cave Hill: Unit of Use of English and Linguistics.

MOLFESE, D. and MOLFESE, V. (1979) 'Left hemisphere involvement of newborn infants in speech perception', Paper presented at the annual meeting of the International Neuropsychological Association, New York.

MOUGEON, R., BENIAK, E. and VALOIS, D. (1985) 'A sociolinguistic study of language contact, shift and change', *Linguistics* **23**:455–89.

MUFWENE, S. (1984) 'The language bioprogram hypothesis, creole studies and linguistic theory', *The Behavioral and Brain Sciences* **7**:202–3.

MUFWENE, S. (1986) 'Number delimitation in Gullah', *American Speech* **61**:33–60.

MUFWENE, S. and DIJKOFF, M. (1986) 'Notes on the so-called infinitive in creoles', Paper presented at the Sixth Biennial Meeting of the Society for Caribbean Linguistics, St. Augustine, Trinidad.

MÜHLHÄUSLER, P. (1974) *Pidginization and Simplification of Language*. Pacific Linguistics B-26. Canberra: Australian National University.

MÜHLHÄUSLER, P. (1979) *Growth and Structure of the Lexicon of New Guinea Pidgin*. Pacific Linguistics C-52. Canberra: Australian National University.

MÜHLHÄUSLER, P. (1980) 'Structural expansion and the process of creolization', in Valdman and Highfield, A. (eds) *pp* 19–55.

MÜHLHÄUSLER, P. (1981a) 'The development of the category of number in Tok Pisin', in Muysken, P. (ed.) *pp* 35–85.

MÜHLHÄUSLER, P. (1981b) 'Foreigner Talk: Tok Masta in New Guinea', *International Journal of the Sociology of Language* **28**:93–113.

MÜHLHÄUSLER, P. (1982) 'Etymology and pidgin and creole languages', *Transactions of the Philological Society* 99–118.

MÜHLHÄUSLER, P. (1984) 'Tracing the roots of Pidgin German', *Language and Communication* **4**:27–57.

MÜHLHÄUSLER, P. (1985a) 'Variation in Tok Pisin', in Wurm, S. A. and Mühlhäusler, P. (eds) *pp* 233–73.

MÜHLHÄUSLER, P. (1985b) 'History of the study of Tok Pisin', in Wurm, S. A. and Mühlhäusler, P. (eds) *pp* 15–33.

MÜHLHÄUSLER P. (1985c) 'Syntax of Tok Pisin', in Wurm, S. A. and Mühlhäusler, P. (eds) *pp* 344–421.

MÜHLHÄUSLER P. (1985d) 'Tok Pisin and its relevance to theoretical issues in creolistics and general linguistics', in Wurm, S. A. and

Mühlhäusler, P. (ed) *pp* 443–83.

MÜHLHÄUSLER, P. (1986) *Pidgin and Creole Linguistics*. Oxford: Blackwell.

MÜHLHÄUSLER, P. (forthcoming) 'An overview of pidgin and creole languages in Australia', in Rigsby, B. and Romaine, S. (eds) *Language in Australia*. Cambridge: Cambridge University Press.

MURPHY, J. (1966) *The book of Pidgin English*. Brisbane: Smith and Patterson.

MUYSKEN, P. (1980) 'Sources for the study of Amerindian contact vernaculars in Ecuador', *Amsterdam Creole Studies* **III**:66–82.

MUYSKEN, P. (1981a) 'Creole tense/mood/aspect systems: the unmarked case', in Muysken, P. (ed.) *pp* 181–99.

MUYSKEN, P. (ed.) (1981b) *Generative Studies on Creole Languages*. Dordrecht: Foris.

MUYSKEN, P. (1981c) 'Halfway between Quechua and Spanish: The case for relexification', in Highfield, A. and Valdman, A. (eds) *pp* 52–79.

MUYSKEN, P. and MEIJER, G. (1979) 'Introduction' to Hesseling, D. C. *On the Origin and Formation of Creoles. A Miscellany of Articles* edited and translated by Markey, T. L. and P. T. Roberge. Ann Arbor: Karoma *pp* vii–xxi.

NADKARNI, M. (1975) 'Bilingualism and syntactic change in Konkani', *Language* **51**:672–83.

NAGARA, S. (1972) *Japanese Pidgin English in Hawaii*. Honolulu: University of Hawaii Press.

NARO, A. J. (1978) 'A study on the origins of pidginization', *Language* **54**:314–47.

NELSON, H. (1972) *Papua New Guinea Black Unity or Black Chaos?* Harmondsworth: Penguin.

NEUMANN, G. (1965) 'Russennorwegisch und Pidginenglisch', *Nachrichten der Giessener Hochschulgesellschaft* **34**:219–32.

NEUMANN, G. (1966) 'Zur chinesisch-russischen Behelfssprache von Kjachta', *Die Sprache* **12**:237–51.

NEVERMANN, H. (1929) 'Des Melanesische Pidjin-Englisch', *Englische Studien* **63**:252–8.

NIDA, E. A. and FEHDERAU, H. W. (1970) 'Indigenous pidgins and koinés', *International Journal of American Linguistics* **32**:146–55.

NOEL, J. (1975) 'Legitimacy of Pidgin in the development of Papua New Guinea toward nationhood', in McElhanon, K. (ed.) *pp* 76–84.

Nupela Testamen Bilong Bikpela Jisas Krais na Buk Bilong Ol Sam. (1966). Port Moresby: The Bible Society of Papua New Guinea.

OCHS, E. (1979) 'Planned and unplanned discourse', in Givón, T. (ed.) *pp* 51–80.

OCHS, F. (1982) 'Talking to children in Western Samoa', *Language in Society* **11**:77–105.

ODO, C. (1975) 'Phonological processes in the English dialect of Hawaii', PhD dissertation, University of Hawaii.

O'DONNELL, W. R. and TODD, L. (1980) *Variety in Contemporary English*. London: George Allen and Unwin.

PELLOWE, J., NIXON, G., STRANG, B. and MCNEANY, V. (1972) 'A dynamic modelling of linguistic variation: the urban (Tyneside) linguistic survey', *Lingua* **30**:1–30.

PENFIELD, W. and ROBERTS, L. (1950) *Speech and Brain Mechanisms*. Princeton: Princeton University Press.

PENNINGTON, M. C. (forthcoming) 'Context and meaning of the English simple tenses: A discourse-based perspective',

PERLMAN, A. (1975) 'Particles, topicalization and defocusing in Hawaiian English', unpublished paper.

PETERS, A. (1984) *The Units of Language Acquisition*. Cambridge: Cambridge University Press.

PLATT, J. T. (1975) 'The Singapore English speech continuum and its basilect "Singlish" as a "Creoloid"', *Anthropological Linguistics* **17**:363–74.

POLOMÉ, E. (1983) 'Creolization and language change', in Woolford, E. and Washabaugh, W. (eds) *pp* 126–37.

POPLACK, S. (1980) 'Sometimes I'll start a sentence in English y termino en español: Toward a typology of code-switching', *Centro Working Papers*. CUNY: Centro de Estudios Puertorriqueños.

POSNER, R. (1983) 'The origins and affinities of French Creoles: New Perspectives', *Language and Communication* **3**:191–202.

POSNER, R. (1985) 'Creolization as typological change. Some examples from Romance syntax', *Diachronica* **II**(2):167–88.

QUIRK, R., GREENBAUM, S., LEECH, G. and SVARTVIK, J. (1972) *A Grammar of Contemporary English*. London: Longman.

REICHENBACH, H. (1947) *Elements of Symbolic Logic*. New York: Macmillan.

REINECKE, J. E. (1937) 'Marginal Languages: A sociological survey of the creole languages and trade jargons', PhD dissertation, Yale University.

REINECKE, J. E. (1971) Tây Bôi: 'Notes on the Pidgin French spoken in Vietnam', in Hymes, D. (ed.) *pp* 47–57.

REINECKE, J. E., DECAMP., HANCOCK, I. and WOOD, R. E. (1975) *A Bibliography of Pidgin and Creole Languages*. Honolulu: University of Hawaii Press.

REUSCH, H. (1895) *Folk og natur i Finmarken*. Oslo.

RICHARDS, J. C. (ed.) (1974). *Error Analysis*. London: Longman.

RICKFORD, J. (1977) 'A review article on Loreto Todd's *Pidgins and Creoles*'. *World Literature Written in English* **16**(2):477–513.

RICKFORD, J. (1979) 'Variation in a creole continuum: Quantitative and implicational approaches', PhD dissertation, University of Pennsylvania.

RICKFORD, J. (1986a) *Dimensions of a Creole Continuum*. Stanford: Stanford University Press.

RICKFORD, J. (1986b) 'Some principles for the study of Black and White speech in the South', in Montgomery, M. and Bailey, G. (eds) *Language Variety in the South: Perspectives in Black and White*. University, Ala.: University of Alabama Press *pp* 38–62.

RICKFORD, J. (1986c) '"Me Tarzan, you Jane!" Adequacy, expressiveness, and the creole speaker', *Journal of Linguistics* **22**:281–311.

ROBERTSON, G. (1948) *The Discovery of Tahiti*. London: The Hakluyt Society.

ROBERTSON, I. (1978) 'Berbice Dutch-Guyanese English and the notion of a post-creole continuum', papers from the Conference of the Society for Caribbean Linguistics, University of the West Indies at Cave Hill, Unit of Use of English and Linguistics.

ROBINS, R. H. (1967) *A Short History of Linguistics*. London: Longman.

ROMAINE, S. (1980) 'The relative clause marker in Scots English: Diffusion, complexity and style as dimensions of syntactic change', *Language in Society* **9**:221–49.

ROMAINE, S. (1982) *Socio-historical Linguistics: Its status and methodology*. Cambridge: Cambridge University Press.

ROMAINE, S. (1983a) 'Syntactic change as category change by reanalysis and diffusion', in Davenport, M., Hansen, E. and Nielsen, H-F. (eds) *Current Topics in English Historical Linguistics*. Odense: Odense University Press *pp* 9–27.

ROMAINE, S. (1983b) 'Review of Derek Bickerton', *Roots of Language', Australian Journal of Linguistics* **3**:115–24.

ROMAINE, S. (1984a) *The Language of Children and Adolescents. The Acquisition of Communicative Competence*. Oxford: Blackwell.

ROMAINE, S. (1984b) 'Relative clauses in child language, pidgins and creoles', *Australian Journal of Linguistics* **4**:257–81.

ROMAINE, S. (1984c) 'Review of P. Muysken, *Generative Studies on Creole Languages*', *Australian Journal of Linguistics* **4**:116–23.

ROMAINE, S. (1984d) 'Review of E. Woolford and W. Washabaugh. *The Social Context of Creolization*', *Linguistics* **22**:137–40.

ROMAINE, S. (1985) 'Grammar and style in children's narratives', *Linguistics* **23**:83–104.

ROMAINE, S. (1986) 'Sprachmischung und Purismus: Sprich mir nicht von Mischmasch', *Lili 62: Sprachverfall?*:92–107.

ROMAINE, S. and WRIGHT, F. (1986) 'A sociolinguistic study of creolization, language acquisition and change in Tok Pisin', a report to the Max-Planck-Institut für Psycholinguistik.

ROMAINE, S. and WRIGHT, F. (1987) 'A short note on short forms in Tok Pisin', *Journal of Pidgin and Creole Languages* **2**:64–7.

ROSS, A. S. C. and MOVERLEY, A. W. (1964) *The Pitcairnese Language*. London: Deutsch.

ROSS, M. (1985) 'Current use and expansion of Tok Pisin: Effects of Tok Pisin on some vernacular languages', in Wurm, S. A. and Mühlhäusler, P. (eds) *pp* 539–56.

RUSSELL, T. (1868) *The Etymology of Jamaica Grammar, by a young gentleman*. Kingston: De Cordova, McDougall.

SAMARIN, W. J. (1962) 'Lingua francas with special reference to Africa', in Rice, F. A. (ed.) *Study of the Role of Second Languages in Asia, Africa and Latin America*. Washington, DC: Center for Applied Linguistics *pp* 54–65.

SAMARIN, W. J. (1971) 'Salient and substantive pidginization', in Hymes, D. (ed.) *pp* 117–40.

SAMARIN, W. J. (1975) 'Historical, ephemeral and inevitable verbal categories', paper presented at the International Conference on Pidgins and Creoles, Honolulu, Hawaii.

SAMARIN, W. J. (1979) 'Simplification, pidginization and language change', in Hancock, I. (ed.) *pp* 55–69.

SAMARIN, W. J. (1980) 'Standardization and instrumentalization of creole languages', in Valdman, A. and Highfield, A. (eds) *pp* 213–37.

SAMARIN, W. J. (1984) 'Socioprogrammed linguistics', *The Behavioral and Brain Sciences* **7**:206–7.

SANDEFUR, J. (1984) 'A language coming of age: Kriol of North Australia', MA thesis, University of Western Australia.

SANKOFF, G. (1972) 'Language use in multilingual societies: Some alternative approaches', in Pride, J. and Holmes, J. (eds) *Sociolinguistics*. Harmondsworth: Penguin *pp* 33–51.

SANKOFF, G. (1977) 'Variability and explanation in language and culture: Cliticization in New Guinea Tok Pisin', in Saville-Troike, M. (ed.) *Linguistics and Anthropology*. Washington, DC: Georgetown University Press *pp* 59–75.

SANKOFF, G. (1979) 'The genesis of a language', in Hill, K. C. (ed.) *pp* 23–47.

SANKOFF, G. (1980) 'Variation, pidgins and creole', in Valdman, A. and Highfield, A. (eds)

SANKOFF, G. (1984) 'Substrate and universals in the Tok Pisin verb phrase', in Schiffrin, D. (ed.) *Meaning, Form and Use in Context: Linguistic Applications*. Washington, DC: Georgetown University Press *pp* 104–120.

SANKOFF, G. and BROWN, P. (1976) 'The origins of syntax in discourse: the case of Tok Pisin relatives', *Language* **52**:631–66.

SANKOFF, G. and LABERGE, S. (1973) 'On the acquisition of native speakers by a language', *Kivung* **6**:32–47.

SATO, C. J. (1978) 'Variation in Hawaii Pidgin and Creole English: go + verb constructions', MA thesis, University of Hawaii.

SATO, C. J. (1985) 'Linguistic inequality in Hawaii: The Post-Creole dilemma', in Wolfson, N. and Manes, J. (eds) *Language of Inequality*. Berlin: Walter de Gruyter *pp* 255–73.

SAUSSURE, F. DE (1969) *Cours de linguistique générale*. Paris: Payot.

SCHACHTER, J, (1974) 'An error in error analysis', *Language Learning* **24**:205–14.

SCHIEFFELIN, B. (1979) *'How Kaluli children learn what to say, what to do, and how to feel: an ethnographic study of the development of communicative competence'*, PhD dissertation, Columbia University.

SCHLIEBEN-LANGE, B. (1976) 'L'Origine des langues romanes – Un cas de créolisation?', in Meisel, J. (ed.) *Langues en contact-Pidgins-Creoles*. Tübingen: Narr. *pp* 81–101, 267–85.

SCHMIDT, R. W. and FROTA, S. N. (1985) 'Developing basic conversational ability in a second language: A case study of an adult learner of Portuguese', in Day, R. (ed.) *Talking to Learn*. Rowley, Mass.: Newbury House. *pp* 237–326.

SCHUCHARDT, H. (1882) 'Kreolische Studien II: Über das Indoportugiesische von Cochim', Vienna: Akademie der Wissenschaften. Sitzungsberichte. Philosophisch-historishe Klasse 102 (II):799–816.

SCHUCHARDT, H. (1883) 'Kreolische Studien IV: Über das Malaiospanische der Philippinen', Vienna: Akademie der Wissenschaften. Sitzungsberichte. Philosophisch-historische Klasse 105:111–50.

SCHUCHARDT, H. (1889) 'Beiträge zur Kenntnis des englishen Kreolisch II. Melaneso-englisches', *Englische Studien* **13**:158–62. [Also in Gilbert, G. (ed.) (1980). *Pidgin and Creole Languages. Selected Essays by Hugo Schuchardt.* Cambridge: Cambridge University Press. *pp* 14–30.]

SCHUCHARDT, H. (1891) 'Beiträge zur Kenntnisse des englishen Kreolisch III. Das Indo-Englische'. *Englische Studien* 15:286–305. [Also in Gilbert, G. (ed.) (1980) *Pidgin and Creole Languages. Selected Essays by Hugo Schuchardt.* Cambridge: Cambridge University Press. *pp* 38–65].

SCHUCHARDT, H. (1909) 'Die Lingua Franca', *Zeitschrift für Romanische Philologie* **33**:441–61.

SCHUCHARDT, H. (1914) *Die Sprache der Saramakkaneger in Surinam.* Verhandelingen der Koninklijke Akademie van Wetenschappen te Amsterdam. Afdeeling Letterkunde, Nieuwe Reeks. Deel XIV, No. 6. [Also in Markey, T. L. (ed. and trans.) (1979) *Hugo Schuchardt. The Ethnography of Variation. Selected Writings on Pidgins and Creoles.* Ann Arbor: Karoma Press *pp* 73–109].

SCHUMANN, J. H. (1978) *The Pidginization Process. A model for second language acquisition.* Rowley, Mass.: Newbury House.

SCHUMANN, J. (1981) 'Discussion of "Two perspectives on pidginization as second language acquisition"', in Andersen, R. (ed.) *pp* 196–201.

SCHUMANN, J. (1986) 'Experimentally created pidgins', Presentation at the Colloquium on Pidgins and Creoles: Issues in Language Acquisition and Education, University of Hawaii at Manoa, August 1–2 1986, Honolulu, Hawaii.

SCOLLON, R. and SCOLLON, S. B. (1978) *Linguistic Convergence. An Ethnography of Speaking at Fort Chipewyan, Alberta.* New York: Academic Press.

SCOTTON, C. (1979) 'The context is the message: morphological, syntactic and semantic reduction and deletion in Nairobi and Kampala varieties of Swahili', in Hancock, I. (ed.) *pp* 111–29.

SCOVEL, T. (1981) 'The effects of neurological age on nonprimary language acquisition', in Andersen, R. (ed.) *pp* 33–42.

SEBBA, M. (1984) 'London Jamaican. A Sociolinguistic Description', unpublished manuscript.

Select Committee on Race Relations and Immigration, Session 1972–3, Education, Volume I: Report. London: HMSO.

Select Committee on Race Relations and Immigration, Session 1976, Education, Volume I: Report. London. HMSO.

SELIGER, H. W. (1978) 'Implications of a multiple critical periods hypothesis for second language learning', in Ritchie, W. C. (ed.) *Second Language Acquisition Research.* New York: Academic Press.

SELIGER, H. W. (1981) 'Exceptions to critical period predictions', in Andersen, R. (ed.) *pp* 47–57.

SELINKER, L. (1972) 'Interlanguage', *International Review of Applied Linguistics* **10**:209–30.

SEUREN, P. A. M. (1984) 'The bioprogram hypothesis: facts and fancy', *The Behavioral and Brain Sciences* **7**:208–9.

SEUREN, P. A. M. and WEKKER, H. (1986) 'Semantic transparency as a factor in creole genesis', in Muysken, P. and Smith, N. (eds) *Universals vs. Substrata in Creole Genesis*. Amsterdam: John Benjamins *pp* 57–71.

SHANKWEILER, D. and STUDDERT-KENNEDY, M (1975) 'A continuum of lateralization for speech perception', *Brain and Language* **2**:212–25.

SHELTON-SMITH, W. (1929) 'Pidgin English in New Guinea', *Rabaul Times* 24 May.

SHILLING, A. (1980) 'Bahamian English – A non-continuum?', in Day, R. (ed.) *pp* 133–47.

SIEGEL, J. (1975) 'Fiji Hindustani', University of Hawaii Working Paper.

SIEGEL, J. (1981) 'Developments in written Tok Pisin', *Anthropological Linguistics* **23**:20–35.

SIEGEL, J. (1983) 'Plantation pidgin Fijian', Paper presented at the 15th Pacific Congress, Dunedin.

SIEGEL, J. (1985) 'Koinés and koineization', *Language in Society* 14:357–79.

SILVA, I. S. (1985) 'Variation and change in the verbal system of Capeverdean Crioulo', PhD dissertation, Georgetown University.

SILVA-CORVALÁN, C. (1983) 'Tense and aspect in oral Spanish narrative', *Language* **59**:769–81.

SILVA-CORVALÁN, C. (1986) 'Tense–mood–aspect across the Spanish-English bilingual continuum', unpublished manuscript, Department of Spanish and Portuguese, University of Southern California.

SILVERSTEIN, M. (1972a) 'Chinook Jargon: Language contact and the problem of multi-level generative systems I and II', *Language* 48:378–406 and 596–625.

SILVERSTEIN, M. (1972b) 'Goodbye Columbus: Language and speech community in Indian-European contact situations', unpublished manuscript.

SILVERSTEIN, M. (1975) 'Dynamics of recent linguistic contact', in Goddard, I. (ed.) *Handbook of North American Indian Languages* 16. Washington, DC: Smithsonian Institution.

SINCLAIR, J. and COULTHARD, M. (1975) *Towards an Analysis of Discourse: the English used by Teachers and Pupils*. London: Oxford University Press.

SKINNER, B. F. (1957) *Verbal Behavior*. New York: Appleton-Century-Crofts.

SLOBIN. D. (1973) 'Cognitive prerequisities for the development of grammar', in Ferguson, C. A. and Slobin, D. (eds) *Studies of Child Language Development*. New York: Holt, Rinehart and Winston *pp* 175–211.

SLOBIN, D. (1977) 'Language change in childhood and in history', in MacNamara, J. (ed.) *Language Learning and Thought*. New York: Holt, Rinehart and Winston *pp* 175–208.

SLOBIN, D. (1978) 'Universal and particular in the acquisition of language', in Gleitman, L. and Wanner, E. (eds) *Language Acquisition: The State of the Art*. Cambridge: Cambridge University Press.

SLOBIN, D. (1984) 'Child language and the bioprogram', *The Behavioral and Brain Sciences* **7**:209–10

SLOBIN, D. (forthcoming) 'The acquisition and use of relative clauses in Turkic and Indo-European languages', in Zimmer, K. and Slobin, D. (eds) *Studies in Turkish Linguistics*. Amsterdam: John Benjamins.

SLOBIN, D. and AKSU, A. A. (1982) 'Tense, aspect and modality in the use of the Turkish evidential', in Hopper, P. (ed.) *Tense–Aspect. Between Semantics and Pragmatics* Amsterdam: John Benjamins *pp* 185–200.

SMITH, C. (1980) 'The acquisition of time talk: relations between child and adult grammars', *Journal of Child Language* **7**:263–78.

SMITH, G. P. (1986) *A preliminary investigation of the spoken Tok Pisin of some urban children in Lae and Goroka*. Department of Language and Social Science, Papua New Guinea University of Technology, Lae, Papua New Guinea.

SMITH, I. R. (1977) 'Sri Lanka Creole Portuguese Phonology', *International Journal of Dravidian Linguistics* **7**:247–406.

SMITH, I. R. (1978) 'Realignment and other convergence phenomena', *University of Melbourne Working Papers in Linguistics* **4**:67–76.

SMITH, N. V. (1973) *The Acquisition of Phonology*. Cambridge: Cambridge University Press.

SMITH, N. V. and WILSON, D. (1979) *Modern Linguistics. The Results of Chomsky's Revolution*. Harmondsworth: Penguin.

SNOW, C. (1977) 'Mothers' speech research: from input to interaction', in Snow, C. and Ferguson, C. (eds).

SNOW, C. and FERGUSON, C. (eds) (1977) *Talking to Children: Language Input and Acquisition*. Cambridge: Cambridge University Press.

SOKOLIK, M. E. (1986) 'Adult second language acquisition in a target free environment', Department of Applied Linguistics, UCLA.

SOUTHWORTH, F. C. (1971) 'Detecting prior creolization: an analysis of the historical origins of Marathi', in Hymes, D. (ed.) *pp* 255–75.

SPEARS, A. K. (1982) 'The Black English semi-auxiliary *come*', *Language* **58**:850–72.

SREEDHAR, M. V. (1977) 'Standardization of Naga Pidgin', *Journal of Creole Studies* **1**:157–70.

STAMMLER, W. (1922–3) 'Das "Halbdeutsch" der Esten', *Zeitschrift für deutsche Mundarten* **XVII**:160–72.

STASSEN, L. (1985) *Comparison and Universal Grammar*. Oxford: Blackwell.

STEFANSSON, V. (1909) 'The Eskimo Trade Jargon of Herschel Island', *American Anthropologist* **11**:217–32.

STEWART, W. A. (1962) 'The functional distribution of Creole and French in Haiti', *Georgetown Monograph Series on Languages and Linguistics* 15. Washington, DC: Georgetown University Press *pp* 149–59.

STEWART, W. A. (1968) 'Continuity and change in American Negro dialects', *Florida FL Reporter* **6**:1.3–4; 14–16; 18.

STEWART, W. A. (1969) 'Historical and structural bases for the recognition of Negro dialect', *Monograph Series on Languages and Linguistics* 24 Georgetown University. Washington, DC: Georgetown University Press *pp* 515–24.

STURTEVANT, E. (1917) *Linguistic Change. An Introduction to the Historical Study of Language*. Chicago: University of Chicago Press.

SUTCLIFFE, D. (1982) *British Black English*. Oxford: Blackwell.

SWADESH, M. (1971) *The Origin and Diversification of Language*. Chicago: Aldine.

SWAN, J. and LEWIS, D. J. (1986) '"There's a lot of it about": Self-estimates of their use of Tok Pisin by students of the Papua New Guinea University of Technology', unpublished manuscript, Department of Language and Communication Studies, Papua New Guinea University of Technology, Lae, Papua New Guinea.

TATE, (1984) [cited in Sebba 1984, but not listed in bibliography].

TAVAKOLIAN, S. (1977) 'Structural principles in the acquisition of complex sentences', PhD dissertation, University of Massachusetts.

TAVAKOLIAN, S. (1978) 'The conjoined-clause analysis of relative clauses and other structures', in Goodluck, H. and Solan, L. (eds) *Papers in the Structure and Development of Child Language. University of Massachusetts Occasional Papers 4*. Amherst, Mass.

TAYLOR, A. (1977) 'Missionary lingue franche: Motu', in Wurm, S. A. (ed.) *Language, Culture, Society, and the Modern World. New Guinea Area Languages and Languages Study* Vol. 3. Pacific Linguistics Series C-40. Canberra: Australian National University *pp* 881–91.

TAYLOR, D. (1957) 'Review of Whinnom, K. *Spanish Contact Vernaculars in the Phillippine Islands*', *Word* **13**:489–288.

TAYLOR, D. (1963) 'The origin of West Indian Creole languages', *American Anthropologist* **65**:800–14.

TAYLOR, D. (1971) Grammatical and lexical affinities of Creoles, in Hymes, D. (ed.), *pp* 293–6.

THOM, R. (1975) *Structural Stability and Morphogenesis: An outline of a general theory of models*. [Fowler, D. (trans.)] Reading, Mass.: W. A. Benjamins.

THOMASON, S. G. (1980) 'On interpreting "The Indian Interpreter"', *Language in Society* **9**:167–93.

THOMASON, S. G. (1983) 'Chinook Jargon in areal and historical context', *Language* **59**:820–71.

THOMPSON, R. W. (1961) 'A note on some possible affinities between the creole dialects of the old world and those of the new', in Le Page, R. B. (ed.) *pp* 107–13.

TODD, L. (1974) *Pidgins and Creoles*. London: Routledge and Kegan Paul.

TODD, L. (1984) *Modern Englishes. Pidgins and Creoles*. Oxford: Blackwell.

TOMAS NAVARRO, T. (1951) 'Observaciones sobre el Papiamento', *Neuva Rivista de Filologia Hispanica* **7**:183–9.

TRAUGOTT, E. C. (1973) 'Some thoughts on natural syntactic processes', in Bailey, C-J. and Shuy, R. (eds) *New Ways of Analyzing Variation in English*. Washington, DC: Georgetown University Press *pp* 313–23.

TRAUGOTT, E. C. (1975) 'Spatial expressions of tense and temporal sequencing: A contribution to the study of semantic fields', *Semiotica* **15**:207–30.

TRAUGOTT, E. C. (1981) 'Introduction', in Highfield, A. and Valdman, A. (eds) *pp* 1–6.

TRAUGOTT, E. C. (1982) 'From propositional to textual and expressive meanings: some semantic and pragmatic aspects of grammaticalization', in Lehmann, W. P. and Malkiel, Y. (eds) *Perspectives on Historical Linguistics*. Amsterdam: John Benjamins *pp* 245–71.

TRUDGILL, P. (1978) 'Creolization in reverse', *Transactions of the Philological Society* 1976–77; 32–50.

TSUZAKI, S. (1971) 'Coexistent systems in language variation: the case of Hawaiian English', in Hymes, D. (ed.) *pp* 327–41.

TURNER, L. D. (1969) *Africanisms in the Gullah Dialect*. New York: Arno Press and the New York Times.

ULTAN, R. (1978) 'The nature of future tenses', in Greenberg, J. (ed.) *Universals of Human Language Vol. IV: Word Structure*. Stanford: Stanford University Press *pp* 83–124.

URRY, J. and WALSH, M. (1981) 'The lost "Macassar language" of Northern Australia' *Aboriginal History* **5**:91–135.

VALDMAN, A. (1973) 'Some aspects of decreolization in Creole French', in Sebeok, T. A. (ed.) *Current Trends in Linguistics*. Vol. XI: *Diachronic, Areal and Typological Linguistics*. The Hague: Mouton *pp* 507–36.

VALDMAN, A. (1977a) 'Elaboration in the development of Creole French Dialects', in Valdman, A. (ed.) *pp* 155–90.

VALDMAN, A. (ed.) (1977b) *Pidgin and Creole Linguistics*. Bloomington: Indiana University Press.

VALDMAN, A. (1978) *Le Créole: Structure, Status et Origine*. Paris: Editions Klincksieck.

VALDMAN, A. and HIGHFIELD, A. (eds) (1980) *Theoretical Orientations in Creole Studies*. New York: Academic Press.

VALKOFF, M. F. (1966) *Studies in Portuguese and Creole: With Special Reference to South Africa*. Johannesburg: Witwatersrand University Press.

VAN DER AUWERA, J. (1985) 'Relative *that* – a centennial dispute', *Journal of Linguistics* **21**:149–79.

VAN WIJK, H. L. A. (1958) 'Origenes y evolucion del Papiamentu', *Neophilologus* **42**:169–82.

VEIGA, M. (1984) *Diskrison Strutural di Lingua Kabuverdianu*. Praia: Institutu Kabuverdianu di Livru.

VOLKER, C. A. (1982) 'An introduction to Rabaul Creole German'. MA thesis, University of Queensland.

VOORHOEVE, J. (1957) 'The verbal system of Sranan', *Lingua* **6**:374–96.

VOORHOEVE, J. (1962) *Sranan Syntax*. Amsterdam.

VOORHOEVE, J. (1973) 'Historical and linguistic evidence in favour of the relexification theory in the formation of creoles', *Language in Society* **2**:133–45.

VOORHOEVE, J. (1981) 'Multifunctionality as a derivational problem', in Muysken, P. (ed.) *pp* 25–34.

WALD, B. (1982) 'Syntacticization in language development: clause status variation', Paper presented at NWAVE XI conference, Georgetown University, Washington, DC

WALLACE, S. (1982) 'Figure and ground: The interrelationships of linguistic categories', in Hopper, P. J. (ed.) *Tense–Aspect: Between Semantics and Pragmatics* Amsterdam: John Benjamins *pp* 201–23.

WALSH, D. S. (1984) 'Is "English-based" an adequately accurate label for Bislama', Paper presented at the 54th ANZAAS Congress, Australian National University, Canberra.

WANG, W. S-Y (1977) *The Lexicon in Phonological Change*. The Hague: Mouton.

WANTOK PUBLICATIONS (no date) *Stail buk bilong Wantok Niuspepa*. Madang.

WASHABAUGH, W. (1977) 'Constraining variation in decreolization', *Language* **53**:329–52.

WASHABAUGH, W. (1980) 'From preposition to complementizer in Caribbean English Creole', in Day, R. (ed.) *Issues in English Creoles*. Heidelberg: Julius Gross Verlag *pp* 97–111.

WASHABAUGH, W. and GREENFIELD, S. M. (1983) 'The development of Atlantic Creole Languages', in Woolford, E. and Washabaugh, W. (eds) *pp* 106–20.

WEINREICH, U. (1953) *Languages in Contact*. The Hague: Mouton.

WEIST, R., WYSOCKA, H., WITKOWSKA-STADNIK, K., BUCZOWSKA, E. and KONIECZNA, E. (1984) 'The defective tense hypothesis: on the emergence of tense and aspect in child Polish', *Journal of Child Language*. **11**:347–74.

WELMERS, W. E. (1973) *African Language Structures*. Berkeley: University of California Press.

WHINNOM, K. (1956) *Spanish Contact Vernaculars in the Philippine Islands*. Oxford and Hong Kong: Oxford and Hong Kong University Press.

WHINNOM, K. (1971) 'Linguistic hybridization and the "special case" of pidgins and creoles', in Hymes, D. (ed.) *pp* 91–115.

WHITE, L. (1985) 'The "Pro-drop" parameter in adult second language acquisition', *Language Learning* 35:47–63.

WIDDOWSON, H. G. (1977) 'Pidgin and babu', in Corder, S. P. and Roulet, E. (eds) *The Notions of Simplification: Interlanguages and Pidgins and Their Relation to Second Language Pedagogy*. Actes du 5ème Colloque de Linguistique Appliquée de Neuchâtel. Geneve: Librairie Droz *pp* 163–70.

WODE, H. (1980) 'Language acquisition, pidgins and creoles', *Arbeitspapiere zum Spracherwerb*. Nr. **21**:21–9. Englisches Seminar der Universität Kiel.

WOITSETSCHLAEGER, E. (1977) 'A semantic theory of the English auxiliary system', PhD thesis, MIT.

WOLFRAM, W. (1974) 'The relationship of white southern speech to vernacular Black English', *Language* **50**:498–527.

WOLFRAM, W. and CHRISTIAN, D. (1976) *Appalachian English*. Arlington, Va.: Center for Applied Linguistics.

WOLFSON, N. (1982) *CHP. The Conversational Historical Present in American English Narrative*. Dordrecht: Foris.

WOODWARD, J. (1973) 'Some characteristics of Pidgin Sign English', *Sign Language Studies* **3**:39–46.

WOOLFORD, E. (1977 'Aspects of Tok Pisin Grammar'. PhD dissertation, Duke University.

WOOLFORD, E. (1979) 'The developing complementizer system of Tok Pisin: syntactic change in progress', in Hill, K. C. (ed.) *pp* 108–24.

WOOLFORD, E. (1983) 'Introduction: The social context of creolization', in Woolford, E. and Washabaugh, W. (eds) *pp* 1–10.

WOOLFORD, E. and WASHABAUGH, W. (eds) (1983) *The Social Context of Creolization*. Ann Arbor: Karoma.

WRIGHT, F. J. (1984) 'A Sociolinguistic Study of Passivization amongst Black Adolescents in Britain'. PhD dissertation, University of Birmingham.

WRIGHT, J. (1898–1905) *The English Dictionary*, 6 vols, London: H. Frowde.

WURM, S. A. (1970) *New Guinea Highlands Pidgin: course materials*. Pacific Linguistics D-3. Canberra: Australian National University.

WURM, S. A. (1971) 'Pidgins, creoles and lingue franche', in Sebeok, T. (ed.) *Current Trends in Linguistics*, Volume 8. *Linguistics in Oceania*. The Hague: Mouton.

WURM, S. A. (1985) 'Writing systems and the orthography of Tok Pisin', in Wurm, S. A. and Mühlhäusler, P. (eds) *pp* 167–76.

WURM, S. A. and MÜHLHÄUSLER, P. (eds) (1985) *Handbook of Tok Pisin* (*New Guinea Pidgin*). Pacific Linguistics C-70. Canberra: Australian National University.

York Papers in Linguistics II (1983). Proceedings of the York Creole Conference. University of York.

ZIPF, G. (1935) *The Psychobiology of Language*. Boston: Houghton Mifflin.

Index

NOTE: For a list of pidgins and creoles by name, please refer to Appendix 1, pp 315–25. References in the index are to the main text only.

accessiblity hierarchy, 132, 235, 251–3
acquisition, language, 2, 6, 20, 21, 46, 68, 156, 204–55, 313–14
  British Blacks, 190, 198–201
  critical period hypothesis, 191
  first, 74–6, 108, 196, 207–8, 218, 228, 294
    context affects, 288–90
    relatives, 231–4, 237–43, 252
    tense/aspect, 278–88
    universals, 275–95
  hierarchies, 198–201, 207–8, 233–4
  interlanguage, 209–10
  irregular forms, 215
  pidginization, 3, 212–15, 224–6
  pro-drop, 27
  second, 6–7, 35, 156, 183
    foreigner talk, 210–12
    native language and, 251–2
    pidginization hypothesis 212–15
    relatives, 251–2
    tense/modality/aspect, 213, 214, 215, 306–8
    universals, 208–9, 302–8
  sign language, 296–9
  universals, 108, 208–9, 275–95, 302–8
acrolect *see* varieties
Adamawa, 137
Adams, R., 83–4
adequacy, 33, 43–4, 67–8
adjectives verbal use, 48, 51, 198, 199, 297
Admiralty Islands, 156–7
adverbs, 41, 47, 153
  complementizer, 133, 140–6
  TMA, 41–2, 268–9, 281–2
adversative connective, 148
African-based pidgins, 63, 137
Afrikaans, 19, 56, 89, 194, 211
  a creole?, 4, 52–63
age-grading, 185
agglutination, 79
agreement systems, 27–8, 39, 78
Ainu, 66
Aitchison, J., 205, 245, 279
Aksu, A. A., 279–80
Aktionsart, 284
Algonquian languages, 120
Alleyne, M. C., 171
allomorphy, 27–9, 39
allotaxy, 29–31
America, North *see* Amerindian; Black English; Canada; Los Angeles; Louisiana: New York; Texas
American-Japanese pidgin, 228
Amerindian pidgins, 14, 30–1, 82, 85, 94, 120
  see also Chinook

Amharic, 66
analyticity, 28–9, 35, 268
anaphora
  Afrikaans/Negerhollands, 55, 60–1
  and relativization, 231, 249, 254
anaphoric unity, 40–1
Andersen, R., 220–7, 276, 307
Angolor, 52
Annam, 73
Annobon, 19, 52
anterior tense, 175, 265–6, 270, 284–5, 287–8, 300–1
Antilles, Lesser, 19
Antinucci, F., 280, 283
aphasia, 215–16, 301
Appalachian English, 187
Arabic, Juba, 304–5
article
  and bioprogram, 260–1
  creole, 47, 48–9, 309
  gender in, 55
  German, 30, 210–12
  sign language, 297–8
Aruba, 19, 59–60
aspect, 264, 270–1
  characteristic creole, 47, 49
  children, 280–1
  go + verb, 272–4
  markers, 41, 280
  primacy of, 266–7, 301
Australia, 14, 18, 99
  creoles, 97, 98, 155, 287
  pidgin English, 94, 99
  see also Kriol
autonomy and typology, 42–4

Babu, 15
baby talk, 72–6, 109–10
back-/foregrounding, 265–6, 308
Bahamian English, 179
Bahasa Indonesia, 42
Bailey, G., 106, 163
baimbai and *bambai*, 58, 69 n4, 119, 138, 152, 285–6
Baker, P., 49, 258
Balaz, J. P., 110–13
Bantu language, 26, 28
  see also Swahili
basilect *see* varieties
Baxter, A., 286–7
Beach-la-Mar, 20, 72, 73, 117
  see also Bichelamar
Beche de Mer *see* Bichelamar
behaviourism/mentalism, 209
Belize, 180–1, 184, 185
Benin, 91
Berbice Dutch, 159
Bhojpuri, 145–6
Bible translations, 45–6, 82, 123
Bichelamar, 19, 98–9, 102, 144, 155
Bickerton, D., 1
  bioprogram hypothesis, 2, 6, 256–309 *passim*, 313
  change and variation, 53–4, 165
  continuum, Tok Pisin, 160–1
  copula, 166–8, 170–1
  creoles, salient features, 47–69
  creolization, 41, 71, 154–5
  fronting rules, 105–6
  Guyanese, 167–8, 170–1, 173–7
  implicational scaling, 186–7, 222–4
  pidginization, 220–9
  relatives, 241–2, 246
  second language acquisition, 219
  social/stylistic factors, 181–2
  tense and aspect, 173–7, 224–5
bioprogram hypothesis, 6, 7, 21, 256–310, 313
Bislama *see* Beach-la-Mar; Bichelamar
Black English
  American, 3, 5, 157, 159, 167–72
  British, 189–203
Bloomfield, L., 40, 73
Bonaire, 19
Borgarmålet, 126
borrowing, 44, 105, 133–5, 136, 150
boundness, morphological, 262, 268

Bradford, West Yorks, 189
brain function, 215–18, 257, 265
Britain, Black speech in, 188–203
Broch, I., 125–6
Broken *see* Torres Straits
'broken language', 81
Bronckart, J-P., 280–4 *passim*
Brown, R., 243–5, 246
Buang, 151
Bush pidgin, 116, 123–4
Butler English, 116
Bybee, J., 267, 287

'cafeteria principle', 108–9
Cameroons Pidgin English, 19, 52, 57, 64, 66, 144
Canada, 45, 120, 301–2
Cape Verde Crioulo, 4, 10, 19, 88, 89, 161, 175, 285, 287, 288
Cape York Creole, 97, 98, 99, 100
Caribbean creoles, 14, 19, 87, 94, 104, 154
  continuum concept, 116, 184
  see also under individual names
case markers, grammaticalized, 153
catastrophe theory, 53–4
causal connectives, 149, 152
causativity, 260, 262–3, 278
Cazden, C., 207–9
Chabacano, 285
change, language, 20, 21, 311, 313–14
  catastrophic/uniformitarian, 53–4
  cycle of (Givón), 139–40
  in decreolization, 184–5
  extreme, and bioprogram, 299
  speed of, in creoles, 165
  'targeted', 160–1
  wave model of, 163
Chee Chee, 15
child language, 6–7, 35, 74–5, 204–5, 209, 267, 289–90
children 140, 290
  affect language development, 68, 129, 135, 136, 293–4
  see also acquisition, first
China, 12–13, 126
China Coast PE, 17, 26, 73, 116
  development, 85, 87, 89, 90–1, 94, 97, 98, 99, 101, 102
Chinook Jargon, 29, 30, 38, 39, 58, 64, 85, 116, 120–2, 259
Chomsky, N. 26–7
  on cognition, 302, 303–4
  LAD 209, 260
  universals, 268, 275, 313
circumlocution, 35, 36, 78
Clark, R., 96–100, 293
clause chaining patterns, 109
cluster analysis, 181
codability, 32–3
code-switching, 191, 194–5
codes, simple, 31–3, 76–7
cognition, 218, 302–4
Collinson, C. W., 8, 9
common core theory, 92
communication, double illusion of, 120–2, 129–30
communicative function, 150–1
comparatives 55, 56–7
complementizers, 47, 49–50
  British Black patois, 199–200
  grammaticalization, 140–6, 152–3
  Hawaii Creole English, 112–13
  in stable pidgins, 132–3
  sign language, 298
completive, 103, 280–4, 287–8, 306
computational component, 302
Comrie, B., 132, 235, 240, 248, 251, 264
conceptual component, 302
conditionals, 149
conjunctions
  complementizers, 140, 142
  relative, 233–4, 242–3
connectives, sentence 146–52
  see also causal
consonant clusters, 63–4, 184
contact, languages in, 228, 257–9
  proficiency continuum, 299–301

continuum
  British Black language, 190–2
  cortical lateralization, 217–18
  creole, 68, 158–88, 209–10, 271–2
  developmental/restructuring, 117
  diachronic, 182–5
  interlanguage, 209–10
  post-pidgin, 304
  pre-pidgin, 116
  proficiency, 299–301
  synchronic, 177–82
contrastive analysis, 206–7
convergence
  lexical, 69 n2
  syntactic, 79–81, 105
copula, 60, 78, 104
  acquisition, 213, 214, 225
  creole, 47, 48, 51, 103, 166–73, 184
  and implicational scaling, 187–8
  patois, 198, 199
  pidgin, 29, 127
  sign language, 297
Corder, S. P., 32, 76–7, 81, 210
Corne, C., 60, 103–5, 258
Costa Rica, 160, 212–15, 220–9
creoles *see Table of contents and individual entries on particular aspects*
creolization, 2, 38–42, 66–7, 154–7, 205, 227, 311–14
  and depidginization, 54, 116–17
creoloid, 160
Crioulo *see* Cape Verde
critical period hypothesis, 205, 215–19, 295
Curaçao, 19

Day, R., 6, 172–3
De Villiers, J. G., 232, 233, 234
deaf, 296–9
death, language, 302
DeCamp, D., 5, 18–19, 23–4, 38, 71, 157, 161–4, 177–8, 180
declaratives, 31
decreolization, 157, 158–61, 227
  of bioprogram data, 294–5
  Black English, 171
  context, 182
  =linguistic variation?, 183–5
defective tense hypothesis, 281, 307
deixis, 248, 249–50, 254
Delaware Indians, 82
deletion rule (equi-NP) 106, 243
  see also copula; relatives, marker, zero
depidginization, 116–17
depth, derivational, 48, 156
Deuchar, M., 15, 295, 296–9
development, language, 54, 155–6
  independent parallel, 92–102, 248–9
  lack of models, 311, 313–14
dialect, 3, 168–72
diffusion, 141, 202
dimensionality, 179–81
discourse-orientation, 241–3
distribution of pidgins and creoles, present, 14–19
Djuka, 56
Doi, T., 65–6, 101–2
Dominican creole, 88
Dorian, N. C., 299, 301
Downs's Syndrome, 218
Dravidian languages, 40, 79–81
Dreyfuss, G., 249–50
Dudley, West Midlands, 194–201
Dutch, 19, 60
  see also Afrikaans; Negerhollands
Dutton, T., 14, 149, 243–5

Early Melanesian Pidgin, 99
Edinburgh, 231–4, 235–9, 241, 245, 246
Edinburgh, Duke of, 1, 2–4
education, 190, 195, 196–7, 296
Edwards, V., 188, 190, 191–2, 194–6, 197–201, 297–8
elaboration of creoles, 41–2
embeddedness, 140, 232–4, 241, 243–5, 251

English
  Afro-Caribbean London, 191, 200
  -based creoles, 19, 101
  -based jargons, 73
  London Jamaican, 191
  Middle, 15, 54, 66, 111–13
  see also Black English
epenthesis, vowel, 63–4
Equi-NP deletion, 106, 243
ergative case, 289, 298
Escure, G., 180, 182, 184, 185
Eskimo Jargon, 31, 85
Estonia, 30
etymologies, 95–6, 137, 144–5
evidential/non-evidential, 280
existentials, 47, 50–1, 55, 60, 112–13
expansion, language, 41–2, 155
expressivity, 253
extinction of creoles, 157
Eze, S. N., 107

factorization principle, 276
family trees 100–2
Fanagalo, 28, 52, 63
Farsi pidgin, experimental, 26, 27, 36, 37, 52, 58, 226, 269
Fasold, R., 169–70
Ferguson, C. F., 76, 77, 81, 177, 303, 304
Fiji, 99
  Pidgin, 30, 34, 46, 83, 263
Flashner, V., 306
focus, 156, 291
  British Black patois, 198, 199
  locative, 235–7
  pidginization 245–6
  relative, 232–4, 235, 237, 241–2, 245–6
  sign language, 298
  temporal, 235–7
  by word order, 47, 48, 104–6
Fon, 103
foreigner talk, 25, 32, 76–84, 98, 108, 210–12
fossilization, 210
French, 66
  -based creoles, 18, 19
  -based jargons, 73
  children's learning, 281–3, 284
  Norman, in England, 54
  Ontarian, 301–2
  TMA, 280, 281–3, 284
  verbal system, 103
function and structure, 108

Gaelic, 159–60
Gass, S. M., 251
Gastarbeiter Deutsch, 15, 81, 210–12
Gbeya, 34
gender systems, 30, 55
genetic relationships, 95
genitive focus, 235, 237
German, 66
  child acquisition, 281–2, 292
  definite article, 210–12
  foreigner talk, 78–9, 80, 81, 210–12
  pidgins, 17, 37, 269
    artificial, 82, 226
    Gastarbeiter, 15, 81, 210–12
  Rabaul Creole, 30
  and Tok Pisin, 88, 90, 101, 122–3, 130
  word order, 29–30
Ghana, 13
Gibson, K., 178, 190, 271–2
Gilbert, G., 211–12
Givón, T., 31, 139–40, 266, 302, 306
glottochronology and glottostatistics, 95
Goodman, M. F., 102, 304–5
grammar, 13–14
  co-existence of two, 141
  creoles, salient features, 47–69
  expanded pidgins, 138
  foreigner talk, 78–9
  jargon, 119, 120, 121
  model of, 148, 149–52
  polylectal, 163
  second language acquisition, 218
  see also universal

grammatical/lexical distinction, 35
grammaticalization, 39, 133, 150
chains of, 100, 150, 152, 252–4
complementizers, 133, 140–6
of relatives, 231, 252–4
sentence connectives, 146–52
TMA, 133, 268, 273
Greek, 211–12
Greenfield, S. M., 312
grid, panlectal, 163
growth, natural internal, 133–4
Guadaloupe, 249
Guinea Bissau Krioulu, 133, 285, 287, 288
Gullah, 57, 64, 94, 137, 157, 295
Gumperz, J. J., 79–81
Guyanese creole, 19, 66, 160
and bioprogram, 258
case relations, 56
causative/non-causative, 262–3
completion marker, 286
consonant clusters, 64
copula, 48, 166–8, 170–1
creole continuum, 158–9, 165, 166, 178, 179, 182, 271–2
negation, 50
questions, 51, 52
specific/non-specific, 261
TMA, 173–7, 271–2, 280, 287

Haiman, J., 29, 35, 42
Haitian creole, 19, 157, 160
comparatives, 57
complementizer, 142–3
discrete systems model, 179
origin, 83, 88, 89
plural marker, 61
question words, 52
reduction, 45
relativization, 249, 250
tense/modality/aspect, 88
verb system, 102, 103
Hall, R. A., 9–10, 11, 33–4, 85, 102
pidgin/creole link, 2, 19–20, 25, 40–1, 92–6, 115
on Tok Pisin, 3–4, 45–6, 134
Halliday, M. A. K., 148, 149–52, 196
Hancock, I. F., 15, 16, 184, 315–25
Hasan, R., 148, 149–52
Hausa, 27, 66, 137
Hawaii
Filipinos in, 157, 220–1, 272, 274, 294
University of, 77
Hawaii Creole English, 66, 258
articles, 49, 309
baimbai, 152
causative/non-causative, 262–3
complementizers, 50
copula, 172–3
development, 53, 116, 154, 290, 293–4
History of Pigeon, Da 110–13
and pidgin, 286, 290, 291, 292–3
relativization, 241–2, 246
repidginization, 157
TMA, 265, 266, 280, 285–6
Hawaii Pidgin English, 14, 17, 120
and creole, 286, 290, 291, 292–3
development, 55, 85, 91, 97, 99
as model for children, 290
possessive, 221–2
specific/non-specific, 261
TMA, 269
Haynes, L., 184
Henzell-Thomas, J., 77, 108
Hesseling, D. C., 4, 52–3, 86
Hindi, 308
Hinnenkamp, V., 78–9, 80, 81
Hiri Motu, 18, 30, 37, 45, 82, 101
historical influence 40–3, 67, 99
linguistic development, 312–13
Hjelmslev, L., 25
Hmong, 308
Hobson-Jobson, 15
Högström, P., 126
Hudson, R., 25, 68

Hyams, N., 27
hybridization, tertiary, 83
Hymes, D., 2, 24, 31–2, 38, 179
hypercorrection, 156

iconicity, 35–6, 39, 105
ideational component, 149–52
identity, expression of, 79, 82, 188, 195–8, 201, 202–3, 295, 312
ideophones, 34
Igbo, 306–7
imitation as origin of pidgin, 73–5
implicational scaling, 178, 179, 186–7
  British Black language use, 194–5
  Jamaican creole continuum, 161–4
  language development, 156
  lects and environments, 166
  negation (Hawaii), 222–4
  plural marking (Tok Pisin), 131–2
  we relative marker, 247–8
Indian Ocean creoles 39, 103, 249, 258, 286
  see also under names of creoles
indicators (defined), 201
Indo-Portuguese, 88
infinitive, 62, 78–9, 198, 199
input
  by children to creole, 293–4
  frequency in, 252
  in language acquisition, 209
  sign language, 296–7, 298–9
interference, 206–8, 210, 251–2, 301
  see also substratum
interlanguage, 209–10, 305–8
interpersonal component, 149–52
intonation
  patois, 198, 199
  questions, 51, 105
  in relativization, 243
  sign language equivalent, 298
Ireland, Northern, 159–60
irrealis *see* realis
Isle de France Creole, 103–5, 113 n1, 203, 258, 284
isolects, 163
isomorphism, 35
Italian, 211–12, 278
  Eritrean, 66
Iwal, 107

Jahr, E. H, 125–6
Jamaican creole, 7
  British Blacks and, 179, 188–9, 190–1, 192–4, 201
  comparatives, 57
  complementizers, 50, 144, 145
  consonant clusters, 64
  continuum, 161–4, 177–8, 179
  copula, 51
  development, 89, 157
  features, defining, 161–3
  localisms, 180
  passives, 52
  plurals, 104
  standardization and, 42
  targeted language change, 160
  tense/modality/aspect, 88, 271–2
Janson, T., 137–8
Japanese, 65–6, 101–2, 220–1, 306–7
  -American pidgin, 228
jargon and jargons
  creolization of, 154–5
  illusion of double communication, 120–2
  nautical, 84–6, 98, 99
  phase, of pidgins, 73–4, 117–24
  trade, 82, 117
  see also Chinook; Eskimo
Java, 88
Jespersen, O., 20, 88, 255 n4
Juba Arabic, 304–5

Kafir, Kitchen-, 7
Kaluli, 110, 289
Kannada, 79–81

Kate, 123
Keenan, E. L., 235, 240, 248, 251, 253
Keesing, R., 100, 134
Kenya Pidgin Swahili, 28, 52
Kiautschou, 90–1
Kikongo, 72–3
Kikongo-Kituba, 259
Kinubi, 66, 304–5
Kitubu, 72–3
Kivung, 4–5
Kjachta, 126
Klein, W., 210, 254 n3
Koefoed, G., 91
koinês and koineization, 26
Kolonialdeutsch, 82
Koopman, H., 46–7, 142–3
Korea, 66, 157
Krakowian, B., 81
Krashen, S. D., 216, 217, 218
Krio, 57, 64, 89, 104, 175–6, 247
Kriol, 42, 133, 287
Kristang, 286–7
Kumpf, L., 306–7
Kunama, 66
Kupwar, 79–81, 94, 105, 299
Kwa, 52, 55–6, 104–5, 107
Kwakiutl, 121

Ll=L2 hypothesis, 208
labelling system, 17–18
Laberge, S., 116–17, 140
Labov, W., 164, 171–2
  on Black youth culture, 196–7
  on copula, 168–9, 170
  on creolization, 41–2
  on jargon, 118–20
  on nativization, 67–8
  on tense, 269
lame (Labov's term), 197, 203
Lamendella, J., 275
Language Acquisition Device, 209, 260
language/dialect distinction, 3
Lappish, 126
lateralization, cortical, 215–18
Le Page, R. B., 24, 180–1, 181–2, 185, 188, 202–3
lects, 158–9, 163, 192–4
Lefebvre, C., 46–7, 142–3
Lehmann, C., 230, 248
Leland, C. G., 13, 73
Lenneberg, E., 215–16, 217
Levelt, W. J. M., 300
lexical/grammatical languages, 35
lexicon, 3, 11–12, 17, 95–6
  creole, 47, 50, 85
  diffusion, 141
  and iconicity, 35–6
  jargons, 117, 120, 123
  multifunctionality, 78–9
  pidgin, 33–8
  syntax convergence, 79–81, 105
  see also relexification
Liberia, 73
life cycle
  creoles, 154–203
  pidgin, 115–53
Lingala, 259
Lingua Franca, 86, 87
Linguistic Minorities Project, 1984, 188
locative, 60
  and existential, 292–3
  focus, 235–7
  and progressive aspect, 187–8
  relatives, 247
  verb (patois), 198, 199
London Jamaican, 184, 188, 191, 200–1
Los Angeles, 240–1, 299–301
loss, language, 302
Louisiana, 19, 82, 89, 249
Loyalty Islands, 99
Lyons, J., 249

Macao, 88
Macassarese, 18
Madras, 116
Mafeni, 68, 116
Malaccan Creole Portuguese, 51, 88
Malay, pidgin, 42
Malayo-Spanish, Philippine, 118
Manam, 107
Marathi, 5, 79–81

Maratsos, M. P., 277–8
markers (linguistic variables), 201
Markey, T. L., 52–63, 183, 184
Martinique creole, 83, 249
Master, P., 36
master-slave relationship, 72, 73–4, 75–6, 82–3
Mauritian Creole, 18, 19, 49–50, 73, 89, 104, 160, 258
Media Lengua, 91
Meisel, J., 32, 281–3
Melanesian pidgins and creoles, 94, 97, 98
  see also under individual names
mentalism/behaviourism, 209
Menyuk, P., 245–6
mesolect *see* varieties
Mihalic, F., 10, 45–6, 96, 143, 146
Miller, R., 280, 283
missionaries, 45, 72–3, 82, 83, 122–3
mixture, language, 44–5, 67, 93
Moag, R. F., 34, 83
Mobilian Trade Jargon, 82
modality, 47, 49, 264
  see also tense/mood/aspect
models, 313–14
  grammaticalization chains, 152–3
  language change, 163, 313–14
Modern Languages Association, 5
Mohan, P., 144, 145–6
monogenesis, 5, 86–91, 93, 182–3
Montagnais, 120
mood *see* modality; TMA
morphology, 79
  inflectional, 25, 37, 74–5, 131
  naturalness, 156
  tense, 281
  valence-changing, 267
  verbal, 224–5, 226
  see also under names of individual components
'motherese', 32, 75–6, 288–90
Motu, 82
  see also Hiri; Police
movement rules, 47, 48, 104–6
  see also focus
Mühlhäusler, P., 1, 7, 20–1
  artificial pidgin German, 82
  common core theory, 92
  creole grammar, 62–3, 67
  creolization, 39, 40, 116
  foreigner talk, 77
  lexicon, 11, 34–5, 37
  origin of pidgins, 12–13, 71–2, 99–102, 116
  pronoun systems, 26
  recognition of pidgins/creoles, 15, 17
  relatives, 247–8
  relexification, 88
  restructuring/development, 155–6
  simplification, 32
  stable pidgins, 48, 130–5, 136, 154–7
  Tok Masta, 12, 81
  Tok Pisin, 46, 96
multidimensional analysis, 180–1
multifunctionality, 37–8
multitude nouns, 137
Muysken, P., 268, 269–71
myelization, 217

Naga Pidgin, 137
Nagara, S., 120, 292–3
Naro, A. J., 82–3, 87, 276
native speakers
  on origins of pidgins, 109–13
  of pidgins, 46
  on varieties, 123–4, 163–4
nativization, 67–9, 227, 304–5
Navajo, Trade, 30–1
negatives
  acquisition, 213–14
  Afrikaans, 55, 58, 59
  attraction/concord, 59
  characteristic creole, 47, 50
  Chinook jargon, 121–2
  patois, 198, 199
  pidgin, 222–4, 226, 227, 228
  sign language, 298
  universal, 228
Negerhollands, 54–5, 56, 157

Nelson, H., 11–12
Neo-Melanesian *see* Tok Pisin
Nevermann, H., 96
New Caledonia, 19, 61, 98–9, 102
New Guinea Pidgins, 17, 31, 97, 99, 102, 116, 122–3
  see also Tok Pisin
New Hebrides pidgin, 19, 97, 98, 99
  Bichelemar, 19, 102, 155
New Testament, 45–6, 123
New York, 191
  see also Labov
New Zealand Pidgin English, 94
Ngatik Men's Language, 99
Nigerian Pidgin English, 46, 107
nominal case inflection, 55–6
Norfolk Island, 65, 99
norms, linguistic, 156, 202
Norway, 124–30
noun compounding, 36
Nubian, 66
Numbani, 107
Nupela Testamen, 45–6, 123

Ochs, E., 289–90
Odo, C., 112, 220–9, 246
O'Donnell, W. R., 158–9, 159–60
orait, 146–51
origin of pidgins, theories of
  baby talk, 72–6
  foreigner talk, 76–84
  imitation, 73–5
  independent parallel development, 92–102
  motherese, 75–6
  monogenesis and relexification, 86–91
  native speakers' theories, 109–13
  nautical jargon, 84–6
  simplification, 72–3, 74
  substratum theories, 102–9
orthography
  Hawaii Creole English, 111–12
  Tok Pisin, 45–6
Ouidah (Juda or Ajuda, Benin), 91
Oxford, University of, 77

Pacific Islands Monthly, 8–9
Pacific Jargon English, 26, 37, 101, 102
Pacific pidgins/creoles, 14, 29, 136–8
  development, 82, 85, 99
Palenquero, 285
Papia Kristang, 285
Papiamentu, 19, 59–60, 87, 88, 89, 116, 137, 159
  TMA, 88, 285, 287, 288
Papua New Guinea
  House of Assembly, 33, 43
  languages used, 18, 19, 43–4, 82
  post pidgin continuum, 304
  University of Technology, 33
  see also New Guinea; Tok Pisin
Papuan Pidgin English, 17, 18, 102
paradigmatic univocity, 25–9
paralanguage, 302
parasitism, 7
participles, past, 282–3
particles
  TMA, 41–2, 49, 285–7
  and verb fronting, 105–6
passives
  Afrikaans/Negerhollands, 55, 59–60
  British Blacks, 190
  characteristic creole, 48, 52
  Pitcairnese, 65
  sign language, 297
patois, British Black, 189–203
perfectivity, 280–4
periphrasis, 36, 78
Petit Negre, 72–3
Philippine Spanish creoles, 73, 87, 88, 118, 285
phonology
  British Black, 191, 198–9
  Chinook jargon, 120–1
  and copula, 168

of creoles, 63–4
in language acquisition, 218
Russenorsk, 129
speech tempo and, 138–40
phonotactics, creole, 63
Piaget, J., 218, 281, 300
pidgin, origin of term, 12–13, 110–13
pidginization, 2, 205, 258
hypothesis, 212–15
second language acquisition compared, 2, 212–15, 220–9
social factors, 311–14
pidgins *see Table of Contents and individual entries on particular aspects*
'pigeon', 13, 22 n3, 110–13
Pitcairn-Norfolk, 64–5, 97, 98, 99, 259
plurals, 25, 27, 74
acquisition, 213, 214, 225–6
in creoles, 60–1
patois, 198, 201
Tok Pisin, 100, 130–2, 133–4
universals, 100, 136–8
Poland, 81, 281
Police Motu, 19, 116
polygenesis, 92
Port Moresby, 82
Portuguese, 13, 307
creoles, 19, 51, 52, 57, 118, 211–12, 286, 287–8, 312
jargons, 73
pidgin, 58, 82–3, 86–8, 89
see also Sri Lankan
Posner, R., 249
possessives
creole, 47, 50–1, 55, 60
in second language acquisition, 213, 214
and pidginization, 221–2
Post Courier, 43
post creoles, 66–7
postpositions, 40, 78
pragmatic/syntactic, 302
predicate markers, 39, 40, 139
prepositions, 29
complementizers, 140–1, 142–3
deletion, 78–9
grammaticalization, 153
Russenorsk, 127–8
and serial verbs, 56
in stable pidgin, 48
prestige, linguistic, 6–14, 17, 18, 123–5, 130, 184, 185, 196–7, 219
Principense, 52, 137
pro-drop parameter, 26–7
progressive aspect, 60, 187–8
acquisition, 213, 214
projection, 202
pronouns, 26–7
African influence on, 104
Afrikaans/Negerhollands, 55, 61–2
anaphoric, 39, 48
in creolization, 39
in indirect speech, 144
inflection of, 61–2
London Jamaican, 201
patois, 198
personal, as relativizers, 242
as plural markers, 137
pro-drop, 26–7
relative, 231, 245, 298
resumptive, 238–41, 250–1
retention in relativization, 240, 251–2, 253, 254
in stable pidgin, 48
in Tok Pisin, 27, 131
propositional/ideational, 149–52
propositional qualifiers, 57–8, 78
prospective/retrospective, 271
Proto-Pidgin English, 93, 94
proto-pidgin, postulated, 86–8, 89
Providence Island Creole, 180
Puerto Ricans in New York, 191
punctuality, 260, 265–6, 271–2, 280–4, 305–6

qualifiers, sentence-external, 48
Quebec, 120
Queensland Plantation pidgin, 99, 101, 102

questions
  acquisition, 208–9
  creole, 48, 51–2
  foreigner talk, 78
  intonation, 105
  patois, 198, 199
  pidginization, 213, 214, 226
  Russenorsk, 128
  sign language, 298
  word order, 31, 48
  -words, 48, 52
Quileute, 121

Rabaul Creole German, 30
Rabaul Times, 10–11
Rambutyo Island, 156–7
Rastafarianism, 189
realis, 49, 173–4, 265–6, 272–4
reanalysis *see* grammaticalization
recognition of pidgin, 15, 17
recreolization, 157, 188–203
reduction, 39, 44, 45,79–81, 138–40
redundancy, 29, 42, 75, 155
reduplication, 133–4
referential function, 150–1, 156, 269
regrammaticalization, 145
regularity, linguistic, 135–6, 215
Reinecke, J. E., 85
relatives, 241–51
  acquisition, 205–6, 226, 229–41, 251–2
  children, 231–4, 237–8, 242–3
  clauses, 229–30, 235
  conjunction, 233–4
  creole, 47, 50, 65, 241–51
  embedding, 233–4
  grammaticalization, 252–4
  independent parallel development, 248–9
  intonation, 243
  marker
    children's use, 237–8
    pronouns, 242, 245
    resumptives, 250–1
    Tok Pisin, 246–7, 248
    zero, 231–2, 237–8, 242, 245
  parataxis, 242–3
  pidginization, 205–6, 226, 229–54
  positioning, 235
  subordination, 230–1
  Tok Pisin, 243–5, 246–8, 250
  universal grammar, 235–41
relexification, 18, 127, 159, 171
  in jargon, 119
  monogenesis and, 86–91
  in pidginization, 220, 228–9
  syntactic convergence and, 79–81
  Tok Pisin, 88, 90, 122–4
repartitions, semantic, 55, 60
repertoire extension, 185
repidginization, 156–7, 294
reportative marker *-ski*, 145
restructuring, 183
  /development, 117, 155–6
  mutual, in foreigner talk, 79
  in pidginization, 220
resumptives, 238–41, 240, 245, 250–1
resyntactification, 79–81
retrospective/prospective, 271
Reunion, 18, 19, 103, 160, 258
Rickford, J., 67, 74, 179, 183
Roper River Creole, 97, 99
Russenorsk, 124–30
Russian, 126, 306

Sabir, 86, 87
St Lucia French, 159, 180–1
Samarin, W. J., 20, 32, 34, 58, 134, 259
Samoa, 123, 288–90
Samoan Plantation Pidgin English, 99, 102, 123, 131, 153 n3
Sandalwood English, 98–9
Sango, 34, 58, 250
Sankoff, G., 39, 108–9, 116–17, 140, 151, 243–5, 246, 258
Saõ Tomense, 19, 52, 56, 288
Saramaccan, 64, 87, 88, 95, 309
Sato, C. J., 54, 272, 293, 294–5
Schieffelin, B., 110, 289–90

Schuchardt, H., 1, 3, 4, 39, 72, 118, 161
Schumann, J. H., 24–5, 26, 212–15, 219, 220–9
scope gradation, 266, 268
Scotland, 237, 301
  see also Edinburgh
Scovel, T., 217, 218
Sebba, M., 188, 191, 200–1
Select Committee on Race Relations and Immigration, 188, 190
Seliger, H. W., 217–18
Selinker, L., 209–10
semantax, natural, 256, 260
sentence connectives, 146–52
sentence structure, 47, 117, 121–2
Serbo-Croat, 278
serialization *see* verb, serial
Seychelles Creole, 39, 49, 137, 258, 287
Seychelles Pidgin, 89
Sierra Leone Creole, 19, 73, 144
sign language, 295, 296–9
significance (statistical), 186–7
Silva-Corvalán, C., 299–301
Silva, I. S., 10, 161, 175, 285, 287–8
Silverstein, M., 120
simplification, 31–3, 82–3, 108
  in foreigner talk, 76, 77, 81
  intuitive strategies of, 83–4
  pidgin origin, 72–3, 74, 109–10
  in post-creoles, 67
  word structure, 63
Singapore English, 160
Sino-Russian pidgins, 126
slave trade, 14, 170, 312
Slaves Narrative Collection, 170
Slobin, D., 229, 233, 276, 279–80, 219–2
Smith, I. R., 40
social factors, 5–6, 17–18, 20–1, 157, 311–14
  in acquisition, 308
  bioprogram, 258–9
  British Black English, 191–2
  continuum, 181–2
  critical period hypothesis, 219
  Gastarbeiter Deutsch, 212
  language change, 68, 202–3
  pidginization, 311
  and reduction, 23, 25
  see also master/slave
socialization, linguistic, 290
solidarity, 43–4, 197–8, 201, 202–3
Solomon Islands, 97, 98, 99, 102, 286
Somare, M., 43–4
Songay, 66
South Africa, 194
South Seas Jargon, 98, 99
Spanish, 206–8, 211–15, 221, 305–6, 307
  -based pidgins/creoles, 14, 19
  see also entries on individual pidgins and creoles
specific/non-specific, 260–1, 277–8
speech, indirect, 143–6, 150
Sranan, 116
  case relations, 56
  change of superstrate, 159
  comparatives, 57
  complementizers, 50, 144
  completive, 288
  consonant clusters, 64
  origin, 83, 87, 94
  relativization, 250
  repidginization, 156
  TMA, 88, 287, 288
  verbal system, 104, 173
  'very', 72
Sri Lanka Creole, 7–8, 40, 145
stabilization of creoles, 68–9
stable pidgins, 39, 48, 124–38
Stail Buk, Wantok, 149
standardization, 42, 45–6
state/process, 260, 279
stereotypes
  British Black, 192–4, 201, 202
  urban/rural, 123–4, 134–5, 179–80
structure
  and function, 108
  of lexicon, 17

logical, and relativization, 253
pidgin and creole, 13–14, 46–7
word, 28–9
Sturtevant, E., 42
stylistics, 181–2, 269
substratum
African, 102, 103, 104, 144–5, 169
diversity of, 108–9
bioprogram, 261
Gastarbeiter Deutsch, 211–12
language acquisition, 210
number for pidginization, 24–5
orait, 151
and pidgin origins, 102–9
relativizers, 248–9
stable pidgins, 133–4
structural expansion, 156
vs. universals, 206–9, 301
superserialization, verbs, 107
superstrate
and bioprogram, 261, 309
and decreolization, 157, 158
relation to creole, 177–9
and structural expansion, 156
see also borrowing
Surinam creoles, 87–8, 95, 156
see also Sranan
Sutcliffe, D., 191, 192–3
Swahili, 19, 25–6, 28, 52, 66
Swedish, 126
synchronic continuum, 177–82
syntactic/pragmatic, 302
syntax
convergence, 79–81, 105
Hawaii Creole English, 112–13
innovation, creole ieature, 53
of motherese, 75
-motivated relatives, 242–3
-motivated speech systems, 241
paratactic, foreigner talk, 108
in pidginization, 220
Russenorsk, 128–9
see also relatives
synthetic structure, 28–9

Taal/Tsotsi Taal, 194
Tagalog, 220–1
Tahiti, 118
Takavolian, S., 233, 234
Taki-Taki, 94
Tây Bôi, 19
Telegu, 79–81
tempo, speech, 138–40
temporality, 147–8, 152, 235–7, 247
tense-modality-aspect system
acquisition
1st language, 278–88
2nd language, 213, 214, 215, 306–8
pidginization, 224–5, 226
anterior, 175, 265–6, 270, 284–5, 287–8, 300–1
in Belize language change, 184
in bioprogram, 260, 264–74
characteristic creole, 47, 49
completedness, 282–3
and creole continuum, 173–7
defective tense hypothesis, 281, 307
evidence for monogenesis, 87–8
Guyanese creole, 173–7
Japanese, 65
in Kriol, 133
map, 152–3
markedness hierarchy, 269–70
markers
adverbial, 41–2, 268–9, .281–2, 285–7
Afrikaans/Negerhollands, 55, 57–9
Haitian creole, 103
particles, 41–2
past participles, 282–3
past tense, used of aspect, 280
pidgin origins of?, 285–7
pididginization and, 224–5, 226
past tense, 25, 112–13, 174–5, 280
patois, 198
sign language, 296–7
Spanish and English, 299–301, 305–6

terminology, problems of, 283–4
Turkish, 279–80
universals, 264–74
see also aspect; modality; relative; temporality
Texas, 169, 172
textual component, 149–52
Thomason, S. G., 39–40, 120
Thompson, R. W., 87–8
time reference, absolute, 264
Times Higher Education Supplement, 13
Todd, L., 20, 24, 71, 88, 89, 115–16, 158–60
Tok Masta, 12, 81
Tok Pisin, 1, 4–5, 14, 18, 45
adequacy, 33, 43–4
agreement markers, 27–8
anglicism, 3–4, 117, 134–6, 150
autonomy, 43
and bioprogram, 259
borrowing, 134–5, 136, 150
causative/non-causative, 263
child acquisition, 136, 294
circumlocution, 35
complementizers, 140–2
completive marker, 103
conditionals, 149
continuum, post-creole, 160–1
creole salient features, 62–3
creolized pidgin, 138, 155
etymologies, 95–6
family trees, 100–2
German influence, 88, 90, 101, 122–3, 130
grammaticalization, 144–5
-im suffix, 32–3
intonation, 243
jargon phase, 122–4
lexicon, 35–6, 37, 38
origin, 109–10
phonological reduction, 138–40
plurals, 100, 130–2, 133–4
predicate markers, 39, 40, 139
pronoun system, 27, 131
propositional qualifiers, 58
question words, 52
range, pidgin-creole, 116
relatives, 243–5, 246–8, 250
relexification, 88, 90, 122–4
repidginization, 156–7
serial verbs, 106, 107
stabilization stage, 130–6
standardization, 45–6
stress patterns, 140
structure, 12
substratum influence, 109, 133
tense marking, 286
'town pidgin', 123–4, 134–5
valence-changing, 267
verb phrase, 109
written, 248
tok ples, 123
Tolai, 40, 96, 101, 102, 131, 133–4
Tomas Navarro, T., 87
Tongo, 88
Torres Strait Pidgin English (Broken), 18, 100, 102, 155, 247
tourists, foreign, 73, 76
town/country, 123–4, 134–5, 179–80
trade languages, 25–6, 35, 83, 117, 124–30
Trader's Jargon, 82
transfer
Gastarbeiter Deutsch, 211–12
pidginization/2nd language, 210, 221, 222, 225, 226, 228–9
relatives, 251–2
vs. universals, 206–9, 301
Traugott, E. C., 23, 32, 150
Trinidad Bhojpuri, 145–6
Turkish
article, 211–12
causative/non-causative, 262, 278
child acquisition, 278, 279, 291–2
copula, 78
German foreigner talk, 78–9, 80, 81
relative clauses, 229
TMA system, 279–80

Twi, 104
typology
  and bioprogram, 267–8
  pidgins and creoles, 42–6
  post-creoles, 66–7

Uganda, 304–5
universals, linguistic, 68, 108, 313
  and acquisition, 183, 132, 204–5, 208–9, 275–95
  article, 211–12
  Chomsky on, 209
  independent parallel development, 92
  negatives, 228
  plurals, 100, 136–8
  relatives, 132, 235–41, 252
  Russenorsk close to, 129
  sign language, 298–9
  simplification, 77
  and stable pidgin, 134
  structural expansion, 156
  tense/modality/aspect, 264–74
  vs. transfer, 21, 206–9, 301
  see also bioprogram
Unserdeutsch, 62–3, 155
urban/rural stereotype, 123–4, 134–5, 179–80
Urdu, 79–81

Vanuatu, 20, 117
variable rule analysis, 164–5
variables, linguistic, 201
variation, 6, 177–9
  creole continuum, 164, 183–5
  and language change, 165
  language restructuring, 156
varieties, language (acro-, basi-, mesolect), 113, 158–64, 166–8, 170–1, 178, 184–5, 190–4
verb
  acquisition, 224–5, 226
  adjectives as, 48, 51, 198, 199, 297
  Afrikaans/Negerhollands, 55, 62
  auxiliary, 213, 214
  complex, 30
  fronting of, 104–6
  of motion, 272–4
  in patois, 198, 199–200, 201
  phrase, Tok Pisin, 109
  Russenorsk, 127
  of saying, 153
  serial, 56, 104, 106–7, 145, 291–2
  Sranan, 173
  stative/non-stative, 174–5, 258–9, 271–2
  telic, 282–3
  topicalization, 104–6
  transitive/intransitive, 262–3
Vietnam, 19
Virgin Islands, 19
vitality, 42, 67–9
Voorhoeve, J., 87, 173
vowel gradation, 58–9

Wald, B., 240–1
Wantok, 43, 46, 123–4, 134, 149, 151–2, 248
War, First World, 82, 125
Warlpiri, 290–1
Washabaugh, W., 180, 311, 312
wave model of change, 163
Weist, R., 281
Weltdeutsch, 82
West African Pidgin English, 46, 57, 94, 101, 176, 247
  range, 116, 138, 155, 304
West Indian creoles, 94, 155
  see also entries on individual creoles
Whinnom, K., 24–5, 83, 87
Wilson, R., 79–81
Wode, H., 21
Woolford, E., 140–2, 311
word formation, 127, 138, 156
word order, 29–31, 48
  acquisition of strategies, 108
  German-Turkish foreigner talk, 78–9
  Hawaii pidgin/creole, 291
  in jargon, 119, 121–2
  patois, 198, 199

pidgin, 26, 29–31, 48, 220–1, 291
Russenorsk, 128
sign language, 298
Sri Lanka Portuguese Creole, 40
stable pidgins, 48
SVO predominance, 55, 61, 108
in Swahili pidgins, 26
questions, 51–2

Wright, F. J., 190, 192–4
Wurm, S. A., 13, 45–6, 243

Yago, 13
Yoruba, 46, 48, 104, 306–7
Yugoslav, 211–12

Zaire, 72–3
Zulu, Pidgin 28, 52, 63